Ancient Christian Commentary on Scripture

Old Testament

I

Genesis 1-11

EDITED BY

Andrew Louth

IN COLLABORATION WITH

Marco Conti

GENERAL EDITOR
Thomas C. Oden

FITZROY DEARBORN PUBLISHERS
CHICAGO · LONDON

For information write to:

FITZROY DEARBORN PUBLISHERS
919 North Michigan Avenue
Chicago, Illinois 60611
USA

or

FITZROY DEARBORN PUBLISHERS
310 Regent Street
London W1R 5AJ
England

Cover photograph: Scala/Art Resource, New York. View of the apse. S. Vitale, Ravenna, Italy.

Spine photograph: Byzantine Collection, Dumbarton Oaks, Washington D.C. Pendant cross (gold and enamel). Constantinople, late sixth century.

British Library and Library of Congress Cataloging in Publication Data is available.

ISBN 1-57958-220-6

Printed in the United States of America ∞

First published in the USA and UK 2001

27	26	25	24	23	22	21	20	19	18	17	16	15	14	13	12	11	10	9	8	7	6	5	4	3	2	1
24	23	22	21	20	19	18	17	16	15	14	13	12	11	10	09	08	07	06	05	04	03	02	01			

"Composed in the style of the great medieval *catenae*, this new anthology of patristic commentary on Holy Scripture, conveniently arranged by chapter and verse, will be a valuable resource for prayer, study and proclamation. By calling attention to the rich Christian heritage preceding the separations between East and West and between Protestant and Catholic, this series will perform a major service to the cause of ecumenism."

AVERY CARDINAL DULLES, S.J.
Laurence J. McGinley Professor of Religion and Society
Fordham University

"The initial cry of the Reformation was *ad fontes*—back to the sources! The Ancient Christian Commentary on Scripture is a marvelous tool for the recovery of biblical wisdom in today's church. Not just another scholarly project, the ACCS is a major resource for the renewal of preaching, theology and Christian devotion."

TIMOTHY GEORGE
Dean, Beeson Divinity School, Samford University

"Modern church members often do not realize that they are participants in the vast company of the communion of saints that reaches far back into the past and that will continue into the future, until the kingdom comes. This Commentary should help them begin to see themselves as participants in that redeemed community."

ELIZABETH ACHTEMEIER
Union Professor Emerita of Bible and Homiletics
Union Theological Seminary in Virginia

"Contemporary pastors do not stand alone. We are not the first generation of preachers to wrestle with the challenges of communicating the gospel. The Ancient Christian Commentary on Scripture puts us in conversation with our colleagues from the past, that great cloud of witnesses who preceded us in this vocation. This Commentary enables us to receive their deep spiritual insights, their encouragement and guidance for present-day interpretation and preaching of the Word. What a wonderful addition to any pastor's library!"

WILLIAM H. WILLIMON
Dean of the Chapel and Professor of Christian Ministry
Duke University

"Here is a nonpareil series which reclaims the Bible as the book of the church by making accessible to earnest readers of the twenty-first century the classrooms of Clement of Alexandria and Didymus the Blind, the study and lecture hall of Origen, the cathedrae of Chrysostom and Augustine, the scriptorium of Jerome in his Bethlehem monastery."

GEORGE LAWLESS
Augustinian Patristic Institute and Gregorian University, Rome

"We are pleased to witness publication of the
Ancient Christian Commentary on Scripture. It is most beneficial for us to learn
how the ancient Christians, especially the saints of the church
who proved through their lives their devotion to God and his Word, interpreted
Scripture. Let us heed the witness of those who have gone before us in the faith."

METROPOLITAN THEODOSIUS
Primate, Orthodox Church in America

"Across Christendom there has emerged a widespread interest
in early Christianity, both at the popular and scholarly level. . . .
Christians of all traditions stand to benefit from this project, especially clergy
and those who study the Bible. Moreover, it will allow us to see how our traditions are
both rooted in the scriptural interpretations of the church fathers while at
the same time seeing how we have developed new perspectives."

ALBERTO FERREIRO
Professor of History, Seattle Pacific University

"The Ancient Christian Commentary on Scripture fills a long overdue need for scholars and
students of the church fathers. . . . Such information will be of immeasurable
worth to those of us who have felt inundated by contemporary interpreters and novel theories
of the biblical text. We welcome some 'new' insight from the
ancient authors in the early centuries of the church."

H. WAYNE HOUSE
Professor of Theology and Law
Trinity University School of Law

Chronological snobbery—the assumption that our ancestors working without benefit of
computers have nothing to teach us—is exposed as nonsense by this magnificent
new series. Surfeited with knowledge but starved of wisdom, many of us are
more than ready to sit at table with our ancestors and listen to their holy
conversations on Scripture. I know I am.

EUGENE H. PETERSON
Professor Emeritus of Spiritual Theology
Regent College

"Few publishing projects have encouraged me as much as the recently announced Ancient Christian Commentary on Scripture with Dr. Thomas Oden serving as general editor.... How is it that so many of us who are dedicated to serve the Lord received seminary educations which omitted familiarity with such incredible students of the Scriptures as St. John Chrysostom, St. Athanasius the Great and St. John of Damascus? I am greatly anticipating the publication of this Commentary."

FR. PETER E. GILLQUIST
Director, Department of Missions and Evangelism
Antiochian Orthodox Christian Archdiocese of North America

"The Scriptures have been read with love and attention for nearly two thousand years, and listening to the voice of believers from previous centuries opens us to unexpected insight and deepened faith. Those who studied Scripture in the centuries closest to its writing, the centuries during and following persecution and martyrdom, speak with particular authority. The Ancient Christian Commentary on Scripture will bring to life the truth that we are invisibly surrounded by a 'great cloud of witnesses.'"

FREDERICA MATHEWES-GREEN
Commentator, National Public Radio

"For those who think that church history began around 1941 when their pastor was born, this Commentary will be a great surprise. Christians throughout the centuries have read the biblical text, nursed their spirits with it and then applied it to their lives. These commentaries reflect that the witness of the Holy Spirit was present in his church throughout the centuries. As a result, we can profit by allowing the ancient Christians to speak to us today."

HADDON ROBINSON
Harold John Ockenga Distinguished Professor of Preaching
Gordon-Conwell Theological Seminary

"All who are interested in the interpretation of the Bible will welcome the forthcoming multivolume series Ancient Christian Commentary on Scripture. Here the insights of scores of early church fathers will be assembled and made readily available for significant passages throughout the Bible and the Apocrypha. It is hard to think of a more worthy ecumenical project to be undertaken by the publisher."

BRUCE M. METZGER
Professor of New Testament, Emeritus
Princeton Theological Seminary

ANCIENT CHRISTIAN COMMENTARY
PROJECT RESEARCH TEAM

GENERAL EDITOR
Thomas C. Oden

ASSOCIATE EDITOR
Christopher A. Hall

OPERATIONS MANAGER
Joel Elowsky

TRANSLATIONS PROJECTS DIRECTOR
Joel Scandrett

RESEARCH AND ACQUISITIONS DIRECTOR
Michael Glerup

EDITORIAL SERVICES DIRECTOR
Warren Calhoun Robertson

ORIGINAL LANGUAGE VERSION DIRECTOR
Konstantin Gavrilkin

GRADUATE RESEARCH ASSISTANTS

Chris Branstetter	*Susan Kipper*
Jeffrey Finch	*Sergey Kozin*
Steve Finlan	*Hsueh-Ming Liao*
Peter Gilbert	*Michael Nausner*
J. Sergius Halvorsen	*Robert Paul Seesengood*
Patricia Ireland	*Baek-Yong Sung*
Alexei Khamine	*Elena Vishnevskaya*
Christian T. Collins Winn	

ADMINISTRATIVE ASSISTANTS
Judy Cox
Åsa Nausner

---

vii

CONTENTS

GENERAL INTRODUCTION

The Ancient Christian Commentary on Scripture (hereafter ACCS) is a twenty-eight volume patristic commentary on Scripture. The patristic period, the time of the fathers of the church, spans the era from Clement of Rome (fl. c. 95) to John of Damascus (c. 645-c. 749). The commentary thus covers seven centuries of biblical interpretation, from the end of the New Testament to the mid-eighth century, including the Venerable Bede.

Since the method of inquiry for the ACCS has been developed in close coordination with computer technology, it serves as a potential model of an evolving, promising, technologically pragmatic, theologically integrated method for doing research in the history of exegesis. The purpose of this general introduction to the series is to present this approach and account for its methodological premises.

This is a long-delayed assignment in biblical and historical scholarship: reintroducing in a convenient form key texts of early Christian commentary on the whole of Scripture. To that end, historians, translators, digital technicians, and biblical and patristic scholars have collaborated in the task of presenting for the first time in many centuries these texts from the early history of Christian exegesis. Here the interpretive glosses, penetrating reflections, debates, contemplations and deliberations of early Christians are ordered verse by verse from Genesis to Revelation. Also included are patristic comments on the deuterocanonical writings (sometimes called the Apocrypha) that were considered Scripture by the Fathers. This is a full-scale classic commentary on Scripture consisting of selections in modern translation from the ancient Christian writers.

The Ancient Christian Commentary on Scripture has three goals: the renewal of Christian *preaching* based on classical Christian exegesis, the intensified study of Scripture by *lay* persons who wish to think with the early church about the canonical text, and the stimulation of Christian historical, biblical, theological and pastoral *scholarship* toward further inquiry into the scriptural interpretations of the ancient Christian writers.

On each page the Scripture text is accompanied by the most noteworthy remarks of key consensual exegetes of the early Christian centuries. This formal arrangement follows approximately the traditional pattern of the published texts of the Talmud after the invention of printing and of the *glossa ordinaria* that preceded printing.[1]

---

[1]Students of the Talmud will easily recognize this pattern of organization. The Talmud is a collection of rabbinic arguments, discussions and comments on the Mishnah, the first Jewish code of laws after the Bible, and the Gemara, an elaboration of the Mishnah. The study of Talmud is its own end and reward. In the Talmud every subject pertaining to Torah is worthy of consideration and analysis. As the Talmud is a vast repository of Jewish wisdom emerging out of revealed Scripture, so are the Fathers the repository of Christian wisdom

Retrieval of Neglected Christian Texts

There is an emerging felt need among diverse Christian communities that these texts be accurately recovered and studied. Recent biblical scholarship has so focused attention on post-Enlightenment historical and literary methods that it has left this longing largely unattended and unserviced.

After years of quiet gestation and reflection on the bare idea of a patristic commentary, a feasibility consultation was drawn together at the invitation of Drew University in November 1993 in Washington, D.C. This series emerged from that consultation and its ensuing discussions. Extensive further consultations were undertaken during 1994 and thereafter in Rome, Tübingen, Oxford, Cambridge, Athens, Alexandria and Istanbul, seeking the advice of the most competent international scholars in the history of exegesis. Among distinguished scholars who contributed to the early layers of the consultative process were leading writers on early church history, hermeneutics, homiletics, history of exegesis, systematic theology and pastoral theology. Among leading international authorities consulted early on in the project design were Sir Henry Chadwick of Oxford; Bishops Kallistos Ware of Oxford, Rowan Williams of Monmouth and Stephen Sykes of Ely (all former patristics professors at Oxford or Cambridge); Professors Angelo Di Berardino and Basil Studer of the Patristic Institute of Rome; and Professors Karlfried Froehlich and Bruce M. Metzger of Princeton. They were exceptionally helpful in shaping our list of volume editors. We are especially indebted to the Ecumenical Patriarch of Constantinople Bartholomew and Edward Idris Cardinal Cassidy of the Pontifical Council for Promoting Christian Unity, the Vatican, for their blessing, steady support, and wise counsel in developing and advancing the Drew University Patristic Commentary Project.

The outcome of these feasibility consultations was general agreement that the project was profoundly needed, accompanied by an unusual eagerness to set out upon the project, validated by a willingness on the part of many to commit valuable time to accomplish it. At the pace of three or four volumes per year, the commentary is targeted for completion within the first decade of the millennium.

This series stands unapologetically as a practical homiletic and devotional guide to the earliest layers of classic Christian readings of biblical texts. It intends to be a brief compendium of reflections on particular Septuagint, Old Latin and New Testament texts by their earliest Christian interpreters. Hence it is not a commentary by modern standards, but it is a commentary by the standards of those who anteceded and formed the basis of the modern commentary.

---

emerging out of revealed Scripture. The Talmud originated largely from the same period as the patristic writers, often using analogous methods of interpretation. In the Talmud the texts of the Mishnah are accompanied by direct quotations from key consensual commentators of the late Judaic tradition. The format of the earliest published versions of the Talmud itself followed the early manuscript model of the medieval *glossa ordinaria* in which patristic comments were organized around Scripture texts. Hence the ACCS gratefully acknowledges its affinity and indebtedness to the early traditions of the catena and *glossa ordinaria* and of the tradition of rabbinic exegesis that accompanied early Christian Scripture studies.

Many useful contemporary scholarly efforts are underway and are contributing significantly to the recovery of classic Christian texts. Notable in English among these are the Fathers of the Church series (Catholic University of America Press), Ancient Christian Writers (Paulist), Cistercian Studies (Cistercian Publications), The Church's Bible (Eerdmans), Message of the Fathers of the Church (Michael Glazier, Liturgical Press) and Texts and Studies (Cambridge). In other languages similar efforts are conspicuously found in Sources Chrétiennes, Corpus Christianorum (Series Graeca and Latina), Corpus Scriptorum Christianorum Orientalium, Corpus Scriptorum Ecclesiasticorum Latinorum, Texte und Untersuchungen zur Geschichte der altchristlichen Literatur, Die griechischen christlichen Schriftsteller, Patrologia Orientalis, Patrologia Syriaca, Biblioteca patristica, Les Pères dans la foi, Collana di Testi Patristici, Letture cristiane delle origini, Letture cristiane del primo millennio, Cultura cristiana antica, Thesaurus Linguae Latinae, Thesaurus Linguae Graecae and the Cetedoc series, which offers in digital form the volumes of Corpus Christianorum. The Ancient Christian Commentary on Scripture builds on the splendid work of all these studies, but focuses primarily and modestly on the recovery of patristic biblical wisdom for contemporary preaching and lay spiritual formation.

Digital Research Tools and Results

The volume editors have been supported by a digital research team at Drew University which has identified these classic comments by performing global searches of the Greek and Latin patristic corpus. They have searched for these texts in the Thesaurus Linguae Graecae (TLG) digitalized Greek database, the Cetedoc edition of the Latin texts of Corpus Christianorum from the Centre de traitement électronique des documents (Université catholique de Louvain), the Chadwyck-Healey Patrologia Latina Database (Migne) and the Packard Humanities Institute Latin databases. We have also utilized the CD-ROM searchable version of the Early Church Fathers, of which the Drew University project was an early cosponsor along with the Electronic Bible Society.

This has resulted in a plethora of raw Greek and Latin textual materials from which the volume editors have made discriminating choices.[2] In this way the project office has already supplied to each volume editor[3] a substantial read-out of Greek and Latin glosses, explanations, observations and comments on each verse or pericope of Scripture text.[4] Only a small percentage of this raw material

---

[2]Having searched Latin and Greek databases, we then solicited from our Coptic, Syriac and Armenian editorial experts selections from these bodies of literature, seeking a fitting balance from all available exegetical traditions of ancient Christianity within our time frame. To all these we added the material we could find already in English translation.

[3]Excepting those editors who preferred to do their own searching.

[4]TLG and Cetedoc are referenced more often than Migne or other printed Greek or Latin sources for these reasons: (1) the texts are more quickly and easily accessed digitally in a single location; (2) the texts are more reliable and in a better critical edition; (3) we believe that in the future these digital texts will be far more widely accessed both by novices and specialists; (4) short selections can be easily downloaded; and (5) the context of each text can be investigated by the interested reader.

has in fact made the grade of our selection criteria. But such is the poignant work of the catenist, or of any compiler of a compendium for general use. The intent of the exercise is to achieve brevity and economy of expression by exclusion of extraneous material, not to go into critical explanatory detail.

Through the use of Boolean key word and phrase searches in these databases, the research team identified the Greek and Latin texts from early Christian writers that refer to specific biblical passages. Where textual variants occur among the Old Latin texts or disputed Greek texts, they executed key word searches with appropriate or expected variables, including allusions and analogies. At this time of writing, the Drew University ACCS research staff has already completed most of these intricate and prodigious computer searches, which would have been unthinkable before computer technology.

The employment of these digital resources has yielded unexpected advantages: a huge residual database, a means of identifying comments on texts not previously considered for catena usage, an efficient and cost-effective deployment of human resources, and an abundance of potential material for future studies in the history of exegesis. Most of this was accomplished by a highly talented group of graduate students under the direction of Joel Scandrett, Michael Glerup and Joel Elowsky. Prior to the technology of digital search and storage techniques, this series could hardly have been produced, short of a vast army of researchers working by laborious hand and paper searches in scattered libraries around the world.

Future readers of Scripture will increasingly be working with emerging forms of computer technology and interactive hypertext formats that will enable readers to search out quickly in more detail ideas, texts, themes and terms found in the ancient Christian writers. The ACCS provides an embryonic paradigm for how that can be done. Drew University offers the ACCS to serve both as a potential research model and as an outcome of research. We hope that this printed series in traditional book form will in time be supplemented with a larger searchable, digitized version in some stored-memory hypertext format. We continue to work with an astute consortium of computer and research organizations to serve the future needs of both historical scholarship and theological study.

The Surfeit of Materials Brought to Light

We now know that there is virtually no portion of Scripture about which the ancient Christian writers had little or nothing useful or meaningful to say. Many of them studied the Bible thoroughly with deep contemplative discernment, comparing text with text, often memorizing large portions of it. All chapters of all sixty-six books of the traditional Protestant canonical corpus have received deliberate or occasional patristic exegetical or homiletic treatment. This series also includes patristic commentary on texts not found in the Jewish canon (often designated the Apocrypha or deuterocanonical writings) but that were included in ancient Greek Bibles (the Septuagint). These texts, although not precisely the same texts in each tradition, remain part of the recognized canons of the

Roman Catholic and Orthodox traditions.

While some books of the Bible are rich in verse-by-verse patristic commentaries (notably Genesis, Psalms, Song of Solomon, Isaiah, Matthew, John and Romans), there are many others that are lacking in intensive commentaries from this early period. Hence we have not limited our searches to these formal commentaries, but sought allusions, analogies, cross-connections and references to biblical texts in all sorts of patristic literary sources. There are many perceptive insights that have come to us from homilies, letters, poetry, hymns, essays and treatises, that need not be arbitrarily excluded from a catena. We have searched for succinct, discerning and moving passages both from line-by-line commentaries (from authors such as Origen, Cyril of Alexandria, Theodoret of Cyr, John Chrysostom, Jerome, Augustine and Bede) and from other literary genres. Out of a surfeit of resulting raw materials, the volume editors have been invited to select the best, wisest and most representative reflections of ancient Christian writers on a given biblical passage.

For Whom Is This Compendium Designed?

We have chosen and ordered these selections primarily for a general lay reading audience of nonprofessionals who study the Bible regularly and who earnestly wish to have classic Christian observations on the text readily available to them. In vastly differing cultural settings, contemporary lay readers are asking how they might grasp the meaning of sacred texts under the instruction of the great minds of the ancient church.

Yet in so focusing our attention, we are determined not to neglect the rigorous requirements and needs of academic readers who up to now have had starkly limited resources and compendia in the history of exegesis. The series, which is being translated into the languages of half the world's population, is designed to serve public libraries, universities, crosscultural studies and historical interests worldwide. It unapologetically claims and asserts its due and rightful place as a staple source book for the history of Western literature.

Our varied audiences (lay, pastoral and academic) are much broader than the highly technical and specialized scholarly field of patristic studies. They are not limited to university scholars concentrating on the study of the history of the transmission of the text or to those with highly focused interests in textual morphology or historical-critical issues and speculations. Though these remain crucial concerns for specialists, they are not the paramount interest of the editors of the Ancient Christian Commentary on Scripture. Our work is largely targeted straightaway for a pastoral audience and more generally to a larger audience of laity who want to reflect and meditate with the early church about the plain sense, theological wisdom, and moral and spiritual meaning of particular Scripture texts.

There are various legitimate competing visions of how such a patristic commentary should be developed, each of which were carefully pondered in our feasibility study and its follow-up. With high respect to alternative conceptions, there are compelling reasons why the Drew University project has been conceived as a practically usable commentary addressed first of all to informed lay readers and more broadly to pastors of Protestant, Catholic and Orthodox traditions. Only in an ancillary way do we have in mind as our particular audience the guild of patristic academics, although we welcome their critical assessment of our methods. If we succeed in serving lay and pastoral readers practically and well, we expect these texts will also be advantageously used by college and seminary courses in Bible, hermeneutics, church history, historical theology and homiletics, since they are not easily accessible otherwise.

The series seeks to offer to Christian laity what the Talmud and Midrashim have long offered to Jewish readers. These foundational sources are finding their way into many public school libraries and into the obligatory book collections of many churches, pastors, teachers and lay persons. It is our intent and the publishers' commitment to keep the whole series in print for many years to come and to make it available on an economically viable subscription basis.

There is an emerging awareness among Catholic, Protestant and Orthodox laity that vital biblical preaching and teaching stand in urgent need of some deeper grounding beyond the scope of the historical-critical orientations that have dominated and at times eclipsed biblical studies in our time.

Renewing religious communities of prayer and service (crisis ministries, urban and campus ministries, counseling ministries, retreat ministries, monasteries, grief ministries, ministries of compassion, etc.) are being drawn steadily and emphatically toward these biblical and patristic sources for meditation and spiritual formation. These communities are asking for primary source texts of spiritual formation presented in accessible form, well-grounded in reliable scholarship and dedicated to practical use.

The Premature Discrediting of the Catena Tradition

We gratefully acknowledge our affinity and indebtedness to the spirit and literary form of the early traditions of the catena and *glossa ordinaria* that sought authoritatively to collect salient classic interpretations of ancient exegetes on each biblical text. Our editorial work has benefited by utilizing and adapting those traditions for today's readers.

It is regrettable that this distinctive classic approach has been not only shelved but peculiarly misplaced for several centuries. It has been a long time since any attempt has been made to produce this sort of commentary. Under fire from modern critics, the catena approach dwindled to almost nothing by the nineteenth century and has not until now been revitalized in this postcritical situation. Ironically, it is within our own so-called progressive and broad-minded century that these texts have been more systematically hidden away and ignored than in any previous century of Christian scholarship. With all our historical and publishing competencies, these texts have been regrettably denied to hearers of Christian preaching in our time, thus revealing the dogmatic biases of modernity (modern chauvinism, naturalism and autonomous individualism).

Nineteenth- and twentieth-century exegesis has frequently displayed a philosophical bias toward naturalistic reductionism. Most of the participants in the ACCS project have lived through dozens of iterations of these cycles of literary and historical criticism, seeking earnestly to expound and interpret the text out of ever-narrowing empiricist premises. For decades Scripture teachers and pastors have sailed the troubled waters of assorted layers and trends within academic criticism. Preachers have attempted to digest and utilize these approaches, yet have often found the outcomes disappointing. There is an increasing awareness of the speculative excesses and the spiritual and homiletic limitations of much post-Enlightenment criticism.

Meanwhile the motifs, methods and approaches of ancient exegetes have remained shockingly unfamiliar not only to ordained clergy but to otherwise highly literate biblical scholars, trained exhaustively in the methods of scientific criticism. Amid the vast exegetical labors of the last two centuries, the ancient Christian exegetes have seldom been revisited, and then only marginally and often tendentiously. We have clear and indisputable evidence of the prevailing modern contempt for classic exegesis, namely that the extensive and once authoritative classic commentaries on Scripture still remain untranslated into modern languages. Even in China this has not happened to classic Buddhist and Confucian commentaries.

This systematic modern scholarly neglect is seen not only among Protestants, but also is widespread among Catholics and even Orthodox, where ironically the Fathers are sometimes piously venerated while not being energetically read.

So two powerful complementary contemporary forces are at work to draw our lay audience once again toward these texts and to free them from previous limited premises: First, this series is a response to the deep hunger for classical Christian exegesis and for the history of exegesis, partly because it has been so long neglected. Second, there is a growing demoralization in relation to actual useful exegetical outcomes of post-Enlightenment historicist and naturalistic-reductionist criticism. Both of these animating energies are found among lay readers of Roman, Eastern and Protestant traditions.

Through the use of the chronological lists and biographical sketches at the back of each volume, readers can locate in time and place the voices displayed in the exegesis of a particular pericope. The chains (catenae) of interpretation of a particular biblical passage thus provide glimpses into the history of the interpretation of a given text. This pattern has venerable antecedents in patristic and medieval exegesis of both Eastern and Western traditions, as well as important expressions in the Reformation tradition.

The Ecumenical Range and Intent

Recognition of need for the Fathers' wisdom ranges over many diverse forms of Christianity. This has necessitated the cooperation of scholars of widely diverse Christian communities to accomplish the task fairly and in a balanced way. It has been a major ecumenical undertaking.

Under this classic textual umbrella, this series brings together in common spirit Christians who have long distanced themselves from each other through separate and often competing church memories. Under this welcoming umbrella are gathering conservative Protestants with Eastern Orthodox, Baptists with Roman Catholics, Reformed with Arminians and charismatics, Anglicans with Pentecostals, high with low church adherents, and premodern traditionalists with postmodern classicists.

How is it that such varied Christians are able to find inspiration and common faith in these texts? Why are these texts and studies so intrinsically ecumenical, so catholic in their cultural range? Because all of these traditions have an equal right to appeal to the early history of Christian exegesis. All of these traditions can, without a sacrifice of intellect, come together to study texts common to them all. These classic texts have decisively shaped the entire subsequent history of exegesis. Protestants have a right to the Fathers. Athanasius is not owned by Copts, nor is Augustine owned by North Africans. These minds are the common possession of the whole church. The Orthodox do not have exclusive rights over Basil, nor do the Romans over Gregory the Great. Christians everywhere have equal claim to these riches and are discovering them and glimpsing their unity in the body of Christ.

From many varied Christian traditions this project has enlisted as volume editors a team of leading international scholars in ancient Christian writings and the history of exegesis. Among Eastern Orthodox contributors are Professors Andrew Louth of Durham University in England and George Dragas of Holy Cross (Greek Orthodox) School of Theology in Brookline, Massachusetts. Among Roman Catholic scholars are Benedictine scholar Mark Sheridan of the San Anselmo University of Rome, Jesuit Joseph Lienhard of Fordham University in New York, Cistercian Father Francis Martin of the Catholic University of America, Alberto Ferreiro of Seattle Pacific University, and Sever Voicu of the Eastern European (Romanian) Uniate Catholic tradition, who teaches at the Augustinian Patristic Institute of Rome. The New Testament series is inaugurated with the volume on Matthew offered by the renowned Catholic authority in the history of exegesis, Manlio Simonetti of the University of Rome. Among Anglican communion contributors are Mark Edwards (Oxford), Bishop Kenneth Stevenson (Fareham, Hampshire, in England), J. Robert Wright (New York), Anders Bergquist (St. Albans), Peter Gorday (Atlanta) and Gerald Bray (Cambridge, England, and Birmingham, Alabama). Among Lutheran contributors are Quentin Wesselschmidt (St. Louis), Philip Krey and Eric Heen (Philadelphia), and Arthur Just, William Weinrich and Dean O. Wenthe (all of Ft. Wayne, Indiana). Among distinguished Protestant Reformed, Baptist and other evangelical scholars are John Sailhamer and Steven McKinion (Wake Forest, North Carolina), Craig Blaising and Carmen Hardin (Louisville, Kentucky), Christopher Hall (St. Davids, Pennsylvania),

J. Ligon Duncan III (Jackson, Mississippi), Thomas McCullough (Danville, Kentucky), John R. Franke (Hatfield, Pennsylvania) and Mark Elliott (Hope University Liverpool).

The international team of editors was selected in part to reflect this ecumenical range. They were chosen on the premise not only that they were competent to select fairly those passages that best convey the consensual tradition of early Christian exegesis, but also that they would not omit significant voices within it. They have searched insofar as possible for those comments that self-evidently would be most widely received generally by the whole church of all generations, East and West.

This is not to suggest or imply that all patristic writers agree. One will immediately see upon reading these selections that within the boundaries of orthodoxy, that is, excluding outright denials of ecumenically received teaching, there are many views possible about a given text or idea and that these different views may be strongly affected by wide varieties of social environments and contexts.

The Drew University project has been meticulous about commissioning volume editors. We have sought out world-class scholars, preeminent in international biblical and patristic scholarship, and wise in the history of exegesis. We have not been disappointed. We have enlisted a diverse team of editors, fitting for a global audience that bridges the major communions of Christianity.

The project editors have striven for a high level of consistency and literary quality over the course of this series. As with most projects of this sort, the editorial vision and procedures are progressively being refined and sharpened and fed back into the editorial process.

Honoring Theological Reasoning

Since it stands in the service of the worshiping community, the ACCS unabashedly embraces crucial ecumenical premises as the foundation for its method of editorial selections: revelation in history, trinitarian coherence, divine providence in history, the Christian *kerygma, regula fidei et caritatis* ("the rule of faith and love"), the converting work of the Holy Spirit. These are common assumptions of the living communities of worship that are served by the commentary.

It is common in this transgenerational community of faith to assume that the early consensual ecumenical teachers were led by the Spirit in their interpretive efforts and in their transmitting of Christian truth amid the hazards of history. These texts assume some level of unity and continuity of ecumenical consensus in the mind of the believing church, a consensus more clearly grasped in the patristic period than later. We would be less than true to the sacred text if we allowed modern assumptions to overrun these premises.

An extended project such as this requires a well-defined objective that serves constantly as the organizing principle and determines which approaches take priority in what sort of balance. This objective informs the way in which tensions inherent in its complexity are managed. This objective has already been summarized in the three goals mentioned at the beginning of this introduction. To alter any one of these goals would significantly alter the character of the whole task. We view our work not only as an academic exercise with legitimate peer review in the academic community, but also as a vocation, a task primarily undertaken *coram Deo* ("before God") and not only *coram hominibus* ("before humanity"). We have been astonished that we have been led far beyond our original intention into a Chinese translation and other translations into major world languages.

This effort is grounded in a deep respect for a distinctively theological reading of Scripture that cannot be reduced to historical, philosophical, scientific or sociological insights or methods. It takes seriously the venerable tradition of ecumenical reflection concerning the premises of revelation, apostolicity, canon and consensuality. A high priority is granted here, contrary to modern assumptions, to theological, christological and triune reasoning as the distinguishing premises of classic Christian thought. This approach does not pit theology against critical theory; instead, it incorporates critical methods and brings them into coordinate accountability within its overarching homiletic-theological-pastoral purposes. Such an endeavor does not cater to any cadre of modern ideological advocacy.

Why Evangelicals Are Increasingly Drawn Toward Patristic Exegesis

Surprising to some, the most extensive new emergent audience for patristic exegesis is found among the expanding worldwide audience of evangelical readers who are now burgeoning from a history of revivalism that has often been thought to be historically unaware. This is a tradition that has often been caricatured as critically backward and hermeneutically challenged. Now Baptist and Pentecostal laity are rediscovering the history of the Holy Spirit. This itself is arguably a work of the Holy Spirit. As those in these traditions continue to mature, they recognize their need for biblical resources that go far beyond those that have been made available to them in both the pietistic and historical-critical traditions.

Both pietism and the Enlightenment were largely agreed in expressing disdain for patristic and classic forms of exegesis. Vital preaching and exegesis must now venture beyond the constrictions of historical-critical work of the century following Schweitzer and beyond the personal existential storytelling of pietism.

During the time I have served as senior editor and executive editor of *Christianity Today*, I have been privileged to surf in these volatile and exciting waves. It has been for me (as a theologian of a liberal mainline communion) like an ongoing seminar in learning to empathize with the tensions, necessities and hungers of the vast heterogeneous evangelical audience.

But why just now is this need for patristic wisdom felt particularly by evangelical leaders and laity? Why are worldwide evangelicals increasingly drawn toward ancient exegesis? What accounts for this rapid and basic reversal of mood among the inheritors of the traditions of Protestant revivalism? It is partly because the evangelical tradition has been long deprived of any vital contact with these patristic sources since the days of Luther, Calvin and Wesley, who knew them well.

This commentary is dedicated to allowing ancient Christian exegetes to speak for themselves. It will not become fixated unilaterally on contemporary criticism. It will provide new textual resources for the lay reader, teacher and pastor that have lain inaccessible during the last two centuries. Without avoiding historical-critical issues that have already received extensive exploration in our time, it will seek to make available to our present-day audience the multicultural, transgenerational, multilingual resources of the ancient ecumenical Christian tradition. It is an awakening, growing, hungry and robust audience.

Such an endeavor is especially poignant and timely now because increasing numbers of evangelical Protestants are newly discovering rich dimensions of dialogue and widening areas of consensus with Orthodox and Catholics on divisive issues long thought irreparable. The study of the Fathers on Scripture promises to further significant interactions between Protestants and Catholics on issues that have plagued them for centuries: justification, authority, Christology, sanctification and eschatology. Why? Because they can find in pre-Reformation texts a common faith to which Christians can appeal. And this is an arena in which Protestants distinctively feel at home: biblical authority and interpretation. A profound yearning broods within the heart of evangelicals for the recovery of the history of exegesis as a basis for the renewal of preaching. This series offers resources for that renewal.

Steps Toward Selections

In moving from raw data to making selections, the volume editors have been encouraged to move judiciously through three steps:

Step 1: *Reviewing extant Greek and Latin commentaries.* The volume editors have been responsible for examining the line-by-line commentaries and homilies on the texts their volume covers. Much of this material remains untranslated into English and some of it into any modern language.

Step 2: *Reviewing digital searches.* The volume editors have been responsible for examining the results of digital searches into the Greek and Latin databases. To get the gist of the context of the passage, ordinarily about ten lines above the raw digital reference and ten lines after the reference have been downloaded for printed output. *Biblia Patristica* has been consulted as needed, especially in cases where the results of the digital searches have been thin. Then the volume editors have determined from these potential digital hits and from published texts those that should be regarded as more serious possibilities for inclusion.

Step 3. *Making selections.* Having assembled verse-by-verse comments from the Greek and Latin digital databases, from extant commentaries, and from already translated English sources, either on disk or in paper printouts, the volume editors have then selected the best comments and reflections of ancient Christian writers on a given biblical text, following agreed upon criteria. The intent is to set apart those few sentences or paragraphs of patristic comment that best reflect the mind of the believing church on that pericope.

The Method of Making Selections

It is useful to provide an explicit account of precisely how we made these selections. We invite others to attempt similar procedures and compare outcomes on particular passages.[5] We welcome the counsel of others who might review our choices and suggest how they might have been better made. We have sought to avoid unconsciously biasing our selections, and we have solicited counsel to help us achieve this end.

In order that the whole project might remain cohesive, the protocols for making commentary selections have been jointly agreed upon and stated clearly in advance by the editors, publishers, translators and research teams of the ACCS. What follows is our checklist in assembling these extracts.

The following principles of selection have been mutually agreed upon to guide the editors in making spare, wise, meaningful catena selections from the vast patristic corpus:

1. From our huge database with its profuse array of possible comments, we have preferred those passages that have enduring relevance, penetrating significance, crosscultural applicability and practical applicability.

2. The volume editors have sought to identify patristic selections that display trenchant rhetorical strength and self-evident persuasive power, so as not to require extensive secondary explanation. The editorial challenge has been to identify the most vivid comments and bring them to accurate translation.

We hope that in most cases selections will be pungent, memorable, quotable, aphoristic and short (often a few sentences or a single paragraph) rather than extensive technical homilies or detailed expositions, and that many will have some narrative interest and illuminative power. This criterion follows in the train of much Talmudic, Midrashic and rabbinic exegesis. In some cases, however, detailed comments and longer sections of homilies have been considered worthy of inclusion.

3. We seek the most representative comments that best reflect the mind of the believing church (of all times and cultures). Selections focus more on the attempt to identify consensual strains of exegesis than sheer speculative brilliance or erratic innovation. The thought or interpretation can emerge out of individual creativity, but it must not be inconsistent with what the apostolic tradition teaches and what the church believes. What the consensual tradition trusts least is individualistic innovation that has not yet subtly learned what the worshiping community already knows.

Hence we are less interested in idiosyncratic interpretations of a given text than we are in those

---

[5]A number of Ph.D. dissertations are currently being written on the history of exegesis of a particular passage of Scripture. This may develop into an emerging academic methodology that promises to change both biblical and patristic studies in favor of careful textual and intertextual analysis, consensuality assessment and history of interpretation, rather than historicist and naturalistic reductionism.

texts that fairly represent the central flow of ecumenical consensual exegesis. Just what is central is left for the fair professional judgment of our ecumenically distinguished Orthodox, Protestant and Catholic volume editors to discern. We have included, for example, many selections from among the best comments of Origen and Tertullian, but not those authors' peculiar eccentricities that have been widely distrusted by the ancient ecumenical tradition.

4. We have especially sought out for inclusion those consensus-bearing authors who have been relatively disregarded, often due to their social location or language or nationality, insofar as their work is resonant with the mainstream of ancient consensual exegesis. This is why we have sought out special consultants in Syriac, Coptic and Armenian.

5. We have sought to cull out annoying, coarse, graceless, absurdly allegorical[6] or racially offensive interpretations. But where our selections may have some of those edges, we have supplied footnotes to assist readers better to understand the context and intent of the text.

6. We have constantly sought an appropriate balance of Eastern, Western and African traditions. We have intentionally attempted to include Alexandrian, Antiochene, Roman, Syriac, Coptic and Armenian traditions of interpretation. Above all, we want to provide sound, stimulating, reliable exegesis and illuminating exposition of the text by the whole spectrum of classic Christian writers.

7. We have made a special effort where possible to include the voices of women[7] such as Macrina,[8] Eudoxia, Egeria, Faltonia Betitia Proba, the Sayings of the Desert Mothers and others who report the biblical interpretations of women of the ancient Christian tradition.

8. In order to anchor the commentary solidly in primary sources so as to allow the ancient Christian writers to address us on their own terms, the focus is on the texts of the ancient Christian writers themselves, not on modern commentators' views or opinions of the ancient writers. We have looked for those comments on Scripture that will assist the contemporary reader to encounter the deepest level of penetration of the text that has been reached by is best interpreters living amid highly divergent early Christian social settings.

Our purpose is not to engage in critical speculations on textual variants or stemma of the text, or

---

[6]Allegorical treatments of texts are not to be ruled out, but fairly and judiciously assessed as to their explanatory value and typicality. There is a prevailing stereotype that ancient Christian exegesis is so saturated with allegory as to make it almost useless. After making our selections on a merit basis according to our criteria, we were surprised at the limited extent of protracted allegorical passages selected. After making a count of allegorical passages, we discovered that less than one twentieth of these selections have a decisive allegorical concentration. So while allegory is admittedly an acceptable model of exegesis for the ancient Christian writers, especially those of the Alexandrian school and especially with regard to Old Testament texts, it has not turned out to be as dominant a model as we had thought it might be.

[7]Through the letters, histories, theological and biographical writings of Tertullian, Gregory of Nyssa, Gregory of Nazianzus, Jerome, John Chrysostom, Palladius, Augustine, Ephrem, Gerontius, Paulinus of Nola and many anonymous writers (of the Lives of Mary of Egypt, Thais, Pelagia).

[8]Whose voice is heard through her younger brother, Gregory of Nyssa.

extensive deliberations on its cultural context or social location, however useful those exercises may be, but to present the most discerning comments of the ancient Christian writers with a minimum of distraction. This project would be entirely misconceived if thought of as a modern commentary on patristic commentaries.

9. We have intentionally sought out and gathered comments that will aid effective preaching, comments that give us a firmer grasp of the plain sense of the text, its authorial intent, and its spiritual meaning for the worshiping community. We want to help Bible readers and teachers gain ready access to the deepest reflection of the ancient Christian community of faith on any particular text of Scripture.

It would have inordinately increased the word count and cost if our intention had been to amass exhaustively all that had ever been said about a Scripture text by every ancient Christian writer. Rather we have deliberately selected out of this immense data stream the strongest patristic interpretive reflections on the text and sought to deliver them in accurate English translation.

To refine and develop these guidelines, we have sought to select as volume editors either patristics scholars who understand the nature of preaching and the history of exegesis, or biblical scholars who are at ease working with classical Greek and Latin sources. We have preferred editors who are sympathetic to the needs of lay persons and pastors alike, who are generally familiar with the patristic corpus in its full range, and who intuitively understand the dilemma of preaching today. The international and ecclesiastically diverse character of this team of editors corresponds with the global range of our task and audience, which bridge all major communions of Christianity.

Is the ACCS a Commentary?

We have chosen to call our work a commentary, and with good reason. A commentary, in its plain sense definition, is "a series of illustrative or explanatory notes on any important work, as on the Scriptures."[9] *Commentary* is an Anglicized form of the Latin *commentarius* (an "annotation" or "memoranda" on a subject or text or series of events). In its theological meaning it is a work that explains, analyzes or expounds a portion of Scripture. In antiquity it was a book of notes explaining some earlier work such as Julius Hyginus's commentaries on Virgil in the first century. Jerome mentions many commentators on secular texts before his time.

The commentary is typically preceded by a proem in which the questions are asked: who wrote it? why? when? to whom? etc. Comments may deal with grammatical or lexical problems in the text. An attempt is made to provide the gist of the author's thought or motivation, and perhaps to deal with sociocultural influences at work in the text or philological nuances. A commentary usually

---

[9]*Funk & Wagnalls New "Standard" Dictionary of the English Language* (New York: Funk and Wagnalls, 1947).

takes a section of a classical text and seeks to make its meaning clear to readers today, or proximately clearer, in line with the intent of the author.

The Western literary genre of commentary is definitively shaped by the history of early Christian commentaries on Scripture, from Origen and Hilary through John Chrysostom and Cyril of Alexandria to Thomas Aquinas and Nicolas of Lyra. It leaves too much unsaid simply to assume that the Christian biblical commentary took a previously extant literary genre and reshaped it for Christian texts. Rather it is more accurate to say that the Western literary genre of the commentary (and especially the biblical commentary) has patristic commentaries as its decisive pattern and prototype, and those commentaries have strongly influenced the whole Western conception of the genre of commentary. Only in the last two centuries, since the development of modern historicist methods of criticism, have some scholars sought to delimit the definition of a commentary more strictly so as to include only historicist interests—philological and grammatical insights, inquiries into author, date and setting, or into sociopolitical or economic circumstances, or literary analyses of genre, structure and function of the text, or questions of textual criticism and reliability. The ACCS editors do not feel apologetic about calling this work a commentary in its classic sense.

Many astute readers of modern commentaries are acutely aware of one of their most persistent habits of mind: control of the text by the interpreter, whereby the ancient text comes under the power (values, assumptions, predispositions, ideological biases) of the modern interpreter. This habit is based upon a larger pattern of modern chauvinism that views later critical sources as more worthy than earlier. This prejudice tends to view the biblical text primarily or sometimes exclusively through historical-critical lenses accommodative to modernity.

Although we respect these views and our volume editors are thoroughly familiar with contemporary biblical criticism, the ACCS editors freely take the assumption that the Christian canon is to be respected as the church's sacred text. The text's assumptions about itself cannot be made less important than modern assumptions about it. The reading and preaching of Scripture are vital to the church's life. The central hope of the ACCS endeavor is that it might contribute in some small way to the revitalization of that life through a renewed discovery of the earliest readings of the church's Scriptures.

A Gentle Caveat for Those Who Expect Ancient Writers to Conform to Modern Assumptions

If one begins by assuming as normative for a commentary the typical modern expression of what a commentary is and the preemptive truthfulness of modern critical methods, the classic Christian exegetes are by definition always going to appear as dated, quaint, premodern, hence inadequate, and in some instances comic or even mean-spirited, prejudiced, unjust and oppressive. So in the interest of hermeneutic fairness, it is recommended that the modern reader not impose on ancient

Christian exegetes lately achieved modern assumptions about the valid reading of Scripture. The ancient Christian writers constantly challenge what were later to become these unspoken, hidden and often indeed camouflaged modern assumptions.

This series does not seek to resolve the debate between the merits of ancient and modern exegesis in each text examined. Rather it seeks merely to present the excerpted comments of the ancient interpreters with as few distractions as possible. We will leave it to others to discuss the merits of ancient versus modern methods of exegesis. But even this cannot be done adequately without extensively examining the texts of ancient exegesis. And until now biblical scholars have not had easy access to many of these texts. This is what this series is for.

The purpose of exegesis in the patristic period was humbly to seek the revealed truth the Scriptures convey. Often it was not even offered to those who were as yet unready to put it into practice. In these respects much modern exegesis is entirely different: It does not assume the truth of Scripture as revelation, nor does it submit personally to the categorical moral requirement of the revealed text: that it be taken seriously as divine address. Yet we are here dealing with patristic writers who assumed that readers would not even approach an elementary discernment of the meaning of the text if they were not ready to live in terms of its revelation, i.e., to practice it in order to hear it, as was recommended so often in the classic tradition.

The patristic models of exegesis often do not conform to modern commentary assumptions that tend to resist or rule out chains of scriptural reference. These are often demeaned as deplorable proof-texting. But among the ancient Christian writers such chains of biblical reference were very important in thinking about the text in relation to the whole testimony of sacred Scripture by the analogy of faith, comparing text with text, on the premise that *scripturam ex scriptura explicandam esse* ("Scripture is best explained from Scripture").

We beg readers not to force the assumptions of twentieth-century fundamentalism on the ancient Christian writers, who themselves knew nothing of what we now call fundamentalism. It is uncritical to conclude that they were simple fundamentalists in the modern sense. Patristic exegesis was not fundamentalist, because the Fathers were not reacting against modern naturalistic reductionism. They were constantly protesting a merely literal or plain-sense view of the text, always looking for its spiritual and moral and typological nuances. Modern fundamentalism oppositely is a defensive response branching out and away from modern historicism, which looks far more like modern historicism than ancient typological reasoning. Ironically, this makes both liberal and fundamentalist exegesis much more like each other than either are like the ancient Christian exegesis, because they both tend to appeal to rationalistic and historicist assumptions raised to the forefront by the Enlightenment.

Since the principle prevails in ancient Christian exegesis that each text is illumined by other texts and by the whole of the history of revelation, we find in patristic comments on a given text many other subtexts interwoven in order to illumine that text. When ancient exegesis weaves many Scriptures together, it does not limit its focus to a single text as much modern exegesis prefers, but constantly relates it to other texts by analogy, intensively using typological reasoning as did the rabbinic tradition.

The attempt to read the New Testament while ruling out all theological and moral, to say nothing of ecclesiastical, sacramental and dogmatic assumptions that have prevailed generally in the community of faith that wrote it, seems to many who participate in that community today a very thin enterprise indeed. When we try to make sense of the New Testament while ruling out the plausibility of the incarnation and resurrection, the effort appears arrogant and distorted. One who tendentiously reads one page of patristic exegesis, gasps and tosses it away because it does not conform adequately to the canons of modern exegesis and historicist commentary is surely no model of critical effort.

On Misogyny and Anti-Semitism

The questions of anti-Semitism and misogyny require circumspect comment. The patristic writers are perceived by some to be incurably anti-Semitic or misogynous or both. I would like to briefly attempt a cautious apologia for the ancient Christian writers, leaving details to others more deliberate efforts. I know how hazardous this is, especially when done briefly. But it has become such a stumbling block to some of our readers that it prevents them even from listening to the ancient ecumenical teachers. The issue deserves some reframing and careful argumentation.

Although these are challengeable assumptions and highly controverted, it is my view that modern racial anti-Semitism was not in the minds of the ancient Christian writers. Their arguments were not framed in regard to the hatred of a race, but rather the place of the elect people of God, the Jews, in the history of the divine-human covenant that is fulfilled in Jesus Christ. Patristic arguments may have had the unintended effect of being unfair to women according to modern standards, but their intention was to understand the role of women according to apostolic teaching.

This does not solve all of the tangled moral questions regarding the roles of Christians in the histories of anti-Semitism and misogyny, which require continuing fair-minded study and clarification. Whether John Chrysostom or Justin Martyr were anti-Semitic depends on whether the term *anti-Semitic* has a racial or religious-typological definition. In my view, the patristic texts that appear to modern readers to be anti-Semitic in most cases have a typological reference and are based on a specific approach to the interpretation of Scripture—the analogy of faith—which assesses each particular text in relation to the whole trend of the history of revelation and which views the difference between Jew and Gentile under christological assumptions and not merely as a matter of genetics or race.

Even in their harshest strictures against Judaizing threats to the gospel, they did not consider

Jews as racially or genetically inferior people, as modern anti-Semites are prone to do. Even in their comments on Paul's strictures against women teaching, they showed little or no animus against the female gender as such, but rather exalted women as "the glory of man."

Compare the writings of Rosemary Radford Ruether and David C. Ford[10] on these perplexing issues. Ruether steadily applies modern criteria of justice to judge the inadequacies of the ancient Christian writers. Ford seeks to understand the ancient Christian writers empathically from within their own historical assumptions, limitations, scriptural interpretations and deeper intentions. While both treatments are illuminating, Ford's treatment comes closer to a fair-minded assessment of patristic intent.

A Note on Pelagius

The selection criteria do not rule out passages from Pelagius's commentaries at those points at which they provide good exegesis. This requires special explanation, if we are to hold fast to our criterion of consensuality.

The literary corpus of Pelagius remains highly controverted. Though Pelagius was by general consent the arch-heretic of the early fifth century, Pelagius's edited commentaries, as we now have them highly worked over by later orthodox writers, were widely read and preserved for future generations under other names. So Pelagius presents us with a textual dilemma.

Until 1934 all we had was a corrupted text of his Pauline commentary and fragments quoted by Augustine. Since then his works have been much studied and debated, and we now know that the Pelagian corpus has been so warped by a history of later redactors that we might be tempted not to quote it at all. But it does remain a significant source of fifth-century comment on Paul. So we cannot simply ignore it. My suggestion is that the reader is well advised not to equate the fifth-century Pelagius too easily with later standard stereotypes of the arch-heresy of Pelagianism.[11]

It has to be remembered that the text of Pelagius on Paul as we now have it was preserved in the corpus of Jerome and probably reworked in the sixth century by either Primasius or Cassiodorus or both. These commentaries were repeatedly recycled and redacted, so what we have today may be regarded as consonant with much standard later patristic thought and exegesis, excluding, of course, that which is ecumenically censured as "Pelagianism."

Pelagius's original text was in specific ways presumably explicitly heretical, but what we have now is largely unexceptional, even if it is still possible to detect points of disagreement with Augustine.

---

[10]Rosemary Radford Ruether, *Gregory of Nazianzus: Rhetor and Philosopher* (Oxford: Clarendon Press, 1969); Rosemary Radford Ruether, ed., *Religion and Sexism: Images of Woman in the Jewish and Christian Traditions* (New York: Simon and Schuster, 1974); David C. Ford, "Men and Women in the Early Church: The Full Views of St. John Chrysostom" (So. Canaan, Penn.: St. Tikhon's Orthodox Theological Seminary, 1995). Cf. related works by John Meyendorff, Stephen B. Clark and Paul K. Jewett.

[11]Cf. Adalbert Hamman, Supplementum to PL 1:1959, cols. 1101-1570.

We may have been ill-advised to quote this material as "Pelagius" and perhaps might have quoted it as "Pseudo-Pelagius" or "Anonymous," but here we follow contemporary reference practice.

What to Expect from the Introductions, Overviews and the Design of the Commentary
In writing the introduction for a particular volume, the volume editor typically discusses the opinion of the Fathers regarding authorship of the text, the importance of the biblical book for patristic interpreters, the availability or paucity of patristic comment, any salient points of debate between the Fathers, and any particular challenges involved in editing that particular volume. The introduction affords the opportunity to frame the entire commentary in a manner that will help the general reader understand the nature and significance of patristic comment on the biblical texts under consideration, and to help readers find their bearings and use the commentary in an informed way.

The purpose of the *overview* is to give readers a brief glimpse into the cumulative argument of the pericope, identifying its major patristic contributors. This is a task of summarizing. We here seek to render a service to readers by stating the gist of patristic argument on a series of verses. Ideally the overview should track a reasonably cohesive thread of argument among patristic comments on the pericope, even though they are derived from diverse sources and times. The design of the overview may vary somewhat from volume to volume of this series, depending on the requirements of the specific book of Scripture.

The purpose of the selection *heading* is to introduce readers quickly into the subject matter of that selection. In this way readers can quickly grasp what is coming by glancing over the headings and overview. Usually it is evident upon examination that some phrase in the selection naturally defines the subject of the heading. Several verses may be linked together for comment.

Since biographical information on each ancient Christian writer is in abundant supply in various general reference works, dictionaries and encyclopedias, the ACCS has no reason to duplicate these efforts. But we have provided in each volume a simple chronological list of those quoted in that volume, and an alphabetical set of biographical sketches with minimal ecclesiastical, jurisdictional and place identifications.

Each passage of Scripture presents its own distinct set of problems concerning both selection and translation. The sheer quantity of textual materials that has been searched out, assessed and reviewed varies widely from book to book. There are also wide variations in the depth of patristic insight into texts, the complexity of culturally shaped allusions and the modern relevance of the materials examined. It has been a challenge to each volume editor to draw together and develop a reasonably cohesive sequence of textual interpretations from all of this diversity.

The footnotes intend to assist readers with obscurities and potential confusions. In the annotations we have identified many of the Scripture allusions and historical references embedded within the texts.

The aim of our editing is to help readers move easily from text to text through a deliberate editorial linking process that is seen in the overviews, headings and annotations. We have limited the footnotes to roughly less than a one in ten ratio to the patristic texts themselves. Abbreviations are used in the footnotes, and a list of abbreviations is included in each volume. We found that the task of editorial linkage need not be forced into a single pattern for all biblical books but must be molded by that particular book.

The Complementarity of Interdisciplinary Research Methods in This Investigation

The ACCS is intrinsically an interdisciplinary research endeavor. It conjointly employs several diverse but interrelated methods of research, each of which is a distinct field of inquiry in its own right. Principal among these methods are the following:

Textual criticism. No literature is ever transmitted by handwritten manuscripts without the risk of some variations in the text creeping in. Because we are working with ancient texts, frequently recopied, we are obliged to employ all methods of inquiry appropriate to the study of ancient texts. To that end, we have depended heavily on the most reliable text-critical scholarship employed in both biblical and patristic studies. The work of textual critics in these fields has been invaluable in providing us with the most authoritative and reliable versions of ancient texts currently available. We have gratefully employed the extensive critical analyses used in creating the Thesaurus Linguae Graecae and Cetedoc databases.

In respect to the biblical texts, our database researchers and volume editors have often been faced with the challenge of considering which variants within the biblical text itself are assumed in a particular selection. It is not always self-evident which translation or stemma of the biblical text is being employed by the ancient commentator. We have supplied explanatory footnotes in some cases where these various textual challenges may raise potential concerns for readers.

Social-historical contextualization. Our volume editors have sought to understand the historical, social, economic and political contexts of the selections taken from these ancient texts. This understanding is often vital to the process of discerning what a given comment means or intends and which comments are most appropriate to the biblical passage at hand. However, our mission is not primarily to discuss these contexts extensively or to display them in the references. We are not primarily interested in the social location of the text or the philological history of particular words or in the societal consequences of the text, however interesting or evocative these may be. Some of these questions, however, can be treated briefly in the footnotes wherever the volume editors deem necessary.

Though some modest contextualization of patristic texts is at times useful and required, our purpose is not to provide a detailed social-historical placement of each patristic text. That would require volumes ten times this size. We know there are certain texts that need only slight contextualization, others that require a great deal more. Meanwhile, other texts stand on their own easily and brilliantly, in some cases aphoristically, without the need of extensive contextualization. These are the texts we have most sought to identify and include. We are least interested in those texts that obviously require a lot of convoluted explanation for a modern audience. We are particularly inclined to rule out those blatantly offensive texts (apparently anti-Semitic, morally repugnant, glaringly chauvinistic) and those that are intrinsically ambiguous or those that would simply be self-evidently alienating to the modern audience.

Exegesis. If the practice of social-historical contextualization is secondary to the purpose of the ACCS, the emphasis on thoughtful patristic exegesis of the biblical text is primary. The intention of our volume editors is to search for selections that define, discuss and explain the meanings that patristic commentators have discovered in the biblical text. Our purpose is not to provide an inoffensive or extensively demythologized, aseptic modern interpretation of the ancient commentators on each Scripture text but to allow their comments to speak for themselves from within their own worldview.

In this series the term *exegesis* is used more often in its classic than in its modern sense. In its classic sense, exegesis includes efforts to explain, interpret and comment on a text, its meaning, its sources, its connections with other texts. It implies a close reading of the text, using whatever linguistic, historical, literary or theological resources are available to explain the text. It is contrasted with *eisegesis,* which implies that the interpreter has imposed his or her own personal opinions or assumptions on the text.

The patristic writers actively practiced *intra*textual exegesis, which seeks to define and identify the exact wording of the text, its grammatical structure and the interconnectedness of its parts. They also practiced *extra*textual exegesis, seeking to discern the geographical, historical or cultural context in which the text was written. Most important, they were also very well-practiced in *inter*textual exegesis, seeking to discern the meaning of a text by comparing it with other texts.

Hermeneutics. We are especially attentive to the ways in which the ancient Christian writers described their own interpreting processes. This hermeneutic self-analysis is especially rich in the reflections of Origen, Tertullian, Jerome, Augustine and Vincent of Lérins.[12] Although most of our volume editors are thoroughly familiar with contemporary critical discussions of hermeneutical and literary methods, it is not the purpose of ACCS to engage these issues directly. Instead, we are concerned to display and reveal the various hermeneutic assumptions that inform the patristic reading of Scripture, chiefly by letting the writers speak in their own terms.

Homiletics. One of the practical goals of the ACCS is the renewal of contemporary preaching in the light of the wisdom of ancient Christian preaching. With this goal in mind, many of the most trenchant and illuminating comments included are selected not from formal commentaries but

---

[12]Our concern for this aspect of the project has resulted in the production of a companion volume to the ACCS written by the ACCS Associate Editor, Prof. Christopher Hall of Eastern College, *Reading Scripture with the Church Fathers* (Downers Grove, Ill.: InterVarsity Press, 1998).

from the homilies of the ancient Christian writers. It comes as no surprise that the most renowned among these early preachers were also those most actively engaged in the task of preaching. The prototypical Fathers who are most astute at describing their own homiletic assumptions and methods are Gregory the Great, Leo the Great, Augustine, Cyril of Jerusalem, John Chrysostom, Peter Chrysologus and Caesarius of Arles.

Pastoral care. Another intensely practical goal of the ACCS is to renew our readers' awareness of the ancient tradition of pastoral care and ministry to persons. Among the leading Fathers who excel in pastoral wisdom and in application of the Bible to the work of ministry are Gregory of Nazianzus, John Chrysostom, Augustine, and Gregory the Great. Our editors have presented this monumental pastoral wisdom in a guileless way that is not inundated by the premises of contemporary psychotherapy, sociology and naturalistic reductionism.

Translation theory. Each volume is composed of direct quotations in dynamic equivalent English translation of ancient Christian writers, translated from the original language in its best received text. The adequacy of a given attempt at translation is always challengeable. The task of translation is intrinsically debatable. We have sought dynamic equivalency[13] without lapsing into paraphrase, and a literary translation without lapsing into wooden literalism. We have tried consistently to make accessible to contemporary readers the vital nuances and energies of the languages of antiquity. Whenever possible we have opted for metaphors and terms that are normally used by communicators today.

What Have We Achieved?

We have designed the first full-scale early Christian commentary on Scripture in the last five hundred years. Any future attempts at a Christian Talmud or patristic commentary on Scripture will either follow much of our design or stand in some significant response to it.

We have successfully brought together a distinguished international network of Protestant, Catholic and Orthodox scholars, editors and translators of the highest quality and reputation to accomplish this design.

---

[13]The theory of dynamic equivalency has been most thoroughly worked out by Eugene A. Nida, *Toward a Science of Translating* (Leiden: Brill, 1964), and Eugene A. Nida and Jan de Waard, *From One Language to Another: Functional Equivalence in Bible Translating* (Nashville, Tenn.: Nelson, 1986). Its purpose is "to state clearly and accurately the meaning of the original texts in words and forms that are widely accepted by people who use English as a means of communication." It attempts to set forth the writer's "content and message in a standard, everyday, natural form of English." Its aim is "to give today's readers maximum understanding of the content of the original texts." "Every effort has been made to use language that is natural, clear, simple, and unambiguous. Consequently there has been no attempt to reproduce in English the parts of speech, sentence structure, word order and grammatical devices of the original languages. Faithfulness in translation also includes a faithful representation of the cultural and historical features of the original, without any attempt to modernize the text." [Preface, *Good News Bible: The Bible in Today's English Version* (New York: American Bible Society, 1976)]. This does not imply a preference for paraphrase, but a middle ground between literary and literal theories of translation. Not all of our volume editors have viewed the translation task precisely in the same way, but the hope of the series has been generally guided by the theory of dynamic equivalency.

This brilliant network of scholars, editors, publishers, technicians and translators, which constitutes an amazing *novum* and a distinct new ecumenical reality in itself, has jointly brought into formulation the basic pattern and direction of the project, gradually amending and correcting it as needed. We have provided an interdisciplinary experimental research model for the integration of digital search techniques with the study of the history of exegesis.

At this time of writing, we are approximately halfway through the actual production of the series and about halfway through the time frame of the project, having developed the design to a point where it is not likely to change significantly. We have made time-dated contracts with all volume editors for the remainder of the volumes. We are thus well on our way toward bringing the English ACCS to completion. We have extended and enhanced our international network to a point where we are now poised to proceed into modern non-English language versions of ACCS. We already have inaugurated editions in Spanish, Chinese, Arabic, Russian and Italian, and are preparing for editions in Arabic and German, with several more languages under consideration.

We have received the full cooperation and support of Drew University as academic sponsor of the project—a distinguished university that has a remarkable record of supporting major international publication projects that have remained in print for long periods of time, in many cases over one-hundred years. The most widely used Bible concordance and biblical word-reference system in the world today was composed by Drew professor James Strong. It was the very room once occupied by Professor Strong, where the concordance research was done in the 1880s, that for many years was my office at Drew and coincidentally the place where this series was conceived. Today *Strong's Exhaustive Concordance of the Bible* rests on the shelves of most pastoral libraries in the English-speaking world over a hundred years after its first publication. Similarly the *New York Times's* Arno Press has kept in print the major multivolume Drew University work of John M'Clintock and James Strong, *Theological and Exegetical Encyclopedia.* The major edition of Christian classics in Chinese was done at Drew University fifty years ago and is still in print. Drew University has supplied much of the leadership, space, library, work-study assistance and services that have enabled these durable international scholarly projects to be undertaken.

Our selfless benefactors have preferred to remain anonymous. They have been well-informed, active partners in its conceptualization and development, and unflagging advocates and counselors in the support of this lengthy and costly effort. The series has been blessed by steady and generous support, and accompanied by innumerable gifts of providence.

Thomas C. Oden
Henry Anson Buttz Professor of Theology, Drew University
General Editor, ACCS

A Guide to Using This Commentary

Several features have been incorporated into the design of this commentary. The following comments are intended to assist readers in making full use of this volume.

Pericopes of Scripture

The scriptural text has been divided into pericopes, or passages, usually several verses in length. Each of these pericopes is given a heading, which appears at the beginning of the pericope. For example, the first pericope in the commentary on Genesis is "1:1 The Beginning of Creation." This heading is followed by the Scripture passage quoted in the Revised Standard Version (RSV) across the full width of the page. The Scripture passage is provided for the convenience of readers, but it is also in keeping with medieval patristic commentaries, in which the citations of the Fathers were arranged around the text of Scripture.

Overviews

Following each pericope of text is an overview of the patristic comments on that pericope. The format of this overview varies within the volumes of this series, depending on the requirements of the specific book of Scripture. The function of the overview is to provide a brief summary of all the comments to follow. It tracks a reasonably cohesive thread of argument among patristic comments, even though they are derived from diverse sources and generations. Thus the summaries do not proceed chronologically or by verse sequence. Rather they seek to rehearse the overall course of the patristic comment on that pericope.

We do not assume that the commentators themselves anticipated or expressed a formally received cohesive argument but rather that the various arguments tend to flow in a plausible, recognizable pattern. Modern readers can thus glimpse aspects of continuity in the flow of diverse exegetical traditions representing various generations and geographical locations.

Topical Headings

An abundance of varied patristic comment is available for each pericope of these letters. For this reason we have broken the pericopes into two levels. First is the verse with its topical heading. The patristic comments are then focused on aspects of each verse, with topical headings summarizing the essence of the patristic comment by evoking a key phrase, metaphor or idea. This feature provides a bridge by which modern readers can enter into the heart of the patristic comment.

Identifying the Patristic Texts

Following the topical heading of each section of comment, the name of the patristic commentator is given. An English translation of the patristic comment is then provided. This is immediately followed by the title of the patristic work and the textual reference—either by book, section and subsection or by book-and-verse references.

The Footnotes

Readers who wish to pursue a deeper investigation of the patristic works cited in this commentary will find the footnotes especially valuable. A footnote number directs the reader to the notes at the bottom of the right-hand column, where in addition to other notations (clarifications or biblical cross references) one will find information on English translations (where available) and standard original-language editions of the work cited. An abbreviated citation (normally citing the book, volume and page number) of the work is provided except in cases where a line-by-line commentary is being quoted, in which case the biblical references will lead directly to the selection. A key to the abbreviations is provided on pages xv-xvi. Where there is any serious ambiguity or textual problem in the selection, we have tried to reflect the best available textual tradition.

For the convenience of computer database users the digital database references are provided to either the Thesaurus Lingua Graecae (Greek texts) or to the Cetedoc (Latin texts) in the appendix found on pages 177-82.

ABBREVIATIONS

ACW	Ancient Christian Writers: The Works of the Fathers in Translation. Mahwah, N.J.: Paulist Press, 1946-.
AF	J. B. Lightfoot and J. R. Harmer, trans. *The Apostolic Fathers*. Edited by M. W. Holmes. 2nd ed. Grand Rapids, Mich.: Baker, 1989.
AHSIS	Dana Miller, ed. *The Ascetical Homilies of Saint Isaac the Syrian*. Boston, Mass.: Holy Transfiguration Monastery, 1984.
ANF	A. Roberts and J. Donaldson, eds. Ante-Nicene Fathers. 10 vols. Buffalo, N.Y.: Christian Literature, 1885-1896. Reprint, Grand Rapids, Mich.: Eerdmans, 1951-1956. Reprint, Peabody, Mass.: Hendrickson, 1994.
ARL	St. Athanasius. *The Resurrection Letters*. Paraphrased and introduced by Jack N. Sparks. Nashville: Thomas Nelson, 1979.
CCL	Corpus Christianorum. Series Latina. Turnhout, Belgium: Brepols, 1953-.
CSCO	Corpus Scriptorum Christianorum Orientalium. Louvain, Belgium, 1903-.
CSEL	Corpus Scriptorum Ecclesiasticorum Latinorum. Vienna, 1866-.
ESOO	J. A. Assemani, ed. *Sancti Patris Nostri Ephraem Syri Opera Omnia*. Rome, 1737.
FC	Fathers of the Church: A New Translation. Washington, D.C.: Catholic University of America Press, 1947-.
FGFR	F. W. Norris. *Faith Gives Fullness to Reasoning: The Five Theological Orations of Gregory Nazianzen*. Leiden and New York: E. J. Brill, 1990.
GNOS	Hadwiga Hörner, ed. *Gregorii Nysseni Opera Supplementum*. Leiden: E. J. Brill, 1972.
HOG	Bede the Venerable. *Homilies on the Gospels*. Translated by L. T. Martin and D. Hurst. 2 vols. Kalamazoo, Mich.: Cistercian Publications, 1990.
HOP	Ephrem the Syrian. *Hymns on Paradise*. Translated by S. Brock. Crestwood, N.Y.: St. Vladimir's Seminary Press, 1990.
HQG	Jerome. *Hebrew Questions on Genesis*. Translated with introduction and commentary by C. T. R. Hayward. Oxford: Clarendon Press, 1995.
JCC	John Cassian. *Conferences*. Translated by Colm Luibheid. Classics of Western Spirituality. Mahwah, N.J.: Paulist Press, 1985.
JMO	Justin Martyr. *Opera*. Edited by J. C. T. Otto. 3 vols. Jena: Mauke, 1842-1848.
LCC	J. Baillie et al., eds. The Library of Christian Classics. 26 vols. Philadelphia: Westminster, 1953-1966.
LCL	Loeb Classical Library. Cambridge, Mass.: Harvard University Press; London: Heinemann, 1912-.

LQAH   W. W. Harvey, ed. *Sancti Irenaei Episcopi Lugunesis Libros Quinque Adversus Haereses.* 2 vols. Cambridge: Academic Press, 1857.

NPNF   P. Schaff et al., eds. A Select Library of the Nicene and Post-Nicene Fathers of the Christian Church. 2 series (14 vols. each). Buffalo, N.Y.: Christian Literature, 1887-1894; Reprint, Grand Rapids, Mich.: Eerdmans, 1952-1956; Reprint, Peabody, Mass.: Hendrickson, 1994.

OFP   Origen. *On First Principles.* Translated by G. W. Butterworth. London: SPCK, 1936; Reprint, Gloucester, Mass.: Peter Smith, 1973.

OSW   Origen. *Selected Writings.* Translated by Rowan A. Greer. Classics of Western Spirituality: A Library of the Great Spiritual Masters. Mahwah, N.J.: Paulist, 1979.

PG   J.-P. Migne, ed. Patrologia Graeca. 166 vols. Paris: Migne, 1857-1886.

PL   J.-P. Migne, ed. Patrologia Latina. 221 vols. Paris: Migne, 1844-1864.

PL Supp.   A. Hamman, ed. Patrologia Latina Supplementum. 5 vols. Paris: Éditions Garnier Frères, 1958-1974.

PMFSH   Pseudo-Macarius. *The Fifty Spiritual Homilies and the Great Letter.* Translated and edited by George A. Maloney, S.J. Classics of Western Spirituality. New York: Paulist, 1992.

PS   R. Graffin, ed. Patrologia Syriaca. 3 vols. Paris: Firmin-Didot et socii, 1894-1926.

PSD   Pseudo-Dionysius. *The Complete Works.* Translated by Colm Luibheid et al. Classics of Western Spirituality. Mahwah, N.J.: Paulist, 1987.

QO   Theodoret of Cyrus. *Quaestiones in Octateuchum.* Edited by N. Fernandez. Madrid: Marcos A. Saenz-Badillos, 1979.

SC   H. de Lubac, J. Daniélou et al., eds. Sources Chrétiennes. Paris: Editions du Cerf, 1941-.

SNTD   Symeon the New Theologian. *The Discourses.* Translated by C. J. DeCatanzaro. Classics of Western Spirituality: A Library of the Great Spiritual Masters. Mahwah, N.J.: Paulist, 1980.

TP   *The Philokalia.* The complete text compiled by St. Nikodimos of the Holy Mountain and St. Makarios of Corinth. Translated and edited by G. E. H. Palmer, Philip Sherrard and Kallistos Ware. 4 vols. London: Faber & Faber, 1979-1995.

INTRODUCTION TO GENESIS 1-11

The early chapters of Genesis had arguably a greater influence on the development of Christian theology than did any other part of the Old Testament. In these early chapters the Fathers have set out the fundamental patterns of Christian theology. Here there was affirmed the doctrine of creation, in accordance with which the created order had been brought into being from nothing by God's Word as something "exceedingly good" (Gen 1:31). One of the most popular genres of scriptural commentary among the Fathers was commentary on the six days of creation, the Hexaemeron. Those by Basil the Great and Ambrose are perhaps the most famous. Although Augustine gave this title to none of his books, he returned at least five times to exposition of the first chapter of Genesis and three times carried his commentary beyond the first chapter (*Two Books on Genesis Against the Manichaeans, On the Literal Interpretation of Genesis* and *City of God* 11-16).

The Fathers also found in Genesis the doctrine of humankind created "according to the image and likeness of God." In addition, they found there the doctrine of the fall and the beginning of fallen human society, as well as hints and guesses about the eventual overcoming of the fallen human condition through the incarnation. There follows an account of the establishment of the human race outside the "paradise of delight," the constant struggle for survival in a natural environment now unfriendly or even actively hostile, the spread of sin and crime, beginning after humanity's first disobedience, with Cain's murder of his brother Abel, but also the discovery of music (Gen 4:21) and metal tools (Gen 4:22). That first attempt to find a way of life outside paradise soon foundered in the proliferation of wickedness by humankind, which was swept away by the flood, Noah and his family alone surviving, together with representatives of the whole animal kingdom. Such wholesale punishment of human wickedness was not, however, to be the rule, and the rainbow became the sign and pledge of God's covenant with humankind, made with Noah (the Noachic covenant, Gen 9:8-17).

After the flood, Noah and his descendants began once again to establish a way of life in the fallen world. Noah became a farmer and planted a vineyard (Gen 9:20). His first experiments with wine making, however, were unfortunate: he succumbed to drunkenness and ended up stretched out in his tent with his clothes in disarray. In this phase of human development, cities began to be established: Babylon and Nineveh are mentioned (Gen 10:10-11). But it became apparent that human solidarity manifest in the building up of ordered human communities, such as cities, could be directed in pride against God and his purposes for humankind, and at the tower of Babel (or "confusion," as the Septuagint has it) human solidarity was broken by the confusion of tongues, the creation of different languages.

It was in this divided world that Abram was born among the Chaldeans. (Neither the Greek Septuagint nor the Latin Vulgate recognized Ur as a place name: the Greek translates it as "place," Jerome takes it to mean "fire" and, in a learned note, connects it with the fire worship of the ancient Zoroastrians.) Genesis 11 ends with Abraham leaving the Chaldeans and settling in Haran in Mesopotamia, where he received God's call to journey still further and become the father of a great nation (Gen 12:1-3). With that call there commence the accounts of the patriarchs, of the revelation of the God of Abraham and Isaac and Jacob, of the calling of the people of Israel and the whole story of the Old Testament, in which there emerges, so Christians with the Fathers believe, the hope for the coming Messiah, a hope fulfilled in the incarnation of the Son of God as Jesus of Nazareth.

Critical Problems of the Text

We shall look in more detail at the theology the Fathers drew out of these chapters later on, but first various critical problems need to be discussed. Compiling a patristic commentary on any part of the Old Testament raises questions not raised by such a commentary on the New Testament. These questions are largely to do with the actual biblical text and to a lesser extent with the higher criticism of that text (that is, questions of composition and authorship). With the New Testament, the English text that we read nowadays is a translation of the New Testament more or less as the Greek fathers themselves knew it (there are sometimes minor differences where textual criticism detects early accretions to the text, for instance at Mk 9:29, but these are few). But with the Old Testament, there is a major difference. For the Christian Old Testament was the Greek Septuagint (usually abbreviated as LXX, the Latin numeral for seventy), whereas what is translated in our Bibles is the Hebrew text, of which the Septuagint was an early translation.

Differences between the Hebrew Bible and the Septuagint. The text of the Hebrew Bible and that of the Septuagint display some major differences. The Septuagint includes books such as Ecclesiasticus (or Sirach, an abbreviation of the full title The Wisdom of Jesus the Son of Sirach) and the Wisdom of Solomon that are not included in the Hebrew Bible. Some books in the Septuagint seem to be later expanded versions of the Hebrew original: for example, Esther and Daniel, which in the Septuagint includes stories about Susanna and Bel and the Dragon, and an expanded account of the Three Young Men in the fiery furnace (including the songs sung by them in praise of God and creation). In other cases, the Septuagint presents the text in a rearranged order (e.g., the book of Jeremiah, which has additions as well). There are also many minor disagreements between the Greek and Hebrew versions.

It is generally held that the Septuagint is a later, embellished version of the original Hebrew text. But this is only partly true. Sometimes, as the Qumran discoveries have revealed, the Septuagint preserves works that might have been included by the rabbis in the Hebrew Bible had the Hebrew original not been lost by the early centuries of the Christian era (or the common era, though it is not clear to whom it is common, apart from Christians and post-Christians); such is the case with Sirach. Furthermore, the text of the Hebrew Bible that we have, the so-called Masoretic text, is the result of critical endeavors on the part of rabbis in the second half of the first millennium. It is, then, a good deal later than the Hebrew text that would have been available to the Greek translators of the Septuagint. Variants in it may well be witnesses to older and better readings than those found in the Masoretic text. (This, too, has been supported by the biblical texts discovered at Qumran.)[1]

The Septuagint: The Christian Old Testament. The early Christians were well aware of these discrepancies between the Greek Old Testament and the Hebrew Bible, but almost universally they regarded the Septuagint and translations from it, notably the Old Latin version, as the authoritative text of the Old Testament of their Christian Scriptures. The main reason for this was that the Septuagint was the version of the Old Testament that they were accustomed to using. It was in Greek that Christianity had spread throughout the Mediterranean world, and it was the Septuagint to which Christian preachers and missionaries appealed as the Scripture. The Septuagint is the version quoted and referred to, for the most part, in the New Testament, which is, of course, in the Greek of the first Christian missionaries and Christian communities. The Old Latin version (or versions) was a translation of the Septuagint and remained the principal text of the Scriptures for those who spoke Latin throughout the patristic period.

When Christianity established itself among the Armenians, the Copts and the Georgians, the Septuagint formed the basis for their vernacular Old Testament. Even among the Syrians, who spoke a Semitic language, Syriac, their translation, the Peshitta, though naturally a translation of the closely related Hebrew, is not without the influence of interpretations inspired by the Septuagint.

The earliest dissenting voice from the primacy of the Septuagint seems to have been the Latin scholar Jerome, whose translation, now called the Vulgate, was inspired by his ideal of Hebrew truth (*Hebraica veritas*), though even here, despite his shrill defense of the priority of the Hebrew, his version frequently follows the text of the Septuagint.[2] At the Reformation, the Renaissance ideal of *ad fontes* ("to the sources") led to Protestant vernacular translations of the Old Testament being based on the Hebrew, and thence to the idea that the Hebrew Bible is the Christian Old Testament.

Although the Roman Catholic Church initially resisted this and insisted on the authority of the Latin Vulgate, Roman Catholic scholarship in the latter half of the twentieth century has tended to follow the Reformers. Christians of the Orthodox tradition (whether Greek, Russian, Romanian or other strands) stick to the traditional notion of the Septuagint or translations of it as the Christian

---

[1]Some scholars are coming to appreciate the value of the Septuagint as a witness to the original Hebrew. In the case of Genesis 1-11, see Ronald S. Hendel, *The Text of Genesis 1-11: Textual Studies and Critical Edition* (New York: Oxford University Press, 1998).
[2]See again for Genesis, C. T. R. Hayward, *Jerome's Hebrew Questions on Genesis* (Oxford: Clarendon Press, 1995).

Old Testament, and they are shored up in this position by the enormous importance of the liturgical texts that are soaked in allusions to and quotations from the Greek text of the Septuagint. In the West, Orthodox Christians are a minority, but it is worth noting that recently a few scholars have called for a return to the original Christian tradition, according to which the Christian Old Testament is the Septuagint.[3]

The legend of the Septuagint. For the Fathers, this tradition was virtually unquestioned. Furthermore, it was enhanced by the widely accepted tradition of the way in which the Septuagint had been translated. According to a legend, first witnessed in the *Letter of Aristeas,* probably written in the second century B.C., the Septuagint was a Greek translation of the Hebrew Scriptures, commissioned by the Egyptian pharaoh Ptolemy II Philadelphus (287-247 B.C.) for his library in Alexandria. The Jewish high priest Eleazar was approached and selected seventy-two scholars, six from each of the tribes of Israel, who traveled to Alexandria and there finished their translation in seventy-two days.[4] Later versions of the legend exist, for instance that recorded by the Christian bishop of Lyons in the later second century, Irenaeus. According to his version the translators numbered seventy and were required each to produce individual translations of the whole of the Hebrew Scriptures, which were miraculously found to be identical.[5] Such stories of its miraculous translation naturally enhanced the authority of the Septuagint (the title derived from the number of the translators) among Greek-speaking Jews, especially in Alexandria, and then among Christians.

The Septuagint between Christians and Jews. By the second century A.D., however, the use of the Septuagint among Christians was producing a reaction against it in Jewish circles, especially those circles influenced by the growing rabbinic movement, which emphasized the supreme authority of the Hebrew version. This division between Christian Greek and Jewish Hebrew was deepened by Christian interpretations of verses from the Greek Septuagint that had no support from the Hebrew text, the most famous of these being the use of Isaiah 7:14 (Isaiah's prophecy that "a virgin shall conceive and bear a son and his name shall be called Emmanuel") as a prophecy of the virginal conception of Jesus Christ (already found in the New Testament at Mt 1:23). While the Septuagint *parthenos* unambiguously means "virgin," the Hebrew word so translated (*'almāh*) means a "young woman." Such discrepancies between the Septuagint and the Hebrew Bible, especially where the Greek version could be read as a prophecy of Christ, became one of the principal issues of early Jewish-Christian polemic (see especially Justin Martyr's *Dialogue with Trypho the Jew,* a work belonging to the mid-second century).

New translations, the Hexapla. In the course of the second century, various translators—Aquila, and later Symmachus and Theodotion—provided Greek versions closer to the original Hebrew.

---

[3]See M. Müller, *The First Bible of the Church: A Plea for the Septuagint,* JSOT Supplement 206 (Sheffield: Sheffield Academic Press, 1996).
[4]Letter to Aristeas, esp. 301-17.
[5]Irenaeus *Adversus Haereses* 3.21.2. Augustine has much the same story, *City of God* 18.42.

These translations, which were presumably intended for Greek-speaking Jews, have not survived, probably because of the supreme value attached by the rabbis to the Hebrew text and the consequent encouragement to learn Hebrew within rabbinic Judaism, save in the fragments that survive of a massive tool for biblical scholarship, the Hexapla, compiled by the great third-century Christian scholar and theologian Origen. The Hexapla, so-called because of its six columns, was a massive synopsis of the versions of the Old Testament with columns containing side by side the Hebrew text, that text transliterated into Greek, and the texts of Aquila, Symmachus, the Septuagint and Theodotion (though there is some dispute about the exact shape of the Hexapla[6]).

It is not clear what its purpose was, though it would alert Christian apologists to places where the Hebrew text did not support the Septuagint. What happened was that the Hexapla supplemented the text of the Septuagint and provided a broader textual basis for scriptural interpretation: this may have been Origen's purpose, for it is borne out by his exegetical practice in his commentaries and homilies. But it also enabled Origen and other scholars to correct the Septuagint against the Hebrew (where it was obscure, for instance), to supplement the Septuagint by the Hebrew where the latter was fuller and to alert the Christian scholar to places in the Septuagint where the Hebrew was lacking. Origen apparently used the marks of ancient scholarship, the obelus ($\div$) and the asterisk (*), to indicate passages unique to the Septuagint and those passages that had been added to the Septuagint from the Hebrew version.

This text—the Septuagint augmented by passages from the translations of the Hebrew, sometimes with the obeli and asterisks written in, sometimes with them omitted—came to circulate among Christians, especially from the fourth century onwards, when the expansion of the now tolerated Christian church led to the demand for copies of the Scriptures (e.g., the fifty copies of the Scriptures ordered from Eusebius of Caesarea by the emperor Constantine for use in churches; see *Life of Constantine* 4.36-37). Such acceptance of both the Hebrew and Septuagint versions of the Old Testament—with the Hebrew supplementing but not correcting the Greek Septuagint, by now traditional among Christians—became the norm among Christians. Augustine gave eloquent expression to this understanding of scriptural authority:

> For the same Spirit that was in the prophets when they delivered those messages was present in person in the seventy men also; and he surely had it in his power to say something else, just as if the prophet had said both, because it was the same Spirit that said both . . . so as to show that the work was not accomplished by a man enslaved to a literal rule of thumb but by the power of God flooding and guiding the intelligence of the translator. . . . If, then, we see, as it behooves us to see, in these Scriptures no words that the Spirit of God did not speak through men, it follows that whatever is in the Hebrew text but not in that of the seventy translators is something that the Spirit of God did not choose to say

---

[6]On the Hexapla, see, most recently, A. Salvesen, ed., *Origen's Hexapla and Fragments: Papers Presented at the Rich Seminar on the Hexapla, Oxford Centre for Hebrew and Jewish Studies*, Texte und Studien zum antiken Judentum 0721-8753; 58 (Tübingen: Mohr Siebeck, 1998).

through the latter, but only through the prophets. On the other hand, where anything that is in the Septuagint is not in the Hebrew text, the same Spirit must have preferred to say it through the former rather than through the prophets, thus showing that these as well as those were prophets. Likewise he spoke, as he pleased, some things through Isaiah, others through Jeremiah, still others through one or another prophet, or the same things but in different form through the latter prophet as well as the former. Moreover, anything that is found in both places is something that one and the same Spirit chose to say through both kinds of instruments, but in such wise that the one kind led the way in prophesying and the other came after with a prophetic translation of their words. For just as a single Spirit of peace inspired the former when they spoke true and concordant words, so the same Spirit manifested himself in the latter when without mutual consultation they nevertheless translated the whole as if with one mouth. (*City of God* 18.43)

Jerome and the Vulgate. Among the Greeks, this view held sway without any serious opposition. The only real dissent came in the West from Jerome, whose Latin translation, which came to be called the Vulgate (the common Bible), was made in the case of the Old Testament, in principle, from the Hebrew. Nevertheless, even he included the books of the Septuagint that are not found in the Hebrew, and frequently his translations, which were generally revisions of the Old Latin rather than fresh translations, reflect the interpretation of the Septuagint. Jerome's preference for Hebrew truth was a lonely stance and attracted criticism from, among others, Augustine.[7] It was only gradually that the Vulgate established itself against the Old Latin, and in the case of the Psalter, Jerome's version from the Hebrew never established itself in liturgical use. The Venerable Bede, writing in England in the early eighth century, is one of the first to make regular use of the Vulgate in his commentaries.

The text in the Ancient Christian Commentary on Scripture. How does this bear on the Ancient Christian Commentary on Scripture, and in particular on this, the first volume, that deals with Genesis 1-11? From what we have seen, it is apparent that the actual text the Fathers used is not something that we can pick up in a current English translation, for English Bibles use the Hebrew text for the Old Testament. Even if there were a reliable translation of the Septuagint available in English, that would not be exactly the text of the Fathers either, for printed versions of the Septuagint text are based on Alfred Rahlfs's edition, first published in 1935, which is an attempt to work back from the texts that have survived to the original text of the Alexandrian translators. But, as we have seen, the text most of the Fathers would have used would have been some form of the so-called Hexaplaric text or at the very least have contained readings derived from the Hexapla.

In this volume we have printed the translation of the Revised Standard Version and noted the variations of this text from the Septuagint (in Rahlfs's critical edition). In the early chapters of Gen-

---

[7]See Carolinne White, *The Correspondence (394-419) Between Jerome and Augustine of Hippo*, Studies in Bible and Early Christianity 23 (Lewiston; Queenston; Lampeter: Edwin Mellen Press, 1990), esp. 35-42. White provides an English translation of the letters.

esis the Septuagint follows the Hebrew closely: there seem to be no Hexaplaric readings, the variations from the Hebrew being mainly matters of interpretation of the Hebrew text or sometimes witnessing to a slightly different form of the text than the Masoretic text. But, as the reader will see, almost all the variant readings of the Septuagint are part of the text that the Fathers had before them and on which they were commenting.

Septuagint variants from the Hebrew in Genesis 1-11. Apart from individual variant readings, there are two striking groups of variants in the first eleven chapters of Genesis, both of which manifest themselves most sharply in the genealogies that form such a prominent feature of these chapters (though one that most modern readers tend to skip). The first concerns names, the second the periods of years mentioned in the genealogies.

The variations in the names are of two kinds. Most commonly, these variants are due to difficulties of transliteration between languages with different alphabets (e.g., Nimrod becomes Nebrod [Gen 10:8]). But it is sometimes a matter of interpretation: the Septuagint may interpret the name rather than transliterating it (e.g., at its first mention, the name *Eve* is translated *Zōē*, "life," rather than transliterated; "Babel" in Gen 11 is translated "confusion"). Or it may do the reverse, taking a word to be a name where modern translators see a noun (e.g., in Gen 2-3, where *Adam* is translated by modern translations as "the man," while the Septuagint sees the name *Adam*). Or it may identify a Hebrew place name (the most striking example being the identification of the "Babel" of Gen 10:10 with Babylon) or fail to identify a place name identified by modern scholars (e.g., in Gen 10:6, 13, where the Septuagint fails to identify Mesraim as Egypt). All significant variations in names are indicated by additional notes to the RSV text.

The discrepancy between the periods of years recorded in the genealogies between the Septuagint and the Hebrew text (presumably due to misreading Hebrew numerals) was noticed in ancient times. The variations are curious in that they usually have the effect of some of the patriarchs having children later in life, while the actual length of their lives remains the same (e.g., according to the Hebrew, Adam became Seth's father when he was 130 and then lived for another 800 years, whereas the Septuagint has him becoming Seth's father at the age of 230 and living for another 700 years; see Gen 5:3-5). These discrepancies, however, caused a problem. In the case of Methuselah (or Mathousala), the Hebrew calculation has him dying, at the age of 969, in the year of the flood (his son Lamech, born in his 187th year [Gen 5:25], became Noah's father when he was 182 [Gen 5:28]; Noah was 600 in the year of the flood: 187 + 182 + 600 = 969), whereas the Septuagint calculation has him dying 14 years after the flood (Lamech, born in Methuselah's 167th year, becomes Noah's father in his 188th year; Noah was 600 in the year of the flood: 167 + 188 + 600 = 955, 14 years short of his death at age 969). But Methuselah was not in the ark, so how did he survive?

Jerome, in his *Hebrew Questions on Genesis,* solved the problem by reference to the Hebrew, a solution accepted by Augustine, who however noted that such correction of the Septuagint by the

Hebrew was warranted only if there was reason to suppose that there had been a simple mistake, for the seventy were to be regarded, as we have seen, not simply as translators but as enjoying the freedom of prophets.[8]

Critical Problems of Composition and Authorship

Most modern readers of the Pentateuch, the first five books of the Bible that constituted the Hebrew law, or Torah, are aware of something of the results of modern scholarship as to composition and authorship. For nearly two centuries it has generally though not universally been held that the Pentateuch was compiled in the postexilic period (that is, after the exile or Babylonian captivity, which lasted from about 597 to 539 B.C.), making use of earlier materials—histories, legends and law codes—and giving them a narrative structure beginning with the creation of the world or perhaps working them into an already existing narrative structure.

The basis for this theory (for it is no more than that) is the existence of parallel passages in which the same event seems to be treated twice and the way in which God is referred to in different passages. So, in the chapters we are concerned with, there seem to be two accounts of creation, Genesis 1:1-2:4a and one beginning with Genesis 2:4b that starts with human creation and continues with an account of the fall. Also, in the account of the flood, there are discrepancies in the number of animals taken into the ark: one account seems to envisage pairs, while the other envisages two groups of animals, those ritually clean and those ritually unclean, the former being preserved in groups of seven, while the latter are preserved in pairs (cf. Gen 6:18-22 with Gen 7:1-5).

The difference in the way God is referred to appears in our chapters in that in Genesis 1:1-2:4a, 5:1-32, 6:9-22, 7:6-10, 8:1-19 and 9:1-17 God is referred to as God (Hebrew *ʾelōhim*; Greek *theos*). Elsewhere God is referred to by using the sacred Tetragrammaton, YHWH (translated into Greek as *kyrios*, "Lord," a practice preserved in English translations until recently and written in capitals, LORD, as in the RSV text), the divine name, only pronounced by the priest in the temple liturgy (as a result we do not know how it is pronounced and can only guess). Following up these clues, scholars have distinguished several different sources for the Pentateuch, often referred to by initials: J (the Yahwist, or Jahwist, source, where God is called from the beginning by the divine name YHWH), E (the Elohist source that calls God *ʾelōhim*), D (the Deuteronomic source, connected with the reform just prior to the exile) and P (the Priestly source, much concerned with liturgical and legal matters). For Genesis 1-11 the principal sources alleged are J and P (which adopts the Elohist practice of referring to God as *ʾelōhim* prior to his revelation to Moses in Exodus 3:13-15).

The Fathers knew nothing of all this, though they were aware of the differences that have led to the postulation of these sources. Such differences they tended to interpret in terms of the pedagogi-

---

[8]See the passages cited below on Genesis 5:25-27.

cal purpose of the narrator who is telling a story on different levels (in this they might be claimed to have anticipated some of the more recent fashions in Old Testament scholarship). For them the narrator was Moses. This conviction the early Christians shared with the Jews, but the theological importance of Genesis, to which we shall shortly turn, and especially its account of creation, led to a shift in the Christian perception of the significance of the figure of Moses, as compared with that of the Jews.

For the Jews, Moses was the great legislator, the one who had received the law on Mt. Sinai; the Pentateuch was for them the Torah. Christian interest in the law had been deflected by the central significance they attached to Christ and to faith in him. Moses is still the lawgiver, the one who received the law on Sinai, but as author of the book of Genesis, he is the one who gave an account of creation, one who could contemplate and accurately describe the created order as God intended it. The story of the creation and of the fall was full of hints and guesses about the coming of Christ and the restoration of the cosmos in him, according to the Fathers. Consequently Moses was as much a prophet as a lawgiver and as much prized for his insight into creation as for his authority as receiver of the law.

Theological Issues

It might seem strange that the Fathers invested so much significance in the early chapters of Genesis. The pattern that it provides of creation and fall is not something that the Jews detected in it: for them the fall was not and is not a cataclysmic event in the history of humankind; it is but one of many examples of human failure to live within the covenant. Why do the early chapters of Genesis assume such significance for patristic and most later Christian theology?

Adam and Christ. One reason is Paul's understanding of Jesus as the Second Adam. "As in Adam all die, so also in Christ shall all be made alive" (1 Cor 15:22); "it is written, 'The first man Adam became a living being'; the last Adam became a life-giving spirit. . . . The first man was from the earth, a man of dust; the second man is from heaven. . . . Just as we have borne the image of the man of dust, we shall also bear the image of the man of heaven" (1 Cor 15:45, 47, 49). If the significance of Christ is summed up through such contrast between him and Adam, then the account of Adam himself assumes archetypal significance for understanding the fallen human condition.

Typology. The tragic parallelism of Adam and Christ became a key to understanding Christ's significance: Adam's disobedience is matched by Christ's obedience, the tree of the knowledge of good and evil is matched by the tree/wood of the cross (especially when the same word, *xylon* in Greek, *lignum* in Latin, means both "tree" and "wood"), Eve is matched by Mary (who truly becomes "mother of the living" [cf. Gen 3:20], while Eve had become rather the mother of the living dead). We can see in this a principle of scriptural interpretation, paralleling the formation of the Christian Bible as consisting of Old Testament and New Testament. It is commonly called typology, though this modern term reifies something that was for the Fathers more a habit of thought than a method or doctrine. The Fathers called it, in the East most commonly, *theoria*, contemplation, looking more deeply into the meaning of Scripture, while the Latin fathers came to use the term for the rhetorical figure that expresses one thing through another: *allegoria*, allegory.

This practice of making the text of Scripture shine like a beam of light, as it were, through the prism of faith in Christ, in whom Adam's sin and ours is canceled and in whom the hopes of Israel and the whole of humankind have been fulfilled, is perhaps, to begin with, the strangest thing about the Fathers' approach to Scripture. Another way of putting it, drawing on some remarks by the French Catholic poet and diplomat Paul Claudel, is to see the Scriptures not as an arsenal of arguments with which to attack one another (as Catholics and Protestants have been doing for years) but as a treasury of the manifold riches of God's grace, a treasury of symbols (for no human words can capture the riches of God's grace) that find their proper orientation in the magnetic field of the rule of faith (an ancient expression for what is nowadays summed up in the creed, or symbol of faith). The use of such imagery to express what is involved in scriptural interpretation points us in the right direction to begin to grasp the approach of the Fathers, which is less scientific than poetic and often finds its fullest expression in the liturgical hymns of the church, woven out of the imagery of the scriptural text.

Creation. The Fathers' sense of the fundamental place of creation in Christian doctrine was a consciously maintained theological premise. Athanasius, at the beginning of his treatise *On the Incarnation*, asserts: "But as we proceed in our exposition of this [the incarnation of the Word], we must first speak about the creation of the universe and its creator, God, so that in this way we may consider as fitting that its renewal was effected by the Word who created it in the beginning."[9]

It is only against the background of a proper understanding of the doctrine of creation that we are able to grasp the significance of the incarnation of the Word. What creation means, as Athanasius goes on to make clear, is that the universe has been created out of nothing by the Word of God. It follows from this that the universe is good, that the reason for its present lamentable state is not to be sought in the Creator but in the fact that the highest created state is that of a free, rational being, so that to create a universe capable of containing the highest form of goodness was to create a universe that depended on the free obedience of rational beings, the fall being the failure of rational beings to remain faithful to the good.

That failure led to a universe characterized by corruption and death. The fall was not, however, the end of the story, for God the Word, who had created the universe, came to live as a human being, among fallen human beings, and thereby to encounter the powers of corruption and death, unleashed in the cosmos by the human failure to cleave to the good, to conquer them in his death

---

[9]Athanasius *On the Incarnation* 1.

and thereby to reveal the power of life in the resurrection and draw humankind into his divine life, where they will be secure in the good. The whole picture is of an arc of the divine purpose passing from creation to deification (to use the traditional term in Greek patristics for the final glorification of creation, including humankind), transcending the lesser arc necessitated by human frailty passing from fall to redemption. Seen in this context, the incarnation is of more than merely human significance but involves the whole cosmic order.

Humanity in the image of God. The cosmic dimension of creation-incarnation-deification does not supplant the human significance of the drama of creation and redemption. In fact, rather the opposite, for the human itself has a cosmic role according to the Greek fathers. This is expressed partly in the doctrine of the human as a microcosm, a "little cosmos," in which the greater cosmos is reflected, a doctrine that the Fathers found in the classical philosophers, notably Plato. There is a tendency in the Fathers to read the creation narrative of Genesis in terms of the cosmological myth of Plato's *Timaeus* and vice versa. As microcosm, the human being is seen as integral to the cosmos, as the "bond *(syndesmos)* of the cosmos." For this reason, the fall of humankind has cosmic consequences: it is not just humankind that has been subjected to corruption and death but the whole cosmic order (cf. Rom 8:20-23).

But the ultimate justification for the high doctrine of the cosmic role of humankind lies in the doctrine, asserted in Genesis 1:26, that human beings were created "in the image and likeness of God." The doctrine of human beings as bearing the divine image is not a doctrine that recurs much in the Old Testament; outside Genesis there are occasional echoes, no more (e.g., Ps 8:6, Wis 2:23). Nor is it very prominent in the New Testament. But to the Fathers it is central: as Père Th. Camelot once remarked, "This theme of the image is, in the theology of the Fathers, above all the Greek fathers, central: in that doctrine there converge at once their christology and theology of the Trinity, their anthropology and psychology, their theology of creation and that of grace, the problem of nature and of the supernatural, the mystery of deification, the theology of the spiritual life and the laws of its development and of its progress."[10]

It is central, one might argue, because the doctrine of the image enabled the Fathers to interpret the teaching they found in the Bible in categories of thought that they, as Greeks, owed in large part to their education, rooted as it was in classical philosophy, especially that of Plato. This can be illustrated in two ways. First, if being "in the image" identified what it was to be human, then this would suggest that to be in the image was to be rational, the Greek for which is *logikos*. God created through his word ("He spoke . . . and it was so"), that is, through his Logos, the Logos that, as John tells us, was "in the beginning," was "with God" and "was God" (Jn 1:1). This suggests a deeper meaning of being rational, *logikos*: to be *logikos* is to participate in the Logos, that is, to participate in

---

[10]Th. Camelot, "La Théologie de l'Image de Dieu," in *Revue des sciences philosophiques et théologiques* 40 (1956): 443-44.

the One who was incarnate as Christ (cf. Jn 1:14).

The language of Genesis 1:26 fits in well with this, for it states that human beings were created according to the image of God, *kat' eikona tou theou*. In other words, there is an image of God, in accordance with which human beings are fashioned, and that image is the Logos (cf. 2 Cor 4:4, which speaks of "Christ, who is the image of God," cf. 1 Cor 11:7; Col 1:15). And that image is also that into which we are transformed, or transfigured, by our response to the grace of God (cf. 2 Cor 3:18, where we are said to be "changed into the same image from glory to glory," and Rom 8:29, where we are destined to be "conformed to the image of his Son").

The notion then of being fashioned in the image deepens the notion of what it is to be human. It makes rationality a participation in the creative Logos of God and links the original human state of being in the image of God with our final state, transfigured by the glory of God into the image of his Son. Being *kat' eikona* (which in later Christian Greek becomes a noun phrase, *to kat' eikona*, "the state of being in the image") is then fundamental to understanding what it is to be human and what it is to be restored to communion with God.

This dynamic sense of a movement in which the fundamental created potentiality of human beings is revealed is linked by most of the Greek fathers to the other word used in Genesis 1:26, which says that humans were made in God's *image and likeness, kat' eikona . . . kai . . . homoiōsin*. For the Greek word *homoiōsis* suggests a process rather than a state (the state of likeness would be *homoiōma* or *homoiotēs*): it was the word used by Plato to denote "likening to God" or "assimilation to God" (*homoiōsis theō*), which was for him the goal of philosophy, as he remarks in a phrase much quoted by the Fathers (*Theaetetus* 176b). Human beings are created in the image of God and, finally transfigured by the glory of God, will display God's likeness.

The whole process of responding to the grace of God by prayer and a demanding life of love brings about an assimilation to God in which humans find their created fulfillment: this assimilation to God is also called *theōsis* (deification, becoming God). But this deification is possible only in and through Christ the incarnate Word, for humans possess only the potentiality for deification, because they are created in accordance with Christ, who is the image of God.

Even in this brief sketch, one can see how the notion of the image of God is an architectonic term in the theology of the Fathers, one in which all the dimensions of their theology converge. This realization perhaps found nowhere such clear expression as in John of Damascus, the Palestinian monk who opposed the destruction of images (iconoclasm) by the Byzantine emperor Leo at the beginning of the eighth century. In his defense of the divine images, he begins his argument by showing how the notion of the image is a central analogical term in Christian theology, so that disrespect for the artistic image, such as the iconoclast emperor displayed, threatened to tear apart the whole fabric of Orthodox theology (see *On the Divine Images* 1.9-13; 3.16-23).

The fall and original sin. Genesis 3 became for Christian theologians an explanation of why the created order, fashioned by God as "exceedingly good," is full of evil and wickedness. As we have already remarked, the fundamental significance seen in the account of humanity's first disobedience is not something Christians inherited from Jewish interpretation of Genesis but probably has much to do with the way in which the story of Adam is seen to mirror in reverse the story of Christ the Second Adam. By his disobedience, Adam destroyed the relationship that God had established with him, not just for himself but for his descendants: they are born into a world alienated from God.

Exactly how Adam came to disobey God is something which the Fathers pondered, and they came up with different solutions, as will be discovered in the patristic commentary that follows. Pride in the sense of setting one's self up against God and ignoring his will, giving in to the allurement of the senses and solidarity on Adam's part with his misguided wife are all interpretations suggested by the Fathers. They also make much of the deceit of the serpent, whom they generally identify with Satan, who had been created as the greatest of the angels but fell, either because of pride that would not permit God to determine his moral world or more commonly because of envy (cf. Wis 2:23-24), envy of the human being whom God had made a microcosm and bond of the cosmos.

This cosmic role that the human being was created to fulfill is invoked by the Greek fathers to explain the fact that Adam's sin affected not just himself but also his descendants. As Athanasius put it, and following him most of the Greek fathers, as a result of Adam's sin, corruption and death have been unleashed into the world. The reason why repentance on Adam's part could not undo the effects of the fall is that the created order is in ruins as a result of Adam's sin, and this ruinous state is manifest in corruption and death that seem to stalk through the cosmos like avenging angels (see *On the Incarnation* 7).

This cosmic understanding of the effects of the fall, characteristic of the Greek fathers, is in some contrast to Augustine's idea of the fall and original sin (an idea already developed by the unknown Latin father called Ambrosiaster, because his works are preserved among the writings of Ambrose), that eventually came to be dominant in the West. Augustine saw Adam's personal sin and guilt as inherited by his descendants, so that they are guilty of original sin and justly suffer its consequences, because they all sinned in Adam (which he found affirmed in Rom 5:12, according to his interpretation of the traditional Latin version). The term *original* sin is not found in the Greek fathers, who in contrast speak of the rather different concept of ancestral sin *(propaterikē hamartia)*.

The archetypal status of Genesis for the Fathers. After the first three chapters of Genesis, the seam of patristic comment becomes much thinner. The account of the flood is paid some attention and seen as a prefiguration of Christian baptism (cf. 1 Pet 3:20-21). But the rest of the account of the development of human society, the seeming parallel growth of human skills and crafts and human wickedness, attracts little comment. Nonetheless these chapters provided preconceptions that affect patristic thought in subliminal ways. The ambivalence of might in the battle of the giants in Genesis

6:1-4 or in the figure of Nimrod (or Nebrod) who, in the Septuagint, is described as a mighty hunter against the Lord, is an example. More obvious and striking is the way in which the account of the origin of the different human languages in the story of the tower of Babel (or Babylon, or "confusion") presents the variety of human languages as a curse separating human beings one from another, in contrast to our modern inclination, the product of Romanticism, to see the multitude of different languages as witness to the untold variety of human experience.

The Fathers read the first chapters of the Bible as unfolding a theological understanding of the human condition. The remarks above are intended to help the reader to profit from such an approach to what much modern scholarship regards as ancient legends of limited theological value. In rediscovering the theological perspective that the Fathers brought to the Scriptures, men and women today will find access to the depths of a theological tradition that still has much to say to them—this is the foundation on which the Ancient Christian Commentary on Scripture has been conceived.[11]

The spadework for this anthology of passages from the Fathers was done by Dr. Marco Conti, though the final version is the result of our collaborative effort. The introduction is mine. In the passages selected, a number of already existent translations have been used, often modified in the interests of accuracy or clarity. No attempt has been made, however, to introduce inclusive gender language; this would have been an elaborate task, since so much of Genesis 1-11 concerns the human condition, and in seeking a variety of strategies to avoid using the term *man* we would have run the risk of obscuring the Fathers' thought. The reader should bear in mind that in the original languages used by the Fathers the noun translated "man" (in Greek *anthrōpos*, in Latin *homo*) embraces both male and female.

University of Durham
Durham, U.K.

---

[11]General editor's note: This volume of the ACCS was prepared and edited—almost completely—before the appearance of *Genesis, Creation and Early Man: The Orthodox Christian Vision* by the late Fr. Seraphim Rose, with an introduction by Phillip E. Johnson (Plantina, Calif.: St. Herman of Alaska Brotherhood, 2000), to which the reader is referred for additional patristic selections and interpretations of Genesis. We are grateful for the massive labors of Fr. Rose, from which our efforts have belatedly benefited. While his work has directed us to selections we otherwise would have bypassed, all our translations have been checked against their original texts, since Fr. Rose worked principally from Russian translations.

1:1 THE BEGINNING OF CREATION

¹In the beginning God created[a] the heavens* and the earth.

a *Or* When God began to create **LXX* heaven

OVERVIEW: God created heaven and earth through the Word, since "in the beginning was the Word" (AUGUSTINE). God made heaven and earth in the beginning, not in the beginning of time but in Christ (ORIGEN, CHRYSOSTOM, AUGUSTINE). God created heaven and earth, that is, the matter of the heavens and the matter of the earth, which came to be from nothing (BASIL, NEMESIUS OF EMESA). The birth of the world was preceded by a condition of things suitable for the exercise of supernatural powers. The meaning of creation is known from divine revelation (BASIL). To Moses, God's revelation of the beginnings was made adequately known, and his account is to be fully trusted (CHRYSOSTOM).

1:1 *In the Beginning God Created the Heavens and Earth*

HEAVEN AND EARTH WERE CREATED THROUGH THE WORD. ORIGEN: What is the beginning of all things except our Lord and "Savior of all,"[1] Jesus Christ "the firstborn of every creature?"[2] In this beginning, therefore, that is, in his Word, "God made heaven and

earth" as the evangelist John also says in the beginning of his Gospel: "In the beginning was the Word, and the Word was with God, and the Word was God. The same was in the beginning with God. All things were made by him, and without him nothing was made."[3] HOMILIES ON GENESIS 1.1.[4]

THE BEGINNING IS THE WORD. ORIGEN: Scripture is not speaking here of any temporal beginning, but it says that the heavens and the earth and all things that were made were made "in the beginning," that is, in the Savior. HOMILIES ON GENESIS 1.1.[5]

HEAVEN AND EARTH ARE THE FORMLESS MATTER OF THE UNIVERSE. AUGUSTINE: Scripture called heaven and earth that formless matter of the universe, which was changed into formed and beautiful natures by God's ineffable command. . . . This heaven and earth, which were confused and mixed up, were suited to receive forms from God their

---

[1]1 Tim 4:10. [2]Col 1:15. [3]Jn 1:1-3. [4]FC 71:47. [5]FC 71:47.

maker. ON THE LITERAL INTERPRETATION OF
GENESIS 3.10.[6]

**GOD CREATED THE MATTER AND THE FORM
OF HEAVENS AND EARTH.** BASIL THE
GREAT: [The Manichaeans assert that] the
form of the world is due to the wisdom of the
supreme Artificer; matter came to the Creator from without; and thus the world results
from a double origin. It has received from
outside its matter and its essence and from
God its form and figure. They thus come to
deny that the mighty God has presided at the
formation of the universe and pretend that
he has only brought a crowning contribution
to a common work, that he has only contributed some small portion to the genesis of
beings. They are incapable from the debase-
ment of their reasoning of raising their
glances to the height of truth. Here below
arts are subsequent to matter—introduced
into life by the indispensable need of them.
Wool existed before weaving made it supply
one of nature's imperfections. Wood existed
before carpentering took possession of it and
transformed it each day to supply new wants
and made us see all the advantages derived
from it, giving the oar to the sailor, the win-
nowing fan to the laborer, the lance to the
soldier. But God, before all those things that
now attract our notice existed, after casting
about in his mind and determining to bring
into being time which had no being, imagined the world such as it ought to be and created matter in harmony with the form that
he wished to give it. He assigned to the heavens the nature adapted for the heavens and
gave to the earth an essence in accordance
with its form. He formed, as he wished, fire,
air and water, and gave to each the essence
that the object of its existence required.

Finally, he welded all the diverse parts of the
universe by links of indissoluble attachment
and established between them so perfect a
fellowship and harmony that the most distant, in spite of their distance, appeared
united in one universal sympathy. Let those
men therefore renounce their fabulous imag-
inations, who, in spite of the weakness of
their argument, pretend to measure a power
as incomprehensible to man's reason as it is
unutterable by man's voice. God created the
heavens and the earth, but not only half—he
created all the heavens and all the earth, creating the essence with the form. HEXAE-
MERON 2.2-3.[7]

GOD CREATED THINGS OUT OF NOTHING.
NEMESIUS OF EMESA: Even if it is granted
that the God of all things followed an order
[in the creation], he is shown to be God and
Creator and to have brought all things into
being out of nothing. ON THE NATURE OF
MAN 26.[8]

**THE CONDITION BEFORE THE BIRTH OF
THE WORLD.** BASIL THE GREAT: It appears,
indeed, that even before this world an order of
things existed of which our mind can form an
idea but of which we can say nothing, because
it is too lofty a subject for men who are but
beginners and are still babes in knowledge.
The birth of the world was preceded by a condition of things suitable for the exercise of
supernatural powers, outstripping the limits
of time, eternal and infinite. The Creator and
Demiurge of the universe perfected his works
in it, spiritual light for the happiness of all
who love the Lord, intellectual and invisible

[6]FC 84:151. [7]FC 46:23-24. [8]LCC 4:317.

natures, all the orderly arrangement of pure intelligences who are beyond the reach of our mind and of whom we cannot even discover the names. They fill the essence of this invisible world, as Paul teaches us. "For by him were all things created that are in heaven and that are in earth, visible and invisible, whether they be thrones or dominions or principalities or powers"[9] or virtues or hosts of angels or the dignities of archangels. To this world at last it was necessary to add a new world, both a school and training place where the souls of men should be taught and a home for beings destined to be born and to die. Thus was created, of a nature analogous to that of this world and the animals and plants which live on it, the succession of time, forever pressing on and passing away and never stopping in its course. Is not this the nature of time, where the past is no more, the future does not exist, and the present escapes before being recognized? And such also is the nature of the creature that lives in time—condemned to grow or to perish without rest and without certain stability. It is therefore fit that the bodies of animals and plants, obliged to follow a sort of current and carried away by the motion that leads them to birth or to death, should live in the midst of surroundings whose nature is in accord with beings subject to change. Thus the writer who wisely tells us of the birth of the universe does not fail to put these words at the head of the narrative. "In the beginning God created"; that is to say, in the beginning of time. Therefore, if he makes the world appear in the beginning, it is not a proof that its birth has preceded that of all other things that were made. He only wishes to tell us that, after the invisible and intellectual world, the visible world, the world of the senses, began to exist. EXEGETIC HOMILIES 1.5.[10]

CREATION KNOWN FROM REVELATION.
BASIL THE GREAT: We are proposing to examine the structure of the world and to contemplate the whole universe, not from the wisdom of the world but from what God taught his servant when he spoke to him in person and without riddles. HEXAEMERON 6.1.[11]

TO MOSES WAS REVEALED THE BEGINNING.
CHRYSOSTOM: Notice this remarkable author, dearly beloved, and the particular gift he had. I mean, while all the other inspired authors told either what would happen after a long time or what was going to take place immediately, this blessed author, being born many generations after the event, was guided by the deity on high and judged worthy to narrate what had been created by the Lord of all from the very beginning. Accordingly he began with these words: "In the beginning God created heaven and earth." He well nigh bellows at us all and says, "Is it by human beings I am taught in uttering these things? It is the one who brought being from nothing who stirred my tongue in narrating them." Since we therefore listen to these words not as the words of Moses but as the words of the God of all things coming to us through the tongue of Moses, so I beg you, let us heed what is said as distinguished from our own reasoning. HOMILIES ON GENESIS 2.5.[12]

TRUST GOD'S REVELATION TO MOSES. CHRYSOSTOM: Let us accept what is said with much gratitude, not overstepping the proper limit nor busying ourselves with matters beyond us. This is the besetting weakness of enemies of

---

[9]Col 1:16. [10]NPNF 2 8:54-55. [11]FC 46:83. [12]FC 74:31-32*; PG 53:28.

the truth, wishing as they do to assign every matter to their own reasoning and lacking the realization that it is beyond the capacity of human nature to plumb God's creation. HOM-ILIES ON GENESIS 2.5.[13]

HEAVEN AND EARTH. CHRYSOSTOM: Why does it proceed, first heaven then earth? The temple's roof made before its pavement? God is not subject to nature's demands nor to the rules of technique. God is the creator and master technician of nature, and art, and everything made or imagined. SERMON 1.3. [14]

---

[13]FC 74:32; PG 53:28. [14]PG 54:585.

1:2 THE FORMLESS EARTH

[2]*The earth was without form and void,* and darkness was upon [the face of][†] the deep;[§] and the Spirit[b] of God was moving over [the face of][†] the waters.[‡]*

b Or wind *LXX invisible and unformed †LXX omits the bracketed portion §LXX abyss ‡LXX water (singular)

OVERVIEW: The earth that God made was invisible and without form before God arranged the forms of all things by ordering and distinguishing them (AUGUSTINE). The darkness and the deep signify the absence of the bodily light that had to be created by God (AUGUSTINE). "Water" is another defini-tion of the formless matter to be arranged by God (AUGUSTINE). The Spirit moving over the face of the waters foreshadows baptism (JEROME). The Spirit, which is compared to a mother bird (EPHREM), is said to hover over the water to accomplish the triune purpose of the Father and the Son (EPHREM, AMBROSE). On the first day the creation was still incom-plete (BASIL). First it was created, and only then was it ordered (AMBROSE).

1:2a The Earth Was Without Form and Void

THE EARTH WAS FORMLESS MATTER. AUGUSTINE: The earth was invisible and unorganized, and darkness was over the abyss. Formlessness is suggested by these words, so that we might grasp the meaning by degrees, for we are unable to think cognitively about an absolute privation of form that still does not go as far as nothing. From this, another visible and organized heaven and earth were to be made. CONFESSIONS 12.15.[1]

WAS CREATION COMPLETE ON THE FIRST DAY? BASIL THE GREAT: Surely the perfect condition of the earth consists in its state of abundance: the budding of all sorts of plants, the putting forth of the lofty trees both fruit-ful and barren, the freshness and fragrance of

---

[1]FC 21:379.

4

flowers, and whatever things appeared on earth a little later by the command of God to adorn their mother. Since as yet there was nothing of this, the Scripture reasonably spoke of it as incomplete. We might say the same also about the heavens; that they were not yet brought to perfection themselves, nor had they received their proper adornment, since they were not yet lighted around by the moon nor the sun, nor crowned by the choirs of the stars. For these things had not yet been made. Therefore you will not err from the truth if you say that the heavens also were incomplete. HEXAEMERON 2.1.[2]

CREATING PRECEDES ORDERING. AMBROSE: The good architect lays the foundation first and afterward, when the foundation has been laid, plots the various parts of the building, one after the other, and then adds to it the ornamentation. . . . Scripture points out that things were first created and afterward put in order lest it be supposed that they were not actually created and that they had no beginning, just as if the nature of things had been, as it were, generated from the beginning and did not appear to be something added afterward. HEXAEMERON 1.7.[3]

1:2b Darkness Was on the Face of the Deep

GOD DWELT IN SUPERNAL LIGHT BEFORE CREATING A DIFFERENT PHYSICAL LIGHT. AUGUSTINE: "And darkness was over the abyss." The Manichaeans find fault with this and say, "Was God then in darkness, before he made the light?" They themselves are truly in the darkness of ignorance, and for that reason they do not understand the light in which God was before he made this light. For they know only the light they see with the eyes of

the flesh. And therefore they worship this sun that every creature sees. But let us understand that there is a different light in which God dwells. TWO BOOKS ON GENESIS AGAINST THE MANICHAEANS 1.3.6.[4]

THE DARKNESS AND THE DEEP ARE THE MERE ABSENCE OF LIGHT. AUGUSTINE: One who diligently considers what darkness is really finds only the absence of light. Thus it said, "darkness was over the abyss," as if to say, "There was no light over the abyss." Hence, this matter that is ordered and distinguished by the next work of God is called the invisible and unformed earth and the deep that is lacking light. This is what was above called heaven and earth, like the seed of heaven and earth. ON THE LITERAL INTERPRETATION OF GENESIS 4.12.[5]

1:2c The Spirit Was Moving over the Face of the Waters

CREATED BY THE SPIRIT. AMBROSE: The Spirit fittingly moved over the earth, destined to bear fruit because by the aid of the Spirit it held the seeds of new birth which were to germinate according to the words of the prophet: "Send forth thy Spirit and they shall be created and thou shalt renew the face of the earth."[6] HEXAEMERON 1.8.[7]

WATER IS EASILY MOVABLE FORMLESS MATTER. AUGUSTINE: The matter is first called by the name of the universe, that is, of heaven and earth, for the sake of which it was made from absolutely nothing. Second, its

---

[2]FC 46:22. [3]FC 42:26, 29. [4]FC 84:53. [5]FC 84:152. [6]Ps 104:30. [7]FC 42:32-33.

formlessness is conveyed by the mention of the unformed earth and the abyss, because among all the elements earth is more formless and less bright than the rest. Third, by the name *water*, there is signified matter that is subject to the work of the Maker, for water can be moved more easily than earth. And thus on account of the easiness by which it can be worked and moved, the matter subject to the Maker should be called water rather than earth. ON THE LITERAL INTERPRETATION OF GENESIS 4.13.[8]

A SYMBOL OF BAPTISM. JEROME: In the beginning of Genesis, it is written: "And the Spirit was stirring above the waters." You see, then, what it says in the beginning of Genesis. Now for its mystical meaning—"The Spirit was stirring above the waters"—already at that time baptism was being foreshadowed. It could not be true baptism, to be sure, without the Spirit. HOMILIES 10.[9]

CREATION INITIATED THROUGH THE SPIRIT. EPHREM THE SYRIAN: [The Holy Spirit] warmed the waters with a kind of vital warmth, even bringing them to a boil through intense heat in order to make them fertile. The action of a hen is similar. It sits on its eggs, making them fertile through the warmth of incubation. Here then, the Holy Spirit foreshadows the sacrament of holy baptism, prefiguring its arrival, so that the waters made fertile by the hovering of that same divine Spirit might give birth to the children of God. COMMENTARY ON GENESIS 1.[10]

THE SPIRIT HOVERED. EPHREM THE SYRIAN: It was appropriate to reveal here that the Spirit hovered in order for us to learn that the work of creation was held in common by the Spirit with the Father and the Son. The Father spoke. The Son created. And so it was also right that the Spirit offer its work, clearly shown through its hovering, in order to demonstrate its unity with the other persons. Thus we learn that all was brought to perfection and accomplished by the Trinity. COMMENTARY ON GENESIS 1.[11]

---

[8]FC 84:153. [9]FC 48:74. The water of creation prefigures the water of baptism. [10]ESOO 1:118. [11]ESOO 1:117.

1:3-5 CREATION OF THE LIGHT

[3]*And God said, "Let there be light"; and there was light.* [4]*And God saw that the light was good; and God separated the light from the darkness.* [5]*God called the light Day, and the darkness he called Night. And there was evening and there was morning, one day.*

OVERVIEW: "Let there be light" was spoken ineffably. The light that God created is the bodily light. "And God saw that the light was good" signifies that God approved his work, not that he found before him a good that he had not known (AUGUSTINE). God is the author of light (AMBROSE). Light in its primordial form did not come from the sun, which had not yet been created (EPHREM). "God called the light day, and the darkness he called night" means that God made a distinction between light and darkness (BASIL, EPHREM, AUGUSTINE). The first day and night were not ruled yet by solar motion (BASIL). The concept of a "day" is not to be allegorized (EPHREM). The invisible spiritual world is created before the physical world (AMBROSE, EPHREM). Creation out of nothing is distinguished from that which is created out of what existed before (EPHREM).

1:3 Let There Be Light

THE AUTHOR OF LIGHT. AMBROSE: God is the author of light, and the place and cause of darkness is the world. But the good Author uttered the word *light* so that he might reveal the world by infusing brightness therein and thus make its aspect beautiful. Suddenly then, the air became bright and darkness shrank in terror from the brilliance of the novel brightness. HEXAEMERON 1.9.[1]

INEFFABLE COMMAND. AUGUSTINE: We ought to understand that God did not say "Let there be light" by a sound brought forth from the lungs or by the tongue and teeth. Such thoughts are those of persons physically preoccupied. To be wise in accord with the flesh is death. "Let there be light" was spoken ineffably. ON THE LITERAL INTERPRETATION OF GENESIS 5.19.[2]

THE LIGHT BORN FROM GOD DISTINGUISHED FROM THE LIGHT MADE BY GOD.

AUGUSTINE: As the words themselves make sufficiently clear, we are told that this light was made. The light born from God is one thing; the light that God made is another. The light born from God is the very Wisdom of God, but the light made by God is something mutable, whether corporeal or incorporeal. ON THE LITERAL INTERPRETATION OF GENESIS 5.20.[3]

THE LIGHT DID NOT COME FROM THE SUN. EPHREM THE SYRIAN: The light was released so that it might spread over everything without being fastened down. It dispersed the darkness that was over everything although it did not move. It was only when [the light] went away and when it came that it moved, for when [the light] went away the rule was given to the night, and at [the light's] coming there would be an end to [the night's] rule. After the brightness [of the light] rendered its service for three days . . . the sun was in the firmament in order to ripen whatever had sprouted under that first light. COMMENTARY ON GENESIS 1.8.3; 9.2.[4]

1:4 The Light Was Good

SEPARATION OF LIGHT FROM DARKNESS. BASIL THE GREAT: Evening, then, is a common boundary line of day and night; and similarly morning is the part of night bordering on day. In order, therefore, to give the prerogative of prior generation to the day, Moses mentioned first the limit of the day and then that of the night, as night followed the day. The condition in the world before the creation of light was not night but darkness. That

---

[1]FC 42:39. [2]FC 84:156-57. [3]FC 84:158. [4]FC 91:81.

which was opposed to the day was named night. HEXAEMERON 2.8.[5]

GOD APPROVES HIS WORK. AUGUSTINE: We should understand that this sentence does not signify joy as if over an unexpected good but an approval of the work. For what is said more fittingly of God—insofar as it can be humanly said—than when Scripture puts it this way: "he spoke," and "it was made," "it pleased him." Thus we understand in "he spoke" his sovereignty, in "it was made" his power and in "it pleased him" his goodness. These ineffable things had to be said in this way by a man to men so that they might profit all. ON THE LITERAL INTERPRETATION OF GENESIS 5.22.[6]

AUGUSTINE: "God saw that the light was good," and these words do not mean that God found before him a good that he had not known but that he was pleased by one that was finished. TWO BOOKS ON GENESIS AGAINST THE MANICHAEANS 1.8.13.[7]

THE ORIGINAL GOODNESS, THE FINAL GLORY OF GOODNESS. AMBROSE: God, as judge of the whole work, foreseeing what is going to happen as something completed, commends the part of his work which is still in its initial stages, being already cognizant of its termination. HEXAEMERON 2.5.[8]

1:5a Day and Night

DISTINCTION BETWEEN LIGHT AND DARK-NESS. AUGUSTINE: "And God divided the light and the darkness, and God called the light day and he called the darkness night." It did not say here "God made the darkness," because darkness is merely the absence of

light. Yet God made a division between light and darkness. So too we make a sound by crying out, and we make a silence by not making a sound, because silence is the cessation of sound. Still in some sense we distinguish between sound and silence and call the one sound and the other silence. . . . "He called the light day, and he called the darkness night" was said in the sense that he made them to be called, because he separated and ordered all things so that they could be distinguished and receive names.[9] TWO BOOKS ON GENESIS AGAINST THE MANICHAEANS 1.9.15.[10]

1:5b The First Day

NOT RULED BY SOLAR MOTION. BASIL THE GREAT: Now, henceforth, after the creation of the sun, it is day when the air is illuminated by the sun shining on the hemisphere above the earth, and night is the darkness of the earth when the sun is hidden. Yet it was not at that time according to solar motion, but it was when that first created light was diffused and again drawn in according to the measure ordained by God, that day came and night succeeded. EXEGETIC HOMILIES 2.8.[11]

DISTINGUISHING CREATION OUT OF NOTH-ING FROM ALL ELSE CREATED OUT OF WHAT EXISTED BEFORE. EPHREM THE SYR-IAN: Heaven, earth, fire, wind and water were created from nothing as Scripture bears witness, whereas the light, which came to be on the first day along with the rest of the things that came to be afterward, came to be from

---

[5]FC 46:33. [6]FC 84:158-59. [7]FC 84:61. [8]FC 42:65. [9]That God has distinguished light from dark does not make darkness more than the absence of light but rather enables light and dark to be distinguished. [10]FC 84:62-63. [11]FC 46:33.

something. . . . Therefore those five created things were created from nothing, and everything else was made from those [five] things that came to be from nothing. COMMENTARY ON GENESIS 1.14.1; 15.1.[12]

THE SIX DAYS ARE RELIABLY DESCRIPTIVE. EPHREM THE SYRIAN: So let no one think that there is anything allegorical in the works of the six days. No one can rightly say that the things pertaining to these days were symbolic, nor can one say that they were meaningless names or that other things were symbolized for us by their names. Rather, let us know in just what manner heaven and earth were created in the beginning. They were truly heaven and earth. There was no other thing signified by the names "heaven" and "earth." The rest of the works and things made that followed were not meaningless significations either, for the substances of their natures correspond to what their names signify. COMMENTARY ON GENESIS 1.1.[13]

THE CREATION OF SPIRITUAL BEINGS. BASIL THE GREAT: In fact, there did exist something, as it seems, even before this world which our mind can attain by contemplation but which has been left uninvestigated because it is not adapted to those who are beginners and as yet infants in understanding. This was a certain condition older than the birth of the world and proper to the supramundane powers, one beyond time, everlasting, without beginning or end. In it the Creator and Producer of all things perfected the works of his art, a spiritual light befitting the blessedness of those who love the Lord, rational and invisible natures, and the whole orderly arrangement of spiritual creatures which surpass our understanding and of which it is impossible even to discover the names. These fill completely the essence of the invisible world. HEXAEMERON 1.5.[14]

THE INVISIBLE WORLD CREATED. AMBROSE: The angels, dominions and powers, although they began to exist at some time, were already in existence when the [visible] world was created. HEXAEMERON 1.5.[15]

---

[12]FC 91:85. [13]FC 91:74. [14]FC 46:8-9. [15]FC 42:18.

1:6-8 CREATION OF THE FIRMAMENT

[6]*And God said, "Let there be a firmament in the midst of the waters,* and let it separate the waters from the waters."*† [7]And God made the firmament and separated the waters which were under the firmament from the waters which were above the firmament. [And it was so.]‡ [8]And God called the firmament Heaven.§ And there was evening and there was morning, a second day.*

*LXX water (singular) †LXX adds And it was so. ‡LXX omits the bracketed portion §LXX adds And God saw that it was good.

OVERVIEW: God formed the stable substance of the firmament by transforming the naturally fluid waters (CYRIL OF JERUSALEM). The firmament separated the corporeal matter of visible things from the incorporeal matter of invisible things (AUGUSTINE). The waters that are above and under the firmament do not symbolize spiritual, incorporeal powers (BASIL). The firmament is the corporeal heaven, which God made after creating the heavens (ORIGEN). He called the firmament heaven because it divides the heavenly matter from the perishable matter (AUGUSTINE).

1:6 A Firmament in the Waters

NATURE OF THE FIRMAMENT. CYRIL OF JERUSALEM: For what fault have they to find with the vast creation of God, who out of the fluid nature of the waters formed the stable substance of the heavens? For God said, "Let there be a firmament in the midst of the waters." God spoke once for all, and it stands fast, never failing. CATECHETICAL LECTURES 9.5.[1]

BASIL THE GREAT: And surely we need not believe, because [the firmament] seems to have had its origin, according to the general understanding, from water, that it is like either frozen water or some such material that takes its origin from the percolation of moisture, such as is a crystalline rock. HEXAEMERON 3.8.[2]

1:7 Separating the Waters

THE FIRMAMENT DIVIDES VISIBLE AND INVISIBLE THINGS. AUGUSTINE: The waters were divided so that some were above the firmament and others below the firmament. Since we said that matter was called water,[3] I believe that the firmament of heaven separated the corporeal matter of visible things from the incorporeal matter of invisible things. TWO BOOKS ON GENESIS AGAINST THE MANICHAEANS 1.11.17.[4]

AUGUSTINE: The matter was separated by the interposition of the firmament so that the lower matter is that of bodies and the higher matter that of souls. ON THE LITERAL INTERPRETATION OF GENESIS 8.29.[5]

THE WATERS NOT REDUCED TO SYMBOLS ONLY. BASIL THE GREAT: But as far as concerns the separation of the waters I am obliged to contest the opinion of certain writers in the church who, under the shadow of high and sublime conceptions, have launched out into metaphor and have seen in the waters only a figure to denote spiritual and incorporeal powers. In the higher regions, accordingly, above the firmament, dwell the better; in the lower regions, earth and matter are the dwelling place of the malignant. So, say they, God is praised by the waters that are above the heavens, that is to say, by the good powers, the purity of whose soul makes them worthy to sing the praises of God. And the waters that are under the heavens represent the wicked spirits, who from their natural height have fallen into the abyss of evil. Turbulent, seditious, agitated by the tumultuous waves of passion, they have received the name of sea, because of the instability and the inconstancy of their movements. Let us reject these theories as dreams and old women's tales. HEXAEMERON 3.9.[6]

---

[1]NPNF 2 7:52. [2]FC 46:43. [3]Cf. *Comm. on Gen.* 1:2. [4]FC 84:64. [5]FC 84:165*. [6]NPNF 2 8:70-71.

THE FLOW OF WATER DOWNWARD. BASIL THE GREAT: Someone may ask this: Why does the Scripture reduce to a command of the Creator that tendency to flow downward which belongs naturally to water? . . . If water has this tendency by nature, the command ordering the waters to be gathered together into one place would be superfluous. . . . To this inquiry we say this, that you recognized very well the movements of the water after the command of the Lord, both that it is unsteady and unstable and that it is borne naturally down slopes and into hollows; but how it had any power previous to that, before the motion was engendered in it from this command, you yourself neither know nor have you heard it from one who knew. Reflect that the voice of God makes nature, and the command given at that time to creation provided the future course of action for the creatures. HEXAE-MERON 4.2.[7]

1:8 The Firmament Is Heaven

THE FIRMAMENT IS THE CORPOREAL

HEAVEN. ORIGEN: Although God had already previously made heaven, now he makes the firmament. For he made heaven first, about which he says, "Heaven is my throne."[8] But after that he makes the firmament, that is, the corporeal heaven. For every corporeal object is, without doubt, firm and solid; and it is this that "divides the water which is above heaven from the water which is below heaven." HOMILIES ON GENESIS 1.2.[9]

THE MATTER BELOW THE FIRMAMENT IS CORPOREAL. AUGUSTINE: Since Scripture called heaven the firmament, we can without absurdity hold that anything below the ethereal heaven, in which everything is peaceful and stable, is more mutable and perishable and is a kind of corporeal matter prior to the reception of beauty and the distinction of forms. ON THE LITERAL INTERPRETATION OF GENESIS 8.29.[10]

[7]FC 46:56-57. [8]Is 66:1. [9]FC 71:48-49. [10]FC 84:165-66.

1:9-10 THE DRY LAND AND THE SEAS APPEAR

[9]And God said, "Let the waters* under the heavens* be gathered together into one place, and let the dry land appear." And it was so.† [10]God called the dry land Earth, and the waters that were gathered together he called Seas. And God saw that it was good.

*LXX water (singular) †LXX adds And the water beneath the heaven was gathered into these places, and dry land appeared.

OVERVIEW: The waters were segregated from the earth (JOHN OF DAMASCUS). Through the gathering together of the waters and the appearance of the dry land the confused and formless matter was ordered by receiving its proper, different forms (AUGUSTINE, CHRYSOSTOM). The waters may symbolize the sins and vices of the body, which must be separated from the dry land, that is, from the deeds done in the flesh (ORIGEN). It is impossible for the human mind to fathom how precisely God creates (GREGORY OF NYSSA).

1:9-10 Creation of Earth and Seas

HOW THE SEAS WERE FORMED. JOHN OF DAMASCUS: Now, the fact that Scripture speaks of one gathering does not mean that they were gathered together into one place, for notice that after this it says: "And the gathering together of the waters he called seas." Actually, the account meant that the waters were segregated by themselves apart from the earth. And so the waters were brought together into their gathering places and the dry land appeared. ORTHODOX FAITH 2.9.[1]

TRANSFORMATION OF THE FORMLESS MATTER. AUGUSTINE: Now when Scripture says, "Let the water which is below the heavens be gathered into one gathering," these words mean that this corporeal matter is to be formed into the beauty that these visible waters have. This gathering into one place is the formation of these waters that we see and touch. For every form is reduced to a rule of unity. What else should we understand is meant by the words "let the dry land appear" than this matter receives the visible form that this earth that we see and touch now has? Hence the previous expression "the earth was invisible and without form" signified the confusion and obscurity of matter, and the expression "the water over which the spirit of God was borne" signified that same matter.

But now this water and earth are formed from that matter that was called by their names before it had received the forms that we now see. TWO BOOKS ON GENESIS AGAINST THE MANICHAEANS 1.12.18.[2]

THE ELEMENTS RECEIVE THEIR FAMILIAR FORMS. AUGUSTINE: Hence, at the words "Let the waters be gathered together, and let dry land appear," these two things [earth and water] received their proper forms familiar to us and perceived by our senses, water being made fluid and earth solid. Of water, therefore, it is said, "Let it be gathered"; of earth, "Let it appear." For water tends to ebb and flow, but earth remains immobile. ON THE LITERAL INTERPRETATION OF GENESIS 2.11.24.[3]

THE LORD NAMES THE ELEMENTS. CHRYSOSTOM: Have you seen, dear brother, how God, in a sense, stripped the earth, which was invisible and formless, and was covered by the waters as if they were veils, and showed us its face, after he had imposed an appropriate name on it as well? "And the gatherings of the waters he called seas." So the waters also got their name. In fact, as an excellent craftsman, who sets out to make with his art a certain vase, does not give it a name until he has completed it, so the good Lord does not impose names on the elements until he has put them in their proper place according to his command. Therefore after the earth had received its name and had reached its proper form, the gathered waters were called with their own name. HOMILIES ON GENESIS 5.10.[4]

---

[1]FC 37:224-25. [2]FC 84:65-66. [3]ACW 41:62. [4]FC 74:71.

SYMBOLISM OF THE SEAS AND THE DRY LAND. ORIGEN: Let us labor, therefore, to gather "the water that is under heaven" and cast it from us that "the dry land," which is our deeds done in the flesh, might appear. When this has been done, "men seeing our good works may glorify our Father who is in heaven."[5] For if we have not separated from us those waters that are under heaven, that is, the sins and vices of our body, our dry land will not be able to appear nor have the courage to advance to the light. . . . The dry land, after the water was removed from it, did not continue further as "dry land" but was named "earth" by God. In this manner also our bodies, if this separation from them takes place, will no longer remain "dry land." They will, on the contrary, be called "earth" because they can now bear fruit for God. HOMILIES ON GENESIS 1.2.[6]

HOW DID GOD CREATE? GREGORY OF NYSSA: As for the question of precisely how any single thing came into existence, we must banish it altogether from our discussion. Even in the case of things which are quite within the grasp of our understanding and of which we have sensible perception, it would be impossible for the speculative reason to grasp the "how" of the production of the phenomenon, so much so that even inspired and saintly men have deemed such questions insoluble. For instance, the apostle says, "Through faith we understand that the worlds were framed by the word of God, so that things which are seen are not made of things which do appear."[7] . . . Let us, following the example of the apostle, leave the question of the "how" in each created thing without meddling with it at all but merely observing incidentally that the movement of God's will becomes at any moment that he pleases a fact, and the intention becomes at once realized in nature. ON THE SOUL AND THE RESURRECTION.[8]

---

[5]Mt 5:16. [6]FC 71:50-51. [7]Heb 11:3. [8]NPNF 2 5:457-58.

1:11-13 THE CREATION OF PLANTS

[11]And God said, "Let the earth put forth vegetation, plants yielding seed,* and fruit trees bearing fruit in which is their seed, each according to its kind, upon the earth." And it was so. [12]The earth brought forth vegetation, plants yielding seed according to their own kinds,† and trees bearing fruit in which is their seed, each according to its kind.‡ And God saw that it was good. [13]And there was evening and there was morning, a third day.

*LXX adds according to their kind and likeness †LXX adds and likeness ‡LXX adds upon the earth

OVERVIEW: Since plants are different in species from earth and water, they are created separately from these elements (AUGUSTINE). God's command "Let the earth bring forth vegetation" became a law of nature and remained in the earth (BASIL). The earth did not of itself produce plants that were hidden primordially in its womb; rather, plants were created through the Word (BASIL). Although the grasses and the trees were only a moment old at their creation, they appeared as if they were months and years old. They were created as food for the animals and for Adam and his descendants (EPHREM). Poisonous and thorny plants were created after the original sin (AUGUSTINE). In the beginning the fruits, grains and vegetables were ripened by the Creator, not by the sun, which of itself is not to be worshiped (BASIL, AMBROSE, CHRYSOSTOM). The grain came from the ear, not the ear from the grain (GREGORY OF NYSSA).

1:11 Creation of Plants and Trees

PLANTS CREATED SEPARATELY FROM EARTH AND WATER. AUGUSTINE: Here we must note the plan of the Ruler of the world. Since the crops and trees created are different in species from earth and water and so cannot be counted among the elements, the decree by which they are to proceed from the earth is given separately, and the customary phrases describing their creation are put down separately. Thus Scripture says, "And so it was done," and then there is a repetition of what was done. There is separate mention also of the fact that God saw that it was good. But since these creatures cling fast to the earth and are joined to it by their roots, God wished them also to belong to the same day [of creation]. ON THE LITERAL INTERPRETATION OF GENESIS 2.12.25.[1]

THE GERMINATION OF THE EARTH. BASIL

THE GREAT: After the earth, rid of the weight of the water, had rested, the command had come to it to bring forth first the herbs, then the trees. And this we see still happening even at the present time. For the voice that was then heard and the first command became, as it were, a law of nature and remained in the earth, giving it the power to produce and bear fruit for all succeeding time. HEXAEMERON 5.1.[2]

PLANTS CREATED THROUGH THE WORD. BASIL THE GREAT: When the earth heard, "Let it bring forth vegetation and the fruit trees," it did not produce plants that it had hidden in it; nor did it send up to the surface the palm or the oak or the cypress that had been hidden somewhere down below in its womb. On the contrary, it is the divine Word that is the origin of things made. HEXAEMERON 8.1.[3]

THE MIRACLE OF VEGETATION. BASIL THE GREAT: "Let the earth bring forth herbs." And in the briefest moment of time the earth, beginning with germination in order that it might keep the laws of the Creator, passing through every form of increase, immediately brought the shoots to perfection. The meadows were deep with the abundant grass; the fertile plains, rippling with standing crops, presented the picture of a swelling sea with its moving heads of grain. And every herb and every kind of vegetable and whatever shrubs and legumes there were rose from the earth at that time in all profusion. HEXAEMERON 5.5-6.[4]

1:12 Bringing Forth Vegetation

---

[1]ACW 41:63. [2]FC 46:67. [3]FC 46:117. [4]FC 46:74.

FROM THE EAR CAME THE GRAIN. GREGORY OF NYSSA: In the beginning, we see, it was not an ear rising from a grain but a grain coming from an ear, and after that, the ear grows round the grain. ON THE SOUL AND THE RESURRECTION.[5]

DO NOT WORSHIP THE SUN. BASIL THE GREAT: The adornment of the earth is older than the sun, that those who have been misled may cease worshiping the sun as the origin of life. HEXAEMERON 5.1.[6]

THE FRUITS WERE RIPENED BY THE CREATOR. CHRYSOSTOM: Hence Scripture shows you everything completed before the creation of this body [the sun] lest you attribute the production of the crops to it instead of to the Creator of all things. HOMILIES ON GENESIS 6.12.[7]

THE SUN DID NOT CREATE VEGETATION. AMBROSE: Let everyone be informed that the sun is not the author of vegetation.... How can the sun give the faculty of life to growing plants when these have already been brought forth by the life-giving creative power of God before the sun entered into such a life as this? The sun is younger than the green shoot, younger than the green plant. HEXAEMERON 3.6.[8]

HOW THE PLANTS APPEARED. EPHREM THE SYRIAN: Although the grasses were only a moment old at their creation, they appeared as if they were months old. Likewise, the trees, although only a day old when they sprouted forth, were nevertheless like trees years old as they were fully grown and fruits were already budding on their branches. The grass that would be required as food for the animals that were to be created two days later

was thus made ready. And the new corn that would be food for Adam and his descendants, who would be thrown out of paradise four days later, was thus prepared. COMMENTARY ON GENESIS 1.22.1-2.[9]

THE POISONOUS AND THORNY PLANTS. AUGUSTINE: The Manichaeans are accustomed to say, "If God commanded that the edible plants and the fruit trees come forth from the earth, who commanded that there come forth so many thorny or poisonous plants that are useless for food and so many trees that bear no fruit?"... We should say then that the earth was cursed by reason of the sin of man so that it bears thorns, not that it should suffer punishment since it is without sensation but that it should always set before the eyes of man the judgment upon human sin. Thus men might be admonished by it to turn away from sins and to turn to God's commandments. Poisonous plants were created as a punishment or as a trial for mortals. All this is the result of sin. TWO BOOKS ON GENESIS AGAINST THE MANICHAEANS 1.13.19.[10]

THE EARTH PUT FORTH VEGETATION. BASIL THE GREAT: At this saying all the dense woods appeared; all the trees shot up.... Likewise all the shrubs were immediately thick with leaf and bushy; and the so-called garland plants ... all came into existence in a moment of time, although they were not previously on the earth....

"Let the earth bring forth." This brief command was immediately a mighty nature and

[5]NPNF 2 5:467. [6]FC 46:67. [7]FC 74:84; PG 53:58. [8]FC 42:87. [9]FC 91:90. [10]FC 84:66-67.

an elaborate system which brought to perfection more swiftly than our thought the countless properties of plants. HEXAEMERON 5.6, 10.[11]

VEGETATION NOT A SYMBOL. BASIL THE GREAT: When I hear "grass," I think of grass, and in the same manner I understand everything as it is said: a plant, a fish, a wild animal and an ox. Indeed, "I am not ashamed of the gospel."[12] . . . (Some) have attempted by false arguments and allegorical interpretations to bestow on the Scripture a dignity of their own imagining. But theirs is the attitude of one who considers himself wiser than the revelations of the Spirit and introduces his own ideas in pretense of an explanation. Therefore, let it be understood as it has been written. HEXAEMERON 9.1.[13]

GOD, NOT THE SUN, CREATED DAY. JOHN CHRYSOSTOM: He created the sun on the fourth day lest you think it is the cause of the day. HOMILIES ON GENESIS 6.14.[14]

---

[11]FC 46:74, 82. [12]Rom 1:16. [13]FC 46:135-36. [14]FC 74:85; PG 53:58.

1:14-19 CREATION OF THE HEAVENLY BODIES

[14]And God said, "Let there be lights in the firmament of the heavens*† to separate the day from the night; and let them be for signs and for seasons and for days and years, [15]and let them be lights‡ in the firmament of the heavens to give light upon the earth." And it was so. [16]And God made the two great lights, the greater light to rule the day, and the lesser light to rule the night; he made the stars also. [17]And God set them in the firmament of the heavens* to give light upon the earth, [18]to rule over the day and over the night, and to separate the light from the darkness. And God saw that it was good. [19]And there was evening and there was morning, a fourth day.

*LXX heaven (singular) †LXX adds for the illumination of the earth ‡LXX for illumination

OVERVIEW: The heavenly bodies are the receptacles of the primordial light, which God created on the first day (JOHN OF DAMASCUS). Their function is to rule the days, the seasons and the years (BASIL, CYRIL OF JERUSALEM). Their signs fix distinct intervals of time (AUGUSTINE). The order of creation is precisely defined (CHRYSOSTOM) with primordial light preceding the sun (AMBROSE). After the stars, the sun and the moon were created, the day and the night were divided among the heavenly bodies. The heavenly bodies must be observed as natural phenomena but not in order to forecast the future (AUGUSTINE). The sun symbolizes the divine goodness (PSEUDO-DIONYSIUS). The sun and the moon symbolize Christ and the church. The stars are symbols of the saints and the prophets (ORIGEN).

1:14-15 *Lights in the Firmament*

NATURE OF THE HEAVENLY BODIES. JOHN OF DAMASCUS: Fire is one of the four elements. It is light and more buoyant than the others, and it both burns and gives light. It was made by the Creator on the first day, for sacred Scripture says, "And God said: Be light made. And light was made." According to what some say, fire is the same thing as light. . . . And into the luminaries of the firmament the Creator put the primordial light, not that he was in want of any other light but that that particular light might not remain idle. For the luminary is not the light itself but its receptacle. ORTHODOX FAITH 2.7.[1]

THEIR FUNCTION. BASIL THE GREAT: "Let them serve," he says, "for the fixing of days," not for making days but for ordering the days. For day and night are earlier than the generation of the luminaries.[2] This the psalm declares to us when it says: "He placed the sun to rule the day, the moon and stars to rule the night."[3] How, then, does the sun rule the day? Because, whenever the sun, carrying the light around with it, rises above our horizon, it puts an end to the darkness and brings us the day. Therefore one would not err if he would define the day as air, lighted by the sun, or as the measure of time in which the sun tarries in the hemisphere above the earth. But the sun and the moon were also appointed to be for the years. The moon, when it has completed its course twelve times, measures a year, except that it frequently needs an intercalary month for the accurate determination of the seasons, as the Hebrews and the most ancient Greeks formerly measured the year. The solar year is the return of the sun from a certain sign to that same sign in its regular revolution. HEXAEMERON 6.8.[4]

WELL-ORDERED MOVEMENTS. CYRIL OF JERUSALEM: Men ought to have been astonished and amazed not only at the arrangement of the sun and moon but also at the well-ordered movements of the stars and their unfettered courses and the timely rising of each of them; how some are signs of summer, others of winter; how some indicate the time for sowing, others the times of navigation. CATECHETICAL LECTURES 9.8.[5]

WHAT PRECEDED THE SUN. AMBROSE: Look first on the firmament of heaven, which was made before the sun. Look first on the earth, which began to be visible and was already formed before the sun put in its appearance. Look at the plants of the earth, which preceded in time the light of the sun. The bramble preceded the sun. The blade of grass is older than the moon. Therefore, do not believe that object to be a god to which the gifts of God are seen to be preferred. Three days have passed. No one, meanwhile, has looked for the sun, yet the brilliance of light has been in evidence everywhere. For the day too has its light, which is itself the precursor of the sun. HEXAEMERON 4.1.[6]

THE ORDER OF CREATION. CHRYSOSTOM: For that reason the blessed Moses, inspired by the divine Spirit, teaches us with great precision, lest we fall victim to the same things as they, instead of being able to know clearly both the sequence of created things and how each thing was created. You see, if God in his

---

[1]FC 37:215-16. [2]Day and night were created before the stars. [3]Ps 135:8-9. [4]FC 46:97. [5]FC 61:189. [6]FC 42:126.

care for our salvation had not directed the tongue of the biblical author in this way, it would have been sufficient to say that God made heaven and earth, the sea and living things, and not add the order of the days nor what was created first and what later. HOMILIES ON GENESIS 7.10.[7]

EXACT MEANING OF "SIGNS." AUGUSTINE: We should not interpret the signs as something other than times. For Scripture is now speaking of these times that by their distinct intervals convey to us that eternity remains immutable above them so that time might appear as a sign, that is, as a vestige of eternity. Likewise, when it adds, "and for days and for years," it shows of what times it is speaking. These days come about by the revolution of the fixed stars, and from this it becomes obvious when the sun completes its starry course in a particular year. ON THE LITERAL INTERPRETATION OF GENESIS 13.38.[8]

1:16-18 Greater and Lesser Lights

THE DAYS BEFORE AND AFTER THE CREATION OF THE SUN AND THE MOON. AUGUSTINE: The Manichaeans ask how it could be that the heavenly bodies, that is, the sun and the moon and the stars, were made on the fourth day. How could the three previous days have passed without the sun? For we now see that a day passes with the rising and setting of the sun, while night comes to us in the sun's absence when it returns to east from the other side of the world. We answer them that the previous three days could each have been calculated by as great a period of time as that through which the sun passes, from when it rises in the east until it returns again to the east. . . . This would be our answer if we were

not held back by the words "and evening came and morning came,"[9] for we see that this cannot now take place without the movement of the sun. Hence we are left with the interpretation that in that period of time the divisions between the works were called evening because of the completion of the work that was done and morning because of the beginning of the work to come. Scripture says this after the likeness of human works, since they generally begin in the morning and end at evening. . . . [Then Scripture says, "And God set them in the firmament of the heavens to give light upon the earth, to rule over the day and over the night, and to divide the light from the darkness."] Again they ask, "How did God previously divide the light and the darkness[10] if he made the heavenly bodies on this the fourth day?" Therefore these words, "to divide the light from the darkness," mean "to divide among themselves the light and the darkness, so that the day is given to the sun and the night to the moon and the other stars." The day and the night had already been distinguished[11] but not yet in relation to the heavenly bodies. TWO BOOKS ON GENESIS AGAINST THE MANICHAEANS 1.14.20-23.[12]

THE STARS DO NOT FORECAST THE FUTURE. AUGUSTINE: Everyone understands that there is a great difference between astrological prediction and observing the stars as natural phenomena, in the way that farmers and sailors do, either to verify geographical areas or to steer their course somewhere, as pilots of ships do, and travelers, making their way through the sandy wastes of the south

---

[7]FC 74:96-97; PG 53:65. [8]FC 84:173*. [9]Gen 1:5; 1:8; 1:13. [10]Cf. Gen 1:4-5. [11]Cf. Gen 1:4-5. [12]FC 84:68-70.

with no sure path; or to explain some point of doctrine by mentioning some of the stars as a useful illustration. As I said, there is a great difference between these practical customs and the superstitions of men who study the stars not to forecast the weather or to find their way or for spiritual parables but in an effort to peer into the predestined outcome of events. LETTERS 55.[13]

THE SUN AS ECHO OF THE DIVINE GOODNESS. PSEUDO-DIONYSIUS: The great, shining, ever-lighting sun is the apparent image of the divine goodness, a distant echo of the good. It illuminates whatever is capable of receiving its light, and yet it never loses the utter fullness of its light. It sends its shining beams all around the visible world, and if anything fails to receive them the fault lies not in the weakness or defect of the spreading light but in the unsuitability of whatever is unable to have a share in light. DIVINE NAMES 4.697D.[14]

SUN AND MOON ARE SIGNS OF THE TRUE LIGHT. ORIGEN: As those lights of heaven that we see have been set "for signs and seasons and days and years," that they might give light from the firmament of heaven to those who are on the earth, so also Christ, illuminating his church, gives signs by his precepts, that one might know how, when the sign has

been received, to escape the "wrath to come,"[15] lest "that day overtake him like a thief,"[16] but that rather he can reach "the acceptable year of the Lord."[17] Christ, therefore, is the "true light which enlightens every man coming into this world."[18] From his light the church itself also having been enlightened is made "the light of the world" enlightening those "who are in darkness,"[19] as also Christ himself testifies to his disciples saying, "You are the light of the world."[20] HOMILIES ON GENESIS 1.6.[21]

THE STARS AS SYMBOLS. ORIGEN: Just as the sun and the moon are said to be the great lights in the firmament of heaven, so also are Christ and the church in us. But since God also placed stars in the firmament, let us see what are also stars in us, that is, in the heaven of our heart. Moses is a star in us, which shines and enlightens us by his acts. And so are Abraham, Isaac, Jacob, Isaiah, Jeremiah, Ezekiel, David, Daniel, and all to whom the Holy Scriptures testify that they pleased God. For just as "star differs from star in glory"[22] so also each of the saints, according to his own greatness, sheds his light upon us. HOMILIES ON GENESIS 1.7.[23]

---

[13]FC 12:272-73. [14]PSD 74. [15]1 Thess 1:10. [16]1 Thess 5:4. [17]Is 61:2. [18]Jn 1:9. [19]Rom 2:19. [20]Mt 5:14. [21]FC 71:54-55. [22]1 Cor 15:41. [23]FC 71:55.

1:20-23 GOD CREATES THE BIRDS AND THE AQUATIC CREATURES

²⁰And God said, "Let the waters bring forth swarms of living creatures, and [let birds fly]* above the earth across the firmament of the heavens."† ²¹So God created the great [sea monsters]‡ and [every living creature that moves],§ with which the waters swarm, according to their kinds, and every winged bird according to its kind. And God saw that it was good. ²²And God blessed them, saying, "Be fruitful and multiply and fill the waters in the seas, and let birds multiply on the earth." ²³And there was evening and there was morning, a fifth day.

*LXX and birds flying †LXX adds And it was so. ‡LXX whales §LXX the whole soul (life?) of creeping animals

OVERVIEW: God gave waters their proper ornament by creating swimming creatures and birds (BASIL). The birds did not originate from water but from the cloudy air saturated with water, out of which they "came forth" (AUGUSTINE). The fish and birds respectively symbolize the evil and the good thoughts in the human mind (ORIGEN). God also created the sea monsters, in order to raise fear and consternation in humans (BASIL). After creating the animals of the water and the birds, God gave them the power of procreation by saying "increase and multiply" (AUGUSTINE).

Many creatures were created on the same day (AMBROSE), each of its own kind (BASIL) with differences sustained through the generations, the succession of each species preserved (BASIL) with the properties it especially received from God. Hybrids are the work of humans, not of God (AMBROSE). The soul is not pre-existently eternal as though sharing in God's essence, and the soul does not immigrate from body to body (GREGORY OF NYSSA). The coming to life of a seed after being buried in the ground is a prefiguration of the resurrection (AMBROSE, GREGORY OF NYSSA).

1:20 Living Creatures in Waters and Sky

ADORNING THE WATERS. BASIL THE GREAT: After the creation of the lights, then the waters were filled with living creatures, so that this portion of the world also was adorned. The earth had received its ornamentation from its own plants. The heavens had received the flowers of stars and had been adorned with two great lights as if with the radiance of twin eyes. It remained for the waters, too, to be given their proper ornament. The command came. Immediately rivers were productive, and marshy lakes were fruitful of species proper and natural to each. The sea was astir with all kinds of swimming creatures, and not even the water that remained in the slime and ponds was idle or without its contribution in creation. For clearly frogs and mosquitoes and gnats were generated from them. HEXAEMERON 7.1.[1]

HOW BIRDS AND FISH MOVE SIMILARLY.

---

[1]FC 46:105.

BASIL THE GREAT: God also said, "Let birds fly above the earth across the firmament of the heavens." Why did he give winged creatures also their origin from the waters? Because the flying animals have a certain relationship, as it were, with those that swim. For just as the fish cut the water, going forward with the motion of their fins and guiding their turns and forward movements by the change of their tails, so also in the case of birds, they can be seen cutting and moving through air on wings in the same manner. HEXAEMERON 8.2.[2]

SIMULTANEOUS CREATION OF MANY LIVING BEINGS. AMBROSE: The rivers were in labor. The lakes produced their quota of life. The sea itself began to bear all manner of reptiles.... We are unable to record the multiplicity of the names of all those species which by divine command were brought to life in a moment of time. At the same instant substantial form and the principle of life were brought into existence.... The whale, as well as the frog, came into existence at the same time by the same creative power. HEXAEMERON 5.2-3, 5.[3]

BIRDS GENERATED FROM AIR SATURATED WITH WATER. AUGUSTINE: [The Manichaeans] usually find fault, questioning and often misrepresenting Scripture for saying that not merely those animals that live in the water but also those that fly in the air and all winged creatures were born from the waters. Let them know that learned men who carefully investigate these matters usually include with the water this cloudy and moist air in which the birds fly. For it comes together and becomes dense with the exhalations and what I might call vapors of

the sea so that it can support the flight of birds. Thus on calm nights it produces dew, and drops of this dew are found on the grass in the morning. TWO BOOKS ON GENESIS AGAINST THE MANICHAEANS 1.15.24.[4]

SYMBOLISM OF THE SWIMMING AND FLYING CREATURES. ORIGEN: According to the letter[5] "swimming creatures" and "birds" are brought forth by the waters at the command of God, and we recognize by whom these things that we see have been made. But let us see how also[6] these same things come to be in our firmament of heaven, that is, in the firmness of our mind or heart. I think that if our mind has been enlightened by Christ, our sun, it is ordered afterward to bring forth from these waters that are in it "swimming creatures" and "birds that fly," that is, to bring out into the open good or evil thoughts that there might be a distinction of the good thoughts from the evil, which certainly both proceed from our heart as from the waters. But by the word and precept of God let us offer up both to God's view and judgment so that, with his enlightenment, we may be able to distinguish what is evil from the good. HOMILIES ON GENESIS 1.8.[7]

1:21 Creation of Sea Monsters

WHY THE SEA MONSTERS WERE CREATED. BASIL THE GREAT: "God created the great sea monsters." And not because they are larger than the shrimp and herring are they called great, but because with their immense bodies

[2]FC 46:120-21. [3]FC 42:160-62. [4]FC 84:71. [5]The literal or plain sense of the text. [6]In a spiritual sense. [7]FC 71:57.

they are like huge mountains. Indeed, they frequently look like islands when they swim upon the surface of the water.... Such are the animals that have been created for our fear and consternation.... And thus the Creator wants you to be kept awake by them, in order that, through hope in God, you might escape the harm that comes from them. Hexaemeron 7.6.[8]

Of Its Own Kind. Basil the Great: There is nothing truer than this, that either each plant has seed or there exists in it some generative power. And this accounts for the expression "of its own kind." For the shoot of the reed is not productive of an olive tree, but from the reed comes another reed, and from seeds spring plants related to the seeds sown. Thus what was put forth by the earth in its first generation has been preserved until the present time, since the kinds persisted through constant reproduction. Hexaemeron 5.2.[9]

Succession Preserved. Basil the Great: The nature of existing objects, set in motion by one command, passes through creation without change, by generation and destruction, preserving the succession of the kinds through resemblance until it reaches the very end. It begets a horse as the successor of a horse, a lion of a lion and an eagle of an eagle. It continues to preserve each of the animals by uninterrupted successions until the consummation of the universe. No length of time causes the specific characteristics of the animals to be corrupted or extinct, but, as if established just recently, nature, ever fresh, moves along with time. Hexaemeron 9.2.[10]

Species Peculiar Properties Received from God. Ambrose: In the pine cone nature seems to express an image of itself. It preserves its peculiar properties which it received from that divine and celestial command, and it repeats in the succession and order of the years its generation until the end of time is fulfilled. Hexaemeron 3.16.68.[11]

Differences Sustained. Ambrose: The Word of God permeates every creature in the constitution of the world. Hence, as God had ordained, all kinds of living creatures were quickly produced from the earth. In compliance with a fixed law they all succeed each other from age to age according to their aspect and kind. The lion generates a lion; the tiger, a tiger; the ox, an ox; the swan, a swan; and the eagle, an eagle. What was once enjoined became in nature a habit for all time. Hence the earth has not ceased to offer the homage of its service. The original species of living creatures is reproduced for future ages by successive generations of its kind. Hexaemeron 6.3.9.[12]

1:22 And God Blessed Them

Hybrids Are the Work of Humans, Not of God. Ambrose: What pure and untarnished generations follow without intermingling one after another, so that a thymallus produces a thymallus; a sea-wolf, a sea-wolf. The sea-scorpion, too, preserves unstained its marriage bed.... Fish, therefore, know nothing of union with alien species. They do not have unnatural betrothals

---

[8]FC46:115-16. [9]FC 46:69. [10]FC 46:137. [11]FC 42:119-20. [12]FC 42:232.

such as are designedly brought about between animals of two different species as, for instance, the donkey and the mare, or again the female donkey and the horse, both being examples of unnatural union. Certainly there are cases in which nature suffers more in the nature of defilement rather than that of injury to the individual. Man as an abettor of hybrid barrenness is responsible for this. He considers a mongrel animal more valuable than one of a genuine species. You mix together alien species and you mingle diverse seeds. HEXAEMERON 5.3.9.[13]

SEEDS PREFIGURE RESURRECTION. AMBROSE: Seeds of one kind cannot be changed into another kind of plant nor bring forth produce differing from its own seeds, so that men should spring from serpents and flesh from teeth. How much more, indeed, is it to be believed that whatever has been sown rises again in its own nature and that crops do not differ from their seed, that soft things do not spring from hard nor hard from soft, nor is poison changed into blood, but that flesh is restored from flesh, bone from bone, blood from blood, the humors of the body from humors. ON BELIEF IN THE RESURRECTION 2.70.[14]

BODY INTEGRITY IN THE RESURRECTION LIKE GREENER INTEGRITY IN THE SEED. GREGORY OF NYSSA: We learn from Scripture in the account of the first creation that first the earth brought forth "the green herb" (as the narrative says), and then from this plant seed was yielded, from which, when it was shed on the ground, the same form of the original plant again sprang up. The apostle, it is to be observed, declares that this very same thing happens in the resurrection also. And so

we learn from him the fact not only that our humanity will be then changed into something nobler but also that what we have therein to expect is nothing else than that which was at the beginning. ON THE SOUL AND THE RESURRECTION.[15]

SOULS DO NOT MIGRATE. GREGORY OF NYSSA: Those who would contend that the soul migrates into natures divergent from each other seem to me to obliterate all natural distinctions—to blend and confuse together in every possible respect the rational, the irrational, the sentient and the insensate; if, that is, all these are to pass into each other with no distinct natural order secluding them from mutual transition. To say that one and the same soul, on account of a particular environment of body, is at one time a rational and intellectual soul, and that then it is caverned along with the reptiles, or herds with the birds, or is a beast of burden, or a carnivorous one, or swims in the deep; or even drops down to an insensate thing so as to strike out roots or become a complete tree, producing buds on branches, and from those buds a flower, or a thorn, or a fruit edible or noxious—to say this is nothing short of making all things the same and believing that one single nature runs through all beings; that there is a connection between them which blends and confuses hopelessly all the marks by which one could be distinguished from another. ON THE SOUL AND THE RESURRECTION.[16]

[13]FC 42:166. [14]NPNF 2 10:185. [15]NPNF 2 5:467. [16]NPNF 2 5:454.

PURPOSE OF THE BLESSING. AUGUSTINE: God wanted the blessing to have the power of fecundity, which is revealed in the succession of offspring. Thus, though the animals were made weak and mortal, they might by that blessing preserve their kind by giving birth. ON THE LITERAL INTERPRETATION OF GENESIS 15.50.[17]

[17]FC 84:180.

1:24-25 CREATION OF THE ANIMALS OF THE EARTH

[24]*And God said, "Let the earth bring forth [living creatures]* according to their kinds: cattle† and creeping things and beasts of the earth according to their kinds." And it was so.* [25]*And God made the beasts of the earth according to their kinds and the cattle according to their kinds, and everything that creeps upon the ground according to its kind. And God saw that it was good.*

*LXX a living soul (life?) †LXX quadrupeds

OVERVIEW: The animals of the earth are not created by the earth but by God on the earth through the divine Word. God's command to the earth remains, and the earth continues to bring forth animals (BASIL). The general description in Genesis 1:24-25 might refer to the creation of three distinct classes of animals: reptiles, predators and herds (AUGUSTINE). Each species of animal resembles various human characteristics (CYRIL OF JERUSALEM). The animals of the earth symbolize the impulses of the outer, earthly person (ORIGEN). The souls of beasts did not exist before creation (BASIL). The glory of God is revealed in the beauty and wealth of created beings (CHRYSOSTOM).

1:24-25 Creation of Beasts of the Earth

SOULS OF BEASTS DID NOT EXIST BEFORE CREATION. BASIL THE GREAT: The soul of brute beasts did not emerge after having been hidden in the earth, but it was called into existence of the time of the command. HEXAEMERON 9.3.[1]

CREATED BY GOD IN THE EARTH. BASIL THE GREAT: Formerly God had said: "Let the waters bring forth crawling creatures that have life,"[2] here, "Let the earth bring forth living creatures." Is the earth, then, possessed of life? And do the mad-minded Manichaeans hold the advantage, since they assume that the earth has a soul? No, when he said, "Let it

[1]FC 46:138. [2]Gen 1:20.

bring forth," it did not produce what was stored up in it, but he who gave the command also bestowed upon it the power to bring forth. Neither did the earth, when it heard, "Let it bring vegetation and the fruit trees,"[3] produce plants that it had hidden in it. . . . On the contrary, it is the divine Word that is the origin of things made. "Let the earth bring forth"—meaning not let it put forth what it already has but let it acquire what it does not have, since God is enduing it with the power of active force. HEXAEMERON 8.1.[4]

GOD'S COMMAND REMAINS CONSTANTLY ACTIVE. BASIL THE GREAT: "Let the earth bring forth living creatures according to their kinds: cattle and creeping things and beasts of the earth according to their kinds." Consider the word of God moving through all creation, having begun at that time, active up to the present and efficacious until the end, even to the consummation of the world. As a ball, when pushed by someone and then meeting with a slope, is borne downward by its own shape and the inclination of the ground and does not stop before some level surface receives it, so too the nature of existing objects, set in motion by one command, passes through creation, without change, by generation and destruction, preserving the succession of the species through resemblance, until it reaches the very end. HEXAEMERON 9.2.[5]

HYMN OF PRAISE FOR THE BEAUTY OF CREATION. BASIL THE GREAT: Let us glorify the Master Craftsman for all that has been done wisely and skillfully, and from the beauty of the visible things let us form an idea of him who is more than beautiful. And from the greatness of these perceptible and circum-

scribed bodies let us conceive of him who is infinite and immense and who surpasses all understanding in the plenitude of his power. For even if we are ignorant of things made, yet at least that which in general comes under our observation is so wonderful that even the most acute mind is shown to be at a loss as regards the least of the things in the world, either in the ability to explain it worthily or to render due praise to the Creator, to whom be all glory, honor and power forever. HEXAEMERON 1.11.[6]

THE WEALTH OF GOD'S CREATIONS. CHRYSOSTOM: It wasn't simply for our use that he produced all these things; it was also for our benefit in the sense that we might see the overflowing abundance of his creatures and be overwhelmed at the Creator's power, and be in a position to know that all these things were produced by a certain wisdom and ineffable love out of regard for the human being that was destined to come into being. HOMILIES ON GENESIS 7.13.[7]

THREE CLASSES OF ANIMALS? AUGUSTINE: We might infer that because the writer says three times "according to their kinds," our attention is called to three classes. First quadrupeds and creeping things according to their kinds, and here I believe he has indicated what quadrupeds he means, namely, those that belong to the class of creeping things, such as lizards, amphibians, and the like. Thus, in repeating the enumeration of animals, the author did not repeat the name *quadrupeds* apparently because he included them in

---

[3]Gen 1:11. [4]FC 46:117. [5]FC 46:136-37. [6]FC 46:19. [7]FC 74:99; PG 53:66.

the term "creeping things." With this in view, he did not say simply "creeping things" but rather "all creeping things of earth." "Of earth" is added because there are also creeping things in the waters, and "all" is added to include those also that move on four feet, the class specifically intended above by the term *quadruped*. Next, the beasts are another class, indicated also by the expression "according to their kinds," and they are all those animals, excluding reptiles, that prowl about with fearsome mouths and claws. Finally, the herds make up a third class designated by the phrase "according to their kinds." These have no such fierce and violent ways as wild beasts, although some may attack with their horns. ON THE LITERAL INTERPRETATION OF GENESIS 3.11.17.[8]

THE ANIMALS RESEMBLE DIFFERENT HUMAN CHARACTERS. CYRIL OF JERUSALEM: God said: "Let the earth bring forth living creatures according to their kinds: cattle and creeping things and beasts of the earth according to their kinds." Different natures of animals sprang forth from the one earth at a single command—the gentle sheep and the carnivorous lion—and the various tendencies of irrational animals that display analogies to various human characteristics. Thus the fox typifies the craftiness of men, the snake the venomous treachery of friends and the neighing horse the wanton young man. There is the busy ant to rouse the indolent and sluggish;

for when a man spends an idle youth, then he is instructed by the irrational creatures, being chided by the sacred Scripture, which says, "Go to the ant, O sluggard, and considering her ways, emulate her and become wiser than she."[9] For when you observe her treasuring up food for herself in good season, imitate her. Treasure up for yourself the fruits of good works for the world to come. CATECHETICAL LECTURES 9.13.[10]

THE ANIMALS SYMBOLIZE HUMAN IMPULSES. ORIGEN: In the present text, I think the impulses of our outer man, that is, of our carnal and earthly man, are indicated by this which is said: "Let the earth bring forth the living creatures according to their kind, four-footed creatures, creeping creatures and beasts on the earth according to their kind." In brief the text indicated nothing winged in these things[11] that are said about the flesh, but only "four-footed creatures, creeping creatures and beasts of the earth." According to that, to be sure, which is said by the apostle, that "no good dwells in my flesh"[12] and that "the wisdom of the flesh is hostile to God,"[13] those are certainly things that the earth, that is, our flesh, produces. HOMILIES ON GENESIS 1.11.[14]

---

[8]ACW 41:86. [9]Prov 6:6. [10]FC 61:191-92. [11]Cf. Gen 1:20. [12]Rom 7:18. [13]Rom 8:7. [14]FC 71:60-61.

1:26-27 GOD CREATES MAN AND WOMAN

26Then God said, "Let us make man [in our image, after our likeness];* and let them have dominion over the fish of the sea, and over the birds of the air, and over the cattle, and over all the earth, and over every creeping thing that creeps upon the earth." 27So God created man in his own image, in the image of God he created him; male and female he created them.

*LXX according to our image and likeness

OVERVIEW: These verses are perhaps the verses of the Old Testament most commented on by the Fathers. The doctrine of man's creation in the image of God is the foundation of patristic anthropology. The mention of his likeness to God points to the destiny of his sanctification and glorification. On that common basis the Fathers develop the text in various ways. Many comment on God's address to himself in the plural as referring to the Trinity (PRUDENTIUS). Most of the early Fathers and later Greek fathers take the image according to which man is created to be Christ himself; hence man is an "image of the image" (CLEMENT OF ALEXANDRIA, MARIUS VICTORINUS).

Among the Greeks there is generally a distinction drawn between the image and the likeness: man is created according to the image, and his destiny in freedom is to achieve likeness to God (ORIGEN, DIADOCHUS). Augustine argued that man's soul is created in the image of God directly. Accordingly he maintained that the human soul is an image of the triune God and therefore intrinsically trinitarian (FULGENTIUS).

As to what constitutes the image of God in man, Irenaeus maintained that this included both the corporeal and spiritual aspect of man. Most, however, found it in man's soul or spiritual aspect (ORIGEN, JOHN CASSIAN, AMBROSE). According to Sahdona the concept of the image of God in man had especially an ethical connotation: man achieved a likeness to God when he was renewed in the Christian faith. A peculiar view was expressed by Potamius of Lisbon, who saw the actual human body as a concrete representation of the Trinity (POTAMIUS). It refers to both our relationship to God and our being placed over the created order. It constitutes our royal state and is manifest in our possession of divine reason, in our freedom, immortality, virtue and justice (GREGORY OF NYSSA, JOHN OF DAMASCUS, CHRYSOSTOM).

Both man and woman are created in the image of God. The divine image transcends sexual difference (GREGORY OF NYSSA). The complementarity of female and male is represented in various ways: the female was already in the male when Adam was created (EPHREM); the male symbolizes the spirit, while the female represents the soul. Scripture says "male and female he created them," anticipating what was to happen later, after the blessing "increase and multiply" allowed human beings to reproduce through the union of male and female (ORIGEN).

Human dignity is honored by the unique triune consultation prior to the creation of Adam, as revealed in Scripture (BASIL, CHRYSOSTOM). "The image of God" is a comprehensive phrase (GREGORY OF NYSSA). It is given; the likeness is to be freely chosen (BASIL). The twofold nature of humanity is seen in the terms *image* and *likeness*, and *man* and *woman* (GREGORY OF NYSSA). The fall preceded cohabitation (CHRYSOSTOM).

1:26a *Let Us Make Man*

THE TRIUNE CONSULTATION OVER THE CREATION OF HUMANS. GREGORY OF NYSSA: This same language was not used for (the creation) of other things. The command was simple when light was created; God said, "let there be light." Heaven was also made without deliberation. . . . These, though, were before (the creation of) humans. For humans, there was deliberation. He did not say, as he did when creating other things, "Let there be a human." See how worthy you are! Your origins are not in an imperative. Instead, God deliberated about the best way to bring to life a creation worthy of honor. ON THE ORIGIN OF MAN.[1]

HUMAN DIGNITY HONORED BY THIS DELIBERATION. CHRYSOSTOM: To begin, it is worthwhile to ask why God did not say, when the heavens were created, "Let us make the heavens" but instead, "Let there be a heaven. . . . Let there be light," and similarly for each other aspect of creation. "Let us make" suggests deliberation, collaboration and conference with another person. So what is it whose

pending creation is granted so great an honor? It is humanity, the greatest and most marvelous of living beings, and the creation most worthy of honor before God. . . . There is here this deliberation, collaboration and communion not because God needs advice—God forbid saying such a thing!—but so that the very impact of the language of our creation would show us honor. SERMONS ON GENESIS 2.1.[2]

ASCENT FROM LOWER TO HIGHER. GREGORY OF NYSSA: If, therefore, Scripture tells us that man was made last, after every animate thing, the lawgiver is doing nothing else than declaring to us the doctrine of the soul, considering that what is perfect comes last, according to a certain necessary sequence in the order of things. . . . Thus we may suppose that nature makes an ascent as it were by steps—I mean the various properties of life—from the lower to the perfect form. ON THE CREATION OF MAN 8.7.[3]

THE CREATION OF HUMANITY. GREGORY OF NYSSA: Scripture informs us that the Deity proceeded by a sort of graduated and ordered advance to the creation of man. After the foundations of the universe were laid, as the history records, man did not appear on the earth at once, but the creation of the brutes preceded him, and the plants preceded them. Thereby Scripture shows that the vital forces blended with the world of matter according to a gradation; first it infused itself into insensate nature; and in continuation of this advanced into the sentient world; and then ascended to intelligent and rational beings. . . . The creation of man is related as coming last, as of one who took up

[1]GNOS 5-6, 8. [2]PG 54:587-88. [3]NPNF 2 5:394.

into himself every single form of life, both that of plants and that which is seen in brutes. His nourishment and growth he derives from vegetable life; for even in vegetables such processes are to be seen when aliment is being drawn in by their roots and given off in fruit and leaves. His sentient organization he derives from the brute creation. But his faculty of thought and reason is incommunicable, and a peculiar gift in our nature. . . . It is not possible for this reasoning faculty to exist in the life of the body without existing by means of sensations, and since sensation is already found subsisting in the brute creation, necessarily, as it were, by reason of this one condition, our soul has touch with the other things which are knit up with it; and these are all those phenomena within us that we call "passions." ON THE SOUL AND THE RESURRECTION.[4]

THE FATHER AND THE SON CREATE MAN. PRUDENTIUS:

> The inspired historian makes it very clear
> That at earth's dawn the Father not alone
> Nor without Christ his new creation
>   formed.
> "God fashioned man," he says, "and gave to
>   him
> The face of God." What but to say that he
> Was not alone, that God stood by God's
>   side
> When the Lord made man in image of the
>   Lord? POEMS.[5]

1:26b Made in God's Image and Likeness

CHRIST THE IMAGE. CLEMENT OF ALEXANDRIA: For "the image of God" is his Word (and the divine Word, the light who is the archetype of light, is a genuine son of Mind [the Father]); and an image of the Word is the true man, that is, the mind in man, who on this account is said to have been created "in the image" of God and "in his likeness," because through his understanding heart he is made like the divine Word or Reason [Logos], and so rational [logikos]. EXHORTATION TO THE GREEKS 10.[6]

ACCORDING TO OUR IMAGE. MARIUS VICTORINUS: Moses says what was said by God: "Let us make man according to our image and likeness." God says that. He says "let us make" to a co-operator, necessarily to Christ. And he says "according to the image." Therefore man is not the image of God, but he is "according to the image." For Jesus alone is the image of God, but man is "according to the image," that is, image of the image. But he says "according to our image." Therefore both Father and Son are one image. AGAINST ARIUS 1A.20.[7]

DISTINCTION BETWEEN IMAGE AND LIKENESS. ORIGEN: In recording the first creation of man, Moses before all others says, "And God said, Let us make man in our own image and likeness." Then he adds afterwards, "And God made man; in the image of God made he him; male and female made he them, and he blessed them." Now the fact that he said "he made him in the image of God" and was silent about the likeness points to nothing else but this, that man received the honor of God's image in his first creation, whereas the perfection of God's likeness was reserved for him at the consummation. The purpose of this was that man should acquire it for himself by his own earnest efforts to imitate God, so that while the possibility of attaining perfection was given to him in the beginning through the

---

[4]NPNF 2 5:441-42. [5]FC 52:15. [6]LCL 215. [7]FC 69:117.

honor of the "image," he should in the end through the accomplishment of these works obtain for himself the perfect "likeness." ON FIRST PRINCIPLES 3.6.1.[8]

IMAGE FREELY RECEIVED. DIADOCHUS OF PHOTICE: All men are made in God's image; but to be in his likeness is granted only to those who through great love have brought their own freedom into subjection to God. For only when we do not belong to ourselves do we become like him who through love has reconciled us to himself. No one achieves this unless he persuades his soul not to be distracted by the false glitter of this life. ON SPIRITUAL PERFECTION 4.[9]

IN OUR IMAGE. AUGUSTINE: For why the "our," if the Son is the image of the Father alone? But it is on account of the imperfect likeness, as we have said, that man is spoken of as "after our image," and so "our," that man might be an image of the Trinity. This image is not equal to the Trinity, as the Son is to the Father, but approaching it, as is said, by a certain likeness; as in things distinct there can be closeness, not however in this case as if a spatial closeness but by imitation. ON THE TRINITY 7.6.12.[10]

AUGUSTINE: Not everything that among creatures bears some likeness to God is rightly called his image, but only that than which God alone is more exalted. That is directly drawn from him, if between himself and it there is no interposed nature. ON THE TRINITY 11.5.8.[11]

AUGUSTINE: For God said, "Let us make man in our image and likeness": a little later, however, it is said "And God made man in the image of God." It would certainly not be correct to say "our," because the number is plural, if man were made in the image of one person, whether Father, Son or Holy Spirit. But because he is made in the image of the Trinity, consequently it was said "in our image." Again, lest we choose to believe in three gods in the Trinity, since the same Trinity is one God, he said, "And God made man in his image," as if he were to say "in his [own triune] image." ON THE TRINITY 12.6.6.[12]

WHO SPEAKS OF "OUR"? FULGENTIUS OF RUSPE: Therefore let us hold that the Father and the Son and the Holy Spirit are by nature one God; neither is the Father the one who is the Son, nor the Son the one who is the Father, nor the Holy Spirit the one who is the Father or the Son. For the essence, that which the Greeks call the *ousia*, of the Father and the Son and the Holy Spirit is one, in which essence the Father is not one thing and the Son a second thing and the Holy Spirit still a third thing, although in person the Father is different, the Son is different, and the Holy Spirit is different. All of this is demonstrated for us in the strongest fashion at the very beginning of the Holy Scriptures, when God says, "Let us make human beings in our image and likeness." When, using the singular number, he says "image," he shows that the nature is one, in whose image the human being was made. But when he says "our" in the plural, he shows that the very same God in whose image the human being was made is not one in person. For if in that one essence of Father, Son and Holy Spirit there were one person, "to our

---

[8]OFP 244. [9]SC 5:86. [10]FC 45:241*. [11]FC 45:327-28*. [12]FC 45:348*.

image" would not have been spoken but "in my image." Nor would he have said "let us make" but "I shall make." If in reality in those three persons three substances were to be understood or believed, "to our image" would not have been said; rather, "to our images"; for there could not be one image of three unequal natures. But while the human being is said to be made according to the one image of the one God, the divinity of the Holy Trinity in one essence is announced. Then and shortly thereafter, in place of what he had said above, "Let us make human beings in our image and likeness," Scripture thus told of the making of the human being by saying, "And God created humankind in his image; in the image of God he created them." TO PETER ON THE FAITH 5.[13]

THE INVISIBLE FATHER THROUGH THE VISIBLE WORD. IRENAEUS: In previous times man, it is true, was said to have been made according to the image of God, but he was not revealed as such. For the Word according to whose image man was made was still invisible. Therefore also man easily lost the likeness. But when the Word of God was made flesh, he confirmed both image and likeness. For on the one hand he truly showed the image by becoming what his image was. On the other hand he firmly established the likeness by the co-assimilation of man to the invisible Father through the visible Word. AGAINST HERESIES 5.16.2.[14]

OR SPIRITUAL? ORIGEN: We do not understand, however, this man indeed whom Scripture says was made "according to the image of God" to be corporeal. For the form of the body does not contain the image of God, nor is the corporeal said to be "made" but "formed," as is written in the words that follow. For the text says, "And God formed man,"

that is fashioned, "from the slime of the earth."[15] But it is our inner man, invisible, incorporeal, incorruptible and immortal, that is made "according to the image of God." For it is in such qualities as these that the image of God is more correctly understood. But if anyone supposes that this man who is made "according to the image and likeness of God" is made of flesh, he will appear to represent God himself as made of flesh and in human form. It is most clearly impious to think this about God. HOMILIES ON GENESIS 1.13.[16]

IMAGE SPIRITUALLY INTERPRETED. JOHN CASSIAN: Placing him in the midst of all the brothers, he inquired as to how the Catholic churches throughout the East interpreted what is said in Genesis: "Let us make man according to our image and likeness." Then he explained that the image and likeness of God was treated by all the heads of the churches not according to the lowly sound of the letter but in a spiritual way, and he proved this with a long discourse and many examples from Scripture, showing that nothing of this sort could be the case with that immeasurable and incomprehensible and invisible majesty—that it could be circumscribed in a human form and likeness, that indeed a nature that was incorporeal and uncomposed and simple could be apprehended by the eye or seized by the mind. CONFERENCE 10.3.2-3.[17]

SPATIAL AND VISUAL METAPHORS PERCEIVED BY THE POWER OF THE MIND. AMBROSE: But let us define more accurately the meaning of the phrase "to the image of

---

[13]FC 95:63. [14]LQAH 2:368. [15]Gen 2:7. [16]FC 71:63. [17]ACW 57:372.

God." Is it true that the flesh is made "to the image of God"? In that case, is there earth in God, since flesh is of earth? Is God corporeal, that is to say, weak and subject like the flesh to the passions? Perhaps the head may seem to you to be made in the likeness of God because it stands aloft, or the eyes because they observe or the ears because they hear? As to the question of height, are we to consider ourselves to be tall just because we tower a little over the earth? Are we not ashamed to be thought of as like to God merely because we are taller than serpents or other creeping creatures or even than deer, sheep or wolves? In that respect, how much taller are elephants and camels in comparison with us! Sight is important to us in order to enable us to behold the things of the world and to have knowledge of what is not reported by any person but is grasped by our sense of sight. How significant, in fact, is this power of sight! Because of it we may be said to have the likeness of God, who sees all, observes all, comprehends our hidden emotions and searches into the secrets of our hearts! Am I not ashamed to admit that it is not in my power to see parts of my body? What is in front of me I can see, but I am unable to see what is behind me. I have no view of my neck or of the back of my head, and I cannot see my loins. In like manner, what avail is our sense of hearing if we cannot either see or hear what is only a short distance away? If walls should intervene, both sight and hearing are impeded. Furthermore, our bodies are fixed and enclosed in a narrow space, whereas all wild animals have a wider range and are also swifter than men. The flesh, therefore, cannot be made to the image of God. This is true, however, of our souls, which are free to wander far and wide in acts of reflection and of counsel. Our souls

are able to envisage and reflect on all things. We who are now in Italy have in mind what seems to pertain to affairs in the East or in the West. We seem to have dealings with men who dwell in Persia. We envision those who have their homes in Africa, if there happen to be acquaintances of ours who enjoy the hospitality of that land. We accompany these people on their departure and draw near to them in their voyage abroad. We are one with them in their absence. Those who are separated far from us engage us in conversation. We arouse the dead even to mutual interchange of thoughts and embrace them as if they were still living. We even go to the point of conferring on these people the usages and customs of our daily life. That, therefore, is made to the image of God that is perceived not by the power of the body but by that of the mind. It is that power that beholds the absent and embraces in its vision countries beyond the horizon. Its vision crosses boundaries and gazes intently on what is hidden. In one moment the utmost bounds of the world and its remote secret places are under its ken. God is attained, and Christ is approached. There is a descent into hell, and aloft in the sky there is an ascent into heaven. Hear, then, what Scripture says: "But our citizenship is in heaven." Is not that, therefore, in which God is ever-present made to the likeness of God? Listen to what the apostle says in that regard: "We all, therefore, with faces unveiled, reflecting as in a mirror the glory of God, are being transformed into his very image from glory to glory, as through the Spirit of the Lord."[18] Hexaemeron 6.8.44-45.[19]

---

[18]2 Cor 3:18. [19]FC 42:256-58.

Humanity Receives Likeness to God by Becoming a Living Sacrifice. SAHDONA: These are the virtues that man acquires by considering and controlling his own senses. He "takes off the old man, who was corrupted in the convolutions of his error,"[20] "and wears the new one, who is renewed in knowing the image of his Creator,"[21] and he becomes as a whole an effigy, likeness and image of his God. Like a living sacrifice, suitable and pleasing to God, he employs his body for his rational service. He consecrates and somehow presents to God the vows and the offerings of all his limbs and offers the sacrifices suitable for the action of grace, which are the rational fruits of the lips of those who confess his name by incessantly celebrating God in their body and soul, God to whom they belong now in definitive oblations. BOOK OF PERFECTION 3.145.[22]

The Image Given, the Likeness to Be Freely Chosen. GREGORY OF NYSSA: "Let us make man in our image, after our likeness." We possess the one by creation; we acquire the other by free will. In the first structure it is given us to be born in the image of God; by free will there is formed in us the being in the likeness of God. . . . "Let us make man in our image": Let him possess by creation what is in the image, but let him also become according to the likeness. God has given the power for this. If he had created you also in the likeness, where would your privilege be? Why have you been crowned? And if the Creator had given you everything, how would the kingdom of heaven have opened for you? But it is proper that one part is given you, while the other has been left incomplete: this is so that you might complete it yourself and might be worthy of the reward which comes from God. ON THE ORIGIN OF MAN.[23]

The Human Body a Physical Epitome of the Trinity. POTAMIUS OF LISBON: In order that the unity itself of the threefold majesty and imprint should encounter our understanding, the invisible majesty itself states so: "Let us make man in our image and according to our likeness." Look! He has demonstrated what we believe. God has engraved his image on the face of the human and has said "in our image." The knowledge of Father and Son is impressed upon the face of man; and the very features of his face, by means of the clay by which we are formed, revealed in the human original model how the Father and the Son were, so that man could admire God in man. LETTER ON THE SUBSTANCE 356-64.[24]

Humankind as Flesh and Spirit. GREGORY OF NAZIANZUS: This was to show that he could call into being not only a nature akin to himself but also one altogether alien to him. For akin to Deity are those natures which are intellectual and only to be comprehended by mind; but all of which sense can take cognizance are utterly alien to it, and of these the furthest removed from it are all those which are entirely destitute of soul and power of motion.

Mind, then, and sense—thus distinguished from each other—had remained within their own boundaries and bore in themselves the magnificence of the Creator-Word, silent praisers and thrilling heralds of his mighty work. Not yet was there any mingling of both, nor any mixture of these opposites, tokens of a greater wisdom and generosity in the creation of natures; nor as yet were the whole

---

[20]Eph 4:22. [21]Col 3:10. [22]CSCO 200:69. [23]GNOS 10. [24]PLS 1:210; CCL 69A:241.

riches of goodness made known. Now the Creator-Word, determining to exhibit this and to produce a single living being out of both (the invisible and the visible creation, I mean) fashions man; and taking a body from already existing matter, and placing in it a breath taken from himself (which the Word knew to be an intelligent soul and the image of God), as a sort of second world great in littleness, he placed him on the earth—a new angel, a mingled worshiper initiated fully into the visible creation but only partially into the intellectual; king of all on earth but subject to the King above; earthly and heavenly; temporal and yet immortal; visible and yet intellectual; halfway between greatness and lowliness; in one person combining spirit and flesh. Spirit because of the favor bestowed on him, flesh on account of the height to which he had been raised; the one that he might continue to live and glorify his benefactor, the other that he might suffer and by suffering be put in remembrance, and be corrected if he became proud in his greatness; a living creature, trained here and then moved elsewhere; and to complete the mystery, made godly by its inclination to God. SECOND ORATION ON EASTER 6-7.[25]

THE IMAGE OF GOD IS A COMPREHENSIVE PHRASE. GREGORY OF NYSSA: God creates man for no other reason than that God is good; and being such, and having this as his reason for entering upon the creation of our nature, he would not exhibit the power of this goodness in an imperfect form, giving our nature some one of the things at his disposal and grudging it a share in another: but the perfect form of goodness is here to be seen by his both bringing man into being from nothing and fully supplying him with all good gifts.

But since the list of individual good gifts is a long one, it is out of the question to apprehend it numerically. The language of Scripture therefore expresses it concisely by a comprehensive phrase, in saying that man was made "in the image of God," for this is the same as to say that he made human nature participant in all good; for if the Deity is the fullness of good, and this is his image, then the image finds its resemblance to the archetype in being filled with all good. ON THE CREATION OF MAN 16.10.[26]

DEFINITION OF THE IMAGE. GREGORY OF NYSSA: Let us add that [man's] creation in the image of the nature that governs all demonstrates precisely that he has from the beginning a royal nature. Following common usage, painters of portraits of princes, as well as representing their features, express their royal dignity by garments of purple, and before this image one is accustomed to say "the king." Thus human nature, created to rule the world because of his resemblance to the universal King, has been made like a living image that participates in the archetype by dignity and by name. He is not clothed in purple, scepter and diadem, for these do not signify his dignity (the archetype himself does not possess them). But in place of purple, he is clothed with virtue, the most royal of garments. Instead of a scepter, he is endowed with blessed immortality. Instead of a royal diadem, he bears the crown of justice, in such a way that everything about him manifests royal dignity, by his exact likeness to the beauty of the archetype. ON THE CREATION OF MAN 4.[27]

---

[25]NPNF 2 7:424-25. [26]NPNF 2 5:405. [27]NPNF 2 5:391**.

IMAGE AND LIKENESS. JOHN OF DAMASCUS: Since this is so, God created man out of visible and invisible nature with his own hands according to the image and likeness, forming the body from the earth and through his own breathing upon it giving it a rational and intellectual soul, which we call the divine image. That which is "according to the image" is manifest in the intellect and free will. That which is "according to the likeness" is manifest in such likeness in virtue as is possible. ORTHODOX FAITH 2.12.[28]

IMAGE OF COMMAND. CHRYSOSTOM: Some others base themselves on our arguments by asserting that God possesses an image in common with us, but they do not understand correctly what has been said. We did not speak about an image of being but about an image of command, as we will explain below. In fact, as a proof that divinity has no human form, listen to Paul's words: "But for a man it is not right to have his head covered, since he is the image and glory of God; but woman is the glory of man."[29] This is why—he says—"she must wear a veil on her head."[30] And in truth, in this passage he has called "image" this absence of difference of form with regard to God, and man is called image of God because God also possesses this figure: in their opinion, therefore, it should not be said that man only is the image of God but the woman as well. For man and woman have in common a single figure, character and resemblance. Why then is man called image of God, while the woman is not? Because Paul does not mean the image appearing in the form but the image concerning the command, which was given to man, not woman. Man in fact is subject to no creature, while woman is subject to man, according to God's words: "Your movement will be toward your husband, and he will rule you."[31] This is why man is the image of God. He has no creature over him, and there is nobody over God: he rules on everything. Woman, on the other hand, is the glory of man, because she is subject to man. SERMONS ON GENESIS 2.[32]

1:27 *Male and Female Created in God's Image*

BOTH MAN AND WOMAN IN GOD'S IMAGE. GREGORY OF NYSSA: Let us carefully examine these expressions. We shall discover this: what is in the image is one thing, what we see now in our unhappiness is another. "God made man," says Scripture. "He made him in the image of God." One who is made in the image of God has the task of becoming who he is. Then Scripture takes up the account of creation and says, "God made them male and female." Everyone knows, I think, that this aspect is excluded from the archetype: "In Christ Jesus," as the apostle says, "there is neither male nor female."[33] And yet Scripture affirms that man has been divided sexually. Thus the creation of our nature must in some way have been double; that which renders us like God and that which establishes the division of the sexes. And indeed such an interpretation is suggested by the very order of the account. Scripture says in the first place, "God made man; in the image of God, he made him." Only after that is it added, "He made them male and female," a division foreign to the divine attributes. ON THE CREATION OF MAN 16.[34]

---

[28]FC 37:234-35**. [29]1 Cor 11:7. [30]1 Cor 11:6. [31]Gen 3:16. [32]PG 54:589. [33]Gal 3:28. [34]NPNF 2 5:405**.

Eve Was in Adam at the Moment of His Creation. Ephrem the Syrian: Then Moses said, "Male and female he created them," to make known that Eve was already inside Adam, in the rib that was drawn out from him. Although she was not in his mind she was in his body, and she was not only in his body with him but also in soul and spirit with him, for God added nothing to that rib that he took out except the structure and the adornment. If everything that was suitable for Eve, who came to be from the rib, was complete in and from that rib, it is rightly said that "male and female he created them." Commentary on Genesis 1.29.2.[35]

Productive Concord Between Male and Female. Origen: Our inner man consists of spirit and soul. The spirit is said to be male; the soul can be called female. If these have concord and agreement between themselves, they increase and multiply by the very accord among themselves and they produce sons, good inclination and understandings or useful thoughts, by which they fill the earth and have dominion over it. Homilies on Genesis 1.15.[36]

Anticipating Human Reproduction Through the Union of Male and Female. Origen: It seems to be worth inquiring in this passage how, according to the letter, when the woman was not yet made, the Scripture says, "Male and female he made them." Perhaps, as I think, it is because of the blessing with which he blessed them saying, "Increase and multiply and fill the earth."[37] Anticipating what was to be, the text says, "Male and female he made them," since indeed man could not otherwise increase and multiply except with the female.

Therefore, that there might be no doubt about his blessing that is to come, the text says, "Male and female he made them." For in this manner man, seeing the consequence of increasing and multiplying to be from the fact that the female was joined to him, could cherish a more certain hope in the divine blessing. For if the Scripture had said, "Increase and multiply and fill the earth and have dominion over it," not adding this, "Male and female he made them," doubtless he would have disbelieved the divine blessing. Homilies on Genesis 1.14.[38]

Image and Likeness, Male and Female. Gregory of Nyssa: I think that by these words Holy Scripture conveys to us a great and lofty doctrine, and the doctrine is this. While two natures—the divine and incorporeal nature, and the irrational life of brutes—are separated from each other as extremes, human nature is the mean between them. For in the compound nature of man we may behold a part of each of the natures I have mentioned—of the divine, the rational and intelligent element, which does not admit the distinction of male and female; of the irrational, our bodily form and structure, divided into male and female—for each of these elements is certainly to be found in all that partakes of human life. That the intellectual element, however, precedes the other we learn as from one who gives in order an account of the making of man; and we learn also that his community and kindred with the irrational is for man a provision for reproduction. . . . He formed for our nature that contrivance for increase which befits those who had fallen

---

[35]FC 91:94. [36]FC 71:68. [37]Gen 1:28. [38]FC 71:67.

into sin, implanting in mankind, instead of the angelic majesty of nature, that animal and irrational mode by which they now succeed one another. ON THE CREATION OF MAN 16.7-9; 17.4.[39]

THE FALL PRECEDED COHABITATION. CHRYSOSTOM: Consider when this happened. After their disobedience, after their loss of the garden, then it was that the practice of intercourse had its beginning. You see, before their disobedience they followed a life like that of the angels, and there was no mention of intercourse. How could there be when they were not subject to the needs of the body? So at the outset and from the beginning the practice of virginity was in force, but when through their indifference disobedience came on the scene and the ways of sin were opened, virginity took its leave for the reason that they had proved unworthy of such a degree of good things, and in its place the practice of intercourse took over for the future. HOMILIES ON GENESIS 18.12.[40]

---

[39]NPNF 2 5:405, 407. [40]FC 82:10-11; PG 53:153.

1:28 HUMAN PROCREATION AND LORDSHIP OVER CREATION

[28]*And God blessed them, and God said to them, "Be fruitful and multiply, and fill the earth and subdue it; and have dominion over the fish of the sea and over the birds of the air and over every living thing that moves upon the earth."*

OVERVIEW: The increase of the human race posed problems for the Fathers. Generally they affirmed that the command to increase and multiply referred to the period before the fall, when human reproduction would have taken place by some means other than through sexual intercourse (AUGUSTINE, MAXIMUS THE CONFESSOR), for they generally maintained that Adam and Eve had been intended to form a virginal couple. Augustine, however, came to the view that sexual differentiation and sexual union were part of God's original plan, even though the fall intervened. The extent of human authority over the animals was a sign of God's love for humanity (CHRYSOSTOM). However, this power was lost after the sin (AUGUSTINE).

Male and female are commanded to increase and multiply (JOHN OF DAMASCUS). There is no depreciation of marriage in the patristic interpretation of Genesis 1:28 (GREGORY OF NYSSA). Two kinds of increase must be distinguished: of body and of soul (BASIL). Since our humanity partakes of the animal nature (GREGORY OF NYSSA), we are called to gain control over the irrational aspects of ourselves (BASIL). Although sexual intercourse followed the expulsion from paradise, sufficient grace was provided for honorable nuptial union, the glory of which is in the nurture of children (AUGUSTINE).

TWO KINDS OF INCREASE. GREGORY OF NYSSA: There are two ways to "increase": in the body and in the soul. The soul increases by education, progressing toward completion; the body increases (by growing) from small to large. He told, therefore, the senseless animals to increase by the development of the body. But to us he said "increase" in the inner person along ways which lead toward God. This was what Paul did, in his stretching out toward what lay ahead and forgetting what lie behind.[1] This is godly increase. ON THE ORIGIN OF MAN.[2]

NO DEPRECIATION OF MARRIAGE. GREGORY OF NYSSA: Let no one think that we depreciate marriage as an institution. We are well aware that it is not a stranger to God's blessing. . . . But our view of marriage is this: that while the pursuit of heavenly things should be a man's first care, yet if he can use the advantages of marriage with sobriety and moderation, he need not despise this way of serving. ON VIRGINITY 8.[3]

"INCREASE AND MULTIPLY" REFERS TO THE PERIOD BEFORE SIN. AUGUSTINE: One is completely right to ask in what sense we should understand the union of male and female before sin, as well as the blessing that said "Increase and multiply, and generate and fill the earth." Should we understand it in a physical manner or spiritually? For we are

permitted to understand it spiritually and to believe that it was changed into sexual fecundity after sin. For there was first the chaste union of male and female, of the former to rule, of the latter to obey, and there was the spiritual offspring of intelligible and immortal joys filling the earth, that is, giving life to the body and ruling it. That is, man so held [the body] subject that he experienced from it no opposition or trouble. We should believe that it was this way, since they were not yet children of this world before they sinned. For the children of this world generate and are generated, as the Lord says, when he shows that we should relatively disregard this carnal generation in comparison with the future life that is promised to us. TWO BOOKS ON GENESIS AGAINST THE MANICHAEANS 1.19.30.[4]

WHETHER CHRIST OVERCOMES THE DIVISION BETWEEN MALE AND FEMALE. MAXIMUS THE CONFESSOR: Indeed being in himself the universal union of all, [Christ] has started with our [sexual] division and become the perfect human being, having from us, on our account and in accordance with our nature, everything that we are and lacking nothing, "apart from sin,"[5] and having no need of the natural intercourse of marriage. In this way he showed, I think, that there was perhaps another way, foreknown to God, for human beings to increase, if the first human being had kept the commandment and not cast himself down to an animal state by abusing his own proper powers. Thus God-made-man has done away with the difference and division of

---

[1]Phil 3:13. [2]GNOS 46-47. [3]NPNF 2 5:352-53. [4]FC 84:77-78. [5]Heb 4:15.

nature into male and female, which human nature in no way needed for generation, as some hold, and without which it would perhaps have been possible. BOOK OF DIFFICULTIES 41.[6]

ADAM AND EVE A SEXUAL COUPLE BEFORE THE FALL. AUGUSTINE: If one should ask why it was necessary that a helper be made for man, the answer that seems most probable is that it was for the procreation of children, just as the earth is a helper for the seed in the production of a plant from the union of the two. This purpose was declared in the original creation of the world: "Male and female he made them. And God blessed them and said, 'Increase and multiply and fill the earth and subdue it.'" This reason for creation and union of male and female, as well as this blessing, was not abrogated after the sin and punishment of man. It is by virtue of this blessing that the earth is now filled with human beings who subdue it. Although it was after the expulsion of the man and woman from paradise that they came together in sexual intercourse and begot children, according to Scripture, nevertheless I do not see what could have prohibited them from honorable nuptial union and "the bed undefiled"[7] even in paradise. God could have granted them this if they had lived in a faithful and just manner in obedient and holy service to him, so that without the tumultuous ardor of passion and without any labor and pain of childbirth, offspring would be born from their seed. In this case, the purpose would not be to have children succeeding parents who die. Rather those who had begotten children would remain in the prime of life and would maintain their physical strength from the tree of life that had been planted in paradise. Those

who would be born would develop to the same state and eventually, when the determined number would be complete, if all live just and obedient lives, there would be a transformation. Thus without any death their natural bodies would receive a new quality since they obeyed every command of the spirit that ruled them. With the spirit alone vivifying them, without any help from corporeal nourishment, they would be called spiritual bodies. This could have been if the transgression of God's command had not merited the punishment of death. ON THE LITERAL INTERPRETATION OF GENESIS 9.3.5-6.[8]

THE NUPTIAL BLESSING REMAINED AFTER SIN APPEARED. AUGUSTINE: Far be it then from us to believe that the couple that were placed in paradise would have fulfilled through this lust, which shamed them into covering those organs, the words pronounced by God in his blessing: "Increase and multiply and fill the earth." For it was only after man sinned that his lust arose; it was after man sinned that his natural being, retaining the sense of shame but losing that dominance to which the body was subject in every part, felt and noticed, then blushed at and concealed that lust. The nuptial blessing, however, whereby the pair, joined in marriage, were to increase and multiply and fill the earth, remained in force even when they sinned. Yet it was given before they sinned, for its purpose was to make it clear that the procreation of children is a part of the glory of marriage and not of the punishment of sin. CITY OF GOD 14.21.[9]

---

[6]PG 91:1307-10. [7]Heb 13:4. [8]ACW 42:73-74. [9]LCL 371-73.

GAINING DOMINION OVER THE BEASTS WITHIN. GREGORY OF NYSSA: "You will rule over savage beasts." How though, you may ask, since I have a beast within? Actually, there are a myriad, a countless number of beasts within you. You should not take offense in these words. Rage is a small beast, yet when it growls in the heart is any dog more savage? Is not the treacherous soul like fresh bait staked in front of a bear's den? Is not the hypocrite a beast? . . . [Rule] then over the beasts inside you. Rule your thoughts so that you will become a ruler over all things. So the same one who provides the power to rule over all living things provides power for us to rule over ourselves. ON THE ORIGIN OF MAN.[10]

HUMANITY PARTAKES OF ANIMAL NATURE. GREGORY OF NYSSA: As brute life first entered into the world and man . . . took something of their nature (I mean the mode of generation), he accordingly took at the same time a share of the other attributes contemplated in that nature. For the likeness of man to God is not found in anger, nor is pleasure a mark of the superior nature; cowardice also, and boldness, and the desire of gain, and the dislike of loss, and all the like, are far removed from that stamp which indicates divinity. These attributes, then, human nature took to itself from the side of the brutes. ON THE CREATION OF MAN 18.1-2.[11]

AUTHORITY OVER BEASTS REFRACTS GOD'S LOVE FOR HUMANITY. CHRYSOSTOM: So, after saying "male and female he made them" as though to bestow a blessing on each of them, he goes on, "God blessed them in the words, 'Increase and multiply, fill the earth and gain dominion over it, and have control of

the fish of the sea.'" Behold the remarkable character of the blessing! I mean, those words, "increase and multiply and fill the earth," anyone could see are said of the brute beasts and the reptiles alike, whereas "gain dominion and have control" are directed to the man and woman. See the Lord's loving kindness: even before creating them, he makes them share in this control and bestows on them the blessing. "Have control" the text says, "of the fish of the sea, the birds of heaven and all the cattle, the whole earth and all the reptiles creeping on the earth." Did you notice the definitive character of this authority? Did you notice all created things placed under the control of this particular being? So no longer entertain casual impressions of this rational being but rather realize the extent of the esteem and the Lord's magnanimity toward it and be amazed at his love beyond all telling. HOMILIES ON GENESIS 10.9.[12]

HUMAN POWER OVER THE BEASTS. AUGUSTINE: At times the Manichaeans also ask, "In what sense did man receive power over the fish of the sea and the birds of heaven and all the cattle and wild animals? For we see that men are killed by many wild animals and that many birds harm us when we want to avoid them or to capture them, though we often cannot. In what sense then did we receive power over these?" On this point they should first be told that they make a big mistake when they consider man after sin, when he has been condemned to the mortality of this life and has lost that perfection by which he was made in the image of the God. But even man's state of condemnation involves such

---

[10]GNOS 36-37, 39. [11]NPNF 2 5:407-8. [12]FC 74:134.

power that he rules many animals. For though he can be killed by many wild animals on account of the fragility of his body, he can be tamed by none, although he tames very many and nearly all of them. TWO BOOKS ON GENESIS AGAINST THE MANICHAEANS 1.18.29.[13]

INCREASE AND MULTIPLY. JOHN OF DAMASCUS: After the transgression, . . . to prevent the wearing out and destruction of the race by death, marriage was devised that the race of men may be preserved through the procreation of children.

But they will perhaps ask, What then is the meaning of "male and female" and "Be fruitful and multiply"? In answer we shall say that "Be fruitful and multiply" does not altogether refer to the multiplying by the marriage connection. For God had power to multiply the race also in different ways, if they kept the precept unbroken to the end. But God, who knows all things before they have existence, knowing in his foreknowledge that they would fall into transgression in the future and be condemned to death, anticipated this and made "male and female," and bade them "be fruitful and multiply." ON THE ORTHODOX FAITH 4.24.[14]

---

[13]FC 84:76-77. [14]NPNF 2 9:96-97.

1:29-30 PLANTS AND FRUITS ARE FOOD FOR HUMANS AND BEASTS

[29]*And God said, "Behold, I have given you every plant yielding seed which is upon the face of all the earth, and every tree with seed in its fruit; you shall have them for food.* [30]*And to every beast of the earth, and to every bird of the air, and to everything that creeps on the earth, everything that has the breath of life, I have given every green plant for food." And it was so.*

OVERVIEW: Originally God permitted the use of foods from vegetation, that is, vegetables and the fruits of the trees (ORIGEN, NOVATIAN, GREGORY OF NYSSA). Both sexes, male and female, used this food for the body that the other animals used and received fitting sustenance from it (AUGUSTINE). The food from vegetation also symbolizes human affections (ORIGEN).

1:29-30 God Gives Plants for Food

THE FIRST FOOD WAS FROM VEGETATION. ORIGEN: The historical meaning, at least, of this sentence indicates clearly that originally God permitted the use of foods from vegetation, that is, vegetables and the fruits of trees. But the opportunity of eating flesh is given to men later when a covenant was made with Noah after the flood.[1] HOMILIES ON GENESIS 1.17.[2]

HUMBLING TO LOWLY SOIL. NOVATIAN: Man's first food was solely fruit and produce from trees. Man's guilt subsequently introduced the use of bread. The posture of his body shows forth the state of his conscience. As long as man's conscience did not reproach him, innocence raised him up toward the heavens to pluck his food from the trees. Once sin had been committed, it bowed man down to the soil of the earth to get grain. Still later the use of meat was added.[3] JEWISH FOODS 2.6.[4]

TO EVERY BEAST I HAVE GIVEN EVERY PLANT. GREGORY OF NYSSA: We note, however, many wild beasts do not eat fruit. What fruit does the panther eat? What fruit makes the lion strong? But nevertheless these creatures, when submitting to the laws of nature, ate fruits. And likewise when the [first] man changed his way of life and voided the limits set upon him, the Lord, after the flood, knowing humans were wasteful, allowed them to use all foods: "Eat every food as if it were edible plants."[5] Since [humans] were allowed this [concession], the other animals [also] received the liberty to eat. So the lion is [now] a meat-eater, and the vulture looks for carrion.

But vultures were not yet circling above the earth to find carrion when the animals originated; nothing created nor imagined had yet died in order to be food for the vul-

tures. Nature had not yet been divided; everything was completely fresh. Hunters did not capture prey, since people did not yet practice this. The beasts did not yet tear apart prey, since they were not meat eaters yet. . . . So was the first creation, and to this creation will be restored after this [age]. Humans will return to their original creation, rejecting hostility, a life encumbered with care, the slavery of the world to daily worries. Once they have renounced all this, they will return to that utopian life which is not enslaved to the passions of the flesh, which is freedom, the closeness to God, a partaker of the life of the angels. ON THE ORIGIN OF MAN.[6]

SUSTENANCE PRECLUDES LUST. AUGUSTINE: I myself hold with those who, considering the words, "Male and female he created them, saying, 'Increase and multiply and fill the earth,'"[7] interpret them as referring to visible and bodily sex. This is clear, in view of what follows: "And God said, 'Behold, I have given you every plant yielding seed which is upon the face of all the earth, and every tree with seed in its fruit; you shall have them for food. And to every beast of the earth, and to every bird of the air, and to everything that creeps on the earth, everything that has the breath of life, I have given every green plant for food.'" Note that both male and female used the food for the body that the other animals used. They received fitting sustenance from it. This was necessary for the animal body lest it suffer from hunger. But it was received in a certain immortal way and from

---

[1]Cf. Gen 9:3. [2]FC 71:69. [3]Cf. Gen 9:3. [4]FC 67:145. [5]Gen 9:3. [6]GNOS 49-50, 51. [7]Gen 1:26-28.

the tree of life, lest they die of old age. I would never believe that, in a place of such great happiness, either the flesh lusted against the spirit or the spirit against the flesh, and there was no internal peace.... We conclude, therefore, that there was no carnal concupiscence in that place. Such was the manner of life that all

necessities were taken care of by the proper functions of the members, without arousing lust. AGAINST JULIAN 4.4.69.[8]

---

[8]FC 35:226*.

1:31 GOD SEES THAT CREATION IS VERY GOOD

[31]*And God saw everything that he had made, and behold, it was very good. And there was evening and there was morning, a sixth day.*

OVERVIEW: Individual things created by God are good, but the entire creation is very good (AUGUSTINE). There is a similarity between created things, which were created good, and their Creator (AUGUSTINE). From the good in nature one can apprehend the supreme and everlasting good (AMBROSE). As God made man in his image on the sixth day, so the Son came in the sixth age of the human race to re-form us in accordance with the image of God (AUGUSTINE).

The "days of creation" set forth a sequence of divine creation (GREGORY OF NAZIANZUS) that proceeded from lower to higher forms of being (GREGORY OF NYSSA). The concept of a "day" cannot be reduced to an instant but implies a process (CHRYSOSTOM).

1:31 God Saw Everything That He Had Made

GOD SAW THAT THE ENTIRE CREATION WAS GOOD. AUGUSTINE: Certainly we should not carelessly pass over the words of Scripture that say, "And God saw that all the things that he had made were very good." For when dealing with individual things, it only says, "God saw that it is good," but in speaking of all things, it was not enough to say "good" without adding "very" as well. For if prudent observers consider the single works of God, they find that individually in their own species, they have praiseworthy measures, numbers and orders. How much more then will this be true of all of them together, that is, of the universe that is filled with these individual things gathered into unity? For every beauty that is composed of parts is much more praiseworthy in the whole than in a part. TWO BOOKS ON GENESIS AGAINST

THE MANICHAEANS 1.21.32.[1]

SIMILARITY BETWEEN CREATED THINGS AND CREATOR.

AUGUSTINE: No one doubts that God himself is the primal good. Indeed things can be said to be similar to God in many ways. Some, created in accordance with power and wisdom, are similar to God because uncreated power and wisdom are in him. Other created things are similar to God in the simple fact that they are alive, and God is incomparably alive and the source of life. Other created things are similar to God in that they have being, for God is the highest being and the source of being. And even those things that merely exist and yet do not live or know are in his likeness, not completely but in a slight degree, because even they are good in their own order, while God is incomparably good in a way transcending all other goods and from whom everything good proceeds. EIGHTY-THREE QUESTIONS 51.2.[2]

THE DIVINE GOOD CAN BE PERCEIVED THROUGH CREATION.

AMBROSE: From the goods that inhere in the nature of creation—they are indeed very good, even as the Lord said—one can apprehend the supreme and everlasting good. The order of the universe, its arrangement and its beauty—is not a man moved by this to love his Creator, even if he is slow in ability? For if we love our parents because they have produced us, how much more ought we to love the Creator of our parents and our own Creator! Therefore the power of God is a creating power. Even if God is not seen, he is judged from his works, and his works betray the workman, so that he who is not comprehended may be perceived. FLIGHT FROM THE WORLD 2.10.[3]

THE SIXTH DAY OF HUMAN CREATION AND THE SIXTH AGE OF THE HUMAN RACE.

AUGUSTINE: Sacred Scripture commends the perfection of the number six to us especially in this, that God completed his works in six days and made man in the image of God on the sixth day. And the Son of God came in the sixth age of the human race and was made the Son of man, in order to re-form us in the image of God. This is the age in which we are at present, whether a thousand years are assigned to each age or whether we settle upon memorable and notable personages as turning points of time. Thus the first age is found from Adam to Noah, the second from that time to Abraham, and after that . . . from Abraham to David, from David to the carrying away to Babylon, and from then to the birth of the Virgin. These three ages added to those make five. Hence the birth of the Lord inaugurated the sixth age, which is now in progress up to the hidden end of time. ON THE TRINITY 4.4.7.[4]

THE DAYS OF CREATION.

GREGORY OF NAZIANZUS: He made a first day, a second, a third, and so forth until the seventh day which was a rest from work. According to these days, everything created was subdivided, brought into an order by inexpressible laws. So creation was not an instantaneous act by the all-powerful Word; for him to think or to speak is to accomplish a task. If humans were last to enter the world—and in such a way as to honor God's handiwork with God's image—is this not marvelous? It is like saying that as a king he prepared the palace and then, as king, when everything was already pre-

---

[1]FC 84:80. [2]FC 70:86*. [3]FC 65:287. [4]FC 45:139.

pared, led in the procession. HOMILIES ON GENESIS 44.[5]

IN A SINGLE DAY. CHRYSOSTOM: I mean, his all-powerful hand and boundless wisdom were not at a loss even to create everything in one day. Why say "one day"? Even in a brief moment. Yet it was not because of its utility to him that he produced anything that exists, since being self-sufficient he is in need of nothing. It was rather out of his loving kind-ness and goodness that he created everything; accordingly he created things in sequence and provided us with a clear instruction about cre-ated things through the tongue of the blessed author, so that we might learn about them precisely and not fall into the error of those led by purely human reasoning. HOMILIES ON GENESIS 3.12.[6]

---

[5]PG 36:612. [6]FC 74:44-45; PG 53:35.

2:1-3 GOD RESTS ON THE SEVENTH DAY

[1]*Thus the heavens* and the earth were finished, and [all the host][†] of them. [2]And on the seventh[‡] day God finished his work[§] which he had done, and he rested on the seventh day from all his work[§] which he had done. [3]So God blessed the seventh day and hallowed it, because on it God rested from all his work which he had done[#] in creation.*

*LXX heaven (singular) [†]LXX the whole cosmos [‡]LXX sixth [§]LXX works (plural) [#]LXX begun to do

OVERVIEW: God's rest on the seventh day is a metaphor that depicts the mystery of the true rest given to people in the eternal world (EPHREM) and alludes to the rest of the Son before his resurrection. It also signifies that the good works done in the present age, which is comprised of six periods, lead humanity to sabbath, that is, to eternal rest (BEDE). The seventh day is sanctified by God's rest. The faithful will be a seventh day when they shall be filled with God's blessing (AUGUSTINE). God rests on the seventh day, but his gover-nance continues (CHRYSOSTOM). Creatures created on the sixth day appear to be old but are young, since they were only just created by God (EPHREM) in the springtime of creation (AMBROSE).

2:1-2 God Rested on the Seventh Day

THE MEANING OF GOD'S REST. EPHREM THE SYRIAN: From what toil did God rest? For the creatures that came to be on the first day came to be by implication, except for the light, which came through his word.[1] And the rest of the works that came to be afterward came to be through his word. What toil is there for

---

[1]Their creation is implied and not stated in the account of cre-ation for the first day.

---

us when we speak one word? So what toil could there have been for God to speak one word a day? Moses, who divided the sea by his word and his rod, did not tire. Joshua, son of Nun, who restrained the luminaries by his word, did not tire. So what toil could there have been for God when he created the sea and the luminaries by his word? It was not because he rested on that day that God, who does not weary, blessed and sanctified the seventh day. Nor was it because he was to give it to that people, who did not understand that since they were freed from their servitude, they were to give rest to their servants and maidservants. He gave it to them so that, even if they had to be put under requirement, they would rest. It was given to them in order to depict by a temporal rest, which he gave to a temporal people, the mystery of the true rest, which will be given to the eternal people in the eternal world. COMMENTARY ON GENESIS 1.32-33.[2]

GOD'S REST AND CHRIST'S RESURRECTION. LETTER OF BARNABAS: God says to the Jews: "I will not abide your new moons and your sabbaths."[3] You see what he means: The present sabbaths are not acceptable to me, but that sabbath which I have made, in which, after giving rest to all things, I will make the beginning of the eighth day, that is, the beginning of another world. Therefore, we also celebrate with joy the eighth day on which Jesus also rose from the dead after his rest, was made manifest and ascended into heaven. LETTER OF BARNABAS 15.8.[4]

GOD RESTS BUT HIS GOVERNANCE CONTINUES. CHRYSOSTOM: You see, in saying at this point that God rested from his works, Scripture teaches us that he ceased creating

and bringing from nonbeing into being on the seventh day, whereas Christ, in saying that "my father is at work up until now and I am at work,"[5] reveals his unceasing care for us: he calls "work" the maintenance of created things, bestowal of permanence on them and governance of them through all time. If this wasn't so, after all, how would everything have subsisted, without the guiding hand above directing all visible things and the human race as well? HOMILIES ON GENESIS 10.18.[6]

THE GOOD WORKS DONE IN LIFE LEAD TO ETERNAL REST. BEDE: Under the law the people were ordered to work for six days and to rest on the seventh . . . because the Lord completed the creation of the world in six days and desisted from his work on the seventh. Mystically speaking, we are counseled by all this that those who in life devote themselves to good works for the Lord's sake are in the future led by the Lord to sabbath, that is, to eternal rest. HOMILIES ON THE GOSPELS 2.17.[7]

2:3 The Seventh Day Hallowed

THE SPRINGTIME OF CREATION. AMBROSE: He created heaven and earth at the time when the months began, from which time it is fitting that the world took its rise. Then there was the mild temperature of spring, a season suitable for all things. Consequently the year too has the stamp of a world coming to birth. . . . In order to show that the creation of the world took place in the spring, Scripture says: "This month shall be to you the beginning of

---

[2]FC 91:96. [3]Is 1:13. [4]AF 152*. [5]Jn 5:17. [6]FC 74:139-40; PG 53:89. [7]HOG 2:174-75.

months, it is for you the first in the months of the year,"[8] calling the first month the spring-time. It was fitting that the beginning of the year be the beginning of generation. HEXAE-MERON 1.4.13.[9]

THE FAITHFUL WILL BE A SEVENTH DAY. AUGUSTINE: Heaven, too, will be the fulfill-ment of that sabbath rest foretold in the com-mand: "Be still and see that I am God."[10] This, indeed, will be that ultimate sabbath that has no evening and that the Lord foreshadowed in the account of his creation: "And God rested on the seventh day from all his work that he had done. And he blessed the seventh day and sanctified it: because in it he had rested from all his work that God created and made." And we ourselves will be a "seventh day" when we shall be filled with his blessing and remade by his sanctification. In the stillness of that rest we shall see that he is the God whose divinity we desired for ourselves when we listened to the seducer's words, "You shall be as gods,"[11] and so fell away from him, the true God who would have given us a divinity by participa-

tion that could never be gained by desertion. For where did the doing without God end but in the undoing of man through the anger of God? Only when we are remade by God and perfected by a greater grace shall we have the eternal stillness of that rest in which we shall see that he is God. CITY OF GOD 22.30.[12]

ALL THE FIRST CREATURES WERE BOTH YOUNG AND OLD. EPHREM THE SYRIAN: Just as the trees, the vegetation, the animals, the birds and even humankind were old, so also were they young. They were old according to the appearance of their limbs and their sub-stances, yet they were young because of the hour and moment of their creation. Likewise, the moon was both old and young. It was young, for it was but a moment old, but was also old, for it was full as it is on the fifteenth day. COMMENTARY ON GENESIS 1.24.1.[13]

---

[8]Ex 12:2. [9]FC 42:12. [10]Ps 45:11. [11]Gen 3:5. [12]FC 24:509. [13]FC 91:91.

2:4-7 GOD FORMS MAN OUT OF DUST

[4][These are the generations]* of the heavens† and the earth when they were created.

In the day that the LORD God made the earth and the heavens,† [5]when no plant of the field was yet in the earth and no herb of the field had yet sprung up—for the LORD God had not caused it to rain upon the earth, and there was no man to till the ground; [6]but a mist‡ went up from the earth and watered the whole face of the ground— [7]then the LORD God *formed man of dust from the ground, and breathed into his nostrils[§] the breath of life; and man became a living being.*

c Or flood *LXX This is the book of the generation †LXX heaven ‡LXX spring §LXX face

OVERVIEW: Moses returns to relate how creation was first adorned (EPHREM). The vegetation of the earth and the rain may be viewed as metaphors of the nurture and growth of the human soul in the field of this world (AUGUSTINE), while the spring is a symbol of triune grace (MARIUS VICTORINUS).

God formed the body of Adam out of mud (AUGUSTINE). When God breathed into his nostrils, he united the soul to the body (TERTULLIAN, AUGUSTINE, AMBROSE) and placed some share of his own grace in man (BASIL). But the nature of God was not turned into the soul of man (AUGUSTINE). Even now, when God forms us in the womb of the mother, he also breathes on us as he did in the beginning (TERTULLIAN). Jesus gave us a second breathing and thereby created a new humanity (AUGUSTINE).

Heaven and earth includes all creatures, both spiritual and physical (CHRYSOSTOM). Human beings were formed of the dust of the earth by God's own "hands," viewed spiritually (THEODORET). In human creation the soul is mixed with the dust of the earth (GREGORY OF NAZIANZUS). The soul is created; the flesh is "fashioned." The greatness and the lowliness of humanity is seen in the breathing of a living soul into the dust (BASIL), which forms a living unity (CHRYSOSTOM). Humanity is not to be reduced to animal existence (BASIL). The rational human soul makes use of bodily members (CHRYSOSTOM). The soul did not pre-exist before creation (JOHN OF DAMASCUS).

2:4-6 *The Generations of the Heavens and the Earth*

THE HEAVEN AND EARTH INCLUDES ALL CREATURES. CHRYSOSTOM: I mean, when it said heaven and earth, it included everything together in those words, both things on earth and things in heaven. So just as in its account of created things it doesn't mention them all one by one but gives a summary of related items and makes no further attempt to describe them to us, so too it called the whole book the book about the origins of heaven and earth, even though it contains many other things, evidently leaving us to work out from the reference to these two that all visible things are of necessity contained in this book, both those in heaven and those on earth. HOMILIES ON GENESIS 12.4.[1]

THE LORD MADE EVERY HERB. CHRYSOSTOM: The earth in compliance with the Lord's word and direction produced plants and was stirred into pangs of fertility without depending on the sun for assistance (how could it, after all, the sun not yet being created?), nor on the moisture from showers, nor on human labor (human beings, after all, not having been brought forth). HOMILIES ON GENESIS 12.5.[2]

RESUMING THE ACCOUNT OF THE CREATION. EPHREM THE SYRIAN: Understand, O hearer, that although the days of creation

---

[1]FC 74:158; PG 53:99. [2]FC 74:159; PG 53:100.

were finished and God had blessed the sabbath day, which was sanctified, and he had completed his account, Moses still returned to tell the story of the beginning of creation even after the days of creation had been finished. "These are the generations of the heavens and the earth," that is, this is the account of the fashioning of heaven and earth on the day when the Lord made heaven and earth, for as yet "no plant of the field was in the earth and no herb of the field had yet sprung up." Even if these things were not actually created on the first day—for they had been made on the third day—still Moses did not rashly introduce, on the first day, the report of those things that were created on the third day. For Moses said, "No plant of the field was yet in the earth and no herb of the field had yet sprung up—for the Lord God had not caused it to rain upon the earth, but a mist went up from the earth and watered the whole face of the ground." Because everything that has been born and will be born from the earth will be through the conjunction of water and earth, Moses undertook to show that no plant or vegetation had been created along with the earth, because the rain had not yet come down. But after the great mist rose up from the great abyss and watered the whole face of earth and after the waters had been gathered together on the third day, then the earth brought forth all the vegetation. COMMENTARY ON GENESIS 2.2.1-2.3.1.[3]

SPIRITUAL MEANING OF THE VEGETATION AND THE RAIN. AUGUSTINE: Why after mentioning heaven and earth does this passage add "vegetation of the field and food" while remaining silent about so many other things that are in heaven and earth or even the sea, unless it wants "vegetation of the field" to be understood as an invisible created thing such as the soul?

For "field" is often used figuratively in Scripture to represent the world. . . . Further on it adds "before they were upon the earth," which means "before the soul sinned." For once the soul was soiled with earthly desires, it was as if the soul was born on the earth, or its essence derived from the earth. TWO BOOKS ON GENESIS AGAINST THE MANICHAEANS 2.3.4-2.4.5.[4]

AUGUSTINE: Now God also makes the vegetation of the field, but by raining upon the earth; that is, he makes souls become green again by his word. But he waters them from the clouds, that is, from the writings of the prophets and apostles. TWO BOOKS ON GENESIS AGAINST THE MANICHAEANS 2.4.5.[5]

THE SPRING SYMBOLIZES CHRIST. MARIUS VICTORINUS: Christ is that spring of which the prophet says, "It irrigates and waters the whole earth." But Christ irrigates the whole universe, both visible and invisible; with the spring of life he waters the substance of everything that exists. Yet insofar as he is life, he is Christ; insofar as he waters, he is the Holy Spirit; insofar as he is the power of vitality, he is Father and God; but the whole is one God. AGAINST ARIUS IA.47.[6]

THE FACE OF THE EARTH IS AN ALLEGORY OF MARY. AUGUSTINE: The gentle face of the earth, that is, the dignity of the earth, may be correctly viewed as the mother of the Lord, the Virgin Mary, who was watered by the Holy Spirit, who is signified in the Gospel by the term *water*.[7] TWO BOOKS ON GENESIS AGAINST THE MANICHAEANS 2.24.37.[8]

---

[3]FC 91:97-98. [4]PL 34:198. [5]FC 84:98. [6]FC 69:166*. [7]Cf. Jn 7:38-39. [8]FC 84:134.

2:7 *God Forms Man from the Ground*

GOD FORMS MAN FROM MUD. AUGUSTINE:
First of all, the fact that God formed man from
the mud of the earth usually raises a question
about the sort of mud it was or the kind of
material the term *mud* signifies. Those enemies
of the Old Book [the Manichaeans], looking at
everything in a carnal manner and therefore
always being in error, bitingly find fault with
this point as well, namely, that God formed
man from the mud of the earth. For they say,
"Why did God make man from mud? Did he
lack a better and heavenly material from which
he could make man, that he formed him fragile
and mortal from this earthly corruption?" To
begin with, they do not understand how many
meanings either earth or water has in the Scriptures, for mud is a mixture of earth and water.
Also we say that the human body began to
waste away and to be fragile and mortal after
sin. But the Manicheans abhor in our body only
the mortality that we merited as punishment.
But even if God made man from the mud of this
earth, still what is there that is strange or difficult for God in making the human body such
that it would not be subject to corruption if, in
obedience to God's commandment, he had not
willed to sin? For we say that the beauty of
heaven was made from nothing or from formless matter, because we believe that the Maker
is almighty. Why is it strange that the almighty
Maker could make the body from some sort of
mud of the earth so that before sin it afflicted
man with no trouble or need and wasted away
from no corruption? TWO BOOKS ON GENESIS
AGAINST THE MANICHAEANS 2.7.8.[9]

THE BREATH OF GOD MIXES WITH DUST.
GREGORY OF NAZIANZUS: The soul is the
breath of God, a substance of heaven mixed
with the lowest earth, a light entombed in a
cave, yet wholly divine and unquenchable.
. . . He spoke, and taking some of the newly
minted earth his immortal hands made an
image into which he imparted some of his own
life. He sent his spirit, a beam from the invisible divinity. DOGMATIC HYMNS 7.[10]

HOW ADAM BECAME A LIVING SOUL. CHRY-
SOSTOM: It was pleasing to God's love of
humanity to make this thing created out of
earth a participant of the rational nature of
the soul, through which this living creature
was manifest as excellent and perfect. "And he
breathed into his nostrils the breath of life,"
that is, the inbreathing communicated to the
one created out of earth the power of life, and
thus the nature of the soul was formed.
Therefore Moses added "And man became a
living soul"; that which was created out of
dust, having received the inbreathing, the
breath of life, "became a living soul." What
does "a living soul" mean? An active soul,
which has the members of the body as the
implements of its activities, submissive to its
will. HOMILIES ON GENESIS 12.15.[11]

ORIGIN OF THE SOUL. TERTULLIAN: The
soul has its origin in the breath of God and
did not come from matter. We base that statement on the clear assertion of divine revelation, which declares that "God breathed the
breath of life into the face of man, and man
became a living soul." ON THE SOUL 3.4.[12]

**GOD UNITES THE HUMAN SOUL TO THE
BODY BY HIS BREATH.** AUGUSTINE: Scrip-

---

[9]FC 84:102-3. [10]PG 37:446. [11]PG 53:103; FC 74:166. [12]FC 10:186.

ture says, "And he breathed into him the breath of life, and man became a living soul." If up to this point there was only the body, we should understand that the soul was at this point joined to the body. Perhaps the soul had been already made but was still as if in the mouth of God, that is, in his truth and wisdom. But it did not depart from there as if separated by places, when it was breathed forth. For God is not contained by place but is present everywhere. TWO BOOKS ON GENESIS AGAINST THE MANICHAEANS 2.8.10.[13]

NATURE OF THE SOUL. AMBROSE: Therefore the soul is not blood, because blood is of the flesh; nor is the soul a harmony, because harmony of this sort is also of the flesh; neither is the soul air, because blown breath is one thing and the soul something else. The soul is not fire, nor is the soul actuality, but the soul is living, for Adam "became a living soul," since the soul rules and gives life to the body, which is without life or feeling. ISAAC, OR THE SOUL 2.4.[14]

FLESH FASHIONED, SOUL CREATED. GREGORY OF NYSSA: God made the inner person; he molded the outer. "Molding" is suitable for clay, but "making" is [fitting] for an image. So on the one hand, he "molded" flesh, but on the other, he "made" the soul. ON THE ORIGIN OF MAN.[15]

THE GREATNESS AND LOWLINESS OF HUMANITY. GREGORY OF NYSSA: "God took of the dust of the earth and fashioned man." In this world I have discovered the two affirmations that man is nothing and that man is great. If you consider nature alone, he is nothing and has no value; but if you regard the honor with which he has been treated, man is something great. ON THE ORIGIN OF MAN.[16]

THE UNITY OF BODY AND SOUL. GREGORY OF NYSSA: Others, on the contrary, marking the order of the making of man as stated by Moses, say that the soul is second to the body in order of time, since God first took dust from the earth and formed man, and then animated the being thus formed by his breath. By this argument they prove that the flesh is more noble than the soul, that which was previously formed [more noble] than that which was afterward infused into it. . . . Nor again are we in our doctrine to begin by making up man like a clay figure and to say that the soul came into being for the sake of this, for surely in that case the intellectual nature would be shown to be less precious than the clay figure. But as man is one, the being consisting of soul and body, we are to suppose that the beginning of his existence is one, common to both aspects, so that he should not be found to be antecedent and posterior to himself, as if the bodily element were first in point of time and the other were a later addition. ON THE CREATION OF MAN 28.1-29.1.[17]

GOD PLACES A SHARE OF HIS GRACE IN THE SOUL. BASIL THE GREAT: "And he breathed into his nostrils," that is to say, he placed in man some share of his own grace, in order that he might recognize likeness through likeness. Nevertheless, being in such great honor because he was created in the image of the Creator, he is honored above the heavens, above the sun, above the choirs of stars. For which of the heavenly bodies was said to be an image of the most high God?[18] EXEGETIC HOMILIES ON THE PSALMS 19.8.[19]

---

[13]FC 84:104. [14]FC 65:13. [15]GNOS 44. [16]GNOS 42. [17]NPNF 2 5:419-20. [18]Cf. Ps 8:5/ Heb 1:5. [19]FC 46:324-25.

**HOW GOD CREATED HUMANS IN A DIFFER-
ENT WAY FROM ANIMALS.** GREGORY OF
NYSSA: Above, the text says that God created;
here it says how God created. If the verse had
simply said that God created, you could have
believed that he created [humanity] as he did
for the beasts, for the wild animals, for the
plants for the grass. This is why, to avoid your
placing him in the class of wild animals, the
divine word has made known the particular
art which God has used for you: "God took of
the dust of the earth." ON THE ORIGIN OF
MAN.[20]

**THE SOUL MAKES USE OF BODILY MEM-
BERS.** CHRYSOSTOM: Thus when you hear that
God "breathed into his face the breath of life,"
understand that just as he brought forth the
bodiless powers, so also he was pleased that the
body of man, created out of dust, should have a
rational soul which could make use of the
bodily members. HOMILIES ON GENESIS 13.9.[21]

**THE NATURE OF GOD WAS NOT TURNED
INTO THE SOUL OF MAN.** AUGUSTINE: We
ought to understand this passage so that we
do not take the words "he breathed into him
the breath of life, and man became a living
soul" to mean that a part, as it were, of the
nature of God was turned into the soul of
man. . . . The nature of God is not mutable,
does not err and is not corrupted by the stains
of vices and sins. . . . Scripture clearly says
that the soul was made by the almighty God
and that it is therefore not a part of God or
the nature of God. TWO BOOKS ON GENESIS
AGAINST THE MANICHAEANS 2.8.11.[22]

**WHEN GOD FORMS US IN THE WOMB, HE
BREATHES ON US.** TERTULLIAN: Thus you
read the word of God, spoken to Jeremiah:

"Before I formed you in the womb, I knew
you."[23] If God forms us in the womb, he also
breathes on us as he did in the beginning:
"And God formed man and breathed into him
the breath of life." Nor could God have known
man in the womb unless he were a whole
man. ON THE SOUL 26.5.[24]

**HUMANITY RAISED AGAIN THROUGH HIS
BREATHING.** AUGUSTINE: After his resurrection, when he first appeared to his disciples,
he said to them, "Receive the Holy Spirit."
About this giving, then, it was said, "The
Spirit had not yet been given because Jesus
had not yet been glorified." "And he breathed
upon their face."[25] The One who first gave life
to man by breathing and raised him up from
the mire and by breathing gave a soul to his
members is the same One who breathed upon
their face that they might rise up from the
slime and renounce filthy works. TRACTATES
ON THE GOSPEL OF JOHN 32.6.3.[26]

FORMED OF DUST BY GOD'S OWN HANDS.
THEODORET OF CYR: When we hear Moses'
writings describe how God took dust from the
earth with his hands in order to make man, we
try to understand what such language might
mean. It means this: the whole of God[27] had a
special interest in the creation of the human
nature. The great prophet proclaims this very
thing, since everything else in creation was
made by spoken command. Man, however,
was made by God's "hands." . . . Just like an

---

[20]GNOS 44-45. [21]PG 53:107; FC 74:173. [22]FC 84:106*. [23]Jer
1:5. [24]FC 10:242. [25]Jn 20:22. [26]FC 88:46* [27]In his reference to
the "whole of God," Theodoret is here addressing, in part, the
heresy of Audius, a fourth-century Syrian deacon and monastic
from Edessa who was accused by Epiphanius of anthropomor-
phizing God.

embryo is planted in the mother's womb and develops from the material which has surrounded it from the beginning, so also God wanted to take the material for the human body from the earth. Thus, clay became flesh and blood, and skin, and nerves, and veins, and arteries, and the brain, and bone marrow and supporting bones, and so on. COMPENDIUM OF HERETICAL MYTHS.[28]

THE SOUL DID NOT PRE-EXIST. JOHN OF

DAMASCUS: From the earth he formed his body and by his own inbreathing gave him a rational and understanding soul, which we say is the divine image. . . . The body and the soul were formed at the same time—not one before and the other afterward, as the ravings of Origen would have it. ON THE ORTHODOX FAITH 2.12.[29]

[28]PG 83:477-80. [29]FC 37:235.

2:8-9 THE GARDEN OF EDEN AND THE TREE OF LIFE

[8] And the LORD God planted a garden* in Eden,[†] in the east; and there he put the man whom he had formed. [9] And out of the ground the LORD God made to grow every tree that is pleasant to the sight and good for food, the tree of life also in the midst of the garden, and the tree of the knowledge of good and evil.

*LXX paradise (i.e., a park or enclosed garden) [†]*LXX Edem*

OVERVIEW: Eden is the land of paradise that God made before he formed man (EPHREM, AUGUSTINE). It also prefigures the church (CYPRIAN). The trees planted in the middle of the garden symbolize life, knowledge and wisdom (LETTER TO DIOGNETUS, JEROME). Christ restores us to life through the tree of life (GREGORY OF NAZIANZUS). From Paul we learn that the location of paradise is not to be simplistically treated, since it belongs to mystical understanding (AMBROSE). That God planted a garden in Eden must be understood in a way

befitting to God (CHRYSOSTOM).

2:8 God Planted a Garden in Eden

EDEN WAS CREATED ON THE THIRD DAY. EPHREM THE SYRIAN: Eden is the land of paradise, and God had already planted it on the third day. Moses explains this by saying, "The Lord caused every tree that is pleasant to the sight and good for food to sprout forth from the earth." And to show that he was talking about paradise, he added, "And the tree of life was in the midst of paradise, and the tree of the knowledge of good and evil." COMMENTARY ON GENESIS 2.5.2.[1]

THE NARRATIVE REFERS TO PREVIOUS EVENTS LEFT UNMENTIONED. AUGUSTINE: In the Scriptures some things are related in such a way that they seem to be following the order of time or occurring in chronological succession, when actually the narrative, without mentioning it, refers to previous events that had been left unmentioned. Unless we understand this distinction, we shall fall into error. For example, we find in Genesis: "And the Lord God planted a paradise of pleasure in the east; and there he put the man whom he had formed. And out of the ground the Lord God made to grow every tree that is pleasant to the sight and good for food." This last mentioned event would seem to have occurred after God had made man and placed him in paradise. After both of these facts have been mentioned briefly (that is, that God planted a paradise and there "placed man whom he had formed"), the narrative turns back by means of recapitulation and relates what had been planted and that "God brought forth out of the ground all manner of trees fair to behold and pleasant to eat of." CHRISTIAN INSTRUCTION 2.36.52.[2]

GOD PLANTED A GARDEN. CHRYSOSTOM: And when, dearly beloved, you hear that "God planted a garden in Eden in the east," take the word *planted* in a sense appropriate to God—namely, that he commanded this happen—and about the next phrase, believe that a garden came into being in the place that Scripture indicated. HOMILIES ON GENESIS 13.13.[3]

EDEN REPRESENTS THE CHURCH. CYPRIAN: The church, expressing the image of paradise, encloses fruitful trees within its walls. From these whatever does not make good fruit is cut off and cast into the fire. LETTERS 73.10.[4]

WHETHER PARADISE IS IN A SPECIFIC TIME-SPACE LOCATION. AMBROSE: If paradise, then, is of such a nature that Paul alone, or one like Paul, could scarcely see it while alive and still was unable to remember whether he saw it in the body or out of the body, and moreover heard words that he was forbidden to reveal—if this be true, how will it be possible for us to declare the position of paradise which we have not been able to see and, even if we had succeeded in seeing it, we would be forbidden to share with others? And again, since Paul shrank from exalting himself by reason of the sublimity of the revelation, how much more ought we to strive not to be too anxious to disclose that which leads to danger by its very revelation! The subject of paradise should not, therefore, be treated lightly. PARADISE 1.[5]

WHY CHRISTIANS PRAY FACING EAST. BASIL THE GREAT: For this reason we all look to the east in our prayers, but few know that this is because we are seeking the ancient fatherland, which God planted in Eden, toward the east. ON THE HOLY SPIRIT 27.66.[6]

2:9 The Tree of Life and the Tree of the Knowledge of Good and Evil

THE CLOSENESS OF THE TREES SIGNIFIES THE CLOSE RELATION BETWEEN LIFE AND KNOWLEDGE. ANONYMOUS: Indeed, there is a

---

[1]FC 91:99-100. [2]FC 2:162*. [3]FC 74:175. [4]FC 51:274. [5]FC 42:287-88. [6]NPNF 2 8:42**.

deep meaning in the passage of Scripture that tells how God in the beginning planted a tree of knowledge and a tree of life in the midst of paradise, to show that life is attained through knowledge. It was because the first men did not use this knowledge with clean hearts that they were stripped of it by the deceit of the serpent. For there cannot be life without knowledge any more than there can be sound knowledge without genuine life. So the two trees were planted close together. LETTER TO DIOGNETUS 12.2.[7]

THE TREE OF LIFE SYMBOLIZES WISDOM AND CHRIST. JEROME: Now if wisdom is the tree of life, Wisdom itself indeed is Christ.[8] You understand now that the man who is blessed and holy is compared to this tree—that is, he is compared to Wisdom. Consequently, you see too that the just man, that blessed man who has not followed the counsel of the wicked— who has not done that but has done this—is

like the tree that is planted near running water.[9] He is, in other words, like Christ, inasmuch as he "raised us up together and seated us together in heaven."[10] You see then that we shall reign together with Christ in heaven. You see too that because this tree has been planted in the garden of Eden, we have all been planted there together with him. HOMILIES 1.[11]

CHRIST RESTORES US TO LIFE BY THE TREE OF LIFE. GREGORY OF NAZIANZUS: Christ is brought up to the tree and nailed to it—yet by the tree of life he restores us. Yes, he saves even a thief crucified with him; he wraps all the visible world in darkness. THEOLOGICAL ORATIONS 29.20.[12]

---

[7]FC 1:368**. [8]Viewed from the perspective of the subsequent history of revelation. [9]Ps 1:3. [10]Eph 2:6. [11]FC 48:7. [12]FGFR 259-60.

2:10-14 THE RIVER OF EDEN

[10]*A river flowed out of Eden* to water the garden,† and there it divided and became four rivers.‡ [11]The name of the first is Pishon;§ it is the one which flows around the whole land of Havilah,# where there is gold; [12]and the gold of that land is good; [bdellium and onyx stone]** are there. [13]The name of the second river is Gihon;†† it is the one which flows around the whole land of Cush.‡‡ [14]And the name of the third river is Tigris, which flows [east of]§§ Assyria. And the fourth river is the Euphrates.*

*LXX Edem †LXX paradise †literally heads; LXX sources §LXX Pison #LXX Evilat **LXX anthrax and the green stone ††LXX Geon ‡‡LXX Ethiopia §§LXX out against

---

OVERVIEW: When the river of Eden flows out of the garden, it divides into four rivers, which

are different in nature and taste from the head (EPHREM). Each river symbolically represents a virtue of Christian faith (Ambrose). The river of Eden might be identified with the ocean that encircles the earth (John of Damascus). It also appears to be a symbolic representation of the resourceful, comforting and life-giving church (Cyprian, Chrysostom). But the rivers must not be treated so allegorically that they are assumed to have no actual existence (Chrysostom).

2:10-14 *A River Flowed from Eden*

DESCRIPTION OF THE RIVER OF EDEN.
EPHREM THE SYRIAN: Moses turned to write about the river that flowed out from paradise and that, once outside of it, divided into four distinct sources, saying, "A river flowed out of Eden to water paradise." Here too Moses calls the delightful land of paradise Eden. If that river had indeed watered paradise, it would not have divided into the four rivers outside it. I would suggest that it was perhaps due to convention that it is said "to water," since the spiritual trees of paradise had no need of water. But if someone should say that because they are spiritual, they drink from the blessed and spiritual waters there, I would not quarrel over this. The four rivers that flowed from that river were not similar in taste to the headspring. For if the waters of our lands vary, all being placed under the sentence of a curse, how much more distinct should the taste of the blessed land of Eden be from the taste of that land that had been placed under the curse of the Just One due to Adam's transgression of the commandment? The four rivers, then, are these: the Pishon, which is the Danube; the Gihon, which is the Nile; and then the Tigris and the Euphrates, between which we dwell. Although the places from which they flow are known, the source of the spring is not known.

Because paradise is set on a great height, the rivers are swallowed up again, and they go down to the sea as if through a tall water duct, and so they pass through the earth that is under the sea into this land. The earth then spits out each one of them: the Danube, which is the Pishon, in the west; the Gihon in the south; and the Euphrates and the Tigris in the north. COMMENTARY ON GENESIS 2.6.[1]

SYMBOLIC MEANING OF THE FOUR RIVERS.
AMBROSE: "The river," we are told, "is separated into four branches." The name of one is Pishon, which encircles all the land of Hevila, where there is gold. And the gold of that land is good; bdellium and onyx are there. The name of the second river is Gihon. This river encircles all the land of Ethiopia. The name of the third river is Tigris, which river flows by the Assyrians. And the fourth river is the Euphrates. There are, therefore, four rivers. Pishon—so called by the Hebrews but named Ganges by the Greeks—flows in the direction of India. Gihon is the river Nile, which flows around the land of Egypt or Ethiopia. The land enclosed by the Tigris and Euphrates rivers is called Mesopotamia because it lives between these two rivers. This name conveys its location even to far-distant peoples and besides expresses popular belief. But how is the fount called the Wisdom of God? That this is a fount the Gospel tells us in the words "If anyone thirst, let him come to me and drink."[2] Wisdom is a fount according to the prophet: "Come and eat my bread and drink the wine which I have mingled for you."[3] As Wisdom is the fountain of life, it is also the fountain of spiritual grace. It is also the fountain of other virtues that

---

[1]FC 91:100-101. [2]Jn 7:37. [3]Prov 9:15.

guide us to the course of eternal life. Therefore, the stream that irrigates paradise rises from the soul when well tilled, not from the soul that lies uncultivated. The results from it are fruit trees of diverse virtues. There are four principal trees that constitute the divisions of Wisdom. These are the well-known four principal virtues: prudence, temperance, fortitude and justice. The wise men of this world have adopted this division from us and transferred it to their writings. Hence, Wisdom acts as the source from which these four rivers take their rise, producing streams that are composed of these virtues.

Pishon, therefore, stands for prudence. Hence it has pure gold, brilliant rubies and topaz stones. We often refer to wise discoveries as gold, as the Lord says, speaking through the prophet: "I gave to them gold and silver."[4] Daniel says of the wise: "If you sleep among the midst of the lots, you shall be as the wings of the dove covered with silver and the hinder parts of her back like to gold."[5] In this way one who puts his trust in the aid of the Old and New Testament can by resourceful inquiry attain the inmost secrets of the Wisdom of God. Here, therefore, is found pure gold, not the metal that is melted, which belongs to this earth and is subject to corruption. In this land, we are told, there is found the brilliant ruby stone in which there exists the vital spark of our souls. Here, too, is the topaz stone that by the nature of its color reveals an effect of greenness and vitality. Plants that are alive give forth green sprouts, while those that are dead are sapless and dry. The earth grows green when it is in bloom. The seeds, too, sprout forth green shoots in their periods of growth. The river Pishon is rightfully given first place. The Hebrews call it Pheoyson, which means "change of mouth," because it flows even

through Lydia and not merely around one nation, for Wisdom, which is of benefit to all men, is productive and useful. Hence, if a person were to leave paradise, this river of Wisdom would be the first object he would meet. Thus he may not become inert and arid and his return to paradise may be facilitated. Many men resort to this river, which is considered to have marvelous beauty and fecundity. Accordingly it is regarded as a figure of Wisdom, which confers manifold fruits in the coming of the Lord of salvation. It flows to the very ends of the earth, because by Wisdom all have been redeemed. Thus it is written: "Their sound has gone forth into all the earth and their words unto the end of the world."[6]

The second river is Gihon, by which, when they were sojourning in Egypt, was laid down the law of the Israelites that they should depart from Egypt,[7] and having girded their loins they should as a sign of temperance partake of a lamb. It is fitting that the chaste and the sanctified should celebrate the Pasch of the Lord. For that reason, the observance of the law was first carried out beside that river, the name of which signifies an opening of the earth. Therefore, just as an opening absorbs the earth and whatever defilements and refuse there may be in it, in like manner chastity tends to consume all the passions of the body. Appropriately, then, the observance of the established law first took place there, because carnal sin is absorbed by the law. And so Gihon, which is a figure of chastity, is said to surround the land of Ethiopia in order to wash away our lowly bodies and quench the fires of our vile flesh. The meaning of Ethiopia in Latin is "holy and vile." What is more lowly,

---

[4]Hos 2:8. [5]Ps 67:14. [6]Ps 18:5. [7]Ex 12:11.

what is more like Ethiopia, than our bodies, blackened, too, by the darkness of sin?

The third river is the Tigris, which flows by the Assyrian land. To this river the deceiver Israel was dragged as a prisoner. This river is the swiftest of all rivers. The Assyrians dwell by it, guarding its course—for this is the meaning of its name. Hence those who by their fortitude hold in check the guileful vices of the body and direct themselves to higher things are thought to have something in common with this river. For that same reason fortitude emanates from that source in paradise. Fortitude in its rapid course tosses aside everything standing in its path and like this river is not hindered by any material obstacle.

The fourth river is the Euphrates, which means in Latin "fecundity and abundance of fruits." It presents a symbol of justice, the nourishment of every soul. No virtue produces more abundant benefits than equity or justice, which is more concerned with others than with itself, neglecting its own advantages and preferring the common good. Many derive Euphrates from the Greek *apo tou euphrainesthai*, that is, from a "feeling of gladness," because the human race rejoices in nothing more than it does in justice and equity. The question as to why, although the location itself of other rivers is reported, we have no description of the regions through which the river Euphrates flows calls for an answer. The waters of this river are considered to have a vital quality that fosters growth and increase. Wherefore the wise men among the Hebrews and the Assyrians called this river Auxen ["increase"] in contradistinction to the water of other rivers. The opposition has been well established between wisdom and malice, fortitude and irascibility, temperance, and other vices. Justice, on the other hand, is the most important as it represents the concord of all the other virtues. Hence it is not known from the places from which it flows, that is to say, it is not known in part. Justice is not divisible into parts. It is, as it were, the mother of all virtues. In these four rivers are symbolized therefore the four principal virtues. PARADISE 3.14-18.[8]

REAL RIVERS. CHRYSOSTOM: Perhaps, however, those people who like to talk from their own wisdom do not concede again that these rivers are rivers or these waters really waters but propound some different interpretation to people ready to lend them their ears. Let us, however, I beg you, not be convinced by them but block our ears against them; let us instead place our credence in sacred Scripture and heed what is told us there. HOMILIES ON GENESIS 13.15-16.[9]

THE RIVER OF EDEN IS THE OCEAN THAT ENCIRCLES THE EARTH. JOHN OF DAMASCUS: Then there is the ocean that encircles the entire earth like a sort of river and to which it seems to me that Scripture referred when it said that "a river flowed out of paradise." It has sweet potable water and supplies the seas, but because the water remains stagnant in the seas for a long time it becomes brackish. The sun and the waterspouts are constantly drawing up the less dense water, and from this the clouds are formed and the rain comes, the water becoming sweet by filtration. This ocean is divided into four heads, of four rivers. The name of the first is Pishon; this is the Ganges of India. The name of the second is Gehon; this is the Nile, which comes down from Ethiopia into Egypt. The name of the third is Tigris, and of

---

[8]FC 42:295-99. [9]PG 53:110; FC 74:177-78.

the fourth, Euphrates. ORTHODOX FAITH 2.9.[10]

THE RIVER OF EDEN SYMBOLICALLY PRE-FIGURES THE CHRISTIAN CHURCH. CYP-RIAN: The church encloses fruitful trees within its walls. It waters these trees with four rivers, that is, with the four Gospels, from which it bestows the grace of baptism by the salutary and heavenly inundation. Can he who is not inside the church be watered from the fountains of the church? How could one who is perverse and condemned by himself and banished beyond the fountains of para-dise provide a healthful resource of water? How could one who has dried up and has failed with the dryness of eternal thirst bestow upon another the salutary drinks of paradise? LETTERS 63.10.[11]

THE COOLING STREAMS OF PARADISE. CHRYSOSTOM: Awe-inspiring, in truth, are the mysteries of the church. Awesome truth is its altar. A fountain sprang up out of paradise, sending forth not only visible streams but also spiritual streams arising as a fountain from this high tableland. Alongside this fountain there have grown, not willows without fruit but abundant trees reaching to heaven itself, with fruit ever in season and remaining still incorrupt. If someone is intensely hot, let him come to this fountain and cool down this feverish heat. It dispels parching heat and gently cools all things that are very hot—not only those literally inflamed by the sun's heat but also those set on fire by sin's burning arrows. It does so because it takes its begin-ning from above and has its source from there, and from there it is fed. Many are the streams of this fountain, streams that the Paraclete sends forth; and the Son becomes its custo-dian, not keeping its channel open with a mat-tock but by making our hearts receptive. HOMILIES ON JOHN 46.4.[12]

---

[10]FC 37:225. [11]FC 51:274. [12]NPNF 1 14:167*.

2:15-17 GOD COMMANDS THE MAN NOT TO EAT OF THE TREE OF THE KNOWLEDGE OF GOOD AND EVIL

[15]*The LORD God took the man* and put him in the garden of Eden† to till it and keep it.* [16]*And the LORD God commanded the man,‡ saying, "You may freely eat of every tree of the garden;* [17]*but of the tree of the knowledge of good and evil you shall not eat, for in the day that you eat of it you shall die."*

*LXX adds whom he had made †*For garden of Eden LXX reads* paradise *(in some manuscripts:* of delight) ‡*LXX* Adam

---

OVERVIEW: To till and keep the garden means to believe in God and to keep the command-ments (CHRYSOSTOM). The first man was cre-ated perfect and for this reason was placed in

Eden to guard it (Origen). He worked and guarded the garden of Eden, but his work was not toilsome (Augustine). The work of the first man demonstrates that there is a natural bent for work in man (Symeon the New Theologian).

The tree of knowledge is a boundary to the inner region of paradise (Ephrem). The tree of the knowledge of good and evil got its name before man broke God's commandment by touching it (Augustine). God's decree, which states that man must not eat of the tree, is a sign of his grace (Athanasius). The death imposed by God on those who will transgress his decree is a complete death (Augustine). The tree brought mortality to men, but in the form of the cross it will bring them into paradise (Cyril of Jerusalem). The tree of knowledge symbolically represents the power of discernment (John of Damascus).

In paradise Adam lived in his body on earth but in his spirit among the angels. In Eden he could eat of every tree freely (John of Damascus) but within the boundaries set (Chrysostom). The tree of the knowledge of good and evil points to the sweetness of divine contemplation (John of Damascus). The law is given as a material for free will to act upon (Gregory of Nazianzus) in order to encourage the exercise of virtue (Chrysostom).

2:15 The Man Put in the Garden to Till It

The First Man Placed in Eden Because of His Perfection. Origen: How would God have placed what was altogether imperfect in paradise to work and guard it? For he who is capable of tending "the tree of life" and everything that God planted and caused to spring up afterwards would not reasonably be called imperfect. Perhaps, then, although he

was perfect, he became imperfect in some way because of his transgression and was in need of one to perfect him from his imperfection. And the Savior was sent for these reasons. Commentary on John 13.240-41.[1]

Man's Work in Eden Was Not Toilsome. Augustine: Although man was placed in paradise so as to work and guard it, that praiseworthy work was not toilsome. For the work in paradise is quite different from the work on the earth to which he was condemned after the sin. The addition "and to guard it" indicated the sort of work it was. For in the tranquility of the happy life, where there is no death, the only work is to guard what you possess. Two Books on Genesis Against the Manichaeans 2.11.15.[2]

Tilling and Keeping the Garden. Severian of Gabala: Tilling the earth, keeping the commandments of God and fidelity to those commandments was the "labor" of God. . . . Just as believing in Christ is a "work," so also was Adam's faithful keeping of God's command. If he touched the tree, he would die, but if he did not, he would live. "Work" was keeping the spiritual words. . . .

The text says "work" and "protect it." From what? There were no thieves, travelers or people with bad intentions. "Protect it" from what? From himself. Do not lose it by transgressing the command. Instead, he would preserve the commandment and in so doing preserve himself in paradise. On the Creation of the World 5.5.[3]

This Work Demonstrates Man's Natural Bent for Work. Symeon the New

---

[1]FC 89:117-18. [2]FC 84:111. [3]PG 56:478.

THEOLOGIAN: In the beginning man was created with a nature inclined to work, for in paradise Adam was enjoined to till the ground and care for it, and there is in us a natural bent for work, the movement toward the good. Those who yield themselves to idleness and apathy, even though they may be spiritual and holy, hurl themselves into unnatural subjection to passions. DISCOURSES 10.3.[4]

2:16-17 Man Forbidden to Eat of the Tree of the Knowledge of Good and Evil

THE TREE OF KNOWLEDGE A BOUNDARY MARK. EPHREM THE SYRIAN:
In the very midst he planted
the Tree of Knowledge,
endowing it with wonder,
hedging it in with dread,
so that it might straightway serve
as a boundary to the inner region of
   paradise.
Two things did Adam hear
in that single decree:
that they should not eat of it
and that, by shrinking from it,
they should perceive that it was not lawful
to penetrate further, beyond that tree.
HYMNS ON PARADISE 3.3.[5]

THE VALUE OF EVERY TREE. JOHN OF DAMASCUS: For God says, "Of every tree of paradise you shall eat," meaning, I think, by means of all created things you will be drawn up to me, their Creator, and from them reap the one fruit which is myself, who am the true life. Let all things be fruitful life to you, and make participation in me to be the substance of your own existence, for thus you shall be immortal. ORTHODOX FAITH 2.11.[6]

WHEN DID THE TREE OF THE KNOWLEDGE OF GOOD AND EVIL GET ITS NAME? AUGUSTINE: Without good reason certain writers are deeply puzzled when they seek to discover how the tree of the knowledge of good and evil could have been so called before man broke God's commandment by touching it and from experience discerning the difference between the good that he lost and the evil that he committed. Now, this tree was given this name so that our first parents might observe the prohibition and not touch it, taking care to avoid suffering the consequences of touching it against the prohibition. It was not because they subsequently went against the commandment and ate the fruit that the tree became the tree of the knowledge of good and evil. Even if they had remained obedient and had taken nothing against that commandment, it would be correctly called by what would happen to them there if they had taken the fruit. ON THE LITERAL INTERPRETATION OF GENESIS 8.15.33.[7]

THE TWO TREES. SEVERIAN OF GABALA: The Tree of Life stood in the middle of paradise like a trophy. The Tree of Knowledge stood as a contest. If you keep the commandment of this tree, you will receive a prize. So consider this marvelous thought: Every tree in paradise was in bloom, and fruit was in abundance everywhere. Only in the center are the duo of competition and struggle. ON THE CREATION OF THE WORLD 6.1.[8]

GOD'S PROHIBITION A SIGN OF HIS GRACE. ATHANASIUS: Knowing once more how the

---

[4]SNTD 164*. [5]HOP 91. [6]FC 37:233. [7]ACW 42:55-56. [8]PC 56:484.

will of man could sway to either side, in anticipation God secured the grace given them by a
command and by the place where he put them.
For he brought them into his own garden and
gave them a law so that, if they kept the grace
and remained good, they might still keep the
life in paradise without sorrow or pain or care,
besides having the promise of incorruption in
heaven. But if they transgressed and turned
back and became evil, they might know that
they were incurring that corruption in death
that was theirs by nature, no longer to live in
paradise but cast out of it from that time forth
to die and abide in death and corruption. ON
THE INCARNATION 3.4.[9]

THE LAW GIVEN TO ADAM IN PARADISE.
GREGORY OF NAZIANZUS: [God gave Adam] a
law as a material for his free will to act on.
This law was a commandment as to what
plants he might partake of and which one he
might not touch. This latter was the tree of
knowledge; not, however, because it was evil
from the beginning when planted, nor was it
forbidden because God grudged it to us—let
not the enemies of God wag their tongues in
that direction or imitate the serpent. But it
would have been good if partaken of at the
proper time. The tree was, according to my
theory, contemplation, which is safe only for
those who have reached maturity of habit to
enter upon, but which is not good for those
who are still somewhat simple and greedy, just
as neither is solid food good for those who are
yet tender and have need of milk. SECOND
ORATION ON EASTER 8.[10]

**BY TRANSGRESSING GOD'S PROHIBITION
HUMANITY IS CONDEMNED TO A COMPLETE
DEATH.** AUGUSTINE: God, referring to the
forbidden fruit, said to the first man whom

he had established in paradise: "In the day
that you shall eat of it, you shall die the
death." His threat included not only the first
part of the first death, that is, the soul's deprivation of God; not only the second part of
the first death, that is, the body's deprivation
of the soul; not only the whole of the first
death in which the soul, separated from both
God and the body, is punished; but whatever
of death is up to and including that absolutely final and so-called second death . . . in
which the soul, deprived of God but united
to the body, suffers eternal punishment.
CITY OF GOD 13.12.[11]

**THE TREE IN THE FORM OF THE CROSS
BRINGS SALVATION TO HUMANITY.** CYRIL OF
JERUSALEM: Although to Adam it was said
"For the day you eat of it, you must die,"
today[12] you have been faithful. Today will
bring you salvation. The tree brought ruin to
Adam; the tree [of life] shall bring you into
paradise. Fear not the serpent; he shall not
cast you out, for he has fallen from heaven. I
say not to you, "This day you shall depart,"
but "This day you shall be with me."[13] CATE-
CHETICAL LECTURES 13.31.[14]

**THE TREE OF KNOWLEDGE REPRESENTS
THE POWER OF DISCERNMENT.** JOHN OF
DAMASCUS: The tree of knowledge of good
and evil is the power of discernment by multi-
dimensional vision. This is the complete
knowing of one's own nature. Of itself it manifests the magnificence of the Creator, and it is
good for them that are full-grown and have

---

[9]NPNF 2 4:37-38. [10]NPNF 2 7:425. [11]FC 14:315-16*. [12]At the
conclusion of catechesis in preparation for baptism. [13]Lk 23:43.
[14]FC 64:24-25.

walked in the contemplation of God—for them that have no fear of changing, because in the course of time they have acquired a certain habit of such contemplation. It is not good, however, for such as are still young and are more greedy in their appetites, who, because of the uncertainty of their perseverance in the true good and because of their not yet being solidly established in their application to the only good, are naturally inclined to be drawn away and distracted by their solicitude for their own bodies. ORTHODOX FAITH 2.11.[15]

THE TREE OF LIFE. JOHN OF DAMASCUS: Some have imagined paradise to have been material, while others have imagined it to have been spiritual. However, it seems to me that just as man was created both sensitive and intellectual, so did this most sacred domain of his have the twofold aspect of being perceptible both to the senses and to the mind. For while in his body he dwelt in this most sacred and superbly beautiful place, as we have related, spiritually he resided in a loftier and far more beautiful place. There he had the indwelling God as a dwelling place and wore him as a glorious garment. He was wrapped about with his grace, and like some one of the angels he rejoiced in the enjoyment of that one most sweet fruit which is the contemplation of God, and by this he was nourished. Now this is indeed what is fittingly called the tree of life, for the sweetness of divine contemplation communicates a life uninterrupted by death to them that partake of it. ON THE ORTHODOX FAITH 2.11.[16]

---

[15]FC 37:232-33. [16]FC 37:232.

2:18-20 A HELPER FIT FOR THE MAN IS NOT YET FOUND

[18]Then the LORD God said, "It is not good that the man should be alone; I will make him a helper fit for him." [19]So out of the ground the LORD God formed every beast of the field and every bird of the air, and brought them to the man* to see what he would call them; and whatever the man* called every living creature, that was its name. [20]The man* gave names to all cattle, and to the birds of the air, and to every beast of the field; but for the man* there was not found a helper fit for him.

*LXX Adam

OVERVIEW: Man needed a helper because he still had to be regenerated in Christ (CHRY- sostom). God brought the animals to Adam by the ministry of angels (AUGUSTINE) in order to demonstrate that a complete harmony between man and the animals existed before the sin (EPHREM) and that the man was superior to them all (AUGUSTINE). In our age, thanks to Christ, the humble people are treated by animals like the first man in Eden (ISAAC OF NINEVEH).

In the naming of animals, humanity is honored (CHRYSOSTOM). Adam exhibits a wise love for the animals (EPHREM), which are brought to him by the Lord (CHRYSOSTOM). Here the dominion of reason over flesh is maintained (AMBROSE).

2:18 *"It Is Not Good That the Man Should Be Alone"*

MAN NEEDED A HELPER BEFORE HIS REGENERATION IN CHRIST. CHRYSOSTOM: At that time[1] God said, "Let us make for him a helper," but in these times[2] God says no such thing. Will he who has received the grace of the Spirit need any other help? How much need of assistance in the future has he who fills out the body of Christ? At that time he made man to the image of God, but now he has united him to God himself. At that time he commanded the man to rule over the fishes and the beasts. Now he has received our firstlings in heaven. Now he has given us the paradise to inhabit it. Now he has opened the gate of heaven to us. At that time man was formed on the sixth day, because the aeon had to be completed. Now he is formed on the first day and from the beginning and in the light. HOMILIES ON JOHN 25.2.[3]

WOMAN A BLESSING. TERTULLIAN: [In goodness God] provided also a help meet for [the man] that there might not be anything in his lot that was not good. For God said that it is

not good for the man to be alone. He knew full well what a blessing the gender of Mary would be to him and also to the church. AGAINST MARCION 2.4.[4]

2:19-20 *The Man Names the Animals*

ADAM'S HOME WAS PARADISE. SEVERIAN OF GABALA: While Adam had been given the whole earth, he had been given paradise for his home. He could leave and go out of paradise, but there was not a habitable place for humans beyond its borders—only for senseless animals, four-footed animals, wild monsters and crawling bugs. His "basilica" and "palace" was located in paradise.

Because of this, God brought the living creatures to Adam; they had been separated from him. For slaves do not always stand in their master's presence; they are present only when needed. The living creatures were named and immediately sent away. Adam, however, remained in paradise. ON THE CREATION OF THE WORLD 6:1.[5]

HOW DID GOD BRING THE ANIMALS TO ADAM? AUGUSTINE: Now we should not imagine God bringing the animals to Adam in a crudely material way. What I have said in the preceding book about the twofold working of divine Providence should be a help here. We must not suppose that the animals were brought to Adam as when hunters and fowlers seek them out and drive them into their nets when they engage in the chase. Nor was there a command spoken by a voice from a cloud in words that rational creatures on hearing

---

[1]In Genesis, according to the Old Testament. [2]In the Gospels, according to the New Testament. [3]NPNF 1 14:88*. [4]ANF 3:300*. [5]PG 56:485.

would understand and obey. Beasts and birds have not received such power. But according to their nature they obey God, not by a rational free choice of the will but according to the plan by which God moves all creatures at the appropriate times. Although he is himself unmoved in time, the angels who minister to him understand in his Word what things are to be done at appointed times. And hence, without any temporal motion in God, the angels are moved in time to accomplish his will in the creatures that are subject to them. ON THE LITERAL INTERPRETATION OF GENESIS 9.14.24.[6]

A COMPLETE HARMONY BETWEEN MAN AND THE ANIMALS. EPHREM THE SYRIAN: Moses said, "God brought them to Adam." This happened in order that God might make known the wisdom of Adam and the harmony that existed between the animals and Adam before he transgressed the commandment. The animals came to Adam as to a loving shepherd. Without fear they passed before him in orderly fashion, by kinds and by species. They were neither afraid of him nor were they afraid of each other. A species of predatory animals would pass by with a species of animal that is preyed upon following safely right behind. COMMENTARY ON GENESIS 2.9.3.[7]

MAN IS SUPERIOR TO ANY ANIMAL. AUGUSTINE: God first showed man how much better he was than cattle and all irrational animals. This is signified by the statement that all the animals were brought to him that he might see what he would call them and give them names. This shows that man is better equipped than the animals in virtue of reason, since only reason that judges concerning

them is able to distinguish and know them by name. The one idea is an easy one to grasp, for man quickly understands that he is better equipped than cattle. The other idea is a difficult one to grasp, namely, that by which he understands that the rational part in him that rules is distinct from the animal part, which is ruled. TWO BOOKS ON GENESIS AGAINST THE MANICHAEANS 2.11.16.[8]

THE HUMBLE MAN IS LIKE ADAM IN EDEN. ISAAC OF NINEVEH: He who speaks contemptuously against the humble man and does not consider him an animate creature is like one who has opened his mouth against God. And though the humble man is contemptible in his eyes, his honor is esteemed by all creation. The humble man approaches ravenous beasts, and when their gaze rests upon him, their wildness is tamed. They come up to him as to their Master, wag their heads and tails and lick his hands and feet, for they smell coming from him that same scent that exhaled from Adam before the fall, when they were gathered together before him and he gave them names in paradise. This was taken away from us, but Jesus has renewed it and given it back to us through his coming. This it is that has sweetened the fragrance of the race of men. ASCETICAL HOMILIES 77.[9]

IMPORTANCE OF NAMING THE ANIMALS. CHRYSOSTOM: Those names that [Adam] imposed on them remain up to the present time. In this way God determined that we might retain a constant reminder of the esteem which the human being from the outset received from the Lord of all and might

---

[6]ACW 41, 42. [7]FC 91:103. [8]FC 84:112. [9]*AHSIS* 383.

attribute responsibility for its removal to a person who by sin put an abrupt end to his authority. HOMILIES ON GENESIS 14:20.[10]

ANIMALS REPRESENT HUMAN PASSIONS. AMBROSE: The beasts of the field and the birds of the air which were brought to Adam are our irrational senses, because beasts and animals represent the diverse passions of the body, whether of the more violent kind or even of the more temperate. . . . God granted

to you the power of being able to discern by the application of sober logic the species of each and every object in order that you may be induced to form a judgment on all of them. God called them all to your attention so that you might realize that your mind is superior to all of them. PARADISE 11:51-52.[11]

[10]FC 74:190-91. [11]FC 42:329-30.

2:21-25 GOD CREATES WOMAN

[21]So the LORD God caused a deep sleep* to fall upon the man,[†] and while he slept took one of his ribs and closed up its place with flesh; [22]and the rib which the LORD God had taken from the man[†] he made[‡] into a woman and brought her to the man. [23]Then the man[†] said,

"This at last is bone of my bones
    and flesh of my flesh;
she shall be called Woman,[d]
    because she was taken out of Man."[e]

[24]Therefore a man leaves his father and his mother and cleaves to his wife, and they[§] become one flesh. [25]And the man and his wife were both naked, and were not ashamed.

d Heb ishshah e Heb ish *LXX an ecstasy †LXX Adam ‡LXX built §LXX the two

OVERVIEW: It is out of a bare bone that God instantly creates the full beauty of woman (EPHREM, CHRYSOSTOM). As Eve was born without a mother, so was Jesus born without a father (CYRIL OF JERUSALEM). God willed that the two, male and female, be established as one (AMBROSE). Eve's creation was painless to the unfallen Adam, in contrast with the pain

of the fallen Eve's birth-giving (CHRYSOSTOM). The woman was made in order to help man in good works (AUGUSTINE) but above all for the sake of bearing children (AMBROSE, AUGUSTINE). She was superior to any animal in her ability to help (EPHREM). When the woman was created from man's rib, he probably dreamed of the rib that was removed from him (EPHREM). When God produced ecstasy in the first man, he made him dream for the first time (TERTULLIAN). The first man possessed the power of prophecy (CLEMENT OF ALEXANDRIA) through which he understood what was finally to come (AUGUSTINE).

The creation of the woman from the man's rib signifies that the woman is one with the man, as Christ is one with the church (AUGUSTINE). Her creation also symbolizes the creation of the church (JEROME, QUODVULTDEUS). The union of man and woman implies a return to their origin (EPHREM). It also symbolizes the spiritual marriage of human beings with the church (AUGUSTINE) and their union with Christ (AMBROSE). However, they must be interpreted as an invitation to chastity and celibacy (APHRAHAT). The church is the mother of the new humanity, as Eve was of the old (QUODVULTDEUS). Before sin man and woman were naked and not ashamed, because they were clothed with glory (EPHREM). Their sexual organs could not offend, because they were not stirred by concupiscent desire (AUGUSTINE). We are baptized naked in order to remind us of our former nakedness in paradise, when we were naked and not ashamed (CHRYSOSTOM).

In creation man and woman were naked and not ashamed. They were not weighed down by bodily needs as they cleaved to each other (CHRYSOSTOM). The relation of man and woman in paradise is anticipatory of the resurrection of the faithful (GREGORY OF NYSSA). After the fall came alienation (DOROTHEUS OF GAZA).

2:21-23 *She Shall Be Called Woman*

ANOTHER IS PROMISED TO BE BORN. CYRIL OF JERUSALEM: Of whom in the beginning was Eve begotten? What mother conceived her, the motherless? But the Scripture says that she was born out of Adam's side. Is Eve then born out of man's side without a mother, and is a child not to be born without a father, of a virgin's womb? This debt of gratitude was due to men from womankind: for Eve was begotten of Adam and not conceived of a mother, but as it were brought forth of man alone. CATECHETICAL LECTURES 12.29.[1]

A DEEP SLEEP. CHRYSOSTOM: "God caused drowsiness to come upon Adam," the text says, "and he slept." It wasn't simply drowsiness that came upon him nor normal sleep; instead the wise and skillful creator of our nature was about to remove one of Adam's ribs. Lest the experience cause Adam afterward to be badly disposed toward the creature formed from his rib and through memory of the pain bear a grudge against this being at its formation, God induced in him this kind of sleep. God caused a drowsiness to come upon him and bid him be weighed down as though by some heavy weight. HOMILIES ON GENESIS 15.7.[2]

FROM ADAM'S RIB. SEVERIAN OF GABALA: Did Adam not suffer pain? Did he not experience agony? A single hair is plucked from the body and we feel pain. Even if one is deeply asleep, he will awake from the pain. Here, however, many hairs are plucked out, even a rib torn out, and the sleeper does not awake? God did not remove the rib violently, which would awaken Adam. He did not wrench it out. Instead Scripture, desiring to reveal the quickness of God's technique, says "he took a rib out of him and he did not awake." ON THE CREATION OF THE WORLD 5.8.[3]

[1]NPNF 2 7:80. [2]PG 53:120; FC 74:198. [3]PG 56:481-82.

This Is Now Bone of My Bone. Ephrem the Syrian: "This now"—that is, the one who has come to me after the animals—is not such as they; they came from the earth, but she is "bone of my bone and flesh of my flesh." Adam said this either in a prophetic way or, as noted above, according to his vision in sleep. And just as on this day all the animals received from Adam their names according to their kinds, so also the bone, made into a woman, he called not by her proper name, Eve, but by the name of woman, the name belonging to the whole kind. Commentaries on Genesis 2.13.2.[4]

The Woman Is Man's Helper. Augustine: Scripture says that the woman was made as man's helper so that by spiritual union she might bring forth spiritual offspring, that is, the good works of divine praise, while he rules and she obeys. He is ruled by wisdom; she, by the man. For Christ is the head of the man, and the man is the head of the woman.[5] Two Books on Genesis Against the Manichaeans 2.11.15.[6]

The Woman Is Created for Bearing Children. Ambrose: Not without significance, too, is the fact that woman was made out of the rib of Adam. She was not made of the same earth with which he was formed, in order that we might realize that the physical nature of both man and woman is identical and that there was one source for the propagation of the human race. For that reason, neither was man created together with a woman, nor were two men and two women created at the beginning, but first a man and after that a woman. God willed it that human nature be established as one. Thus from the very incep-

tion of the human stock he eliminated the possibility that many disparate natures should arise. He said, "Let us make him a helper like himself." We understand that to mean a helper in the generation of the human family—a really good helper. If we take the word *helper* in a good sense, then the woman's cooperation turns out to be something of major import in the process of generation, just as the earth by receiving, confining and fostering the seed causes it to grow and produce fruit in time. In that respect, therefore, woman is a good helper even though in a position of lesser strength. We find examples of this in our own experience. We see how people in high and important offices often enlist the help of people who are below them in rank and esteem. Paradise 10.48.[7]

A Helper for Bearing Children. Augustine: Now suppose the woman was not made for the man to be his helper in begetting children, then how would she be able to help him? It would hardly be the case that she would be made to till the earth with him, for there was not yet any labor required to make her help necessary. In any case, if there were any such need, a male helper would be better, and the same could be said of the comfort of another's presence if Adam were perhaps weary of solitude. How much more agreeably could two male friends, rather than a man and a woman, enjoy companionship and conversation in a life shared together. And if they had to make an arrangement in their common life for one to command and the other to obey in order to make sure that opposing wills would not disrupt the peace of

---

[4]FC 91:105. [5]1 Cor 11:13. [6]FC 84:111. [7]FC 42:327.

the household, there would have been proper rank to assure this, since one would be created first and the other second, and this would be further reinforced if the second were made from the first, as was the case with the woman. Surely no one will say that God was able to make from the rib of the man only a woman and not also a man if he had wished to do so. Consequently, I do not see in what sense the woman was made as a helper for the man if not for the sake of bearing children. ON THE LITERAL INTERPRETATION OF GENE-SIS 9.5.9.[8]

THE ANIMALS NOT ABLE TO HELP MAN AS THE WOMAN. EPHREM THE SYRIAN: Inside the paradise, the woman was very diligent; she was also attentive to the sheep and cattle, the herds and droves that were in the fields. She would also help the man with the buildings, pens, and with any other task that she was capable of doing. The animals, even though they were subservient, were not able to help him with these things. For this reason God made for the man a helper who would be concerned for everything for which God himself would be concerned. She would indeed help him in many things. COMMENTARY ON GENE-SIS 2.11.[9]

ADAM DREAMED WHEN WOMAN WAS CRE-ATED. EPHREM THE SYRIAN: That man, awake, anointed with splendor, and who did not yet know sleep, fell on the earth naked and slept. It is likely that Adam saw in his dream what was done to him as if he were awake. After Adam's rib had been taken out in the twinkling of an eye, God closed up the flesh in its place in the blink of an eyelash. The bare bone took on the full appearance and all the beauty of a woman. God then brought

her to Adam, who was both one and two. He was one in that he was Adam, and he was two because he had been created male and female.[10] COMMENTARY ON GENESIS 2.12.[11]

GOD PRODUCES IN THE FIRST MAN THE ECSTASY OF DREAM. TERTULLIAN: We hold the soul to be perennially active because of its continual movement, which is a sign both of its divinity and its immortality. So, then, when rest comes—rest, that special comfort of bodies—the soul disdains an idleness that is alien to its nature and, deprived of the faculties of the body, makes use of its own. This power we call ecstasy. This occurs when we are deprived of the activity of the senses. Lacking sensory input the soul reflects conditions akin to delirium.[12] Thus, in the beginning, sleep was preceded by ecstasy, as we read: "God sent an ecstasy upon Adam, and he slept." Sleep brought rest to the body, but ecstasy came over the soul and prevented it from resting, and from that time this combination constitutes the natural and normal form of the dream. ON THE SOUL 45.1-3.[13]

THE FIRST MAN POSSESSED THE POWER OF PROPHECY. CLEMENT OF ALEXANDRIA: Among the Hebrews the prophets spoke by the power and inspiration of God. Before the law there was Adam, who used a power of prophecy over the woman and over the naming of animals; Noah, preaching repentance;

---

[8]ACW 42:75. [9]FC 91:104. [10]Before Eve, Adam was two in that Eve was already implicitly within him. After Eve was created, he was two because he had been created male and female. Yet in all this duality he did not cease to be a single person, hence one. Cf. Gen 1:27. [11]FC 91:105. [12]Or enchantment, or a deprivation of the activity of the senses. [13]FC 10:280**.

Abraham, Isaac and Jacob offering a clear fore-shadowing of a large number of events future or imminent. STROMATEIS 1.135.3.[14]

ADAM UNDERSTANDS IN HIS ECSTASY WHAT IS TO COME.

AUGUSTINE: Hence we are justified in concluding that the ecstasy in which Adam was caught up when God cast him into a sleep was given to him so that his mind in that state might participate with the host of angels and, entering into the sanctuary of God, understand what was finally to come. When he awoke, he was like one filled with the spirit of prophecy, and seeing his wife brought before him, he immediately opened his mouth and proclaimed the great mystery that St. Paul[15] teaches: "This now is bone of my bones and flesh of my flesh; she shall be called woman, because she has been taken out of man. And for this reason a man shall leave his father and his mother and shall cleave to his wife; and they shall be the two in one flesh." These were the words of the first man according to the testimony of Scripture, but in the Gospel our Lord declared that God spoke them. For he says, "Have you not read that he who made them from the beginning made them male and female and said, 'For this reason a man shall leave his father and mother and shall cleave to his wife, and they shall be two in one flesh'"?[16] From this we should understand, therefore, that because of the ecstasy that Adam had just experienced he was able to say this as a prophet under divine guidance. ON THE LITERAL INTERPRETATION OF GENESIS 9.19.36.[17]

THE WOMAN IS ONE WITH THE MAN AS CHRIST IS ONE WITH THE CHURCH.

AUGUSTINE: Even in the beginning, when woman was made from a rib in the side of the sleeping man, that had no less a purpose than to symbolize prophetically the union of Christ and his church. Adam's sleep was a mystical foreshadowing of Christ's death, and when his dead body hanging from the cross was pierced by the lance, it was from his side that there issued forth that blood and water that, as we know, signifies the sacraments by which the church is built up. "Built" is the very word the Scripture uses in connection with Eve: "He built the rib into a woman." . . . So too St. Paul speaks of "building up the body of Christ,"[18] which is his church. Therefore woman is as much the creation of God as man is. If she was made from the man, this was to show her oneness with him; and if she was made in the way she was, this was to pre-figure the oneness of Christ and the church. CITY OF GOD 22.17.[19]

THE CREATION OF THE WOMAN SYMBOL-IZES THE CREATION OF THE CHURCH.

JEROME: "God took a rib from the side of Adam and made it into a woman." Here Scripture said *aedificavit* ("built"). The concept of building intends to denote the construction of a great house; consequently Adam's rib fashioned into a woman signifies, by apostolic authority,[20] Christ and the church, and that is why Scripture said he formed (*aedificavit*) a woman from the rib. We have heard about the first Adam; let us come now to the second Adam and see how the church is made (*aedificatur*) from his side. The side of the Lord Savior as he hung on the cross is pierced with a lance, and from it there comes forth blood and water. Would you like to know how the church is built up from water

---

[14]FC 85:124. [15]Cf. Eph 5:31-32. [16]Mt 19:4. [17]ACW 42:95. [18]Cf. Eph 4:12. [19]FC 24:464-65. [20]Cf. Eph 5:32.

and blood? First, through the baptism of water, sins are forgiven; then, the blood of martyrs crowns the edifice. HOMILIES 66.[21]

THE CHURCH AS MOTHER OF THE NEW HUMANITY. QUODVULTDEUS: The apostle Paul testifies that this passage has both a plain and an allegorical meaning. Discussing it in his letter to the Ephesians, he asserts, "This is a great mystery, but I speak concerning Christ and the church."[22] The great mystery is that Adam hopes after receiving the promise. He sees that the spouse in whom he believed is now united to him. Therefore he symbolically announces to us that through faith the church will be the mother of humankind. It is evident that since Eve had been created from the side of the sleeping Adam, he has foreseen that from the side of Christ hanging on the cross the church, which is in truth the mother of the whole new humankind, must be created. In fact the church is "the woman who is guarded for a time, and times, and half a time, from the face of the serpent."[23] BOOK OF PROMISES AND PREDICTIONS OF GOD 1.3.[24]

2:24 Becoming One Flesh

MAN AND WOMAN UNITE AGAIN. EPHREM THE SYRIAN: Then Adam said, "Let the man leave his father and his mother and cling to his wife so that they might be joined and the two might become one" without division as they were from the beginning. COMMENTARY ON GENESIS 2.13.3.[25]

UNION OF MAN AND WOMAN SYMBOLIZES OUR UNION TO THE CHURCH AND TO CHRIST. AUGUSTINE: Scripture said, "A man will leave father and mother, and he will cling

to his wife, and they will be two in one flesh." This is what generally happens in the human race. There is no other way to view its plain, historical sense. But more so, this is all prophecy, and the apostle reminds us of this when he says, "For this reason a man will leave his father and mother and he will cling to his wife, and they will be two in one flesh. This is a great mystery; I mean in Christ and in the church."[26] TWO BOOKS ON GENESIS AGAINST THE MANICHAEANS 2.13.19.[27]

THE BONE AND FLESH OF THE CHURCH. AMBROSE: If the union of Adam and Eve is a great mystery in Christ and in the church, it is certain that as Eve was bone of the bones of her husband and flesh of his flesh, we also are members of Christ's body, bones of his bones and flesh of his flesh. LETTERS TO LAYMEN 85.[28]

CLEAVING TO GOD AND CLEAVING TO THE WORLD. APHRAHAT: From the law we heard: "Therefore a man leaves his father and his mother and cleaves to his wife, and they will become one flesh." This is a great and sublime prophecy. Who actually leaves his father and mother when he takes a wife? This is the meaning of the words: man in his original condition loved and worshiped God, his father, and the Holy Spirit, his mother. He did not have any other love. In order to take a wife, man leaves his mother and father, those whom I mentioned above. His mind is thereby diverted by this world. His soul and mind are driven away from God and drawn into this

---

[21]FC 57:65. [22]Eph 5:32. [23]Rev 12:14. [24]PL 51:735; CCL 60:13; SC 101:159-61. [25]FC 91:105-6. [26]Eph 5:31-32. [27]FC 84:115. [28]FC 26:476.

world that he adores and loves "as a man loves the wife of his youth."[29] The love for this wife is different from the love for the father and the mother. Scripture adds, "They will become one flesh." It is true that as some men make one flesh and soul with their wife, and their mind and thoughts are driven away from their father and mother, so those who never take a wife and stay alone may have a single spirit and mind with their father. DEMONSTRATIONS 18.10-11.[30]

A MAN SHALL CLEAVE TO HIS WIFE. CHRYSOSTOM: Where, tell me, did these things come from for him to utter? From what source did he gain knowledge of future events and the fact that the race of human beings should grow into a vast number? Whence, after all, did he come to know that there would be intercourse between man and woman? I mean, the consummation of that intercourse occurred after the fall; up till that time they were living like angels in paradise and so were not burning with desire, not assaulted by other passions, not subject to the needs of nature; on the contrary, they were created incorruptible and immortal, and on that account at any rate they had no need to wear clothes. . . . So from what source, tell me, did these things come for him to utter? Surely it's obvious that before his disobedience he had a share in prophetic grace and saw everything through the eyes of the Spirit. HOMILIES ON GENESIS 15-16.[31]

2:25 Both Were Naked and Were Not Ashamed

MAN AND WOMAN WERE CLOTHED WITH GLORY BEFORE SIN. EPHREM THE SYRIAN: They were not ashamed because of the glory

with which they were clothed. It was when this glory was stripped from them after they had transgressed the commandment that they were ashamed because they were naked. COMMENTARY ON GENESIS 2.14.2.[32]

THEIR SEXUAL ORGANS COULD NOT OFFEND. AUGUSTINE: [Man and woman] were aware, of course, of their nakedness, but they felt no shame, because no desire stirred their organs in defiance of their deliberate decision. The time had not yet come when the rebellion of the flesh was a witness and reproach to the rebellion of man against his Maker. CITY OF GOD 14.17.[33]

WHY CHRISTIANS ARE BAPTIZED NAKED. CHRYSOSTOM: After stripping you of your robe, the priest himself leads you down into the flowing waters. But why naked? He reminds you of your former nakedness, when you were in paradise and you were not ashamed. For Holy Writ says, "Adam and Eve were naked and were not ashamed," until they took up the garment of sin, a garment heavy with abundant shame. BAPTISMAL INSTRUCTION 11.28.[34]

NAKED BUT NOT ASHAMED. CHRYSOSTOM: "They were both naked," the text says, remember, "and were not ashamed." You see, while sin and disobedience had not yet come on the scene, they were clad in that glory from above which caused them no shame. But after the breaking of the law, then entered the scene both shame and awareness of their nakedness. HOMILIES ON GENESIS 15.14.[35]

---

[29]Prov 5:18. [30]PS 1 1:839-42. [31]PG 53:123; FC 74:202-3. [32]FC 91:106. [33]FC 14:389. [34]ACW 31:170. [35]PG 53:123; FC 74:203.

Resurrection Restores Paradise Lost.
Gregory of Nyssa: The resurrection promises us nothing else than the restoration of the
fallen to their ancient state; for the grace we
look for is a certain return to the first life,
bringing back again to paradise those who
were cast out from it. If then the life of those
restored is closely related to that of the angels,
it is clear that the life before the transgression
was a kind of angelic life, and hence also our
return to the ancient condition of life is compared to the angels. On the Creation of
Man 17.[36]

Reprise. Dorotheus of Gaza: In the
beginning, when God created man, he set him
in paradise (as the divine holy Scripture says)
adorned with every virtue and gave him a
command not to eat of the tree in the middle
of paradise. Adam was provided for in paradise, in prayer and contemplation in the midst
of honor and glory, healthy in his emotions
and sense perceptions, and perfect in his
nature as he was created. For to the likeness of
God did God make man, that is, immortal,
having the power to act freely and adorned
with all the virtues. When he disobeyed the
command and ate of the tree that God commanded him not to eat of, he was thrown out
of paradise and fell from a state in accord with
his nature to a state contrary to nature, a prey
to sin, to ambition, to a love of the pleasures
of this life and to the other passions; and he
was mastered by them and became a slave to
them through his transgression. Spiritual
Instructions 1.[37]

---

[36]NPNF 2 5:407. [37]CS 33:77.

3:1-6 THE DECEIT OF THE SERPENT

[1]*Now the serpent was more subtle than any other wild creature that the Lord God had
made. He said to the woman, "Did God say, 'You shall not eat of any tree of the garden'?"*
[2]*And the woman said to the serpent, "We may eat of the fruit of the trees of the garden;*
[3]*but God said, "You shall not eat of the fruit of the tree which is in the midst of the garden,*
neither shall you touch it, lest you die.'" [4]*But the serpent said to the woman, "You will not
die.* [5]*For God knows that when you eat of it your eyes will be opened, and you will be like
God, knowing good and evil."* [6]*So when the woman saw that the tree was good for food, and
that it was a delight to the eyes, and that the tree was to be desired to make one wise, she
took of its fruit and ate; and she also gave some to her husband, and he ate.*

*LXX paradise

OVERVIEW: The serpent was more clever than the other beasts but was not raised to the level of human rationality (EPHREM). Before the fall the serpent was on intimate terms with man (JOHN OF DAMASCUS). The serpent as created was winsome and able to communicate with Adam and Eve, and hence became a tool of deception used by the devil (CHRYSOSTOM, EPHREM), who was envious of Adam and Eve's special role in paradise (AMBROSE). By questioning Eve the serpent ascertained the mystery of the tree (EPHREM). The devil spoke first to the woman apart from the man, who had received directly from God the command not to eat of the tree (AMBROSE). The serpent realized that God had forewarned Adam and Eve about even looking at the tree in order that they not become enamored by its beauty (EPHREM). The serpent symbolizes pleasure (AMBROSE). It also signifies the devil (AUGUSTINE).

The words of the serpent, "You shall be as gods," demonstrate that pride is the beginning of all sin (AUGUSTINE). Humans were harmed by their own desire (EPHREM). They had already begun in a preliminary way to seek satisfaction in themselves when they were tempted by the serpent. In paradise rebellion began in the soul with the breaking of the commandment. The whole person committed the sin (AUGUSTINE). Adam and Eve did not preserve temperance but voluntarily ate of the fruit (AMBROSE). The Eucharist is the remedy against the poison that ruined human nature when Eve and Adam ate of the fruit (GREGORY OF NYSSA). Since Adam and Eve fell through pride, their posterity would be required to return to God through humility (AUGUSTINE). Mary represents a second Eve, who frees humankind from the sin of the first Eve (IRENAEUS). That Eve disobeyed before Adam is taken by some fathers to be an usurpation of his headship (EPHREM).

3:1-3 *The Serpent Talks to the Woman*

THE CLEVERNESS OF THE SERPENT WAS LIMITED. EPHREM THE SYRIAN: Although the serpent was cunning, it was only more cunning than the dumb animals that were governed by Adam. It is not true that because the serpent surpassed the level of animals in cleverness, it was immediately raised up to the level of human rationality. It was only more clever than those animals that lack reason and was only more crafty than the animals that had no mind. For it is clear that the serpent, which did not have the mind of man, did not possess the wisdom of mankind. Adam was also greater than the serpent by the way he was formed, by his soul, by his mind, by his glory and by his place. Therefore it is evident that in cunning also Adam was infinitely greater than the serpent. COMMENTARY ON GENESIS 2.15.1.[1]

WHY THE SERPENT WAS A TOOL FOR DECEPTION. SEVERIAN OF GABALA: Do not think of the snake the way he currently is, since we now run from him and are disgusted by him. It was not this way in the beginning; the snake was a friend of humanity, even the closest of servants. What, then, made him our enemy? The declaration of God: "You are more cursed than all the cattle, and more than every wild animal. I will place hostility between you and the woman."[2] This hostility destroyed the friendship. I say "friendship," but I do not mean an intellectual relationship, it was

---

[1]FC 91:107. [2]Gen 3:14-15.

instead one which mindless creatures are capable of having. The snake used to serve humans in the same way the dog displaces friendship—not with word but by body language. Since it was a creature who held such great closeness to humanity, the snake was a convenient tool for the devil. . . .

So the devil spoke through the snake in order to deceive Adam. Please hear me in love and do not receive my words carelessly. My question is not easy to take. Many scoff, "how did the snake speak, with a human's voice or with a snake's hiss?" or "how did Eve understand him?" Before the fall, Adam was filled with wisdom, discernment and prophecy. . . . When the devil noticed the snake's intelligence and Adam's high opinion of it (Adam considered the snake very wise), the devil spoke through the snake so that Adam would think that the snake, being intelligent, was able to imitate even human speech. ON THE CREATION OF THE WORLD 6.2.[3]

HOW THE SERPENT WAS ON INTIMATE TERMS WITH MAN. JOHN OF DAMASCUS: Before the fall, all things were subject to the control of man, because God had made him ruler over all the things on the earth and in the water. And the serpent was on intimate terms with man, associating with him more than all the rest and conversing agreeably with him. For that reason it was through this relation that the devil, who is the source of evil, made that most evil suggestion to our first parents. ORTHODOX FAITH 2.10.[4]

HOW THE SERPENT COMMUNICATED WITH MAN. EPHREM THE SYRIAN: As for the serpent's speech, either Adam understood the serpent's own mode of communication, or Satan spoke through it, or the serpent posed

the question in his mind and speech was given to it, or Satan sought from God that speech be given to the serpent for a short time. COMMENTARY ON GENESIS 2.16.1.[5]

THE SERPENT QUESTIONS EVE. EPHREM THE SYRIAN:

> The serpent could not
> enter paradise,
> for neither animal
> nor bird
> was permitted to approach
> the outer region of paradise,
> and Adam had to go out
> to meet them;
> so the serpent cunningly learned,
> through questioning Eve,
> the character of paradise,
> what it was and how it was ordered.
> When the accursed one learned
> how the glory of that inner tabernacle,
> as if in a sanctuary,
> was hidden from them,
> and that the Tree of Knowledge,
> clothed with an injunction,
> served as the veil
> for the sanctuary,
> he realized that its fruit
> was the key of justice
> that would open the eyes of the bold
> and cause them great remorse. HYMNS ON
> PARADISE 3.4-5.[6]

EVE ENTICED TO LOOK UPON THE TREE. EPHREM THE SYRIAN: The tempter then turned its mind to the commandment of the One who had set down the commandment. Adam and Eve were commanded not only to

---

[3]PG 56:485-86. [4]FC 37:228-29. [5]FC 91:107-8. [6]HOP 91-92.

not eat from the tree, but they were not even to draw near to it. The serpent then realized that God had forewarned them about even looking at it lest they become entrapped by its beauty. With this in mind, the serpent enticed Eve to look upon it. COMMENTARY ON GENESIS 2.20.1.[7]

THE DEVIL'S ENVY. AMBROSE: The cause of envy was the happiness of man placed in paradise, because the devil could not brook the favors received by man. His envy was aroused because man, though formed in slime, was chosen to be an inhabitant of paradise. The devil began to reflect that man was an inferior creature yet had hopes of an eternal life, whereas he, a creature of superior nature, had fallen and had become part of this mundane existence. PARADISE 12.[8]

THE SERPENT AS A SYMBOL OF PLEASURE. AMBROSE: Since every creature is subject to passion, lust stole into man's affection with the stealth of a serpent. Moses was quite right in representing pleasure in the likeness of a serpent. Pleasure is prone on its belly like a serpent, not walking on feet or raised on legs. It glides along, so to speak, with the slippery folded curves of its whole body. Earth is its food, as it is the serpent's, for it has no comprehension of heavenly food. It feeds on things of the body, and it is changed into many sorts of pleasures and bends to and fro in twisting wreaths. It has venom in its fangs, and with these the dissolute individual is disemboweled, the glutton destroys himself, the spendthrift is undone. LETTERS TO BISHOPS 25.[9]

THE DEVIL TOOK ADVANTAGE OF THE WOMAN. AMBROSE: [The Devil] aimed to circumvent Adam by means of the woman. He did not accost the man who had in his presence received the heavenly command. He accosted her who had learned of it from her husband and who had not received from God the command which was to be observed. There is no statement that God spoke to the woman. We know that he spoke to Adam. Hence we must conclude that the command was communicated through Adam to the woman. PARADISE 12.[10]

THE SERPENT SIGNIFIES THE DEVIL. AUGUSTINE: The serpent signifies the devil, who was certainly not simple. His cleverness is indicated by the fact that he is said to be wiser than all the beasts. The serpent was not said to be in paradise, though the serpent was among the beasts that God made. For paradise signifies the happy life, from which the serpent was absent, since it was already the devil. He had fallen from his beatitude because he did not stay in the truth. And we must not be confused as to how the serpent could speak to the woman, when she was in paradise and it was not. The serpent entered the paradise spiritually and not bodily, as the apostle suggests: "You were living by the principles of this world, obeying the ruler who dominates the air, the spirit who is at work in those who rebel."[11] TWO BOOKS ON GENESIS AGAINST THE MANICHAEANS 2.14.20.[12]

3:4-5 *Knowing Good and Evil*

THE DEVIL'S STRATEGY. CHRYSOSTOM: Do you see how the devil led her captive, handi-

---

[7]FC 91:111. [8]FC 42:332-33. [9]FC 26:131-32. [10]FC 42:333. [11]Eph 2:2. [12]FC 84:116*.

capped her reasoning and caused her to set her thoughts on goals beyond her real capabilities, in order that she might be puffed up with empty hopes and lose her hold on the advantages already accorded her? HOMILIES ON GENESIS 16.11.[13]

PRIDE IS THE BEGINNING OF ALL SIN. AUGUSTINE: But it is most truly said . . . "Pride is the beginning of all sin,"[14] for it was this sin that overthrew the devil, from whom arose the origin of sin and who, through subsequent envy, overturned the man who was standing in the righteousness from which he had fallen. For the serpent, seeking a way to enter, clearly sought the door of pride, when he declared, "You shall be as gods." That is why it is written, "Pride is the beginning of all sin,"[15] and "The beginning of the pride of man is to fall away from God."[16] ON NATURE AND GRACE 29.33.[17]

ALREADY SEEKING SATISFACTION IN SELF. AUGUSTINE: The conclusion is that the devil would not have begun by an open and obvious sin to tempt man into doing something that God had forbidden, had not man already begun to seek satisfaction in himself and consequently to take pleasure in the words "you shall be as gods." The promise of these words, however, would much more truly have to pass if, by obedience, Adam and Eve had kept close to the ultimate and true source of their being and had not, by pride, imagined that they were themselves the source of their being. . . . Whoever seeks to be more than he is becomes less. Whenever he aspires to be self-sufficing, he retreats from the One who is truly sufficient for him. CITY OF GOD 14.13.[18]

3:6 The Man and Woman Eat the Fruit

TEMPTED BY THEIR OWN DESIRE. EPHREM THE SYRIAN: The words of the tempter would not have caused those two to be tempted to sin if their avarice had not been so helpful to the tempter. Even if the tempter had not come, the tree itself, by its beauty, would have caused them a great struggle due to their avarice. Their avarice then was the reason that they followed the counsel of the serpent. The avarice of Adam and Eve was far more injurious to them than the counsel of the serpent. COMMENTARY ON GENESIS 2.16.[19]

THE REBELLION BEGAN IN THE SOUL. AUGUSTINE: In paradise, rebellion certainly began in the soul. There began the process of giving consent to breaking the commandment. This is why the serpent said, "You shall be as gods." But the whole man committed the sin. It was then that the flesh was made sinful flesh, whose faults could be healed only by the One who came in the likeness of sinful flesh. AGAINST JULIAN 5.4.17.[20]

TEMPERANCE NOT OBSERVED BY ADAM AND EVE. AMBROSE: It is temperance that cuts off desires. God commanded the first humans to hold to it, for he said, "What is in the middle of the garden, you shall not eat, neither shall you touch it, lest you die." And because they did not preserve temperance, the transgressors of this signal virtue were made exiles from paradise, with no share in immortality. For the law teaches temperance and pours it into the hearts of all. JACOB AND THE HAPPY LIFE 2.8.[21]

---

[13]PG 53:129; FC 74:214. [14]Sir 10:15. [15]Sir 10:15. [16]Sir 10:15. [17]FC 86:46-47. [18]FC 14:382-83. [19]FC 91:108. [20]FC 35:261*. [21]FC 65:124*.

The Senses Distract the Heart. Diadochus of Photice: Eve is the first to teach us that sight, taste and the other senses, when used without moderation, distract the heart from its remembrance of God. So long as she did not look with longing on the forbidden tree, she was able to keep God's commandment carefully in mind. She was still covered by the wings of divine love and thus was ignorant of her own nakedness. But after she had looked at the tree with longing, touched it with ardent desire and then tasted its fruit with intense sensuality, she at once felt drawn to physical intercourse, and, being naked, she gave way to passion. All her desire was now to enjoy what was immediately present to her senses, and through the pleasant appearance of the fruit she involved Adam in her fall. On Spiritual Perfection 56.[22]

Christ Is the Remedy Against the Sin. Gregory of Nyssa: Those who have been tricked into taking poison offset its harmful effect by another drug. The remedy, moreover, just like the poison, has to enter the system, so that its remedial effect may thereby spread through the whole body. Similarly, having tasted the poison, that is the fruit, that dissolved our nature, we were necessarily in need of something to reunite it. Such a remedy had to enter into us, so that it might by its counteraction undo the harm the body had already encountered from the poison. And what is this remedy? Nothing else than the body that proved itself superior to death and became the source of our life. Address on Religious Instruction 37.[23]

Those Who Fall Through Pride Will Be Restored Only Through Humility. Augustine: Through [Christ] a pattern of life has been given us, that is to say, a sure path by which we may come to God. For we who have fallen through pride could only return to God through humility. Thus was it said to the first creature of our race: "Taste, and you shall be as God." As I was saying, our Savior has himself condescended to exemplify in his own person that humility which is the path over which we have to travel on our return to God. For "he did not think it robbery to be equal to God but emptied himself, taking the form of a slave."[24] Hence, the Word through whom all things in the beginning were made was created man. On Faith and the Creed 4.6.[25]

Surpassing Adam's Headship. Ephrem the Syrian: She hastened to eat before her husband that she might become head over her head, that she might become the one to give command to that one by whom she was to be commanded and that she might be older in divinity than that one who was older than she in humanity. Commentary on Genesis 2.20.3.[26]

The Sin of the First Woman Ameliorated by the Obedience of Mary. Irenaeus: As Eve was seduced by the word of a [fallen] angel to flee from God, having rebelled against his word, so Mary by the word of an angel received the glad tidings that she would bear God by obeying his word. The former was seduced to disobey God [and so fell], but the latter was persuaded to obey God, so that the Virgin Mary might become the advocate of the virgin Eve. As the human race was subjected to death through the act of

---

[22]TP 1:269. [23]LCC 3:318. [24]Phil 2:6-7. [25]FC 27:322-23. [26]FC 91:113.

a virgin, so was it saved by a virgin, and thus the disobedience of one virgin was precisely balanced by the obedience of another.

AGAINST HERESIES 5.19.1.[27]

---

[27]*LQAH* 2:376.

3:7-8 THE FALL

[7]*Then the eyes of both were opened, and they knew that they were naked; and they sewed fig leaves together and made themselves aprons.*

[8]*And they heard the sound* of the LORD God walking in the garden† in the cool of the day, and the man‡ and his wife hid themselves from the presence of the LORD God among the trees of the garden.†*

*LXX voice †LXX paradise ‡LXX Adam

OVERVIEW: The temptation moved from the eyes to disobedience (CHRYSOSTOM). The law of God, which forbade the eating of the fruit, cannot be regarded as the cause of the fall (CHRYSOSTOM). Even though God foreknew the result, he allowed Adam to be tempted because man would not have deserved great praise if he was good for the simple reason that he was never tempted to be wicked (AUGUSTINE).

After the sin the eyes of sense were opened, while the eyes of the mind, through which Adam and Eve had beheld God, were closed (ORIGEN). Now they saw the difference between the good they had lost and the evil into which they had fallen (AUGUSTINE). And their soul lost mastery over the body (AUGUSTINE). Fig leaves may symbolize the pleasure of lying (AUGUSTINE), the tendency toward sin (BEDE) or an act of repentance (IRENAEUS).

God endowed his silent footsteps with sound so that Adam and Eve might be prepared to make supplication before him (EPHREM). The cool of day (the evening) in which God seeks out Adam signifies that the first man had already lost the sunlight of his innocence (JEROME). So Adam and Eve hid themselves in the garden, because they had lost the light of the truth (CHRYSOSTOM, AUGUSTINE).

3:7 The Eyes of Both Were Opened

DISOBEDIENCE PRIOR TO EATING. CHRYSOSTOM: It wasn't the eating from the tree that opened their eyes: they could see even before eating. Instead the eating from this tree was the symptom of their disobedience and the breaking of the command given by God; and through their guilt they consequently divested themselves of the glory surrounding them, rendering themselves unworthy of such wonderful esteem. Hence Scripture takes up the point in its customary way with the words, "They both ate. Their eyes were opened, and they realized they were naked." Because of the fall they were stripped of grace from above, and they felt the sense of their obvious nakedness so that through the shame that overcame them they might know precisely what peril they had been led into by breaking the Lord's command. HOMILIES ON GENESIS 16.14.[1]

THE LAW CANNOT BE CONSIDERED THE CAUSE OF THE FALL. CHRYSOSTOM: I know that some at this point might accuse the Lawgiver and assert that the law is the cause of the fall. We absolutely must oppose that argument. We must plainly argue and demonstrate that God gave the law not because he hated humanity or wanted to mark our nature with shame but because he loved us and cared for us. In order that you learn that the law was given as a means to help, listen to the words of Isaiah: "He gave the law in our support."[2] One who pursues hatred does not give help. Again the prophet declares, "Your word is the lamp guiding my steps and the light for my paths."[3] But one who pursues hatred does not dispel the darkness with his lamp, nor does he provide light to one who is wandering. Solomon says, "The command of the law is the lamp, the light, the life, the reproach and the rule."[4] So the law is not only a help, not only a lamp but also light and life. Therefore these things are not for those who pursue hatred, not for those who will to be lost, but for those who hold out and lift up their hand. HOMILIES ON GENESIS 8.[5]

WHY DID GOD ALLOW ADAM TO BE TEMPTED? AUGUSTINE: If someone asks, therefore, why God allowed man to be tempted when he foreknew that man would yield to the tempter, I cannot sound the depths of divine wisdom, and I confess that the solution is far beyond my powers. There may be a hidden reason, made known only to those who are better and holier than I, not because of their merits but simply by the grace of God. But insofar as God gives me the ability to understand or allows me to speak, I do not think that a man would deserve great praise if he had been able to live a good life for the simple reason that nobody tempted him to live a bad one. For by nature he would have it in his power to will not to yield to the tempter, with the help of him, of course, "who resists the proud and gives his grace to the humble."[6] Why, then, would God not allow a man to be tempted, although he foreknew he would yield? For the man would do the deed by his own free will and thus incur guilt, and he would have to undergo punishment according to God's justice to be restored to right order. Thus God would make known his will to a proud soul for the instruction of the saints in ages to come. For wisely he uses even bad wills of souls when they perversely abuse their nature, which is good. ON THE LITERAL INTERPRETATION OF GENESIS 11.4.6.[7]

AFTER THE SIN THE EYES OF SENSE ARE OPENED. ORIGEN: The eyes of sense were then opened, which they had done well to keep shut, that they might not be distracted and hindered from seeing with the eyes of the mind. It was those eyes of the mind which in

---

[1]PG 53:131; FC 74:216. [2]Is 8:20. [3]Ps 118:105. [4]Prov 6:23. [5]PG 54:617. [6]1 Pet 5:5. [7]ACW 42:137.

consequence of sin, as I imagine, were then closed. To that time they had enjoyed the delight of beholding God and his paradise. This twofold kind of vision in us was familiar to our Savior, who said, "For judgment I have come into this world, that those who see not might see and that those who see might be made blind"[8]—meaning by "the eyes that see not" the eyes of the mind, which are enlightened by his teaching; and "the eyes that see," meaning the eyes of sense, which his words render blind. AGAINST CELSUS 7.39.[9]

ADAM AND EVE SEE THE EVIL INTO WHICH THEY HAVE FALLEN. AUGUSTINE: It was not in order to see outward things that "their eyes were opened," because they could see such things already. It was in order that they might see the difference between the good they had lost and the evil into which they had fallen. That is why the tree is called the tree of the knowledge of good and evil. They had been forbidden to touch it because if they did it would bring on the experience of this distinction. It takes the experience of the pains of sickness to open our eyes to the pleasantness of health. CITY OF GOD 14.17.[10]

THEIR SOUL LOSES ITS MASTERY OVER THE BODY. AUGUSTINE: As soon as our first parents had disobeyed God's commandment, they were immediately deprived of divine grace and were ashamed of their nakedness. They covered themselves with fig leaves, which perhaps were the first thing noticed by the troubled pair. The parts covered remained unchanged except that previously they occasioned no shame. They felt for the first time a movement of disobedience in their flesh, as though the punishment were meant to fit the crime of their own disobedience to God. The

fact is that the soul, which had taken perverse delight in its own liberty and disdained the service of God, was now deprived of its original mastery over the body. Because it had deliberately deserted the Lord who was over it, it no longer bent to its will the servant below it, being unable to hold the flesh completely in subjection as would always have been the case, if only the soul had remained subject to God. From this moment on, then, the flesh began to lust against the spirit. With this rebellion we are born, just as we are doomed to die and because of the first sin to bear, in our members and vitiated nature, either the battle with or defeat by the flesh. CITY OF GOD 13.13.[11]

SYMBOLISM OF THE FIG LEAVES. AUGUSTINE: Then they saw that they were naked by perverted eyes. Their original simplicity, signified by the term *nakedness*, now seemed to be something to be ashamed of. And so that they might no longer be simple, they made aprons for themselves from the leaves of the fig tree, as if to cover their private parts, that is, to cover their simplicity, of which that cunning pride was ashamed. The leaves of the fig tree signify a certain itching, if this is correctly said in the case of incorporeal things, which the mind suffers in wondrous ways from the desire and pleasure of lying. As a result those who love to joke are even called "salty" in Latin. For in jokes pretense plays a primary role. TWO BOOKS ON GENESIS AGAINST THE MANICHAEANS 2.15.23.[12]

THE TENDENCY TOWARD SIN. BEDE: Since

---

[8]Jn 9:39. [9]ANF 4:626*. [10]FC 14:390. [11]FC 14:316. [12]FC 84:119.

our first parents, shamed by guilt for their transgression, made aprons for themselves from fig leaves, the fig tree can fittingly designate the tendency toward sin. Sin appears wrongfully to be filled with sweetness for the human race. HOMILIES ON THE GOSPELS 1.17.[13]

THEIR CLOTHING. IRENAEUS: Now "the fear of the Lord is the beginning of wisdom."[14] The understanding of transgression leads to penitence, and God extends his kindness to those who repent. For [Adam] showed his repentance in making a girdle, covering himself with fig leaves, when there were many other trees that would have irritated his body less. He, however, in awe of God, made a clothing that matched his disobedience. . . . And he would no doubt have kept this clothing forever, if God in his mercy had not clothed them with tunics of skin instead of fig leaves. AGAINST HERESIES 3.23.5.[15]

3:8 Hiding from the Lord's Presence

THE SOUND OF GOD'S FOOTSTEPS. EPHREM THE SYRIAN: It was not only by the patience he exhibited that God wished to help them; he also wished to benefit them by the sound of his feet. God endowed his silent footsteps with sound so that Adam and Eve might be prepared, at that sound, to make supplication before him who made the sound. COMMENTARY ON GENESIS 2.24.1.[16]

DOES GOD HAVE FEET? CHRYSOSTOM: What are you saying—God strolls? Are we assigning feet to him? Have we no exalted conception of him? No, God doesn't stroll—perish the thought. How could he, present as he is everywhere and filling everything with his presence? Can he for whom heaven is throne and earth a footstool be confined to the garden? What right-minded person could say this?

So what is the meaning of this statement, "They heard the sound of the Lord God as he strolled in the garden in the evening?" He wanted to provide them with such an experience as would induce in them a state of anguish, which in fact happened: they had so striking an experience that they tried to hide from the presence of God. HOMILIES ON GENESIS 17.3-4.[17]

GOD WALKS IN THE COOL OF THE DAY. JEROME: We read in Genesis that when Adam transgressed, when he paid heed to the serpent rather than to God, when he hid himself from the face of God, then God came into the garden and was walking about in the cool of day. Now listen to what the Scripture says. God sought out Adam, not at midday but in the evening. Adam had already lost the sunlight, for his high noon was over. HOMILIES 1.[18]

THE PUNISHMENT OF DEATH MERCIFULLY DELAYED. CHRYSOSTOM: See the Lord's loving kindness and the surpassing degree of his long-suffering. I mean, though being in a position to begrudge such great sinners the right of reply and rather than to consign them at once to the punishment he had determined in anticipation of their transgression, he shows patience and withholds action. He asks a question, receives a reply and questions them further as if inviting them to excuse them-

---

[13]HOG 1:173. [14]Ps 110:10. [15]LQAH 2:128. [16]FC 91:115. [17]PG 53:135; FC 74:223. [18]FC 48:12.

selves so that he might seize the opportunity to display his characteristic love in regard to the sinners, even despite their fall. HOMILIES ON GENESIS 17.13.[19]

ADAM AND EVE HAVE LEFT THE LIGHT OF THE TRUTH. AUGUSTINE: Toward evening God was walking in paradise, that is, he was coming to judge them. He was still walking in paradise before their punishment, that is, the presence of God still moved among them, when they no longer stood firm in his command. It is fitting that he comes toward evening, that is, when the sun was already setting for them, that is, when the interior light of the truth was being taken from them. They heard his voice and hid from his sight. Who hides from the sight of God but he who has abandoned him and is now beginning to love what is his own? For they now were clothed with a lie, and he who speaks a lie speaks from what is his own. This is why they are said to hide near to the tree that was in the middle of paradise, that is, near themselves who were set in the middle rank of things beneath God and above bodies. Hence they became hidden to themselves so that they might be troubled by their wretched errors after they had left the light of truth that they were not. For the human soul can be a partaker in the truth, but the truth is the immutable God above it. Hence whoever turns away from that truth and toward himself, rejoicing not in God who rules and enlightens him but rather in his own seemingly free movements, becomes dark by reason of the lie. TWO BOOKS ON GENESIS AGAINST THE MANICHAEANS 2.16.24.[20]

---

[19]PG 53:138; FC 74:228. [20]FC 84:119-20.

3:9-13 GOD QUESTIONS ADAM AND EVE

[9]*But the LORD God called to the man,* and said to him, "Where are you?"† [10]And he said, "I heard the sound‡ of thee in the garden,§ and I was afraid, because I was naked; and I hid myself." [11]He said, "Who told you that you were naked? Have you eaten of the tree# of which I commanded you not to eat?" [12]The man* said, "The woman whom thou gavest to be with me, she gave me fruit of the tree, and I ate." [13]Then the LORD God said to the woman, "What is this that you have done?" The woman said, "The serpent beguiled me, and I ate."*

*LXX Adam †LXX Adam, where are you? ‡LXX voice §LXX paradise #LXX adds the only one

OVERVIEW: God's words "Where are you?" mean that there was nowhere Adam could be, once God was not in him as a consequence of his sin (AUGUSTINE). The question itself was a reproof (AMBROSE). It was not asked as though God did not know the answer (CHRYsostom). They also emphasize the foolishness of Adam and Eve's transgression (EPHREM) but at the same time predict the salvation of humankind in Christ (NOVATIAN).

Adam's answer to God's question is a wretched error. It also reveals that Adam thinks that his transgression is merely venial (AUGUSTINE). God is patient with Adam, to whom he gives the opportunity to reply. But Adam refuses to confess his sin and puts the blame on Eve (SYMEON THE NEW THEOLOGIAN). By saying that he sinned because of the woman given to him by God, Adam tries to attribute his sinning to God (AUGUSTINE). Eve also fails to confess her sin and says that the serpent beguiled her (SYMEON THE NEW THEOLOGIAN). These evasions and attempts at self-justification show an unwillingness to repent (EPHREM, DOROTHEUS OF GAZA).

3:9 God Calls to the Man

THE QUESTION. AMBROSE: What then does he mean by "Adam, where art thou?" Does he not mean "in what circumstance" are you; not, "in what place?" It is therefore not a question but a reproof. From what condition of goodness, beatitude and grace, he means to say, have you fallen into this state of misery? You have forsaken eternal life. You have entombed yourself in the ways of sin and death. PARADISE 14.70.[1]

GOD DESERTS ADAM'S SOUL. AUGUSTINE: Insofar as a rebellion of the flesh against the rebellious soul prompted our parents to cover their shame, they experienced one kind of death—God's desertion of the soul. It was this death that was intimated when God

asked Adam, who was beside himself with fear and in hiding, "Where are you?" This was not asked, of course, because God did not know the answer. Rather, it was asked in order to scold Adam by reminding him that there really was nowhere that he could be, once God was not in him. CITY OF GOD 13.15.[2]

GOD'S WORDS CONDEMN HUMAN FOOLISHNESS. EPHREM THE SYRIAN: "Where are you, Adam?" Are you trapped in the imagined godlikeness that the serpent falsely promised you? Or are you prepared for the death that I, the Lord, decreed for you? Would that you had considered the fruits! Suppose, Adam, that instead of a serpent who might be the most despicable creature of all, an angel or a god had come to you? Would you have despised the commandment of him who gave you all these things, heeding instead the counsel of one who had not yet done you any good? Would you then have considered evil the very One who formed you out of nothing? Would you despise the One who made you a second god over creation? Would you dare instead to consider good the very fallen one who gave you only a verbal promise of some good? If another god were to come to you in power, should you not have rejected his advice? How much more then in the case of a serpent who came to you with no power, with no wondrous deeds but with only the empty word that it spoke to you? COMMENTARY ON GENESIS 2.26.1-2.[3]

GOD'S SEARCH DOES NOT IMPLY IGNORANCE. NOVATIAN: The fact that God searches for [Adam] does not proceed from

---

[1]FC 42:348. [2]FC 14:318*. [3]FC 91:116*.

any ignorance on the part of God, but it manifests man's hope of a future discovery and salvation in Christ. ON THE TRINITY 1.12.[4]

WHY DID GOD ASK? CHRYSOSTOM: You see, since he was not unaware of the truth when he asked them but rather knew, and knew very well, he shows consideration for their limitations so as to demonstrate his own loving kindness, and he invites them to make admission of their faults. HOMILIES ON GENESIS 17.22.[5]

3:10-12 Fearing and Hiding from God

THE ATTEMPT AT SELF-JUSTIFICATION. EPHREM THE SYRIAN: Instead of confessing what he had done, which would have helped him, he related what had been done to him, which did not help him at all. . . . Adam again failed to confess his folly and blamed the woman. COMMENTARY ON GENESIS 2.27.1-2[6]

GOD IS NOT OFFENDED AT HUMAN NAKEDNESS. AUGUSTINE: When Adam heard God's voice, he answered that he hid because he was naked. His answer was a wretched error, as if a man naked, as God had made him, could be displeasing to him. It is a distinguishing mark of error that whatever anyone finds personally displeasing he imagines is displeasing to God as well. We should understand in a lofty sense the words of the Lord, "Who told you that you were naked, unless because you have eaten from that tree about which I told you that from it alone you should not eat?" Before he was naked of any dissimulation and clothed with the divine light. From this light he turned away and turned toward himself. This is the meaning of his having eaten from that tree. He saw his nakedness, and it was displeasing to himself because he did not have

anything of his own. TWO BOOKS ON GENESIS AGAINST THE MANICHAEANS 2.16.24.[7]

ADAM DOES NOT REALIZE THE GRAVITY OF HIS TRANSGRESSION. AUGUSTINE: Insofar as he as yet had no experience of the divine severity, Adam could be deceived in believing that his transgression was merely venial. And therefore he was at least not deceived in the same way that Eve was. He was merely mistaken concerning the judgment that would follow his attempt to excuse himself: "The woman you placed at my side gave me fruit from the tree, and I ate." To summarize briefly: though not equally deceived by believing the serpent, they equally sinned and were caught and ensnared by the devil. CITY OF GOD 14.11.[8]

THE LACK OF REPENTANCE. EPHREM THE SYRIAN: If Adam and Eve had sought to repent after they had transgressed the commandment, even though they would not have regained that which they had possessed before their transgression of the commandment, they would have escaped from the curses that were decreed on the earth and upon them. COMMENTARY ON GENESIS 2.23.2.[9]

ADAM HID HIS DECEPTION. SYMEON THE NEW THEOLOGIAN: Do you see, dear friend, how patient God is? For when he said, "Adam, where are you?" and when Adam did not at once confess his sin but said, "I heard your voice, O Lord, and realized that I am naked and hid myself," God was not angered, nor did he immediately turn away. Rather, he

---

[4]FC 67:25. [5]PG 53:140; FC 17:233. [6]FC 91:117. [7]FC 84:120-21. [8]FC 14:378-79. [9]FC 91:114-15.

gave him the opportunity of a second reply and said, "Who told you that you are naked? Unless you ate of the tree of which I commanded you not to eat." Consider how profound are the words of God's wisdom. He says, "Why do you say that you are naked but hide your sin? Do you really think that I see only your body but do not see your heart and your thoughts?" Since Adam was deceived he hoped that God would not know his sin. He said something like this to himself, "If I say that I am naked, God in his ignorance will say, 'Why are you naked?' Then I shall have to deny and say, 'I do not know,' and so I shall not be caught by him and he will give me back the garment that I had at first. If not, as long as he does not cast me out, he will not exile me!" While he was thinking these thoughts . . . God, unwilling to multiply his guilt, says, "How did you realize that you are naked? Unless you ate of the tree of which I commanded you not to eat." It is as though he said, "Do you really think that you can hide from me? Do you imagine that I do not know what you have done? Will you not say, 'I have sinned?' Say, O scoundrel, 'Yes, it is true, Master, I have transgressed your command. I have fallen by listening to the woman's counsel, I am greatly at fault for doing what she said and disobeying your word. Have mercy on me!'" But he does not humble himself, he does not bend. The neck of his heart is like a sinew of iron! For had he said this he might have stayed in paradise. By this one word he might have spared himself that whole cycle of evils without number that he endured by his expulsion and in spending so many centuries in hell. DISCOURSES 5.5.[10]

ADAM TRIES TO ATTRIBUTE HIS SINNING TO GOD. AUGUSTINE: Then, as is quite common in cases of pride, he does not accuse himself of having consented to the woman but pushes the fault off upon the woman. Thus, as if out of a cleverness the poor fellow had conceived, he cunningly tried to attribute his sinning to God himself. For he did not just say, "the woman gave to me," but added on, "the woman you gave to me." Nothing is as characteristic of sinners as to want to attribute to God everything for which they are accused. This arises from that vein of pride. For man sinned in wishing to be like God, that is, to be free from his dominion, as God is free from all dominion, since he is the Lord of all. TWO BOOKS ON GENESIS AGAINST THE MANICHAEANS 2.17.25.[11]

3:13 God Questions the Woman

EVE'S EVASIONS. EPHREM THE SYRIAN: Since Adam did not wish to confess his folly, God came down to question Eve and said to her, "What is this that you have done?" Eve too, instead of making supplication with her tears and bearing the fault herself so that mercy might take hold of both her and her husband, responded by saying not "The serpent counseled or seduced me" but "The serpent deceived me and I ate."

When the two of them had been questioned and were both found to be wanting in remorse or true contrition, God went down to the serpent not to make inquiry but to render punishment. For where there is opportunity for repentance, it would be right to inquire, but to one who is a stranger to repentance, judgment is fitting. COMMENTARY ON GENESIS 2.28-29.[12]

---

[10]*SNTD* 95-96. [11]FC 84:121. [12]FC 91:118.

EVE ALSO REFUSES TO CONFESS HER SIN.
SYMEON THE NEW THEOLOGIAN: When God
had left Adam, he came to Eve. He wanted to
show her that she too would be cast out, if she
was unwilling to repent. So he said, "What is
this that you have done?" so that she at least
might be able to say, "I have sinned." Why else
did God need to speak these words to her,
unless indeed to enable her to say, "In my folly,
O Master, I, a lowly wretch, have done this,
and have disobeyed you. Have mercy on me!"
But she did not say this. What did she say?
"The serpent beguiled me." How senseless! So
you have spoken with the serpent, who speaks
against your Master? Him you have preferred
to God who made you. You have valued his
advice more highly and held it to be truer than
the commandment of your Master! So, when
Eve too was unable to say, "I have sinned,"
both were cast out from the place of enjoyment. They were banished from paradise and
from God. DISCOURSES 5.6.[13]

THE UNWILLINGNESS TO REPENT. DOR-
OTHEUS OF GAZA: Again, after Adam had
done wrong God gave him a chance to repent
and be forgiven, and yet he kept on being stiff-
necked and unrepentant. For God came to
him and said, "Adam, where are you?" instead
of saying, "From what glory are you come to
this? Are you not ashamed? Why did you sin?
Why did you go astray?"—as if urging him
sharply to say, "Forgive me!" But there was no
sign of humility. There was no change of heart
but rather the contrary. He replied, "The wife
that you gave me"—mark you, not "my
wife"—"deceived me." "The wife that *you* gave
me," as if to say, "this disaster *you* placed on my
head." So it is, my brethren, when a man has
not the guts to accuse himself, he does not
scruple to accuse God himself. Then God
came to Eve and said to her, "Why did you not
keep the command I gave you?" as if saying, "If
you would only say, 'Forgive me,' to humble
your soul and be forgiven." And again, not a
word! No "forgive me." She only answered,
"The serpent deceived me!"—as if to say, if
the serpent did wrong, what concern is that to
me? What are you doing, you wretches? Kneel
in repentance, acknowledge your fault, take
pity on your nakedness. But neither the one
nor the other stooped to self-accusation, no
trace of humility was found in either of them.

And now look and consider how this was
only an anticipation of our own state! See how
many and great the evils it has brought on
us—this self-justification, this holding fast to
our own will, this obstinacy in being our own
guide. SPIRITUAL INSTRUCTION 1.[14]

---

[13]*SNTD* 97. [14]*CS* 33:82-83.

3:14-15 THE PUNISHMENT OF THE SERPENT

¹⁴*The L*ORD *God said to the serpent,*
  "Because you have done this,
    cursed are you above all cattle,
    and above all wild animals;
  upon* your belly you shall go,
    and dust† you shall eat
    all the days of your life.
  ¹⁵*I will put enmity between you and the woman,*
    and between your seed and her seed;
  he‡ shall bruise§ your head,
    and you shall bruise§ his heel."

*LXX adds your chest and †*LXX* earth ‡*Vulgate* she §*LXX* guard *or* watch for

OVERVIEW: God punishes the serpent without inquiring because it is a stranger to repentance. God curses the serpent above all beasts because it deceived Adam and Eve, who ruled all beasts (EPHREM). Its punishment represents the punishment of the devil (AMBROSE, AUGUSTINE). "Dust you shall eat" means that the devil will look for and destroy those men who are earthly minded and put all their hope in the earth (CAESARIUS OF ARLES). God puts enmity between the serpent and the woman because we cannot be tempted by the devil except through that animal aspect that reveals the image or exemplification of the woman in the one whole man (AUGUSTINE). The serpent is not destroyed by God in order to warn men against the danger of sin (AMBROSE). God's words, "I will put enmity between you and the woman, and between your seed and her seed," can be read as a prefiguring of the victory of Christ over the devil (IRENAEUS).

3:14 God Curses the Serpent

THE SERPENT IS A STRANGER TO REPENTANCE. EPHREM THE SYRIAN: When [Adam and Eve] had been questioned and were both found to be wanting in remorse or true contrition, God went down to the serpent, not to make inquiry but to render punishment. For where there is opportunity for repentance, it would be right to inquire, but to one who is a stranger to repentance, judgment is fitting. It is so that you might know that the serpent is not capable of repentance, that when God said to it, "Because you have done this, cursed are you above every beast," the serpent did not say, "I did not do it," because it was afraid to lie, nor did it say, "I did it," because it was a stranger to repentance. COMMENTARY ON GENESIS 2.29.1.[1]

---

[1] FC 91:118.

88

GOD CURSES IT ABOVE ALL BEASTS.
EPHREM THE SYRIAN: "Cursed are you above every beast," because you deceived those who rule over all the beasts. Instead of being more clever than all the beasts you will be more cursed than all the beasts and "on your belly shall you go," because you brought birth pangs upon the race of women. And "dust you shall eat all days of your life," because you deprived Adam and Eve from eating of the tree of life. COMMENTARY ON GENESIS 2.29.2.[2]

THE ORDER OF CONDEMNATION. AMBROSE: The serpent is a type of the pleasures of the body. The woman stands for our senses and the man for our minds. Pleasure stirs the senses, which in turn have their effect on the mind. Pleasure, therefore, is the primary source of sin. For this reason, do not wonder at the fact that by God's judgment the serpent was first condemned, then the woman and finally the man. The order of condemnation, too, corresponded to that of the crimes committed, for pleasure usually captivates the senses, and the senses captivate the mind. To convince you that the serpent is the type of pleasure, take note of his condemnation. "On your breast and on your belly shall you crawl," we read. Only those who live for the pleasures of the stomach can be said to walk on their bellies, "whose god is their belly and their glory is their shame,"[3] who eat of what is earthy and who, weighed down with food, are bent over toward what is of earth. The serpent is well called the symbol of pleasure in that, intent on food, he seems to feed on the earth: "On your breast and on your belly shall you crawl, dust shall you eat all the days of your life." PARADISE 15.73-74.[4]

THE PUNISHMENT OF THE SERPENT IS THE

PUNISHMENT OF THE DEVIL. AUGUSTINE: The serpent is not now questioned but received punishment first, because he cannot confess his sin. One who cannot confess sin has no ground at all for excusing himself. There is no mention now of that condemnation of the devil that is reserved for the last judgment, of which the Lord speaks when he says, "Depart into the eternal fire, which has been prepared for the devil and his angels."[5] Rather it mentions that punishment of his against which we must be on guard. For his punishment is that he has in his power those who despise the command of God. The words by which sentence is pronounced against him make this clear. The punishment is the greater because he rejoices over this unhappy power, whereas before his fall he was accustomed to rejoice in the sublime truth, in which he did not remain. Hence even the cattle are set ahead of him, not in power but in the preservation of their nature. For cattle did not lose a heavenly happiness that they never had but live their life in the nature that they received. Hence God said to him, "You will creep upon your chest and belly." We can see this in the snake as well, and the expression is transferred from that visible animal to this invisible enemy of ours. For the term *chest* signifies "pride" because the strong drives of the soul rule there. The term *belly* signifies "carnal desire" because that part of the body is recognized as softer. Since by these means he creeps up on those whom he wants to deceive, God said, "You will creep upon your chest and belly." TWO BOOKS ON GENESIS AGAINST THE MANICHAEANS 2.17.26.[6]

---

[2]FC 91:118-19. [3]Phil 3:19. [4]FC 42:351-52. [5]Mt 25:41. [6]FC 84:121-22.

THE DEVIL DESTROYS THOSE WHO ARE EARTHLY MINDED. CAESARIUS OF ARLES:

God said to the devil: "Dust you shall eat." Is it the earth that we tread underfoot that the devil eats, brethren? No, it is people who are earthly minded, sensual and proud, who love the earth and place all their hopes in it. They labor entirely for carnal advantages, rather for such pleasures, and think little or nothing of the salvation of their souls. People like these, then, the devil seeks. He seems to do so justly, for they were assigned to him at the beginning of the world when it was said to him, "Dust you shall eat." Therefore let each one look to his own conscience. If he sees that he has greater care for his body than for his soul, let him fear that he will become the food of the serpent. SERMONS 136.[7]

3:15 Enmity Between the Serpent and the Woman

SYMBOLIC MEANING OF THE ENMITY.

AUGUSTINE: Enmities are not set between the serpent and the man but between the serpent and the woman. This is surely not because he fails to deceive and tempt men, is it? On the contrary, it is clear that he does deceive them. Or is it because he did not deceive Adam but his woman? But is the serpent then not the enemy of the man to whom that deception came through his woman, especially since "I will place enmity between you and the woman" is stated in the future? If the reason is that he did not thereafter deceive Adam, it is also true that he did not thereafter deceive Eve. Hence, why does Scripture put it this way? To show clearly that we cannot be tempted by the devil except through that animal part, which reveals, so to speak, the image or exemplification of the woman in the one

whole man. TWO BOOKS ON GENESIS AGAINST THE MANICHAEANS 2.18.28.[8]

GOD DOES NOT DESTROY THE SERPENT.

AMBROSE: God judged that evil was to be held in check for a time rather than to be destroyed, so that he says to the serpent, "I will put enmity between you and the woman, and between your seed and the seed of the woman. She shall watch for your head and you for her heel." Where enmities remain, there remains discord and the desire to do harm. Where there is the desire to do harm, there evil is established. Therefore there is discord between the serpent and the woman. Evil is at the base of discord; thus evil has not been taken away. Indeed, it has been reserved for the serpent, that he might watch for the woman's heel and the heel of her seed, so as to do harm and infuse his poison. Therefore let us not walk in earthly things, and the serpent will not be able to harm us. Let us put on sandals of the gospel that shut out the serpent's poison and blunt his bites that we may be provided with covering on our feet by the gospel. FLIGHT FROM THE WORLD 7.43.[9]

ENMITY A PREFIGURATION OF THE VICTORY OF CHRIST OVER THE DEVIL. IRENAEUS:

Christ completely renewed all things, both taking up the battle against our enemy and crushing him who at the beginning had led us captive in Adam, trampling on his head, as you find in Genesis that God said to the serpent, "I will put enmity between you and the woman, and between your seed and the seed of the woman. He will be on the watch for your head, and you will be on the watch for

---

[7]FC 47:268. [8]FC 84:123. [9]FC 65:313-14.

his heel." From then on it was proclaimed that he who was to be born of a virgin, after the likeness of Adam, would be on the watch for the serpent's head. This is the seed of which the apostle says in the letter to the Galatians, "The law of works was established until the seed should come to whom the promise was made."[10] He shows this still more clearly in the same epistle when he says, "But when the fullness of time was come, God sent his Son, made of a woman."[11] The enemy would not have been justly conquered unless it had been a man made of woman who conquered him. For it was by a woman that he had power over man from the beginning, setting himself up in opposition to man. Because of this the Lord also declares himself to be the Son of Man, so renewing in himself that primal man from whom the formation of man by woman began, that as our race went down to death by a man who overcame, and as death won the palm of victory over us by a man, so we might by a man receive the palm of victory over death. AGAINST HERESIES 5.21.1.[12]

---

[10]Gal 3:19. [11]Gal 4:4. [12]LQAH 2:381.

3:16-19 THE PUNISHMENT OF ADAM AND EVE

[16]*To the woman he said,*

"I will greatly multiply your pain in childbearing;
in pain you shall bring forth children,
yet your desire shall be for your husband,
and he shall rule over you."

[17]*And to Adam he said,*

"Because you have listened to the voice of your wife,
and have eaten of the tree
of which I commanded you,
'You shall not eat of it,'
cursed is the ground [because of you];*
in toil you shall eat of it all the days of your life;
[18]*thorns and thistles it shall bring forth to you;*
and you shall eat the plants of the field.
[19]*In the sweat of your face*
you shall eat bread
till you return to the ground,

for out of it you were taken;
you are dust,†
    and to dust† you shall return."

*LXX in your works †LXX earth

OVERVIEW: The snake is punished first in order to give Eve and Adam the possibility to repent (EPHREM). The pains imposed on Eve in bringing forth children symbolize the pains that human beings suffer in giving birth to temperance in their soul (AUGUSTINE, CHRYSOSTOM). Marriage is devised in order that the human race might be preserved by the generation of children (JOHN OF DAMASCUS). If Adam and Eve had not sinned, the birthing of children would have taken place in paradise without inordinate concupiscence (AUGUSTINE).

Adam's headship was turned upside down by Eve's action (CHRYSOSTOM). The irony of Adam's curse is that a life of contentment had been promised under set boundaries, but the life he chose apart from those boundaries was thorns, thistles and labor (CYRIL OF ALEXANDRIA, CHRYSOSTOM). The whole creation is destined to share in the curse of man and woman (MACARIUS THE GREAT).

The labors and sorrow imposed on Adam and all human progeny are viewed by the Fathers as both spiritual (AUGUSTINE) and physical (CHRYSOSTOM). The thorns that grow on earth symbolize the sins of humankind removed by Christ (TERTULLIAN). Death was not imposed by God on Adam and Eve but was a consequence of their deliberate sin (AMBROSE). "You shall return to dust" does not mean that human flesh perishes completely but that it is transformed in order to be resurrected by its Creator. Christ, wanting to resurrect that which "had gone into dust," took an earthly body (ORIGEN).

3:16 *The Woman's Punishment*

AFTER THE SERPENT'S PUNISHMENT, ADAM AND EVE DO NOT REPENT. EPHREM THE SYRIAN: The punishment decreed against the serpent was justly decreed. Why? Because it was fitting that punishment return to the place where folly begins. The entire reason God began with this impious creature was so that, when justice appeased its anger on this creature, Adam and Eve should grow afraid and repent so that there might be a possibility for grace to preserve them from the curses of justice. But when the serpent had been cursed and Adam and Eve had still made no supplication, God came to them with punishment. He came to Eve first, because it was through her that the sin was handed on to Adam. COMMENTARY ON GENESIS 2.30.1.[1]

THE WOMAN'S CURSE. CHRYSOSTOM: See the Lord's goodness, how much mildness he employs despite such a terrible fall. "I will greatly aggravate the pain of your labor." My intention had been, he is saying, for you to have a life free of trouble and distress, rid of all pain and grief, filled with every pleasure and with no sense of bodily needs despite your bodily condition. But since you misused such indulgence, and the abundance of good things led you into such ingratitude, accordingly I impose this curb on you to prevent your fur-

---

[1]FC 91:119*.

ther running riot, and I sentence you to painful labor. "I will greatly aggravate the pain of your labor; in pain you will bear children."

I will ensure, he is saying, that the generation of children, a reason for great satisfaction, for you will begin with pain so that each time without fail you will personally have a reminder, through the distress and the pain of each birth, of the magnitude of this sin of disobedience.... In the beginning I created you equal in esteem to your husband, and my intention was that in everything you would share with him as an equal, and as I entrusted control of everything to your husband, so did I to you; but you abused your equality of status. Hence I subject you to your husband. HOMILIES ON GENESIS 17.30-31, 36.[2]

SYMBOLIC MEANING OF THE PUNISHMENT IMPOSED ON EVE. AUGUSTINE: There is no question about the punishment of the woman. For she clearly has her pains and sighs multiplied in the woes of this life. Although her bearing her children in pain is fulfilled in this visible woman, our consideration should nevertheless be recalled to that more hidden woman. For even in animals the females bear offspring with pain, and this is in their case the condition of mortality rather than the punishment of sin. Hence, it is possible that this be the condition of mortal bodies even in the females of humans. But this is the great punishment: they have come to the present bodily mortality from their former immortality. Still there is a great mystery in this sentence, because there is no restraint from carnal desire, which does not have pain in the beginning, until habit has been bent toward improvement. When this has come about, it is as though a child is born, that is, the good habit disposes our

intentions toward the good deed. In order that this habit might be born, there was a painful struggle with bad habit. Scripture adds after the birth, "You will turn to your man, and he will rule over you." ... What can this mean except that when that part of the soul held by carnal joys has, in willing to conquer a bad habit, suffered difficulty and pain and in this way brought forth a good habit, it now more carefully and diligently obeys reason as its husband? And taught by its pains, it turns to reason and willingly obeys its commands lest it again decline to some harmful habit. TWO BOOKS ON GENESIS AGAINST THE MANICHAEANS 2.19.29.[3]

MARRIAGE DEVISED FOR THE PRESERVATION OF HUMANITY. JOHN OF DAMASCUS: Virginity was practiced in paradise. Indeed, sacred Scripture says that "they were naked, to wit, Adam and Eve, and were not ashamed." However, once they had fallen, they knew that they were naked, and being ashamed they sewed together aprons for themselves. After the fall, when Adam heard "Dust thou art, and unto dust you shall return," and death entered into the world through transgression, then Adam knew his wife, who conceived and brought forth. And so to keep the race from dwindling and being destroyed by death, marriage was devised, so that by the begetting of children the race of men might be preserved. ORTHODOX FAITH 4.24.[4]

PROCREATION WOULD HAVE TAKEN PLACE IN PARADISE. AUGUSTINE: Why, therefore, may we not assume that the first couple before they sinned could have given a command to

[2]FC 74:238, 240. [3]FC 84:123-24. [4]FC 37:394.

their genital organs for the purpose of procreation as they did to the other members that the soul is accustomed to move to perform various tasks without any trouble and without any craving for pleasure? For the almighty Creator, worthy of praise beyond all words, who is great even in the least of his works, has given to the bees the power of reproducing their young just as they produce wax and honey. Why, then, should it seem beyond belief that he made the bodies of the first human beings in such a way that, if they had not sinned and had not immediately thereupon contracted a disease that would bring death, they would move the members by which offspring are generated in the same way that one commands his feet when he walks, so that conception would take place without disordered passions and birth without pain? But as it is, by disobeying God's command they deserved to experience in their members, where death now reigned, the movement of a law at war with the law of the mind. This is a movement that marriage regulates and continence controls and constrains, so that where punishment has followed sin, there correction may follow punishment.[5] ON THE LITERAL INTERPRETATION OF GENESIS 9.10.18.[6]

3:17-18 The Man's Punishment

ADAM'S RESPONSIBILITY FOR EVE DEFAULTED. CHRYSOSTOM: After all, you are head of your wife, and she has been created for your sake; but you have inverted the proper order: not only have you failed to keep her on the straight and narrow but you have been dragged down with her, and whereas the rest of the body should follow the head, the contrary has in fact occurred, the head following the rest of the body, turning things upside down. HOMILIES ON GENESIS 17.18.[7]

SPIRITUAL ASPECT OF THE PUNISHMENT IMPOSED ON THE MAN. AUGUSTINE: What shall we say about the judgment pronounced against the man? Are we perhaps to think that the rich, for whom the necessities of life come easily and who do not labor on the earth, have escaped this punishment? It says, "The earth will be cursed for you in all your works, and you shall eat from it in sadness and groaning all the days of your life. It will bring forth thorns and thistles for you, and you will eat the grain of your field. In the sweat of your brow you will eat your bread until you return to the earth from which you were taken, for you are earth, and you will return to the earth." It is certainly clear that no one escapes this sentence. For anyone born in this life has difficulty in discovering the truth because of the corruptible body. For as Solomon says, "The body that is corrupted weighs down the soul, and the earthly habitation presses down the mind that thinks many thoughts."[8] These are the labors and sorrows that man has from the earth. The thorns and thistles are the prickings of torturous questions or thoughts concerned with providing for this life. TWO BOOKS ON GENESIS AGAINST THE MANICHAEANS 2.20.30.[9]

THE PHYSICAL ASPECT OF THE PUNISHMENT OF MAN. CHRYSOSTOM: Since man had shown great disobedience, God cast him forth from his life in paradise. God curbed man's spirit for the future, so that he might not leap farther away. He condemned him to a life of

---

[5]Cf. passages cited on pp. 37-39. [6]ACW 42:81-82. [7]FC 74:231. [8]Wis 9:15. [9]FC 84:125.

toil and labor, speaking to him in some such fashion as this: "The ease and security that were yours in abundance led you to this great disobedience. They made you forget my commandments. You had nothing to do. That led you to think thoughts too haughty for your own nature. . . . Therefore, I condemn you to toil and labor, so that while tilling the earth, you may never forget your disobedience and the vileness of your nature." BAPTISMAL INSTRUCTION 2.4-5.[10]

SYMBOLISM OF THE THORNS. TERTULLIAN: To what kind of a crown, I ask you, did Christ Jesus submit for the salvation of both sexes? He who is the head of man and the glory of woman and the husband of the church—what kind of crown? It was made from thorns and thistles. They stood as a symbol of the sins that the soil of the flesh brought forth for us but that the power of the cross removed, blunting every sting of death since the head of the Lord bore its pain. And beside the symbol, we are reminded also of the scornful abuse, the degradation and the vileness of his cruel tormentors. ON THE CROWN 14.3.[11]

MEANING OF THE CURSES. CHRYSOSTOM: Behold the reminders of the curse: thorns it will bring forth, he says, and thistles so as to give rise to great labor and discomfort, and I will ensure you pass the whole time with pain so that this experience may prove a brake on your getting ideas above your station, and you may instead have a thought to your own makeup and never again bear to be deceived in these matters.

"You are to eat of the grass of the field. In the sweat of your brow may you eat your bread." See how after his disobedience everything is imposed on him in an opposite way to his former life style: My intention in bringing you into the world, he is saying, was that you should live your life without pain or toil, difficulty or sweat, and that you should be in a state of enjoyment and prosperity, and not be subject to the needs of the body but be free from all such and have the good fortune to experience complete freedom. Since, however, such indulgence was of no benefit to you, accordingly I curse the ground so that it will not in future yield its harvest as before without tilling and ploughing. Instead I invest you with great labor, toil and difficulty, and with unremitting pain and despair, and I am ensuring that everything you do is achieved only by sweat so that under pressure from these you may have continual guidance in keeping to limits and recognizing your own makeup. HOMILIES ON GENESIS 17.40-41.[12]

PURPOSE OF THE CREATURE. PSEUDO-MACARIUS: Adam was created pure by God for his service. All these creatures were given to him to serve him. He was destined to be the lord and king of all creatures. But when the evil word came to him and conversed with him, he first received it through an external hearing. Then it penetrated into his heart and took charge of his whole being. When he was thus captured, creation, which ministered and served him, was captured with him. FIFTY SPIRITUAL HOMILIES 11.5.[13]

3:19 *"To Dust You Shall Return"*

MIXING LOVE WITH PUNISHMENT. THE-

---

[10]ACW 31:44-45. [11]FC 40:265. [12]PG 53:146; FC 74:243-44. [13]PMFSH 92.

ODORET OF CYR: Because the devil was envious and the woman was gullible, humankind was immediately cast out of paradise. It was made to walk the very earth from which Adam had just been created, inheriting sweat, toil and hard labor. Along with Adam, the earth and all living things that followed were subjected to evil, being restrained like a horse that is bridled. For since Adam did not use good judgment during the age of paradise— an age which was free from sorrow and pain—he was joined to adversity. Through his suffering he might then get rid of the disease which had come upon him in the midst of paradise.

By punishing us with death, the lawgiver cut off the spread of sin. And yet through that very punishment he also demonstrated his love for us. He bound sin and death together when he gave the law, placing the sinner under punishment of death. And yet he ordered things in such a way that the punishment might in itself serve the goal of salvation. For death brings about separation from this life and brings evil works to an end. It sets us free from labor, sweat and pain, and ends the suffering of the body. Thus the Judge mixes his love for us with punishment. ON THE INCARNATION OF THE LORD 6.1.[14]

GOD DOES NOT IMPOSE DEATH ON ADAM AND EVE. AMBROSE: Still another problem arises. "From what source did death come to Adam? Was it from the nature of a tree of this sort or actually from God?" If we ascribe this to the nature of the tree, then the fruit of this tree seems to be superior to the vivifying power of the breath of God, since its fruit would have drawn into death's toils him on whom the divine breath had bestowed life. If we maintain that God is the responsible

cause of death, then we can be held to accuse him of inconsistency. We seem to accuse him of being so devoid of beneficence as to be unwilling to pardon when he had the power to do so or of being powerless if he was unable to forgive. Let us see, therefore, how this question can be resolved. The solution, unless I am mistaken, lies in the fact that since disobedience was the cause of death, for that very reason not God but man himself was the agent of his own death. If, for example, a physician were to prescribe to a patient what he thought should be avoided, and if the patient felt that these prohibitions were unnecessary, the physician is not responsible for the patient's death. Surely in that case the patient is guilty of causing his own death. Hence God as a good physician forbade Adam to eat what would be injurious to him. PARADISE 7.35.[15]

HUMAN FLESH DOES NOT PERISH COMPLETELY. ORIGEN: Our flesh indeed is considered by the uneducated and by unbelievers to perish so completely after death that nothing whatever of its substance is left. We, however, who believe in its resurrection, know that death only causes a change in it and that its substance certainly persists and is restored to life again at a definite time by the will of its Creator and once more undergoes a transformation. What was at first flesh, "from the earth, a man of dust,"[16] and was then dissolved through death and again made dust and ashes—for "dust you are," it is written, "and unto dust shall you return"—is raised again from the earth. Afterwards, as the merits of the indwelling soul shall demand, the person

[14]PG 75:1424. [15]FC 42:313. [16]Cf. 1 Cor 15:47.

advances to the glory of a spiritual body.[17] On First Principles 3.6.5.[18]

CHRIST RESURRECTS THAT WHICH HAD GONE INTO DUST. ORIGEN: Scripture says, "A consecrated linen tunic will be put on."[19] Think of flax thread that comes from the earth. Imagine that the flax thread becomes a sanctified linen tunic that Christ, the true high priest, puts on when he takes up the nature of an earthly body. Remember that it is said about the body that "it is earth and it will go into the earth." Therefore, my Lord and Savior, wanting to resurrect that which had gone into the earth, took an earthly body that he might carry it raised up from earth to heaven. And the assertion in the law that the high priest is clothed "with a linen tunic" contains this mystery. But that it added "consecrated" must not be heard as superfluous. For the "tunic" that was the flesh of Christ was "consecrated," for it was not conceived from the seed of man but begotten of the Holy Spirit. **HOMILIES ON LEVITICUS 9.2.3.**[20]

---

[17]Cf. 1 Cor 15:44. [18]OFP 251. [19]Lev 16:4. [20]FC 83:178-79.

3:20-21 GOD CLOTHES ADAM AND EVE WITH GARMENTS OF SKIN

[20]*The man called his wife's name Eve,*[f]** because she was the mother of all living.* [21]*And the* LORD *God made for Adam and for his wife garments of skins, and clothed them.*

f *The name in Hebrew resembles the word for "living"* **LXX reads Zōē ("life") here, though in later chapters it reads Eva.*

OVERVIEW: Thanks to the knowledge with which Adam was endowed by God, he was able to give names first to all the animals and then to Eve (EPHREM). Eve, who initiated transgression, was called "Life" because she was given responsibility for the succession of those who came to birth (CLEMENT OF ALEXANDRIA). The garments of skin were probably created by God, and no animal was killed in the presence of Adam and Eve in order to provide them with clothes (EPHREM). Adam and Eve were stripped of their first garment of innocence and immortality, and due to their pride they received garments of skin (AUGUSTINE). These garments of skin are a symbol of the mortality that Adam received because of his skin and of his frailty, which came from the corruption of the flesh (ORIGEN, GREGORY OF NYSSA).

3:20 The Mother of All Living

ADAM FREE TO PURSUE KNOWLEDGE. EPHREM THE SYRIAN:

With that manifest knowledge
which God gave to Adam,
whereby he gave names to Eve
and to the animals,
God did not reveal the discoveries
of things that were concealed;
but in the case
of that hidden knowledge
from the stars downward,
Adam was able to pursue
enquiry into all
that is within this universe.
HYMNS ON PARADISE 12.16.[1]

EVE IS CALLED LIFE. CLEMENT OF ALEXANDRIA: The woman who initiated transgression was called "Life," because she was responsible for the succession of those who came to birth and sinned. She thus became mother of the righteous and unrighteous alike. Each one of us shows himself to be just or willfully renders himself disobedient. STROMATEIS 3.65.1.[2]

3:21 God Clothes Adam and Eve

THE GARMENTS OF SKIN CREATED BY GOD. EPHREM THE SYRIAN: Were these garments from the skins of animals? Or were they created like the thistles and thorns that were created after the other works of creation had been completed? Because it was said that the "Lord made . . . and clothed them," it seems most likely that when their hands were placed over their leaves they found themselves clothed in garments of skin. Why would beasts have been killed in their presence? Perhaps this happened so that by the animal's flesh Adam and Eve might nourish their own bodies and that with the skins they might cover their nakedness, but also that by the death of the animals Adam and Eve might see

the death of their own bodies. COMMENTARY ON GENESIS 2.33.1.[3]

GARMENTS OF SKIN AS A PUNISHMENT OF PRIDE. AUGUSTINE: [Adam and Eve], who were stripped of their first garment [of innocence], deserved by their mortality garments of skin. For the true honor of man is to be the image and the likeness of God that is preserved only in relation to him by whom it is impressed. Hence, he clings to God so much the more, the less he loves what is his own. But through the desire of proving his own power, man by his own will falls down into himself as into a sort of [substitute] center. Since he, therefore, wishes to be like God, hence under no one, then as a punishment he is also driven from the center, which he himself is, down into the depths, that is, into those things wherein the beasts delight. Thus, since the likeness to God is his honor, the likeness to the beasts is his disgrace. ON THE TRINITY 12.11.16.[4]

THE GARMENTS OF SKIN A SYMBOL OF MORTALITY. ORIGEN: It is said that God made those miserable garments with which the first man was clothed after he had sinned. "For God made skin tunics and clothed Adam and his wife." Therefore, those were tunics of skin taken from animals. For with such as these, it was necessary for the sinner to be dressed. It says, "with skin tunics," which are a symbol of the mortality that he received because of his skin and of his frailty that came from the corruption of the flesh. But if you have been already washed from these and purified through the law of God, then Moses

---

[1]HOP 166. [2]FC 85:296. [3]FC 91:121-22. [4]FC 45:358.

will dress you with a garment of incorruptibility so that "your shame may never appear"[5] and "that what is mortal may be swallowed up by life."[6] HOMILIES ON LEVITICUS 6.2.7.[7]

DISORDER AND ORDER. GREGORY OF NYSSA: In the same way, when our nature becomes subject to the disequilibrium and paroxysm of disordered passions, it encounters those conditions that necessarily follow the life of the passions. But when it returns again to the blessedness of an ordered emotive life, it will no longer encounter the consequences of evil. Since whatever was added to human nature from the irrational life was not in us before humanity fell into passion, we shall also leave behind all the conditions that appear along with passion. If a man wearing a ragged tunic should be denuded of his garment, he would no longer see on himself the ugliness of what was discarded. Likewise, when we have put off that dead and ugly garment that was made for us from irrational skins (when I hear "skins" I interpret it as the form of the irrational nature that we have put on from our association with disordered passions), we throw off every part of our irrational skin along with the removal of the garment. These are the disruptions of harmony that we have received from "the irrational skin": sexual intercourse, conception, childbearing, dirt, lactation, nourishment, evacuation, gradual growth to maturity, the prime of life, old age, disease and death. ON THE SOUL AND THE RESURRECTION.[8]

---

[5]Ex 20:26. [6]2 Cor 5:4. [7]FC 83:120. [8]PG 46:61-62; NPNF 2 5:464-65.

3:22-24 ADAM AND EVE ARE EXILED FROM THE GARDEN OF EDEN

[22]Then the LORD God said, "Behold, the man* has become like one of us, knowing good and evil; and now, lest he put forth his hand and take also of the tree of life, and eat, and live for ever"— [23]therefore the LORD God sent him forth from the garden of Eden,† to till the ground from which he was taken. [24][He drove out the man; and at the east of the garden of Eden he placed]‡ the cherubim, and a flaming sword which turned every way, to guard the way to the tree of life.

*LXX Adam †LXX garden of delights ‡LXX He drove out Adam and settled him opposite the garden of delights, and he placed . . .

OVERVIEW: God lampoons Adam when he says, "He has become like one of us, knowing good and evil" (EPHREM). After the sin Adam conceives knowledge of evil that he did not have, but he does not lose the knowledge of good that he already had (JOHN CASSIAN).

Even though the tree of which Adam and Eve eat is called "the tree of the knowledge of good and evil," it gives them no knowledge (CHRYSOSTOM). God prevents Adam from eating again of the tree of life, in order that he may not live forever (EPHREM). Adam is not excluded against his will but dismissed according to his will (EPHREM), drawn down by the weight of his own sins to a place that suited him (AUGUSTINE). The cherubim, whom God places in paradise as the guard of the tree of life, represents the "fullness of knowledge," while the turning sword signifies the "temporal punishment" (AUGUSTINE). The cherubim belong to the highest hierarchical order (PSEUDO-DIONYSIUS). Christ removed the sword from the entry to paradise (EPHREM). The flame by which the cherubim blocked the entry into paradise is extinguished by Christ through the water of the bath of rebirth (BEDE). Martyrdom is a way to pass through the cherubim and the flaming sword that guard the access to the tree of life (ORIGEN).

3:22 Knowing Good and Evil

GOD LAMPOONS ADAM. EPHREM THE SYRIAN: God said, "Behold, Adam has become like one of us, knowing good and evil." Even though by saying, "He has become like one of us," he symbolically reveals the Trinity, the point is rather that God was mocking Adam in that Adam had previously been told, "You will become like God, knowing good and evil." Now even though after they ate the fruit Adam and Eve came to know these two things, before they ate the fruit they had perceived in reality only good, and they heard about evil only by hearsay. After they ate, however, a change occurred so that now they would only hear about good by hearsay,

whereas in reality they would taste only evil. For the glory with which they had been clothed passed away from them, while pain and disease that had been kept away from them now came to hold sway over them. COMMENTARY ON GENESIS 2.34.1-2.[1]

ADAM DOES NOT LOSE HIS KNOWLEDGE OF GOOD. JOHN CASSIAN: And how will that statement of the Lord stand, after the sin of the first man: "Behold, Adam is become like one of us, knowing good and evil?" For he must not to be thought to have been such before the sin that he was wholly ignorant of good. Otherwise, it must be admitted that he was created like an irrational and senseless animal; and this is quite absurd and foreign to the Catholic faith. No, rather, according to the pronouncement of the most wise Solomon, "God made man right,"[2] that is, to enjoy continually the knowledge of good alone. But they sought many thoughts. So they were made, as it was said, "knowing good and evil." After the fall, therefore, Adam conceived a knowledge of evil, which he did not have. But he did not lose the knowledge of good, which he did have. CONFERENCE 3.12.1-2.[3]

THE DEVIL LIES IN PROMISING THAT THE TREE GIVES KNOWLEDGE. CHRYSOSTOM: It is now necessary to say why, even though man did not receive the knowledge from the tree, it is called "the tree that gives the knowledge of good and evil;" for it is not a trifle to learn why a tree has such a name. In fact the devil said, "On the day when you eat of the fruit of the tree, your eyes will be opened and you will be like gods, knowing good and evil."[4] How

---

[1] FC 91:122. [2] Eccles 7:30. [3] ACW 57. [4] Gen 3:5.

can you maintain, you ask me, that it did not provide him with the knowledge of good and evil? Who said, in fact, that it provided him with this knowledge? The devil, you will answer. So do you put forward the testimony of the enemy and the conspirator? The devil said, "You will be gods." Did they really become gods? Therefore, since they did not become gods, they did not receive the knowledge of good and evil either. For the devil is a liar and never speaks the truth. In fact the Gospel says, "He never stays in the truth."[5] HOMILIES ON GENESIS 7.[6]

GOD PREVENTS ADAM FROM EATING OF THE TREE OF LIFE. EPHREM THE SYRIAN: If Adam had rashly eaten from the tree of knowledge he was commanded not to eat, how much faster would he hasten to the tree of life about which he had not been so commanded? But it was now decreed that they should live in toil, in sweat, in pains and in pangs. Therefore, lest Adam and Eve, after having eaten of this tree, live forever and remain in eternal lives of suffering, God forbade them to eat, after they were clothed with a curse, that which he had been prepared to give them before they incurred the curse and when they were still clothed with glory. COMMENTARY ON GENESIS 2.35.1.[7]

3:23 God Sends Adam and Eve from the Garden

GOD BANISHED ADAM FROM THE GARDEN. EPHREM THE SYRIAN:
When Adam sinned
God cast him forth from paradise,
but in his grace he granted him
the low ground beyond it,
settling him in the valley

below the foothills of paradise;
but when mankind even there continued
  to sin
they were blotted out,
and because they were unworthy
to be neighbors of paradise,
God commanded the ark
to cast them out on Mount Qardu.
HYMNS ON PARADISE 1.10.[8]

ADAM IS DISMISSED FROM PARADISE. AUGUSTINE: "And then, lest Adam stretch forth his hand to the tree of life and live forever, God dismissed him from paradise." It is well put, "he dismissed," and not "he excluded," so that he might seem to be drawn down by the weight of his own sins to a place that suits him. A bad man generally experiences this when he begins to live among good men, if he is unwilling to change for the better. He is driven from the company of good men by the weight of his bad habit, and they do not exclude him against his will but dismiss him in accordance with his will. Two BOOKS ON GENESIS AGAINST THE MANICHAEANS 2.22.34.[9]

3:24 The Cherubim and a Flaming Sword

THE CHERUBIM AND THE SWORD. AUGUSTINE: "God placed cherubim and a flaming sword that moves"—this could be said in the one word *movable*—"to guard the way to the tree of life." Those who translate the Hebrew words in Scripture say that "cherubim" means in Latin "the fullness of knowledge." The flaming, movable sword means temporal punishments, because times move in their continual

---

[5]Jn 8:44. [6]PG 54:610. [7]FC 91:122. [8]HOP 81. [9]FC 84:129-30.

variety. It is called flaming because every trib-
ulation burns somehow or other. But it is one
thing to be burned until consumed, another to
be burned until purified. TWO BOOKS ON
GENESIS AGAINST THE MANICHAEANS
2.23.35.[10]

THE POSITION OF THE CHERUBIM IN THE
CELESTIAL HIERARCHY. PSEUDO-DIONY-
SIUS: The name *cherubim* means "fullness of
knowledge" or "outpouring of wisdom." This
first of the hierarchies (including seraphim
and cherubim) is hierarchically ordered by
truly superior beings, for this hierarchy possesses the highest order as God's immediate
neighbor, being grounded directly around
God and receiving the primal theophanies and
perfections. Hence the description is "carrier
of warmth" for the seraphim, and the title is
"outpouring of wisdom" for the cherubim.
These names indicate their similarity to what
God is. . . . The name *cherubim* signifies the
power to know and to see God, to receive the
greatest gifts of his light, to contemplate the
divine splendor in primordial power, to be
filled with the gifts that bring wisdom and to
share these generously with subordinates as a
part of the beneficent outpouring of wisdom.
CELESTIAL HIERARCHIES 7.205B-205C.[11]

CHRIST HAS REMOVED THE FLAMING
SWORD. EPHREM THE SYRIAN: Blessed is he
who was pierced and so removed the sword
from the entry to paradise. HYMNS ON PARA-
DISE 2.1.[12]

CHRIST HAS EXTINGUISHED ITS FLAME.
BEDE: The second Adam, Jesus Christ, points

out that through the water of the bath of
rebirth, the flickering flame—by which the
cherubim guardian blocked the entry into paradise when the first Adam was expelled—
would be extinguished. Where the one went
out with his wife, having been conquered by
his enemy, there the other might return with
his spouse (namely, the church of the saints),
as a conqueror over his enemy. HOMILIES ON
THE GOSPELS 1.12.[13]

MARTYRDOM AS A WAY THROUGH THE
CHERUBIM AND THE SWORD. ORIGEN:
Throughout martyrdom Jesus is with you to
show you the way to the paradise of God and
how you may pass through the cherubim and
the flaming sword that turns every way and
guards the way to the tree of life. For both,
even if they guard the way to pass through to
the tree of life, guard it so that no one unworthy may turn that way to pass through to the
tree of life. The flaming sword will hold fast
those who have built upon the foundation
that is laid, Jesus Christ, with wood, hay or
straw,[14] and the wood of denial, if I may call it
that, which catches fire very easily and burns
all the more. But the cherubim will receive
those who by nature cannot be held by the
flaming sword, because they have built with
nothing that can catch fire. They will escort
them to the tree of life and to all the trees God
planted in the east and made to grow out of
the ground. EXHORTATION TO MARTYRDOM
36.[15]

---

[10]FC 84:131. [11]PSD 161-62*. [12]HOP 85. [13]HOG 1:116-17.
[14]1 Cor 3:11-12. [15]OSW 67-68.

4:1-7 CAIN AND ABEL BRING OFFERINGS TO THE LORD

¹Now Adam knew Eve his wife, and she conceived and bore Cain, saying, "I have gotten^g *a man with the help of the LORD." ²And again, she bore his brother Abel. Now Abel was a keeper of sheep, and Cain a tiller of the ground. ³In the course of time Cain brought to the LORD an offering of the fruit of the ground, ⁴and Abel brought of the firstlings of his flock and of their fat portions. And the LORD had regard for Abel and his offering, ⁵but for Cain and his offering he had no regard. So Cain was very angry, and his countenance fell. ⁶The LORD said to Cain, "Why are you angry, and why has your countenance fallen? ⁷If you do well, will you not be accepted? And if you do not do well, sin is couching at the door; its desire is for you, but you must master it."*

g *Heb* qanah, *get*

OVERVIEW: While Chrysostom argues that there was no talk in Scripture of coitus until after the banishment from paradise, Augustine argues in principle for sufficient grace for honorable nuptial union even in paradise (see Gen 1:28). The birth of Cain is a consequence of Adam's fall, which led him to lose his spiritual wisdom and to acquire a worldly knowledge (SYMEON THE NEW THEOLOGIAN). The name Cain means "ownership." Abel, the second child, served as the first symbol of the City of God of those destined to suffer cruel persecutions on earth (AUGUSTINE).

Sacrifice is an ancient custom that dates from the age of Adam, but God does not need sacrifices (AUGUSTINE). Abel was discerning in his choice of offerings, whereas Cain showed no such discernment (EPHREM). God does not consider Cain's offerings because he knows that his heart is wicked (ORIGEN). Cain's countenance fell when his offering was rejected and his brother's was accepted (CHRYSOSTOM). The first sin of Cain is envy for his brother Abel. Cain refuses God's suggestion to do better with a new offering (CHRYSOSTOM, EPHREM).

4:1-2 The Births of Cain and Abel

ADAM KNEW EVE. CHRYSOSTOM: After his disobedience, after their loss of the garden, then it was that the practice of intercourse had its beginning. You see, before their disobedience they followed a life like that of angels, and there was not mention of intercourse. HOMILIES ON GENESIS 18.12.[1]

CAIN WAS CONCEIVED BECAUSE ADAM TURNED HIS LOVE TO VISIBLE OBJECTS. SYMEON THE NEW THEOLOGIAN: Since Adam had been blinded in the eyes of his soul and had fallen from the life imperishable, he began to look with his physical eyes. He turned the

---

[1]PG 53:153; FC 82:10.

vision of his eyes on visible objects with affectionate desire and "knew Eve his wife, and she conceived and bore Cain." Such knowledge is in reality ignorance of all goodness, for had he not first fallen from the knowledge and contemplation of God he would not have been brought down to this knowledge. DISCOURSES 15.1.[2]

MEANING OF THE NAME CAIN. AUGUSTINE: Note that the name Cain means "ownership," which explains what was said at the time of his birth by his father or mother: "I have come into possession of a man through God." CITY OF GOD 15.17.[3]

ABEL SYMBOLIZES THE CITY OF GOD. AUGUSTINE: Cain was followed by Abel, who was killed by his brother and served as the first prophetic symbol of the City of God. He was like an alien on earth, destined to suffer cruel persecutions at the hands of the wicked men who can properly be called natives of earth because they love this world as their home and find their happiness in the worldly felicity of the earthly city. CITY OF GOD 15.15.[4]

4:3-5 The Offerings of Cain and Abel

GOD DOES NOT NEED SACRIFICES. AUGUSTINE: [The pagans say, "The Christians] censure the ceremonies of sacrifice, the victims, incense and the rest, which are used in temple worship. Yet the same ceremonies of sacrifice were originated by themselves or by the god they worship, in primitive times, when a god was assumed to need their offerings of first fruits." This question is evidently derived from that passage in our Scriptures that tells of Cain making an offering to God

of the fruits of the earth and Abel of the firstlings of his flocks. We answer that the conclusion to be drawn from it is that sacrifice is a very ancient custom, because our true and sacred Books warn us that it is not to be offered except to the one true God. But God does not need sacrifices, as is most clearly expressed in the same sacred Books: "I said to the Lord, thou art my God, for thou hast no need of my goods,"[5] because in accepting or refusing or receiving them he is looking only to man's good. God does not derive any benefit from our worship, but we do. LETTERS 102.3.[6]

ABEL CHOOSES HIS OFFERINGS WITH CARE. EPHREM THE SYRIAN: Abel was very discerning in his choice of offerings, whereas Cain showed no such discernment. Abel selected and offered the choicest of his firstborn and of his fat ones, while Cain either offered young grains or certain fruits that are found at the same time as the young grains. Even if his offering had been smaller than that of his brother, it would have been as acceptable as the offering of his brother, had he not brought it with such carelessness. They made their offerings alternately; one offered a lamb of his flock, the other the fruits of the earth. But because Cain had taken such little regard for the first offering that he offered, God refused to accept it in order to teach Cain how he was to make an offering. COMMENTARY ON GENESIS 3.2.1.[7]

GOD KNOWS THAT CAIN'S HEART IS WICKED. ORIGEN: In the case of Cain his

---

[2]SNTD 193. [3]FC 14:455. [4]FC 14:447-48*. [5]Ps 15:2. [6]FC 18:159-60. [7]FC 91:124*.

wickedness did not begin when he killed his brother. For even before that God, who knows the heart, had no regard for Cain and his sacrifice. But his baseness was made evident when he killed Abel. ON PRAYER 29.18.[8]

CAIN'S COUNTENANCE FELL. CHRYSOSTOM: There were two reasons for his annoyance: not just that he alone had been rejected but also that his brother's gift had been accepted. HOMILIES ON GENESIS 18.21.[9]

CAIN'S ANGER. EPHREM THE SYRIAN: Cain was angry because the offering of his brother had been accepted. Cain became angry on account of the fire that had come down and distinguished between the offerings. His face became gloomy because there was laughter in the eyes of his parents and his sisters when his offering was rejected. They had seen that Cain's offering had been placed in the midst of the fire and yet the fire did not touch it. COMMENTARY ON GENESIS 3.3.3.[10]

4:6-7 Sin Is Couching at the Door

IF YOU DO WELL, WILL YOU NOT BE ACCEPTED? CHRYSOSTOM: God wishes to defuse the wild frenzy and remove the anger by means of his words. You see, he observed the stages of Cain's thinking and realized the savagery of his deadly intention; so he intends at this early stage to sedate his thinking and bring repose to his mind by placing his brother subject to him and not undermining his authority. But even despite such great concern and such potent remedies, Cain gained

nothing from the experience. Such was the degree of difference in their attitudes and the excess of evil intent. HOMILIES ON GENESIS 18.24.[11]

CAIN REFUSES TO MAKE A BETTER OFFERING. EPHREM THE SYRIAN: God said to Cain, "Why are you angry, and why is your face gloomy?" Instead of being filled with anger, you ought to be filled with distress. Instead of your face being gloomy, tears ought to be flowing from your eyes. "If you do well, I will accept it." Notice then that it was not because of the small size of Cain's offering that it was rejected. It was not accepted because of his spitefulness and his lack of good will. "If you do well, I will accept it," even though I did not accept it before, and it will be accepted along with the chosen offering of your brother even though it was not accepted before. "But if you do not do well, sin is couching at the first door." Abel will listen to you through his obedience, for he will go with you to the plain.[12] There you will be ruled over by sin, that is, you shall be completely filled with it. But instead of doing well so that the offering that had been rejected might be credited to Cain as acceptable, he then made an offering of murder to that One to whom he had already made an offering of negligence. COMMENTARY ON GENESIS 3.4.1-3.[13]

---

[8]OSW 161. [9]PG 53:156; FC 82:16. [10]FC 91:125. [11]PG 53:157-58; FC 82:18-19. [12]The field or plain outside of Eden where Abel was killed. [13]FC 91:126.

4:8-15 CAIN KILLS HIS BROTHER ABEL

[8]*Cain said to Abel his brother, "Let us go out to the field."*[h] *And when they were in the field, Cain rose up against his brother Abel, and killed him.* [9]*Then the LORD said to Cain, "Where is Abel your brother?" He said, "I do not know; am I my brother's keeper?"* [10]*And the LORD said, "What have you done? The voice of your brother's blood is crying to me from the ground.* [11]*And now you are cursed from the ground, which has opened its mouth to receive your brother's blood from your hand.* [12]*When you till the ground, it shall no longer yield to you its strength; you shall be a fugitive and a wanderer on the earth."* [13]*Cain said to the LORD, "My punishment is greater than I can bear.* [14]*Behold, thou hast driven me this day away from the ground; and from thy face I shall be hidden; and I shall be a fugitive and a wanderer on the earth, and whoever finds me will slay me."* [15]*Then the LORD said to him, "Not so!*[i] *If any one slays Cain, vengeance shall be taken on him sevenfold." And the LORD put a mark on Cain, lest any who came upon him should kill him.*

h *Sam Gk Syr Compare Vg: Heb lacks* Let us go out to the field i *Gk Syr Vg: Heb* Therefore

OVERVIEW: Cain becomes a murderer by his own evil will (SYMEON THE NEW THEOLOGIAN). The murderer of Abel can be understood as a prefiguring of the passion of Jesus (BEDE). After the murder God questions Cain with solicitude so that he might repent, but Cain shows no repentance (EPHREM). He imagines that he may hide his crime from God (SALVIAN THE PRESBYTER). The innocent blood spilled by Cain cries out not by words but by its very existence (MAXIMUS OF TURIN). This innocent blood also symbolizes the blood of the martyrs (ORIGEN). The punishment imposed on Cain reveals God's great forbearance (CHRYSOSTOM) and mercy for the murderer (CYRIL OF JERUSALEM). Cain receives a mark so that no one might kill him. This is to indicate that evil is not destroyed from the earth. Like Cain, who receives a mark and is shattered by fear, the sinner is a slave to fear, to desire, to guilt and to anger (AMBROSE). Cain, like the serpent, is cursed from the ground (CHRYSOSTOM).

4:8 Cain Kills Abel

CAIN'S EVIL WILL. SYMEON THE NEW THEOLOGIAN: Why did Cain become a fratricide? Was it not by his evil will? He preferred himself to his Creator and followed after evil thoughts and so became abandoned to envy and committed murder. DISCOURSES 4.2.[1]

HOW THE KILLING OF ABEL PREFIGURES THE PASSION OF CHRIST. BEDE: Some understand the murderer Cain as the Jews' lack of faith, the killing of Abel as the passion of the Lord and Savior, and the earth that opened its mouth and received Abel's blood from Cain's

[1]SNTD 72.

hand as the church (which received, in the mystery of its renewal, the blood of Christ poured out by the Jews). Undoubtedly those who have this understanding find water turned into wine, for they have a more sacred understanding of the saying of the sacred law. HOMILIES ON THE GOSPELS 1.14.[2]

4:9-10 Abel's Blood Cries from the Ground

GOD GIVES CAIN THE POSSIBILITY TO REPENT. EPHREM THE SYRIAN: God appeared to Cain with kindness, so that if he repented, the sin of murder that his fingers had committed might be effaced by the compunction on his lips. If he did not repent, however, there would be decreed on him a bitter punishment in proportion to his evil folly. COMMENTARY ON GENESIS 3.6.1.[3]

CAIN REFUSES TO REPENT. EPHREM THE SYRIAN: But Cain was filled with wrath instead of compunction. To him who knows all, who asked him about his brother in order to win him back, Cain retorted angrily and said, "I do not know, am I my brother's keeper?" . . . What then would you say, Cain? Should Justice take vengeance for the blood that cried out to it? Or not? Did it not delay so that you might repent? Did Justice not distance itself from its own knowledge and ask you as if it did not know, so that you might confess? What it said to you did not please you, so you came to that sin to which it had warned you beforehand not to come. COMMENTARY ON GENESIS 3.6.1; 3.7.1.[4]

CAIN THINKS HE MAY COVER HIS CRIME. SALVIAN THE PRESBYTER: Cain was at once the most wicked and foolish of men in believing that for committing the greatest of crimes

it would be sufficient if he avoided other human witnesses. In fact God was the primary witness to his fratricide. Because of this, I think he then shared the opinion held by many today: that God pays no attention to earthly affairs; neither does he see those done by wicked men. There is no doubt that Cain, when summoned by the word of God after his misdeed, answered that he knew nothing of his brother's murder. He believed God was so ignorant of what had been done that he thought this most deadly crime could be covered by a lie. But it turned out otherwise than he thought. When God condemned him, he realized that God, whom he thought had not seen his crime of murder, had seen him. GOVERNANCE OF GOD 1.6.[5]

INNOCENT BLOOD CRIES OUT BY ITS VERY EXISTENCE. MAXIMUS OF TURIN: The divine Scripture always cries out and speaks; hence God also says to Cain, "The voice of your brother's blood cries out to me." Blood, to be sure, has no voice, but innocent blood that has been spilled is said to cry out not by words but by its very existence. [It makes] demands of the Lord not with eloquent discourse but with anger over the crime committed. It does not accuse the wrongdoer with words so much as bind him by the accusation of his own conscience. The evil deed may seem to be excused when it is explained away with words. But it cannot be excused if it is made present to the conscience. For in silence and without contradiction the wrongdoer's conscience always convicts and judges him. SERMONS 88.1.[6]

---

[2]HOG 1:139-40. [3]FC 91:127. [4]FC 91:127. [5]FC 3:39. [6]ACW 50:208.

THE BLOOD OF ABEL SYMBOLIZED THE BLOOD OF THE MARTYRS. ORIGEN: We also know that what was said of Abel, when he was slain by the wicked murderer Cain, is suitable for all whose blood has been shed wickedly. Let us suppose that the verse "The voice of your brother's blood is crying to me from the ground" is said as well for each of the martyrs, the voice of whose blood cries to God from the ground. EXHORTATION TO MARTYRDOM 50.[7]

4:11-15 A Fugitive and a Wanderer

GOD'S SOLICITUDE FOR CAIN. CHRYSOSTOM: The punishment of which God spoke seems to be excessively harsh, but rightly understood it gives us a glimpse of his great solicitude. God wanted men of later times to exercise self-control. Therefore, he designed the kind of punishment that was capable of setting Cain free from his sin. If God had immediately destroyed him, Cain would have disappeared, his sin would have stayed concealed, and he would have remained unknown to men of later times. But as it is, God let him live a long time with that bodily tremor of his. The sight of Cain's palsied limbs was a lesson for all he met. It served to teach all men and exhort them never to dare do what he had done, so that they might not suffer the same punishment. And Cain himself became a better man again. His trembling, his fear, the mental torment that never left him, his physical paralysis kept him, as it were, shackled. They kept him from leaping again to any other like deed of bold folly. They constantly reminded him of his former crime. Through them he achieved greater self-control in his soul. AGAINST JUDAIZING CHRISTIANS 8.2.10.[8]

GOD'S SENTENCE IS LIGHT. CYRIL OF JERUSALEM: Do you, who have but lately come to the catechesis, wish to see the loving kindness of God? Would you want to behold the loving kindness of God and the extent of his forbearance? Listen to the story of [Cain]. . . . Cain, the firstborn man, became a fratricide, from whose wicked designings first stemmed murder and envy. Yet consider his sentence for slaying his brother. "Groaning and trembling shall you be upon the earth."[9] Though the sin was great, the sentence was light. CATECHETICAL LECTURES 2.7.[10]

THE MARK OF CAIN. AMBROSE: Indeed, it was not without reason that the mark was set upon Cain, that no one might kill him. Thus it was indicated that evil is not destroyed or removed from the earth. Cain was afraid that he might be killed, because he did not know how to flee. For evil is augmented and amassed by the practice of evil, and it exists without moderation or limit, fights through guile and deceit and is revealed by its deeds and by the blood of the slain, even as Cain also was revealed. FLIGHT FROM THE WORLD 7.39.[11]

EVERY SINNER IS LIKE CAIN. AMBROSE: Like a slave, Cain received a mark and he could not escape death. Thus is the sinner a slave to fear, a slave to desire, a slave to greed, a slave to lust, a slave to sin, a slave to anger. Though such a man appears to himself free, he is more a slave than if he were under tyrants. LETTERS TO PRIESTS 54.[12]

---

[7]OSW 78-79. [8]FC 68:212-13. [9]Gen 4:12 LXX. [10]FC 61:100. [11]FC 65:310-11. [12]FC 26:297.

CAIN LIKE THE SERPENT. CHRYSOSTOM: You see, since Cain perpetrated practically the same evil as the serpent, which like an instrument served the devil's purposes, and as the serpent introduced mortality by means of deceit, in like manner Cain deceived his brother, led him out into open country, raised his hand in armed assault against him and committed murder. Hence, as God said to the serpent, "Cursed are you beyond all the wild animals of the earth," so to Cain too when he committed the same evil as the serpent. HOMILIES ON GENESIS 19.11.[13]

CAIN CONFESSES TOO LATE. CHRYSOSTOM: Someone may say, "Behold he has confessed, and confessed with great precision"—but all to no avail, dearly beloved: the confession comes too late. You see, he should have done this at the right time when he was in a position to find mercy from the judge. HOMILIES ON GENESIS 19.3.[14]

[13]PG 53:162; FC 82:27. [14]PG 53:163; FC 82:29.

4:16-22 CAIN AND HIS DESCENDANTS

[16]*Then Cain went away from the presence of the LORD, and dwelt in the land of Nod,[j]* east[†] of Eden.*

[17]*Cain knew his wife, and she conceived and bore Enoch; and he built a city, and called the name of the city after the name of his son, Enoch.* [18]*To Enoch was born Irad;[‡] and Irad[‡] was the father of Me-huja-el,[§] and Me-huja-el[§] the father of Me-thusha-el,[#] and Me-thusha-el[#] the father of Lamech.* [19]*And Lamech took two wives; the name of the one was Adah, and the name of the other Zillah.*** [20]*Adah bore Jabal;[††] he was the father of those who dwell in tents and have cattle.* [21]*His brother's name was Jubal; he was the father of all those who play the lyre and pipe.[‡‡]* [22]*Zillah** bore Tubal-cain;[§§] he was the forger of all instruments of bronze and iron. The sister of Tubal-cain[§§] was Naamah.[##]*

j *That is* Wandering *LXX Naid [†]LXX opposite [‡]LXX Gaidad [§]LXX Maiel [#]LXX Mathousala **LXX Sella [††]LXX Iobel [‡‡]LXX psaltery and cittara [§§]LXX Thobel [##]LXX Noema

OVERVIEW: Cain leaves the presence of God because of his wickedness (ATHANASIUS). He separates himself from his kin, because he sees that they would not intermarry with him (EPHREM). The place where he goes and dwells is called Nod, which means "wandering" (EPHREM) or "disturbance" (CLEMENT OF ALEXANDRIA).

It is not possible to ascertain that Cain, after moving to his new dwelling place, generates Enoch as his first son (AUGUSTINE). Cain builds a city, but Abel built none, since the true city of the saints is in heaven (AUGUSTINE). Cain survives through seven generations of descendants (EPHREM). They represent the earthly city that is propagated through physical births (AUGUSTINE). After Cain the family became divided (EPHREM).

4:16 Cain Leaves the Presence of the Lord

CAIN LEAVES BECAUSE OF HIS CRIME. ATHANASIUS: By means of righteousness we come into God's presence, as Moses did when he entered the thick cloud where God was.[1] On the other hand, by the practice of evil a person leaves the presence of the Lord. For example, Cain, when he killed his brother, left the Lord's presence as far as his will was concerned. FESTAL LETTERS 8.[2]

CAIN ALSO LEAVES HIS KIN. EPHREM THE SYRIAN: After Cain received the punishment and the sign had been added to it . . . Moses said that "Cain went away from the presence of the Lord and dwelt in the land of Nod, east of Eden." Cain, therefore, separated himself from his parents and his kin because he saw that they would not intermarry with him. COMMENTARY ON GENESIS 3.11.1.[3]

THE NAME NOD MEANS "WANDERING." EPHREM THE SYRIAN: The land of Nod is so called because it was the land in which Cain wandered about in fear and trembling. But the land also received a second curse when God said, "When you till the earth it shall no longer yield to you its strength." COMMENTARY ON GENESIS 3.11.1.[4]

A DIFFERENT INTERPRETATION OF THE

NAME NOD. CLEMENT OF ALEXANDRIA: The Scripture makes good sense: "Cain left God's presence and went to live in the land of Nod, opposite Eden." Nod means "disturbance," Eden, "the good life." The good life from which the transgressor was expelled consisted in faith, knowledge, peace. Those wise in their own eyes . . . are happy to transfer to the disturbance of a tossing sea. They drop from the knowledge of the One who knows no birth to the realm of birth and death. Their opinions are constantly changing. STROMATEIS 2.51.4-5.[5]

AFTER CAIN THE FAMILY BECAME DIVIDED. EPHREM THE SYRIAN:
There the families
of the two brothers had separated:
Cain went off by himself
and lived in the land of Nod,
a place lower still
than that of Seth and Enosh;
but those who lived on higher ground,
who were called
"the children of God,"
left their own region and came down
to take wives
from the daughters of Cain down below.
HYMNS ON PARADISE 1.11.[6]

4:17 Cain Built a City

IS ENOCH CAIN'S FIRST SON? AUGUSTINE: Consider now the text: "And Cain knew his wife, and she conceived, and brought forth Enoch; and he built a city and called the name thereof by the name of his son Enoch." It does

[1]Ex 19:20. [2]ARL 134. [3]FC 91:130. [4]FC 91:130. [5]FC 85:193. [6]HOP 81-82.

not at all follow from these words that we must believe Cain's first son was Enoch, as though "Cain knew his wife" must refer to their first intercourse. You have the same expression used of the first father, Adam, but not only in reference to the conception of Cain, who seems to have been his firstborn, since a little later Scripture records, "Adam knew his wife, and she conceived and brought forth a son and called his name Seth."[7] CITY OF GOD 15.8.[8]

CAIN BUILDS A CITY, WHILE ABEL BUILT NONE. AUGUSTINE: Now, it is recorded of Cain that he built a city, while Abel, as though he were merely a pilgrim on earth, built none. For the true city of the saints is in heaven, though here on earth it produces citizens in whom it wanders as on a pilgrimage through time looking for the kingdom of eternity. When that day comes, it will gather together all those who, rising in their bodies, shall have that kingdom given to them in which, along with their Prince, the King of Eternity, they shall reign forever and ever. CITY OF GOD 15.1.[9]

4:18-22 The Descendants of Cain

THE SEVEN GENERATIONS OF CAIN. EPHREM THE SYRIAN: That Cain remained alive until the seventh generation is clear. First, . . . it had been so decreed concerning him. Second, the length of the lives of those first generations also testifies to it. For if his father Adam remained alive until the ninth

generation, that of Lamech, and was gathered from the world in the fifty-sixth year of Lamech, it is no great thing that Cain should remain until the seventh generation. COMMENTARY ON GENESIS 3.9.4.[10]

CAIN'S DESCENDANTS REPRESENT THE EARTHLY CITY. AUGUSTINE: The text runs: "Methushael begot Lamech, who took two wives: the name of the one was Ada, and the name of the other Sella. And Ada brought forth Jobel; who was the father of such as dwell in tents, and of herdsmen. His brother's name was Jubal. He was the father of all those who play the psaltery and cittara. Sella bore Tobel; he was the forger of all instruments of bronze and iron. The sister of Tobel was Noema." This is as far as the line of descent from Cain is carried. There are eight generations in all, including Adam. The seventh is that of Lamech, who was the husband of two wives; the eighth is that of his children, among whom is the woman who is mentioned by name. What is here delicately intimated is that to the very end of its existence the earthly city will be propagated by physical births proceeding from the union of the sexes. This is why we are given the proper names of the wives of the last man mentioned as begetting children—a practice unheard of before the flood, except in the case of Eve. CITY OF GOD 15.17.[11]

---

[7]Gen 4:25. [8]FC 14:431. [9]FC 14:415. [10]FC 91:129-30. [11]FC 14:456*.

4:23-24 LAMECH COMMITS MURDER

²³*Lamech said to his wives:*
"Adah and Zillah,* hear my voice;
   you wives of Lamech, hearken to what I say:
I have slain a man for wounding me,
   a young man for striking me.
²⁴*If Cain is avenged sevenfold,*
   truly Lamech seventy-sevenfold."

*LXX Sella

OVERVIEW: Lamech kills a man and a young man in order to propagate further the generations of Cain. According to a different interpretation, Lamech does not kill two unknown persons but Cain himself (EPHREM). The murder of Cain by the hand of Lamech is a legend without foundation. Lamech is a murderer who does not consider the example of the punishment of Cain and is therefore punished more severely (BASIL). Chrysostom opposes Basil's point of view and believes that Lamech considers the example of Cain and through it is brought to a spontaneous confession that enables him to limit his punishment (CHRYSOSTOM). Theodoret, however, sees parallelism here and argues that Lamech is confessing to killing one young man (THEODORET).

4:23-24 Lamech's Vengeance

THE PUNISHMENT OF LAMECH'S MURDER.
EPHREM THE SYRIAN: Some, because they think that Cain was avenged for seven generations, say that Lamech was evil, because God had said, "All flesh has corrupted its path,"[1] and also because the wives of Lamech saw that the line of their generation would be cut off. They were giving birth not to males but to females only, for Moses said that it was "when men multiplied on the earth and daughters were born to them."[2] When these wives saw the plight of their generation, they became fearful and knew that the judgment decreed against Cain and his seven generations had come upon their generation. Lamech, then, in his cleverness, comforted them, saying, "I have killed a man for wounding me and a youth for striking me. Just as God caused Cain to remain so that seven generations would perish with him, so God will cause me to remain, because I have killed two, so that seventy-seven generations should die with me. Before the seventy-seven generations come, however, we will die, and through the cup of death that we taste we will escape from that punishment which, because of me, will extend to seventy-seven generations." COMMENTARY ON GENESIS 4.2.2-3.[3]

---

[1]Gen 6:12. [2]Gen 6:1. [3]FC 91:131-32.

LAMECH MIGHT BE THE MURDERER OF CAIN. EPHREM THE SYRIAN: Still others say that Lamech, who was cunning and crafty, saw the plight of his generation: that the Sethites[4] refused to intermingle with them because of the reproach of their father Cain, who was still alive, and that the lands would become uncultivated from the lack of plowmen and their generation would thus come to an end. Lamech, therefore, moved by zeal, killed Cain together with his one son whom he had begotten and who resembled him, lest through this one son who resembled him the memory of his shame continue through their generations. When he killed Cain, who had been like a wall between the two tribes to keep them from tyrannizing each other, Lamech said to his wives as if in secret, "A man and a youth have been killed, but take and adorn your daughters for the sons of Seth. Because of the murders that I have committed and because of the adornment and beauty of your daughters, those who refused to be married to us in the past six generations might now consent to marry with us in our generation." COMMENTARY ON GENESIS 4.3.1-2.[5]

THE HYPOTHESIS THAT LAMECH MURDERED CAIN MUST BE REJECTED. BASIL THE GREAT: Some think that Cain was destroyed by Lamech on the grounds that he lived until that time to pay the longer penalty. But this is not true. For Lamech seems to have perpetrated two murders from what he tells us. "I have killed a man and a youth"—the man for wounding and the youth for bruising. Now, a wound is one thing and a bruise another; and a man is one thing and a youth another. "For Cain shall be avenged sevenfold, but Lamech seventy times sevenfold." It is right for me to undergo four hundred and ninety chastise-

ments, if truly God's judgment against Cain is just, that he should undergo seven punishments. In fact, as he did not learn to murder from another, so he did not see the murderer undergoing the penalty. But I, having before my eyes the man groaning and trembling and also the greatness of the anger of God, was not brought to my senses by the example. Therefore I deserve to pay four hundred and ninety penalties. LETTERS 260.[6]

THROUGH CONFESSION LAMECH LIMITS HIS PUNISHMENT. CHRYSOSTOM: "Lamech said," the text in fact goes on, "to his wives Ada and Sella,[7] Listen to my voice, wives of Lamech, hearken to my words: I killed a man for wounding me, and a young man for striking me. On Cain fell sevenfold vengeance, but on Lamech seventy times sevenfold." Apply your attention to the utmost. I beseech you, put aside all worldly thoughts and let us study these words with precision so that nothing may escape us, but rather we should proceed to their deepest meaning and be able to light upon the treasure concealed in these brief phrases. "Lamech said to his wives Ada and Sella," the text says, "Listen to my voice, wives of Lamech, hearken to my words." Consider at once, I ask you, from the outset how much benefit this man gained from the punishment inflicted on Cain. Not only does he not await accusation from someone else to the effect that he has been guilty of this sin or some worse one, but without anyone's accusing him or censuring him he confesses his own guilt, admits his crimes and outlines to his wives the magnitude of his sin, as to fulfill the proverb

[4]The generation of Seth; Gen 4:25. [5]FC 91:132. [6]FC 28:228-29. [7]Zillah.

of the inspired writer, "He who accuses himself at the beginning of the speech is in the right."[8] You see, confession is of the greatest efficacy for correction of faults. Thus the denial of guilt after the committing of sin proves worse than the sins themselves. This was the condition of that man who killed his brother and who when questioned by the loving God did not merely decline to confess his crime but even dared to lie to God and thus caused his life to be lengthened. Accordingly Lamech, when he fell into the same sins, arrived at the conclusion that denial would only lead to his receiving a severer punishment, and so he summoned his wives, without anyone's accusing or charging him, and made a personal confession of his sins to them in his own words. By comparing what he had done

to the crimes committed by Cain, he limited the punishment coming to him. HOMILIES ON GENESIS 20.6-7.[9]

LAMECH KILLED ONE YOUTH. THEODORET OF CYR: Some interpreters understand this not of two men or, as others fantasize, of Cain, but of one and the same young man: "a man I have killed for wounding me and a young man for bruising me." That is, a young man approaching maturity. He escapes vengeance through confession of sin, and pronouncing judgment on himself, he prevents divine judgment. QUESTIONS ON GENESIS 44.[10]

---

[8]Prov 18:17. [9]FC 82:38-39. [10]QO 43.

4:25-26 ADAM AND EVE BEGET SETH

[25]*And Adam knew his wife again, and she bore a son and called his name Seth, for she said, "God has appointed for me another child instead of [Abel, for Cain slew him]."** [26]*To Seth also a son was born, and he called his name Enosh. At that time [men began to call]†upon the name of the LORD.*

*LXX Abel, whom Cain slew †LXX he hoped to call

OVERVIEW: The conception of Seth by Adam and Eve signifies the harmony of responsible marriage (CLEMENT OF ALEXANDRIA). The generations originating from Seth represent the heavenly city of God (AUGUSTINE). Since Seth separates himself from the house of Cain, his family is called "the just people of the Lord" (EPHREM). After his birth the Holy

Spirit comes upon Enosh and endows him with the gift of prophecy (CYRIL OF JERUSALEM).

4:25 The Birth of Seth

THE CONCEPTION OF SETH. CLEMENT OF ALEXANDRIA: We agree that weakness of will and sexual immorality are passions inspired by the devil. But the harmony of responsible marriage occupies a middle position. When there is self-control, it leads to prayer; when there is reverent bridal union, to childbearing. At any rate, there is a proper time for the breeding of children, and Scripture calls it knowledge, in the words "Adam knew his wife Eve, and she conceived and bore a son, and called him by the name of Seth, 'for God has raised up for me another child in Abel's place.'" STROMATEIS 3.81.4-5.[1]

IT IS NOT CERTAIN THAT SETH WAS BORN NEXT AFTER CAIN. AUGUSTINE: It is quite possible that when Adam was divinely inspired to say, after Seth was born, "God has given me another seed, for Abel whom Cain slew," there is no implication here that Seth was the next born in the order of time but only that he was destined to be a fit heir in the order of holiness. CITY OF GOD 15.15.[2]

4:26 Sethites Call upon God

THE SETHITES REPRESENT THE CITY OF GOD. AUGUSTINE: We have two lines of succession, one descending from Cain and the other from the son who was born to Adam in order to be the heir of Abel who was killed and to whom Adam gave the name of Seth. He is referred to in the words "God has given me another seed, for Abel whom Cain slew." Thus it is that the two series of generations that are kept so distinct, the one from Seth and the other from Cain, symbolize the two cities with which I am dealing in this work, the heavenly city in exile on earth and the earthly city, whose only search and satisfaction are for and in the joys of earth. CITY OF GOD 15.15.[3]

THE SETHITES ARE THE JUST PEOPLE OF GOD. EPHREM THE SYRIAN: After Seth begot Enosh, Moses wrote "at that time he began to call on the name of the Lord."[4] Because Seth had separated himself from the house of Cain, the Sethites were called by the name of the Lord, that is, the just people of the Lord. COMMENTARY ON GENESIS 5.1.2.[5]

THE HOLY SPIRIT ENDOWS ENOSH WITH THE GIFT OF PROPHECY. CYRIL OF JERUSALEM: The Holy Spirit came upon all the righteous men and prophets, such as Enosh, Enoch, Noah and so on, to Abraham, Isaac and Jacob. CATECHETICAL LECTURES 16.27.[6]

MEANING OF THE NAMES ADAM, SETH AND ENOSH. AUGUSTINE: Seth means "resurrection," and the name of his son Enosh means "man." The name Adam also means "man," but in Hebrew it can be used for any human person, either male or female; as one can see from the text: "He created them male and female; and blessed them and called their name Adam."[7] This text leaves no doubt that Eve was given her proper name, whereas the common noun "adam," or "human being," applied to both Adam and Eve.[8] It was different with the name Enosh. This means "man," Hebrew scholars tell us, in the sense of a man as distinguished from a woman. Thus Enosh was a "son" of "resurrection." CITY OF GOD 15.17.[9]

---

[1]FC 85:306. [2]FC 14:449. [3]FC 14:448. [4]Gen 4:26 LXX. [5]FC 91:133. [6]FC 64:92. [7]Gen 5:1-2. [8]Note that the generic name Adam in Hebrew applies to both Adam and Eve, in the light of the previous explanation that Adam had Eve within himself before the distinction of the sexes. [9]FC 14:455.

5:1-8 SETH AND HIS SON ENOSH

[1]*This is the book of the generations of Adam.* When God created man, he made him in the likeness of God. [2]Male and female he created them, and he blessed them and named them Man† when they were created. [3]When Adam had lived a hundred‡ and thirty years, he became the father of a son in his own likeness, after his image, and named him Seth. [4]The days of Adam after he became the father of Seth were eight hundred§ years; and he had other sons and daughters. [5]Thus all the days that Adam lived were nine hundred and thirty years; and he died.*

[6]When Seth had lived a hundred‡ and five years, he became the father of Enosh. [7]Seth lived after the birth of Enosh eight hundred§ and seven years, and had other sons and daughters. [8]Thus all the days of Seth were nine hundred and twelve years; and he died.

*LXX men †LXX Adam ‡LXX two hundred §LXX seven hundred

OVERVIEW: The beginning of world chronology is not reckoned from the earthly city, not from the generation of Cain. The heavenly city is symbolized in the one "man" (Enosh) born of the "resurrection" (Seth) of the man who was slain (Abel), symbolizing the unity of the whole heavenly city. This is the proper way to present the narrative of world history as symbolized by the two cities (AUGUSTINE). The likeness between Adam and his son Seth is a reflection of the unity between the Father and the Son (ORIGEN). It is likely that Seth's descendants built cities and inhabited them, even though there is no mention of these events in the Scriptures (AUGUSTINE).

5:1-2 The Generations of Adam

WHY DOES THE NARRATIVE OF GENESIS GO BACK TO ADAM? AUGUSTINE: The reason for this break in the narrative [in the description of the genealogies to the flood]

was, I take it, that the writer, as though bidden by God, was unwilling to have the beginning of world chronology reckoned from the earthly city (that is, from the generation of Cain), and so he deliberately went back to Adam for a new beginning. If we ask why this return to recapitulate was made immediately after mentioning Seth's son,[1] the man who hoped to call upon the name of the Lord God, the answer must be that this was the proper way to present the two cities. The one begins and ends with a murderer, for Lamech, too, as he admitted to his two wives, was a murderer.[2] The other city begins with the man who hoped to call upon the name of the Lord God, for the invocation of God is the whole and the highest preoccupation of the city of God during its pilgrimage in this world. It is symbolized in the one "man" (Enosh) born of the "resurrection" (Seth) of

---

[1]Gen 4:25-26. [2]Gen 4:23-24.

116

the man who was slain (Abel). That one man in fact is a symbol of the unity of the whole heavenly city, which is not yet in the fullness that it is destined to reach and which is adumbrated in this prophetic figure. CITY OF GOD 15.21.[3]

5:3-5 Adam's Son Seth in His Likeness

THE UNITY OF THE FATHER AND THE SON IS PREFIGURED IN ADAM AND SETH. ORIGEN: Christ is the invisible image of the invisible God, just as according to the Scripture narrative we say that the image of Adam was his son Seth. It is written thus: "And Adam begot Seth after his own image and after his own kind." This image preserves the unity of nature and substance common to a father and a son. For "whatever the Father does, the Son does likewise."[4] In this very fact—that the Son does all things just as the Father does—the Father's image is reproduced in the Son, whose birth from the

Father is as it were an act of his will proceeding from the mind. ON FIRST PRINCIPLES 1.2.6.[5]

5:6-8 Seth and His Descendants

DID THE DESCENDANTS OF SETH BUILD CITIES? AUGUSTINE: Now notice that when the inspired writer sets forth the length of the lives of the men he mentions, the narrative always ends with the formula "and he begot sons and daughters, and all the time that so and so lived were so many years, and he died." Considering that these sons and daughters are not named and remembering how long people lived in that first period of our history, can anyone refuse to believe that so great a multitude of men was born as to have been able, in groups, to build a great number of cities? CITY OF GOD 15.8.[6]

---

[3]FC 14:466. [4]Jn 5:19. [5]OFP 19. [6]FC 14:430.

5:9-14 ENOSH AND HIS SON KENAN

[9]When Enosh had lived ninety* years, he became the father of Kenan.[†] [10]Enosh lived after the birth of Kenan[†] eight hundred[‡] and fifteen years, and had other sons and daughters. [11]Thus all the days of Enosh were nine hundred and five years; and he died.

[12]When Kenan[†] had lived seventy[§] years, he became the father of Ma-halalel.[#] [13]Kenan[†] lived after the birth of Ma-halalel[#] eight hundred[‡] and forty years, and had other sons and daughters. [14]Thus all the days of Kenan[†] were nine hundred and ten years; and he died.

*LXX a hundred and ninety †LXX Kainan ‡LXX seven hundred §LXX a hundred and seventy #LXX Maleleel

OVERVIEW: The name Enosh means "man" in the language of the Chaldeans as well as in Hebrew (AMBROSE).[1]

5:9-11 Enosh and His Descendants

MEANING OF THE NAME ENOSH. AMBROSE: For a wise man should remove himself from fleshy pleasures, elevate his soul and draw away from the body. This is to know oneself a man—*homo* in Latin but *Enosh* in the language of the Chaldeans. ISAAC, OR THE SOUL 1.1.[2]

---

[1]Cf. comment on Gen 4:26. [2]FC 65:11.

5:15-20 JARED BECOMES THE FATHER OF ENOCH

[15]When Ma-halalel* had lived sixty-five† years, he became the father of Jared. [16]Ma-halalel* lived after the birth of Jared eight hundred‡ and thirty years, and had other sons and daughters. [17]Thus all the days of Ma-halalel* were eight hundred and ninety-five years; and he died.

[18]When Jared had lived a hundred and sixty-two years he became the father of Enoch. [19]Jared lived after the birth of Enoch eight hundred years, and had other sons and daughters. [20]Thus all the days of Jared were nine hundred and sixty-two years; and he died.

*LXX Maleleel †LXX a hundred and sixty-five ‡LXX seven hundred

---

OVERVIEW: Enoch, who is the seventh in the line of descent from Adam, prefigures the sevenfold gifts of the Spirit that would come to rest in Christ (BEDE).

5:18-20 Jared the Father of Enoch

THE CONCEPTION OF ENOCH PREFIGURES THAT OF CHRIST. BEDE: Enoch, in that he was engendered seventh in the line of descent from Adam, prefigured that the Lord would be conceived and born not in the usual way of mortal nature but by the power of the Holy Spirit. He prefigured that the full grace of the Holy Spirit, which is described by the prophet as sevenfold,[1] would come to rest upon Christ in a special way when he was about to be born. And he would baptize in the Holy Spirit and give the gifts of the Spirit to those who believe in him. HOMILIES ON THE GOSPELS 2.15.[2]

---

[1]Is 11:2-3. [2]HOG 2:144.

5:21-27 ENOCH IS TAKEN BY GOD
AND BROUGHT TO HEAVEN

^{21}*When Enoch had lived sixty-five* years, he became the father of Methuselah.† ^{22}Enoch walked with‡ God after the birth of Methuselah† three hundred§ years, and had other sons and daughters. ^{23}Thus all the days of Enoch were three hundred and sixty-five years. ^{24}Enoch walked with God; and he was not, for God took him.$^#$*

^{25}*When Methuselah† had lived a hundred and eighty-seven** years, he became the father of Lamech. ^{26}Methuselah† lived after the birth of Lamech seven hundred and eighty-two†† years, and had other sons and daughters. ^{27}Thus all the days of Methuselah† were nine hundred and sixty-nine years; and he died.*

*LXX a hundred and sixty five †LXX Mathousala ‡LXX was pleasing to §LXX two hundred #LXX Enoch was pleasing to God, and was not found, for God transferred him. **LXX a hundred and sixty seven ††LXX eight hundred and two

OVERVIEW: Enoch is snatched up to heaven on the wings of fire of the Holy Spirit (AMBROSE), showing Adam that paradise is the meeting place of the faithful (EPHREM). God takes Enoch and brings him to paradise because he is pleasing in the sight of God (CYPRIAN). It is uncertain whether this is a consequence or a precondition of Enoch's comprehension of God's nature (GREGORY OF NAZIANZUS). Enoch's life demonstrates that human flesh does not prevent humans from becoming saints (CHRYSOSTOM) and that one who hopes in God does not dwell on earth but is transported and cleaves to God (AMBROSE). Enoch does not experience death but is transported to immortality by God (AUGUSTINE). Enoch is not endowed with eternal life, but his death is only postponed (TERTULLIAN). Enoch was no longer found amid the vanity of the world (JOHN CASSIAN).

Methuselah, the son of Enoch, dies in the year when the flood begins. The discrepancies in the figures mentioned above are discussed by Jerome, who solves the apparent anomaly of Methuselah's dying after the flood by recourse to the Hebrew (JEROME). The discrepancies between the Hebrew and the Septuagint are also discussed by Augustine.

5:21-24 Enoch Walked with God

ENOCH IS TAKEN TO HEAVEN BY THE HOLY SPIRIT. AMBROSE: The Holy Spirit also came down "and filled the whole house, where very many were sitting, and there appeared parted tongues as of fire."[1] Good are the wings of love, the true wings that flew about through the mouths of the apostles, and the wings of fire that spoke the pure word. On these wings Enoch flew when he was snatched up to heaven. ISAAC, OR THE SOUL 8.77.[2]

---

[1]Acts 2:2-3. [2]FC 65:61.

Adam Witnesses the Event. Ephrem the Syrian: Some say that while Adam was looking [at Enoch] God transported him to paradise lest Adam think that Enoch was killed as was Abel and so be grieved. This was so that Adam might also be comforted by this just son of his and that he might know that for all who were like this one, whether before death or after the resurrection, paradise would be their meeting place. **Commentary on Genesis 5.2.1.**[3]

Enoch Pleases God. Cyprian: We also find that Enoch, who pleased God, was transported, as divine Scripture testifies in Genesis and says, "And Enoch pleased God and was not seen later because God took him." This was pleasing in the sight of God—that Enoch merited being transported from the contagion of this world. But the Holy Spirit teaches also through Solomon[4] that those who please God are taken from here earlier and more quickly set free, lest while they are tarrying too long in this world they be corrupted by familiarity with the world. **On Mortality 23.**[5]

Hoping to Invoke the Lord. Gregory of Nazianzus: Enoch "hoped to invoke the Lord."[6] His accomplishment consisted not in hoping for knowledge, mark you, but rather in hoping for invocation of the Lord. Enoch was "transferred"—yes, but it is quite unclear whether this was a consequence or a precondition of his comprehending God's nature. **Theological Orations 28.18.**[7]

Human Flesh Does Not Prevent Enoch from Becoming a Saint. Chrysostom: Well, then, do not say, "I am impeded by the flesh, so I cannot win out or take on myself efforts to acquire virtue." Do not thus accuse your Creator. For if the flesh makes it impossible to possess virtue, the fault is not ours. However, the company of the saints has shown that in reality it does not make this impossible. The nature of the flesh did not prevent Paul, for instance, from becoming such a saint as he became or Peter from receiving the keys of heaven. Further, Enoch, though possessed of the flesh, was taken by God and seen no more. **Homilies on John 75.**[8]

Those Who Hope in God Do Not Dwell on Earth. Ambrose: Enoch called upon God in hope and so is thought to have been transported. And so only that man who puts his hope in God seems to be "man."[9] Moreover, the clear and truthful sense of the passage is that one who puts his hope in God does not dwell on earth but is transported, so to speak, and cleaves to God. **Isaac, or the Soul 1.1.**[10]

Enoch Transcended the Vanity of the World. John Cassian: The mind is so caught up in this way that the hearing no longer takes in the voices outside and images of the passerby no longer come to sight and the eye no longer sees the mounds confronting it or the gigantic objects rising up against it.

No one will possess the truth and the power of all this unless he has direct experience to teach him. The Lord will have turned the eyes of his heart away from everything of the here and now, and he will think of these as not transitory so much as already gone, smoke scattered into nothing. He walks with God,

---

[3]FC 91:133-34. [4]Wis 4:11. [5]FC 36:217-18. [6]Gen 4:26 LXX. [7]FGFR 234. [8]FC 41:313-14. [9]I.e., seems thus far to be truly "man." *Enoch* translates "man." [10]FC 65:11.

like Enoch. He is gone from a human way of life, from human concerns. He is no longer to be found amid the vanity of this present world. The text of Genesis relates that this actually happened to Enoch in the body: "Enoch walked with God and was not to be found because God had taken him away."[11] The apostle says, "Because of his faith, Enoch was taken up so that he did not have to encounter death."[12] CONFERENCE 3.7.[13]

ENOCH DOES NOT EXPERIENCE PRESENT DEATH. AUGUSTINE: Then the Scripture states that after some time had elapsed, there was a man named Enoch, whose justice merited a singular privilege: that he should not experience present death but should be transported to immortality from the midst of mortals. This incident shows that one just man is dearer to God than many sinners. CHRISTIAN LIFE 7.[14]

ENOCH'S DEATH IS ONLY POSTPONED. TERTULLIAN: Enoch and Elijah were transported hence without suffering death, which was only postponed. The day will come when they will actually die that they may extinguish Antichrist with their blood. There was a legend that St. John the Evangelist was to live till the second coming, but he died. ON THE SOUL 50.5.[15]

5:25-27 Methuselah's Age

METHUSELAH DIES IN THE YEAR OF THE FLOOD. JEROME: There is a famous question that has been aired by discussion in all churches: that by a careful reckoning it can be shown that Methuselah lived fourteen years after the flood. It appears that in this case as in many others, in the Septuagint translation

of the Bible there is an error in the numbers. Among the Hebrews and the books of the Samaritans, I have found the text written thus: "Methuselah lived a hundred and eighty-seven years and became the father of Lamech. Methuselah lived after the birth of Lamech seven hundred and eighty-two years and had other sons and daughters. Thus all the days of Methuselah were nine hundred and sixty-nine years; and he died. And Lamech lived one hundred and eighty two years and begot Noah." Accordingly, there are 369 years from the day of Methuselah's birth to the day of Noah's birth; to these add Noah's six hundred years, since the flood occurred in the six hundredth year of his life, and so it works out that Methuselah died in the nine hundred sixty-ninth year of his life, in the same year when the flood began. HEBREW QUESTIONS ON GENESIS 5.25-29.[16]

APOLOGIA FOR DISCREPANCIES BETWEEN HEBREW AND SEPTUAGINT VERSIONS. AUGUSTINE: Moreover the difference in numbers that we find between the Hebrew text and our own[17] constitutes no disagreement about this longevity of the ancients. If any discrepancy is such that the two versions cannot both be true, we must seek the authentic account of events in the language from which our text was translated. Though this opportunity is universally available to those who wish to take it, yet, significantly enough, no one has ventured to correct the Septuagint version from the Hebrew text in the very many places where it seems to offer something different. The reason is that those differences were not

---

[11]Gen 5:24. [12]Heb 11:5. [13]JCC 87. [14]FC 16:21. [15]FC 10:290. [16]HQG 35-36. [17]LXX.

considered falsifications, nor do I think that they should be so regarded in any way. Rather, where no error by the copyist is ascertained and where the sense would be harmonious with the truth and would proclaim the truth, we should believe that they were moved by the Holy Spirit to say something differently, not as part of the service that they did as translators but as exercising the freedom that they enjoyed as prophets. CITY OF GOD 15.14.[18]

[18]LCL 491*.

5:28-32 LAMECH BEGETS NOAH

[28]*When Lamech had lived a hundred and eighty-two* years, he became the father of a son,* [29]*and called his name Noah,† saying, "Out of the ground which the LORD has cursed this one shall bring us relief from our work and from the toil of our hands."‡* [30]*Lamech lived after the birth of Noah† five hundred and ninety-five§ years, and had other sons and daughters.* [31]*Thus all the days of Lamech were seven hundred and seventy-seven years;# and he died.*

[32]*After Noah† was five hundred years old, Noah† became the father of Shem, Ham,** and Japheth.*

*LXX one hundred and eighty-eight †LXX Noe ‡LXX this one will bring us relief from our work and from the griefs of our hands and from the ground that the Lord has cursed §LXX five hundred and sixty-five #LXX seven hundred and fifty-three **LXX Cham

OVERVIEW: Lamech prophesies that Noah, whose name means "relief," will bring relief to humankind (EPHREM). Lamech's prophecy prefigures Christ (ORIGEN). Noah was considered an example of virtue because he preserved his virginity for five hundred years (EPHREM).

5:28-29 Relief from Work and Toil

NOAH WILL BRING RELIEF TO HUMANITY.
EPHREM THE SYRIAN: Enoch begot Methuselah, and Methuselah begot Lamech, and Lamech begot Noah (whose name means "relief" in Hebrew and Syriac). Lamech prophesied about his son and said, "This one shall bring us relief from our work and from the toil of our hands and from the earth which the Lord cursed." His offerings . . . will be pleasing to God who, because of the sin of the earth's inhabitants, will destroy in the waters of wrath the buildings that we have made and the plants over which our hands have toiled. COMMENTARY ON GENESIS 5.2.2.[1]

THIS PROPHECY IS MORE APPROPRIATE FOR CHRIST. ORIGEN: By ascending through

[1]FC 91:134.

the individual levels of the dwellings [in the ark built by Noah during the flood], one arrives at Noah himself, whose name means rest or righteous, who is Jesus Christ. For what Lamech his father says is not appropriate to the ancient Noah. For "this one," he says, "shall give us rest from the labors and the sorrows of our hands and from the earth that the Lord God cursed." For how shall it be true that the ancient Noah gave rest to that Lamech or to that people who were then contained in the lands? How is there a cessation from the labors and sorrows in the times of Noah? Jesus only has given rest to humanity and has freed the earth from the curse with which the Lord God cursed it. HOMILIES ON GENESIS 2.3.[2]

5:32 Noah the Father of Shem, Ham and Japheth

NOAH IS AN EXAMPLE OF VIRTUE. EPHREM THE SYRIAN: After recounting the ten generations from Adam to Noah, Moses said, "Noah was five hundred years old and begot Shem and Ham and Japheth." During this entire time Noah was an example to his sons by his virtue, for he had preserved virginity for five hundred years among those of whom it was said, "All flesh corrupted its path."[3] COMMENTARY ON GENESIS 6.1.1.[4]

---

[2]FC 71:79. [3]Gen 6:12. [4]FC 91:134.

6:1-4 THE SONS OF GOD UNITE WITH THE DAUGHTERS OF MEN

[1]When men began to multiply on the face of the ground, and daughters were born to them, [2]the sons of God saw that the daughters of men were fair; and they took to wife such of them as they chose. [3]Then the LORD said, "My spirit shall not abide in man for ever, for he is flesh, but his days shall be a hundred and twenty years." [4]The Nephilim* were on the earth in those days, and also afterward, when the sons of God came in to the daughters of men, and they bore children to them. These were the mighty men* that were of old, the men of renown.

*LXX giants

OVERVIEW: The sons of God are angels who forsake the beauty of God for perishable beauty and unite themselves with women (CLEMENT OF ALEXANDRIA). Their desires were set on things of earth (NEMESIUS OF EMESA).

Others argue that the sons of God are the sons of Seth, who marry the daughters of Cain (EPHREM).

The words "my spirit shall not abide in man" demonstrate that the whole man had been changed into something worse after the fall of Adam (AUGUSTINE), but God nevertheless grants to this generation of men 120 years for repentance (EPHREM). According to Augustine, who follows the argument of Ephrem, the giants were generated by the sons of Seth and the daughters of Cain (AUGUSTINE), whereas Ambrose, who resumes the view expressed by Clement, maintains that they were born from angels uniting to mortal women (AMBROSE). Both these writers agree that the giants symbolize those persons who are devoted only to earthly desires. Strength tends toward arrogance (BASIL). Their time for repentance was limited (JEROME).

6:1-2 The Sons of God, the Daughters of Men

FALLEN ANGELS ENTICED BY EARTHLY BEAUTY. CLEMENT OF ALEXANDRIA: The mind is led astray by pleasure, and the virgin center of the mind, if not disciplined by the Word, degenerates into licentiousness and reaps disintegration as reward for its transgressions. An example of this for you is the angels who forsook the beauty of God for perishable beauty and fell as far as heaven is from the earth. CHRIST THE EDUCATOR 3.2.14.[1]

THEIR DESIRES SET ON THINGS OF EARTH. NEMESIUS OF EMESA: Of the incorporeal beings, only angels fell away, and not all of them, but some only, that inclined to things below and set their desire on things of earth, withdrawing themselves from their relations with things above, even from God. ON THE NATURE OF MAN 58.[2]

THE SONS OF GOD ARE THE SONS OF SETH.

EPHREM THE SYRIAN: [Moses] called the sons of Seth "sons of God," those who, like the sons of Seth, had been called "the righteous people of God." The beautiful daughters of men whom they saw were the daughters of Cain who adorned themselves and became a snare to eyes of the sons of Seth. Then Moses said "they took to wife such of them as they chose," because when "they took" them, they acted very haughtily over those whom they chose. A poor one would exalt himself over the wife of a rich man, and an old man would sin with one who was young. The ugliest of all would act arrogantly over the most beautiful. COMMENTARY ON GENESIS 6.3.1.[3]

6:3 Humans' Lifespan Limited

ADAM'S SIN HAS CHANGED HUMANITY INTO SOMETHING WORSE. AUGUSTINE: By the justice of God the whole human race was delivered into the power of the devil, the sin of the first man passing originally into all persons of both sexes, who were born through conjugal union, the debt of our first parents binding all their posterity. This delivering was first indicated in Genesis, where, when it was said to the serpent, "Earth shall you eat,"[4] it was said to the man, "Earth you are, and into earth shall you return."[5] The death of the body was foretold by "into earth shall you return," because he would not have experienced it if he had remained upright as he had been created. But what he says to the living man, "earth you are," shows that the whole man has been changed into something worse, for "earth you

---

[1]FC 23:210-11. [2]LCC 4:420. [3]FC 91:134-35. [4]Gen 3:14. [5]Gen 3:19.

are" is just the same as saying "My spirit shall not remain in those men, because they are flesh." Hence God showed that he had then delivered man to the devil, to whom he had said, "Earth shall you eat." ON THE TRINITY 13.12.16.[6]

TIME GRANTED TO THIS GENERATION FOR REPENTANCE. EPHREM THE SYRIAN: This generation will not live nine hundred years like the previous generations, for it is flesh and its days are filled with the deeds of flesh. Therefore, their days will be one hundred and twenty years. If they repent during this time, they will be saved from the wrath that is about to come upon them. But if they do not repent, by their deeds they will call down wrath upon themselves. Grace granted one hundred and twenty years for repentance to a generation that, according to justice, was not worthy of repentance. COMMENTARY ON GENESIS 6.4.1.[7]

THE TIME FOR REPENTANCE. JEROME: Furthermore, lest [God] may seem to be cruel in that he had not given to sinners a place for repentance, he added, "But their days will be 120 years," that is, they will have 120 years to do repentance. It is not therefore that human life was contracted to 120 years, as many wrongly assert, but that 120 years were given to that generation for repentance, since indeed we find that after the flood Abraham lived 175 years and others more than 200 and 300 years. Since indeed they despised to do repentance, God was unwilling for his decree to await its time, but cutting off the space of twenty years he brought on the flood in the one hundredth year that had been destined for doing repentance. QUESTION ON GENESIS 6.3.[8]

6:4 The Men of Renown

THE GIANTS OF OLD. EPHREM THE SYRIAN: The house of Cain, because the earth had been cursed so as not to give them its strength, produced small harvests, deprived of its strength, just as it is today that some seeds, fruits and grasses give strength and some do not. Because at that time they were cursed and sons of the cursed and were dwelling in the land of curses, they would gather and eat produce that lacked nutrition, and those who ate these were without strength just like the food that they ate. As for the Sethites, on the other hand, because they were the descendants of the blessed [Seth] and were dwelling in the land along the boundary of the fence of paradise, their produce was abundant and full of strength. So too were the bodies of those who ate that produce strong and powerful. COMMENTARY ON GENESIS 6.5.1.[9]

THE NEPHILIM ARE A RACE OF GIANTS. AUGUSTINE: All that we indubitably know, from the authentic Scripture in the Hebrew and Christian traditions, is the fact that in the period before the flood there were many giants, all of whom belonged to the earthly city in human society, and that there were sons of God descended from Seth who abandoned their holiness and sank down into this city of men. There is nothing surprising in the fact that giants could be born from men like that. In any case, they were not all giants, even though there were more giants before the flood than in all subsequent ages. They served a divine purpose in that they reveal to anyone who is wise that mere bodily magnitude and

---

[6]FC 45:391. [7]FC 91:135-36. [8]HQG 99. [9]FC 91:136.

might have no more value than bodily beauty. CITY OF GOD 15.23.[10]

FROM FALLEN ANGELS UNITING TO MORTAL WOMEN. AMBROSE: "The giants (Nephilim) were on the earth in those days." The author of the divine Scripture does not mean that those giants must be considered, according to the tradition of poets, as sons of the earth[11] but asserts that those whom he defines with such a name because of the extraordinary size of their body were generated by angels and women. And let us see whether by any chance the men who only take care of their body and not of their soul are similar to the Nephilim and at the same time to those giants who were born from the earth according to the tales of the poets and despised the authority of the gods by confiding in the hugeness of their body. Must we really consider as different from giants those men who, even though they are composed of body and soul, despise the most precious good of the soul, that is, the activity of the mind, and show themselves to be imitators of this flesh, as if confirming that they were heirs of their own mother's foolishness.[12] They only struggle in vain when they

believe that they will conquer the heaven with their bold desires and their earthly activities. On the contrary, by choosing a lower way of life and despising the higher life, they are condemned with greater severity since they are guilty of voluntary sins. ON NOAH 4.8.[13]

STRENGTH ELICITS ARROGANCE. BASIL THE GREAT: Strength of arm, swiftness of foot and comeliness of body—the spoils of sickness and the plunder of time—also awaken pride in man, unaware as he is that "All flesh is grass and all the glory of man as the flower of the field. The grass is withered and the flower is fallen."[14] Such was the arrogance of the giants because of their strength.[15] Such also was the God-defying pride of the witless Goliath.[16] HOMILY 20, OF HUMILITY.[17]

---

[10]FC 14:475. [11]Ambrose alludes to the pagan myth of the giants, who were generated by the earth. Confiding in their huge bodies and strength, according to this myth, they tried to climb Olympus in order to dethrone Zeus but were destroyed by the thunderbolts that the god hurled at them. [12]The foolishness of Eve. [13]PL 14:385; CSEL 32:418. [14]Is 40:6. [15]Gen 6:4; Wis 14:6. [16]1 Sam 17:4-10. [17]FC 9:476-77.

6:5-7 THE LORD DECIDES TO PUNISH HUMAN WICKEDNESS

[5]*The LORD saw that the wickedness of man was great in the earth, and that every imagination of the thoughts of his heart was only evil continually.* [6]*And the LORD was sorry that he had made man on the earth, and it grieved him to his heart.** [7]*So the LORD said, "I will blot out man whom I have created from the face of the ground, man and beast and creeping*

things and birds of the air, for I am sorry that I have made them."

*LXX and he thought [what to do]

OVERVIEW: After the union of the sons of Seth with the daughters of Cain, the wickedness of humankind increases (EPHREM). In his condemnation of humanity God shows both solicitude and severity (SALVIAN THE PRESBYTER). God's anger, expressed by the words "he was sorry that he had made man," implies no inconstancy or perturbation in the divine mind. God does not repent as human beings repent. God announces the death of the animals, which are not guilty of sin, either in order to declare the magnitude of the coming disaster (AUGUSTINE) or because those who had been exclusively created for the sake of man had to perish with him (AMBROSE).

6:5 The Wickedness of Humanity Was Great

CONSEQUENCES OF THE UNION BETWEEN THE SONS OF SETH AND THE DAUGHTERS OF CAIN. EPHREM THE SYRIAN: After Moses spoke about the mighty men[1] who were born into the tribe of Cain, whose women, even though beautiful, were nevertheless smaller than the sons of Seth, he then said, "The Lord saw that the wickedness of man was great in the earth and that every inclination of the thoughts of his heart was always evil," for in the years given to them for repentance[2] they had increased their sins. "The wickedness of mankind was great in the earth," that is, evil extended and spread throughout both those tribes. "The inclination of the thoughts of their hearts was always evil," for their sins were not committed only occasionally, but their sins were incessant. Night and day they would not desist from their wicked thoughts. COMMENTARY ON GENESIS 6.6.1.[3]

6:6-7 The Lord Grieved by Humanity

GOD'S CARE, SORROW AND SEVERITY TOWARD HUMAN SIN. SALVIAN THE PRESBYTER: Let us consider how both the solicitude and severity of the Lord are shown equally in all these words. First, he said, "And God saw that the wickedness of man was great." Second, he said, "He was touched inwardly with sorrow of heart." Third, "I will destroy man whom I have created." In the first statement, wherein it is said that God sees all things, his providential care is shown. In the statement that he has sorrow is shown his solicitude amid the dread of his wrath. The statement about his punishment shows his severity as a judge. Holy Scripture says, "God repented that he had made man on earth." This does not mean that God is affected by emotion or is subject to any passion. Rather, the Divine Word, to impart more fully to us a true understanding of the Scriptures, speaks "as if" in terms of human emotions. By using the term "repentant God," it shows the force of God's rejection. God's anger is simply the punishment of the sinner. GOVERNANCE OF GOD 1.7.[4]

GOD'S ANGER IMPLIES NO PERTURBATION OF THE DIVINE MIND. AUGUSTINE: God's "anger" implies no perturbation of the divine mind. It is simply the divine judgment passing

---

[1]Gen 6:4. [2]Gen 6:3. [3]FC 91:137. [4]FC 3:41.

sentence on sin. And when God "thinks and then has second thoughts," this merely means that changeable realities come into relation with his immutable reason. For God cannot "repent," as human beings repent, of what he has done, since in regard to everything his judgment is as fixed as his foreknowledge is clear. But it is only by the use of such human expressions that Scripture can make its many kinds of readers whom it wants to help to feel, as it were, at home. Only thus can Scripture frighten the proud and arouse the slothful, provoke inquiries and provide food for the convinced. This is possible only when Scripture gets right down to the level of the lowliest readers. CITY OF GOD 15.25.[5]

WHY DOES GOD ANNOUNCE THE DEATH OF THE ANIMALS? AUGUSTINE: When God announces the death of all animals on the earth and in the air, the intention is to declare the magnitude of the coming disaster. There is no question here of punishing with death irra-

tional animals as though they were guilty of sin. CITY OF GOD 15.25.[6]

ANIMALS DESTROYED BECAUSE THEY HAD BEEN CREATED FOR THE SAKE OF HUMANITY. AMBROSE: "I will blot out man and beasts and creeping things and birds of the air." What transgression could the irrational creatures have ever committed? But since they had been created for the sake of man, after that for whom they had been created was wiped out, it was logical that they were destroyed too, because there was no one who could profit from them. This is also clear in a deeper sense. Man is a mind endowed with reason. Man is defined as a living, mortal and rational being. When he, who is the principal element, disappears, every aspect of sensible life also disappears. ON NOAH 4.10.[7]

[5]FC 14:476-77. [6]FC 14:477. [7]PL 14:386; CSEL 32:419.

6:8-10 NOAH IS A RIGHTEOUS MAN IN A CORRUPTED WORLD

[8]*But Noah* found favor in the eyes of the LORD.*
[9]*These are the generations of Noah.* Noah* was a righteous man, blameless[†] in his generation; Noah* walked with[‡] God.* [10]*And Noah* had three sons, Shem, Ham,[§] and Japheth.*

*LXX Noe †LXX perfect ‡LXX was pleasing to §LXX Cham

OVERVIEW: Noah's virtue shines through the widespread corruption of his times (CHRYSOS-

TOM). Noah was perfect as far as citizens of the city of God can be perfect during their pilgrimage in this present earthly life (AUGUS-TINE). He was pious by his own choice at a time when the obstacles to virtue were many (CHRYSOSTOM).

6:8-9 Noah Found Favor with the Lord

NOAH'S VIRTUE IN HIS CORRUPTED TIMES. CHRYSOSTOM: The Scriptures have shown us the gravity of human wickedness and the severity of the punishment that had to be inflicted on it. They then point out to us the one who amid such a multitude had been able to keep a sincere virtue. Virtue in fact is admirable even for itself. If someone cultivates virtue among those who refuse it, he makes it much more worthy of admiration. Therefore the Scriptures, as though in admiration of this just man, point out the contrast: that only one man who was living among those who soon would experience the wrath of God, this Noah, "found favor in the eyes of the Lord God." He "found favor," but "in the eyes of God"; not simply "he found favor" but "in the eyes of the Lord God." This is said in order to show us that he had a single purpose, that is, to be praised by that eye that never sleeps or rests. He had no care for human glory or scorn or irreverence. HOMILIES ON GENESIS 23.4.[1]

IN WHAT SENSE PERFECT? AUGUSTINE: Speaking of Noah, our unerring Scriptures tell us that he "was a just and perfect man in his generation," meaning that he was perfect as far as citizens of the city of God can be perfect during the pilgrimage of this present life, not, of course, as perfect as they are to be in

that immortal life in which they will be as perfect as the angels of God. CITY OF GOD 15.26.[2]

NOAH PIOUS BY HIS CHOICE. CHRYSOSTOM: Do you see how the Lord created our nature to enjoy free will? I mean, how did it happen, tell me, that while those people showed enthusiasm for wickedness and rendered themselves liable to punishment, this man opted for virtue, shunned association with them and thus felt no effect of punishment? Is it not crystal clear that each person chose wickedness or virtue of his own volition? You see, if that were not the case and freedom did not have its roots in our nature, those people would not have been punished, nor would others receive reward for their virtue. Since, however, everything has been allowed to remain with our choice owing to grace from on high, punishment duly awaits the sinners, and reward and recompense those who practice virtue. HOMILIES ON GENESIS 22.5.[3]

IN NOAH'S DAYS IT WAS EXTREMELY DIFFICULT TO BE BLAMELESS. CHRYSOSTOM: Therefore, in praise of Noah, Scripture not merely called him "blameless" but added "among the men of his day" to make it clear that he was so at that time when the obstacles to virtue were many. Besides, other men were illustrious after him, yet he will have no less praise than they. For he was blameless in his own time. HOMILIES ON JOHN 71.[4]

---

[1]FC 82:90*. [2]FC 14:477. [3]FC 82:71. [4]FC 41:266.

6:11-16 GOD ORDERS NOAH TO MAKE AN ARK

¹¹Now the earth was corrupt in God's sight, and the earth was filled with violence. ¹²And God saw the earth, and behold, it was corrupt; for all flesh had corrupted their way upon the earth. ¹³And God said to Noah,* "I have determined to make an end of all flesh;[†] for the earth is filled with violence through them; behold, I will destroy them with the earth. ¹⁴Make yourself an ark of gopher wood;[‡] make rooms in the ark, and cover it inside and out with pitch. ¹⁵This is how you are to make it: the length of the ark three hundred cubits, its breadth fifty cubits, and its height thirty cubits. ¹⁶Make a roof^k for the ark, and finish it to a cubit above; and set the door of the ark in its side; make it with lower, second, and third decks.

k Or window *LXX Noe †LXX The time of all mankind has come before me ‡LXX squared timbers

OVERVIEW: The wives of the sons of Seth, after being abandoned by their husbands, who married the daughters of Cain, lose their modesty, so that "all flesh corrupted its path" (EPHREM). Because of this wickedness and corruption God decided to cause a flood and destroy all men except for Noah and his family (AUGUSTINE). The dimensions in the length, breadth and height of the ark, which God orders Noah to build, have a mystical meaning (JEROME). The ark, in its different aspects, symbolizes Jesus Christ and his church (AUGUSTINE).

6:11-13 The Earth Corrupt in God's Sight

ALL FLESH CORRUPTED. EPHREM THE SYRIAN: Because the sons of Seth were going into the daughters of Cain, they turned away from their first wives whom they had previously taken. Then these wives, too, disdained their own continence and now, because of their husbands, quickly began to abandon their modesty, which up until that time they had preserved for their husbands' sake. It is because of this wantonness that assailed both the men and the women that Scripture says, "All flesh corrupted its path." COMMENTARY ON GENESIS 6.3.3.[1]

GOD CONDEMNS HUMANITY FOR WICKEDNESS. AUGUSTINE: Somebody may say to me, "Was Adam, created by God as the first man in the original state of the world, condemned for lack of faith or for sin?" It was not incredulity but disobedience that was the cause for his condemnation and the reason why all his posterity are punished. Cain too was condemned, not for lack of faith but because he killed his brother. Why need I seek further proof when I read that this whole world was destroyed not for incredulity but for wickedness. CHRISTIAN LIFE 13.[2]

---

[1]FC 91:135. [2]FC 16:35.

6:14 *Instructions for Making the Ark*

Mystical Meaning of the Dimensions of the Ark. Jerome: We read in Genesis that the ark that Noah built was three hundred cubits long, fifty cubits wide and thirty cubits high. Notice the mystical significance of the numbers.[3] In the number fifty, penance is symbolized because the fiftieth psalm of King David is the prayer of his repentance.[4] Three hundred contains the symbol of crucifixion. The letter T is the sign for three hundred, whence Ezekiel says, "Mark THAV on the forehead of those who moan; and do not kill any marked with THAV." No one marked with the sign of the cross on his forehead can be struck by the devil; he is not able to efface this sign, only sin can. We have spoken of the ark, of the number fifty, of the number three hundred. Let us comment on the number thirty because the ark was thirty cubits high and finished above in one cubit. First, we repent in the number fifty; then, through penance, we arrive at the mystery of the cross; we reach the mystery of the cross through the perfect Word that is Christ. As a matter of fact, when Jesus was baptized, according to Luke, "he was thirty years of age." These same thirty cubits were finished off one cubit above. Fifty, and three hundred, and thirty were finished above in one cubit,[5] that is, in one[6] faith of God.[7] Homilies 84.[8]

The Ark as a Symbol of Christ and His Church. Augustine: Undoubtedly the ark is a symbol of the city of God on its pilgrimage in history. It is a figure of the church that was saved by the wood on which there hung the "Mediator between God and men, himself man, Jesus Christ."[9] Even the very measurements of length, height and breadth of the ark are meant to point to the reality of the human body into which he came as it was foretold that he would come. It will be recalled that the length of a normal body from head to foot is six times the breadth from one side to the other and ten times the thickness from back to front. Measure a man who is lying on the ground, either prone or supine. He is six times as long from head to foot as he is wide from left to right or right to left, and he is ten times as long as he is high from the ground up. That is why the ark was made three hundred cubits in length, fifty in breadth and thirty in height. As for the door in the side, that surely, symbolizes the open wound made by the lance in the side of the Crucified—the door by which those who come to him enter in, in the sense that believers enter the church by means of the sacraments that issued from that wound. It was ordered that the ark be made out of squared timbers—a symbol of the four-square stability of a holy life, which, like a cube, stands firm however it is turned. So it is with every other detail of the ark's construction.[10] They are all symbols of something in the church. City of God 15.26.[11]

---

[3]Virtually all biblical numbers had mystical significance for Jerome and for most of the Fathers. [4]The fifty-first psalm in the Hebrew Bible becomes the fiftieth psalm in the LXX. [5]Including the roof. [6]Triune. [7]Thus Jerome sees a progression from repentance to faith in the cross to the maturing of the believer through sanctifying grace, all prefigured in the dimensions of the ark. Although farfetched to a modern culture that is not attuned to the spiritual significance of numbers, such speculations are common among the early Christian writers, who took it as a premise that every word and number in the sacred text had meaning that was inviting investigation. This is less properly designated as allegory than as numerical typology. [8]FC 57:190-91. [9]1 Tim 2:5. [10]The body of Christ is thus prefigured in the ark. [11]FC 14:477-78.

6:17-22 GOD INSTRUCTS NOAH
TO BRING HIS FAMILY AND TWO OF EVERY
SORT OF ANIMAL INTO THE ARK

[17]For behold, I will bring a flood of waters upon the earth, to destroy all flesh in which is the breath of life from under heaven; everything that is on the earth shall die. [18]But I will establish my covenant with you; and you shall come into the ark, you, your sons, your wife, and your sons' wives with you. [19]And of every living thing of all flesh,* you shall bring two of every sort into the ark, to keep them alive with you; they shall be male and female. [20]Of the birds according to their kinds, and of the animals according to their kinds, of every creeping thing of the ground according to its kind, two of every sort shall come in to you, to keep them alive.† [21]Also take with you every sort of food that is eaten, and store it up; and it shall serve as food for you and for them." [22]Noah‡ did this; he did all that God commanded him.

*LXX And of every animal and any creeping thing and of all the beasts and of all flesh †LXX adds male and female ‡LXX Noe

OVERVIEW: God announces that he will wash away with water the sins of the world (JOHN OF DAMASCUS). The words "I will establish my covenant with you" are addressed to all those who are righteous (AMBROSE). God instructs Noah to bring into the ark his family. Noah keeps his sons separated from their wives so that chastity can be preserved throughout the deluge (JOHN OF DAMASCUS). Noah also receives the order to bring two of every sort of animals into the ark and to store food for the period of the deluge (AUGUSTINE) and to keep them alive (EPHREM).

6:17 "Everything That Is on the Earth Shall Die"

GOD WASHES AWAY THE POLLUTION OF SINS WITH WATER. JOHN OF DAMASCUS: From the beginning "the spirit of God moved over the waters,"[1] and over and again Scripture testifies to the fact that water is purifying. It was with water that God washed away the sin of the world in the time of Noah. ORTHODOX FAITH 4.9.[2]

6:18 The Covenant with Noah

THESE WORDS ADDRESSED TO THE RIGHTEOUS. AMBROSE: Every earthly thing dies with the deluge and only the righteous live forever. Thus the words "I will establish my covenant with you" are addressed to the righteous. He is the heir of divine grace, the recipient of the heavenly inheritance, a sharer of the very holy goods. ON NOAH 10.35.[3]

---

[1]Gen 1:2. [2]FC 37:345. [3]PL 14:396; CSEL 32:435.

Noah Keeps His Sons Separated from Their Wives. John of Damascus: When Noah was ordered to enter the ark and was entrusted with the safeguarding of the seed of the earth, he was given this command, which reads: "Come into the ark, you, your sons, your wife and your sons' wives." He separated them from their wives, so that with the help of chastity they might escape the ocean's depths and that worldwide destruction. Orthodox Faith 4.25.[4]

6:19-21 *Two of Every Living Thing*

God Orders Noah to Bring Couples of Animals into the Ark. Augustine: A further question asked by the curious concerns those tiny creatures, smaller even than mice and lizards, such as locusts, beetles, flies and even fleas. Were there not more of these in the ark than the number prescribed by God? Those who raise this difficulty must first be reminded that the words "that creep on the earth" imply that there was no need to preserve in the ark animals that live either in the water like fishes or on the water, as certain birds do. Second, the words "male and female" imply that there was no need to have in the ark such animals as are not born in the normal way but populate from putrid or inanimate matter.[5] Or if they were in the ark, they could have been there as they are in our houses and not in any definite number. On the other hand, if the sacred mystery that was there being enacted demanded down to the last number of nonmarine animals the perfect accord of symbolic figure and historical fact, then God took care of this in his own way and did not leave it to Noah or his family. City of God 15.27.[6]

Keep Them Alive. Ephrem the Syrian: On that same day elephants came from the east, apes and peacocks approached from the south, other animals gathered from the west, and still others hastened to come from the north. Lions came from the jungles, and wild beasts arrived from their lairs. Deer and wild asses came from their lands, and the mountain beasts gathered from their mountains.

When those of that generation gathered [to see] this novel sight, it was not to repent but rather to amuse themselves. Then in their very presence the lions began to enter the ark, and the bulls, with no fear, hurried in right on their heels to seek shelter with the lions. The wolves and the lambs entered together, and the hawks and the sparrows together with the doves and the eagles. Commentary on Genesis 6.9.2.[7]

---

[4]FC 37:394-95. [5]Augustine follows the Aristotelian theory according to which insects generate spontaneously from putrid matter. This theory, technically defined as abiogenesis, was confuted in the seventeenth century by the Italian scientist and poet Francesco Redi. [6]FC 14:482. [7]FC 91:139.

7:1-5 SEVEN PAIRS OF ALL CLEAN ANIMALS
AND ONE PAIR OF ALL UNCLEAN ANIMALS

¹Then the LORD said to Noah,* "Go into the ark, you and all your household, for I have seen that you are righteous before me in this generation. ²Take with you seven pairs† of all clean animals, the male and his mate;‡ and a pair of the animals that are not clean, the male and his mate;‡ ³and seven pairs† of the birds of the air also, male and female,§ to keep their kind alive upon the face of all the earth. ⁴For in seven days I will send rain upon the earth forty days and forty nights; and every living thing# that I have made I will blot out from the face of the ground." ⁵And Noah* did all that the LORD had commanded him.

*LXX Noe †LXX in sevens ‡LXX male and female §LXX adds and a pair of the birds that are not clean, male and female #LXX everything that rises up (*exanastasis*)

OVERVIEW: When God commands Noah to "go into the ark," he symbolically commands the righteous to seek the truth, which, amid the deluge of passions, will direct him to salvation. The numbers seven and two of the pairs of clean and unclean animals received into the ark symbolize the principles of perfection and imperfection (AMBROSE). The ark receiving clean and unclean animals prefigures the church, which allows those who are unclean to dwell as tares with the clean ones by reason of tolerance and not because of a total failure of discipline (AUGUSTINE). God clearly shows the people of Noah's generation that the deluge is about to come, but they do not repent (EPHREM).

7:1-3 God Tells Noah to Go into the Ark

DEEPER MEANING OF THE WORDS "GO INTO THE ARK." AMBROSE: But a deeper meaning leads us to believe that the strength of the mind in the soul and the soul in the body is what the father of a family is in his house. What the mind is in the soul, the soul is in the body. If the mind is certain, the house is safe; the soul is safe if the soul is uninjured; the flesh also is uninjured. A temperate mind restrains every passion, controls the senses, rules the words. Therefore God justly says to the righteous, "Go into," that is, go into yourself, into your mind, in the ruling part of your soul. Salvation is there, the rudder is there; outside the deluge rages, outside there is danger. In truth if you have been inside, you are safe outside too, because when the mind is the straightforward guide of the self, the thoughts are righteous, the actions are righteous. If no vice obscures the mind, the thoughts are trustworthy. ON NOAH 11.38.[1]

SYMBOLISM OF THE PAIRS OF CLEAN AND UNCLEAN ANIMALS. AMBROSE: Let us see now why it was ordered that seven males and seven females of clean animals and two males and two females of unclean ones were received

---

[1]PL 14:397; CSEL 32:436.

into the ark, so that the seed all over the earth might be nourished. And, as I believe, it is said that a clean week begins, since pure and holy is number seven. In fact it is united to no number and generated by no number. Therefore it is said to be virgin, because it generates nothing from itself, and we may add that this is said with good reason, since it is lacking and immune from maternal childbirth and from intercourse with female. The number two, on the other hand, is not full because it is divided; and what is not full has some void in itself. But the number seven is full, because the week is like the decade and is similar to that principal number, because the alpha is similar to that One who always exists. From him the virtues that are in every species take their origin, and by him they are moved. ON NOAH 12.39.[2]

THE ARK AS THE CHRISTIAN CHURCH. AUGUSTINE: Let us recognize that the ark prefigured the church. Let us be the clean beasts in it. Yet let us not refuse to allow the unclean ones to be carried in it with us until the end of the deluge. They were together in the ark, but they were not equally pleasing to the Lord as a savor of sacrifice, for after the deluge, Noah offered sacrifice to God of the clean, not of the unclean. But the ark was not on that account abandoned before the time by any of the clean because of the unclean. LETTERS 108.[3]

THE SINNER IS RECEIVED BY REASON OF TOLERANCE. AUGUSTINE: By this prefigura-tion it is prophesied that in the church there will be the impure by reason of tolerance, not because of corruption of doctrine or dissolution of discipline. Furthermore, the unclean animals did not break their way into the ark through any part of the structure, but because the ark was an integral whole, they entered by the one and only entrance that the architect had made. FAITH AND WORKS 27.49.[4]

7:4-5 Noah Did As the Lord Commanded

GOD SHOWS THAT THE DELUGE IS COMING. EPHREM THE SYRIAN: God granted one hundred years while the ark was being made to that generation, and still they did not repent. God summoned beasts that they had never seen and still they showed no remorse. He established a state of peace between the predatory animals and those who are preyed upon, and still they had no awe. God delayed yet seven more days for them, even after Noah and every creature had entered the ark, leaving the gate of the ark open to them. This is a wondrous thing that no lion remembered its jungle and no species of beast or bird visited its customary haunt! Although those of that generation saw all that went on outside and inside the ark, they were still not persuaded to renounce their evil deeds. COMMENTARY ON GENESIS 6.10.2.[5]

---

[2]PL 14:397; CSEL 32:437. [3]FC 18:236-37. [4]FC 27:280-81. [5]FC 91:140.

7:6-9 NOAH GETS READY
FOR THE COMING DELUGE

⁶*Noah* was six hundred years old when the flood of waters came upon the earth.* ⁷*And Noah* and his sons and his wife and his sons' wives with him went into the ark, to escape the waters of the flood.* ⁸*Of clean animals, and of animals that are not clean, and of birds, and of everything that creeps on the ground,* ⁹*two and two, male and female, went into the ark with Noah,* as God had commanded Noah.**

*LXX Noe

OVERVIEW: Noah prefigures Christ and the wood of the ark the cross which carries us to deliverance. The family of Noah in the ark are a prefiguration of the Christian church (AUGUSTINE). In the ark men and women are separated, and the same rule is observed in the church in baptism (CYRIL OF JERUSALEM).

7:7-9 Noah, His Family and the Animals Enter the Ark

NOAH AND THE ARK AS SYMBOLS OF CHRIST AND THE NATIONS. AUGUSTINE: Christ was also represented in Noah, and the world, in that ark. For why were all living creatures shut up in that ark except to signify all the nations? For God did not lack the capability of creating anew every species of living things. For when no creatures were in existence, did he not say, "Let the earth bring forth"[1] and the earth brought forth? So from the same source as he made them then, he could remake them. God made them by a word, so God could remake them by a word. TRACTATES ON THE GOSPEL OF JOHN 9.11.1.[2]

THE CHURCH IS PREFIGURED IN NOAH AND HIS FAMILY. AUGUSTINE: Was not Noah a holy man, who alone in the whole human race together with his whole house deserved to be delivered from the flood? And is not the church prefigured by Noah and his sons? They escape the flood, with wood (which symbolizes the cross) carrying them. TRACTATES ON THE GOSPEL OF JOHN 11.7.2.[3]

MEN AND WOMEN MUST BE KEPT SEPARATE IN CHURCH. CYRIL OF JERUSALEM: During the actual exorcism, while waiting for the others, let men be with men and women with women. For now I need Noah's ark that I may have Noah and his sons together, separate from his wife and his sons' wives. For although the ark was one and the door was closed, yet decorum was observed. So now, though the church doors are barred and you are all inside, let distinctions be kept: men with men, women with women. Let not the principle of salvation be made a pretext for spiritual license. Keeping close together is a good rule, provided that passion is kept at a distance. CATECHETICAL LECTURES 14.[4]

---

[1]Gen 1:24. [2]FC 78:205. [3]FC 79:16-17. [4]FC 61:80-81, regarding baptism.

7:10-16 GOD CAUSES RAIN TO FALL FOR FORTY DAYS AND FORTY NIGHTS

¹⁰And after seven days the waters of the flood came upon the earth.

¹¹In the six hundredth year of Noah's* life, in the second month, on the seventeenth† day of the month, on that day all the fountains of the great deep burst forth, and the windows‡ of the heavens were opened. ¹²And rain fell upon the earth forty days and forty nights. ¹³On the very same day Noah* and his sons, Shem and Ham§ and Japheth, and Noah's* wife and the three wives of his sons with them entered the ark, ¹⁴they and every beast according to its kind, and all the cattle according to their kinds, and every creeping thing that creeps on the earth according to its kind, every bird according to its kind, every bird of every sort. ¹⁵They went into the ark with Noah,* two and two of all flesh in which there was the breath of life. ¹⁶And they that entered, male and female of all flesh, went in as God had commanded him; and the LORD shut him in.*

*LXX Noe †LXX twenty-seventh ‡LXX cataracts (flood-gates?) §LXX Cham *LXX *adds* from the outside

OVERVIEW: The deluge caused by God demonstrates how he may actively intervene in earthly affairs (SALVIAN THE PRESBYTER). God brings on the deluge for forty days so that some men and women might still repent and somehow escape the ruin (CHRYSOSTOM). The months and years at the time of the deluge have the same duration as our months and years (AUGUSTINE).

After everybody has entered the ark, God shuts the door from the outside because he does not want Noah to be distressed by the sight of the disaster (CHRYSOSTOM). Those who have chosen to be outside the door are thus prevented from breaking it down (EPHREM). Since the family of Noah that enters the ark consists of eight souls, some psalms are entitled "for the octave" as a reference to the saved (JEROME). God closed the ark "from without" not by descending physically but as a witness to his almighty power (JUSTIN MARTYR).

7:10-12 The Flood Comes upon the Earth

THE DELUGE PROVES THAT GOD INTERVENES IN EARTHLY AFFAIRS. SALVIAN THE PRESBYTER: And then what? "All the fountains of the great deep were broken up, and the flood gates of heaven were opened. And the rain fell upon the earth forty days and forty nights." And a little later: "And all flesh was destroyed that moved upon the earth."[1] And again, "And Noah only remained alive and they that were with him in the ark."[2] Here and now I wish to ask them who call God indifferent to human affairs whether they believe that at that time he either cared for

---

[1]Gen 7:21. [2]Gen 7:23.

earthly affairs or intervened in them. GOVER-NANCE OF GOD 1.7.[3]

WHY DOES GOD BRING ON THE DELUGE FOR FORTY DAYS? CHRYSOSTOM: The fact, too, that he brought on the deluge for forty days and nights is a further wonderful sign of his loving kindness. His purpose in his great goodness was that at least some of them might come to their senses and escape that utter ruin, having before their eyes the annihilation of their peers and the destruction about to overwhelm them. I mean, the likelihood is that on the first day some proportion were drowned, an additional number on the second day, and likewise on the third day and so on. His reason for extending it for forty days was that he might remove from them any grounds for excuse. You see, had it been his wish and command, he could have submerged everything in one downpour. Instead, out of fidelity to his characteristic love he arranged for a stay of so many days. HOMILIES ON GENESIS 25.11.[4]

DURATION OF THE MONTHS AND YEARS AT THE TIME OF THE DELUGE. AUGUSTINE: It is now time to examine the evidence that proves convincingly that the biblical years, so far from being only one-tenth as long as ours, were precisely as long as the present solar years. This is true of the years used in giving those extremely long life spans. It is said, for example, that the flood occurred in the six hundredth year of Noah's life. But notice the full text: "The waters of the flood overflowed the earth in the six hundredth year of the life of Noah, in the second month, in the twenty-seventh day of the month." Now those words are inexplicable if a year was so short that it took ten of them to make one of ours. That

would mean that a year had only thirty-six days. For so short a year (if it was actually called a year in ancient usage) either had no months at all, or if it had twelve months, then each month could have had but three days. How, then, [can we] explain the words of the text, "in the six hundredth year . . . in the second month, in the twenty-seventh day of the month," unless the months then were the same as they are now? There is no other way of explaining how the flood could be said to have had a beginning on the twenty-seventh day of the second month. CITY OF GOD 15.14.[5]

7:13-16 The Lord Shut Noah in the Ark

GOD ENSURES NOAH'S WELL-BEING. CHRYSOSTOM: The text goes on, "The Lord God shut the ark from the outside." Notice in this place too the considerateness in the expression "God shut the ark from the outside," to teach us that he had ensured the good man's complete safety. The reason for adding "from the outside" to "he shut" was that the good man might not be in the position of seeing the disaster occur and suffering even greater distress. I mean, if he brooded over that terrible flood and set indelibly in his mind the destruction of the human race, the complete annihilation of all brute beasts and the disappearance, as it were, of people, animals and the earth itself, he would have been disturbed and anguished. HOMILIES ON GENESIS 25.12.[6]

GOD SHUTS THE DOOR TO PREVENT THOSE OUTSIDE FROM BREAKING IN. EPHREM THE SYRIAN: "The Lord shut the door before

---

[3]FC 3:41. [4]FC 82:132. [5]FC 14:444. [6]FC 82:132-33.

Noah," lest those left behind come at the time of the floods and break down the gate of the ark. The deluge came and "God blotted out all flesh. Only Noah was left and those that were with him in the ark." The springs of the abyss and the floodgates of heaven were open forty days and forty nights, and the "ark was afloat for one hundred fifty days."[7] COMMENTARY ON GENESIS 6.11.2.[8]

HOW THE ARK WAS CLOSED FROM WITH- OUT. JUSTIN MARTYR: "God closed the ark of Noah from without."[9] You should not imagine that the unbegotten God himself descended or ascended from any place. For the ineffable Father and Lord of all neither comes to any place, nor walks, nor sleeps, nor arises, but always remains in his place, wherever it may

be, acutely seeing and hearing, not with eyes or ears but with a power beyond description. DIALOGUE WITH TRYPHO 127.[10]

WHY CERTAIN PSALMS ARE TITLED "FOR THE OCTAVE." JEROME: [We see that] certain psalms are titled "for the octave." This is the day on which the synagogue comes to an end and the church is born.[11] This is the day in the number of which eight souls were preserved in the ark of Noah, and "its counterpart, the church," says Peter, "now saves you."[12] HOMI- LIES 93.[13]

---

[7]Gen 7:24. [8]FC 91:141. [9]Gen 7:16. [10]FC 6:345. [11]The day of resurrection, the eighth day. [12]1 Pet 3:21. [13]FC 57:248.

7:17-24 THE DELUGE COVERS THE EARTH

[17]*The flood continued forty days* upon the earth; and the waters increased, and bore up the ark, and it rose high above the earth.* [18]*The waters prevailed and increased greatly upon the earth; and the ark floated on the face of the waters.* [19]*And the waters prevailed so might- ily upon the earth that all the high mountains under the whole heaven were covered;* [20]*the waters prevailed above the mountains, covering them fifteen cubits deep.* [21]*And all flesh died that moved upon the earth, birds, cattle, beasts, all swarming creatures that swarm upon the earth, and every man;* [22]*everything on the dry land in whose nostrils was the breath of life died.* [23]*He blotted out every living thing† that was upon the face of the ground, man and animals and creeping things and birds of the air; they were blotted out from the earth. Only Noah‡ was left, and those that were with him in the ark.* [24]*And the waters pre- vailed upon the earth a hundred and fifty days.*

*LXX adds and forty nights †LXX everything that rises up (anastema) ‡LXX Noe

OVERVIEW: The deluge covers the entire earth and destroys every creature (CHRYSOSTOM). Only the summit of paradise is not reached: the flood stops at its foothills (EPHREM). The sentence "Everything on the dry land in whose nostrils was the breath of life died" refers to every living creature (AUGUSTINE). The deluge symbolizes the judgment of God that those who repent will escape (JUSTIN MARTYR).

The forty days prefigures the subsequent rite of baptism during Quadragesima, the forty days of Lent (MAXIMUS OF TURIN). That the Lord loves righteousness and hates iniquity is made manifest through the deluge (BEDE).

7:17-20 The Flood Continues for Forty Days

THE FORTY DAYS PREFIGURES LENT AND BAPTISM. MAXIMUS OF TURIN: But let us see where this most sacred number of forty days had its beginning. We read first in the Old Testament that in the time of Noah, when criminal wickedness had seized the whole human race, torrents of water poured forth from the opened floodgates of heaven for just as many days.[1] In a kind of mysterious image of Quadragesima, this inundation of the earth refers not so much to a flood as to baptism.[2] This was clearly a baptism in which the wickedness of sinners was removed and Noah's righteousness preserved. For this reason, then, the Lord has given us forty days now as well in imitation of that time, so that for this number of days, while the heavens are opened, a celestial rain of mercy might pour upon us and, with the flood, the water of the saving washing might enlighten us[3] in baptism and—as was the case then—the wickedness of our sins might be quenched in

us by the streams of water and the righteousness of our virtues preserved. For the very same thing is at issue with regard to Noah and in our own day: baptism is a flood to the sinner and a consecration to the faithful; by the Lord's washing, righteousness is preserved and unrighteousness is destroyed. SERMONS 50.2.[4]

THE DELUGE COVERS THE EARTH. CHRYSOSTOM: It is not without purpose that Scripture describes all this to us. Instead, its purpose is for us to learn that not only people, cattle, four-footed beasts and reptiles were drowned but also the birds of heaven and whatever inhabited the mountains, namely, animals and other wild creatures. Hence the text says, "The flood rose fifteen cubits above the mountains," for you to learn that the execution of the Lord's sentence had been effected. He said, remember, "After seven more days I will bring a deluge upon the earth and I will wipe off the face of the earth all the life I have made, from human beings to cattle, and from reptiles to birds of heaven."[5] So Scripture narrates this not simply to teach us the flood level[6] but that we may be able to understand along with this that there was absolutely nothing left standing—no wild beasts, no animals, no cattle—rather, everything was annihilated along with the human race. Since it was for their sake that all these creatures had been created, with the imminent destruction of the human beings it was fitting that these creatures too should

---

[1]Cf. Gen 7:7-20. [2]Cf. 1 Pet 3:20-21. [3]The reference to baptism as enlightenment, which is very common, dates at least to the middle of the second century. [4]ACW 50:119. [5]Gen 7:4. [6]As an objective fact.

meet their end. Then, after teaching us the great height reached by the flood waters and the fact that they rose a further fifteen cubits above the mountain peaks, it further adds out of fidelity to its characteristic precision, "There perished all flesh that moved on the earth—birds, animals, every reptile that moved on the earth, every human being—everything that had breath of life, everything on dry land: all perished."[7] That was not an idle reference in the words "everything on dry land"; instead, its purpose was to teach us that while others perished, the just man with everyone in the ark alone was saved. HOMILIES ON GENESIS 25.20.[8]

ONLY THE SUMMIT OF PARADISE NOT REACHED BY THE FLOOD. EPHREM THE SYRIAN:
With the eye of my mind
I gazed upon paradise.
The summit of every mountain
is lower than its summit,
the crest of the flood
reached only its foothills,
these it kissed with reverence
before turning back
to rise above and subdue the peak
of every hill and mountain.
The foothills of paradise it kisses,
while every summit it buffets.
HYMNS ON PARADISE 1.4.[9]

7:21-22 All Flesh Died

THE BREATH OF LIFE. AUGUSTINE: Then, a little further on in the same book [Genesis], one could just as easily have noticed the verse "Everything on the dry land in whose nostrils was the breath of life died." This means that everything that lived on the earth perished in

the flood. Thus we find that Holy Scripture is accustomed to use both phrases—"living soul" and "the breath of life"—in regard even to beasts, and in the verse "All things wherein there is the breath of life" the Greek text does not use the word *pneuma* but *pnoē*. CITY OF GOD 13.24.[10]

7:23-24 Living Things Blotted Out

THE DELUGE SYMBOLIZES THE JUDGMENT OF GOD. JUSTIN MARTYR: When the sacred text states that the entire earth was inundated, as the water reached a height of twenty-three feet above the highest mountains, it is evident that God was not speaking to your land [that is, Israel] in particular but to all those who are faithful to him, for whom he has arranged a restful haven in Jerusalem. All the signs that accompanied the flood prove my assertion. For by the expression "by water and faith and wood"[11] it is indicated that those who prepare themselves and repent of their sins shall escape the future judgment of God. DIALOGUE WITH TRYPHO 138.[12]

THE LORD LOVES RIGHTEOUSNESS, HATES INIQUITY. BEDE: We read in the story of holy Noah how he miraculously escaped the flood which destroyed the impious by being preserved with his household in the ark.[13] From this it is evident to everyone that the Lord who loves righteousness and hates iniquity[14] knows how to deliver the pious from temptation and to punish the impious with the punishment they deserve. . . . Through spiritual

---

[7]Gen 7:21-22. [8]FC 82:139-40. [9]HOP 78-79. [10]FC 14:343*. [11]Wis 10:4. [12]JMO 2:452-54. [13]Gen 6:13-19. [14]Ps 45:7 (44:8).

understanding this same text is shown to be full of more sacred mysteries, when the ark is discerned to signify the catholic church;[15] the water of the flood, baptism; the clean and unclean animals,[16] those in the church both spiritual and carnal; the wood of the ark which was smooth and covered with pitch,[17] the teachers who are stalwart as a result of their faith. ON THE TABERNACLE 2.7.69.[18]

---

[15]1 Pet 3:20-21. [16]Gen 7:2. [17]Gen 6:14. [18]TTH 18:70.

8:1-5 THE OCCUPANTS OF THE ARK STAY ABOARD FOR A YEAR

¹But God remembered Noah* and all the beasts and all the cattle† that were with him in the ark. And God made a wind blow over the earth, and the waters subsided; ²the fountains of the deep and the windows‡ of the heavens were closed, the rain from the heavens was restrained, ³and the waters receded from the earth continually. At the end of a hundred and fifty days the waters had abated; ⁴and in the seventh month, on the seventeenth§ day of the month, the ark came to rest upon the mountains of Ararat. ⁵And the waters continued to abate until the tenth month; in the tenth month, on the first day of the month, the tops of the mountains were seen.

*LXX Noe †LXX adds and all the birds and all the creeping things ‡LXX cataracts (flood-gates) §LXX twenty-seventh

---

OVERVIEW: The love of God accompanies Noah and all the occupants of the ark throughout the deluge (CHRYSOSTOM). The wind sent by God is the Holy Spirit (AMBROSE). The ark remains afloat for 150 days, but its occupants could not leave it before 365 days (EPHREM).

8:1-3 God Remembered Noah

THE LOVE OF GOD ACCOMPANIES THE ARK.

CHRYSOSTOM: See how God did everything out of his esteem for the human being. As in the case of the destruction of human beings in the flood he destroyed also along with them the whole range of brute beasts, so in this case too, when he intends to show his characteristic love for the good man out of his regard for him, he extends his goodness to the animal kingdom as well, the wild beasts, the birds and the reptiles. "God was mindful of Noah," the text says, "and of all the wild beasts, all the cattle and all the reptiles that were with him in the ark. God sent a wind upon the earth, and the water subsided." Being mindful of Noah, the text says, and of those with him in the ark, he directed the flood of water to halt so that little by little he might show his characteristic love and now give the good man a breath of fresh air, free him from the turmoil of his thoughts and restore him to a state of tranquility by granting him the enjoyment of daylight and a breath of fresh air. "God sent a wind upon the earth, and the water subsided. The torrents of the depths and the sluice gates of heaven were shut off." HOMILIES ON GENESIS 26.10.[1]

THE WIND SENT BY GOD IS THE HOLY SPIRIT.

AMBROSE: "And the Lord sent a breath over the earth and the water subsided." I do not believe that this has been said because under the name of breath we may think of the wind. In fact the wind had no power to dry the deluge. Otherwise the sea, which is moved every day by the winds, would become empty. How would the sea become empty because of the strength of the winds alone? Isn't it true that the strength that overcame the deluge spread all over the earth to the so-called Columns of Hercules[2] and the vast sea boiling over the tops of the highest mountains? There is no doubt, therefore, that that deluge was subsided by the invisible power of the Spirit, not through the wind as such but through divine intervention. ON NOAH 16.58.[3]

8:3-5 The Waters Abated

DURATION OF THE DELUGE.

EPHREM THE SYRIAN: The springs of the abyss and the floodgates of heaven were open forty days and forty nights and "the ark was afloat for one hundred fifty days."[4] But after one hundred fifty days the waters began to subside and the ark came to rest on Mt. Qardu.[5] In the tenth month the tops of the mountains were seen. In the six hundred and first year, in the first month, the first day of the month, the waters were dried from off the earth. In the second month, that is, Iyor, "on the twenty-seventh day of the month, the earth was dry." Therefore Noah and those with him had been in the ark three hundred sixty-five days, for from the seventeenth of the second month, that is, Iyor, until the twenty-seventh of the same month the following year, according to the lunar reckoning, there were three hundred sixty-five days. Notice then that even the generation of the house of Noah employed this reckoning of three hundred sixty-five days in a year. Why then should you say that it was the Chaldeans and Egyptians who invented and developed it? COMMENTARY ON GENESIS 6.11.2-6.12.1.[6]

---

[1]FC 82:151. [2]Now the Strait of Gibraltar. In ancient times it was considered to be the limit of the world. [3]PL 14:408; CSEL 32:453. [4]Gen 7:24. [5]Following the Peshitta, Ephrem locates the resting of the ark not on Ararat but on Mt. Qardu, in northern Iraq. [6]FC 91:141-42.

8:6-12 END OF THE DELUGE

⁶At the end of forty days Noah* opened the window of the ark which he had made, ⁷and sent forth a raven;† and it went to and fro‡ until the waters were dried up from the earth. ⁸Then he sent forth a dove from him,§ to see if the waters had subsided from the face of the ground; ⁹but the dove found no place to set her foot, and she returned to him to the ark, for the waters were still on the face of the whole earth. So he put forth his hand and took her and brought her into the ark with him. ¹⁰He waited another seven days, and again he sent forth the dove out of the ark; ¹¹and the dove came back to him in the evening, and lo, in her mouth a freshly plucked olive leaf; so Noah* knew that the waters had subsided from the earth. ¹²Then he waited another seven days, and sent forth the dove; and she did not return to him any more.

*LXX Noe †LXX to see if the water had abated ‡LXX it went out and did not return §LXX after it

OVERVIEW: The raven, which is sent forth by Noah, is held captive by gluttony and does not return to the ark (PRUDENTIUS, CHRYSOSTOM). The raven symbolizes those Christians who having been baptized have gone astray (AUGUSTINE, BEDE). The dove, which Noah sends after the raven, brings an olive branch back to the ark. This branch not only reveals that the deluge has abated but also is a symbol of the promised everlasting peace (AUGUSTINE). The dove is a symbol of the Holy Spirit (AMBROSE, BEDE), of the anointing by oil in chrismation (BEDE) and of Christ (MAXIMUS OF TURIN). The end of the deluge can be compared with the end of the persecutions that those who live in Christ have to suffer in the world (AUGUSTINE).

8:6-7 Noah Sends a Raven

THE RAVEN DID NOT RETURN. BEDE: Noah wanted to know how things stood on the face of the earth when the inundation had come to an end, and he sent forth a raven, which scorned to return to the ark,[1] signifying those who, although they have been cleansed by the waters of baptism, nevertheless neglect putting off the very black dress of their old selves by living more faultlessly; and lest they deserve to be renewed by the anointing of the Holy Spirit, they at once fall away from the inmost unity of catholic peace and rest by following exterior things, that is, the desires of the world. HOMILY 1.12.[2]

THE RAVEN DOES NOT RETURN TO THE ARK. PRUDENTIUS:
As a sign that the flood had abated
the dove is now bringing
Back to the ark in her beak

---

[1]Gen 8:6-7. [2]HOG 122.

the budding green branch of an olive.
For the raven, held captive by gluttony,
clung to foul bodies,
While the dove brought back
the glad tidings of peace that was given.
SCENES FROM SACRED HISTORY 3.[3]

WHY THE RAVEN DID NOT COME BACK.
CHRYSOSTOM: But for the present we need to
explain the reason why the bird [the raven]
did not come back. Perhaps, with the waters
subsiding, the bird, being unclean, happened
upon corpses of men and beasts and, finding
nourishment to its liking, stayed there! This
would have been something that proved to be
no little sign of hope and encouragement for
the just man [if the raven had returned].
HOMILIES ON GENESIS 26.12.[4]

THE TIRESOME SOUND OF THE CROW.
AUGUSTINE: You do not know when that last
hour is going to come and yet you say, "I am
reforming." When are you going to reform?
When are you going to change? "Tomorrow,"
you say. Behold, how often you say, "Tomorrow, tomorrow."[5] You have really become a
crow. Behold, I say to you that when you make
the noise of a crow, ruin is threatening you. For
that crow whose cawing you imitate went forth
from the ark and did not return. SERMONS ON
THE LITURGICAL SEASON 224.4.[6]

8:8-11 Noah Sends a Dove

**THE OLIVE BRANCH SYMBOLIZES EVER-
LASTING PEACE.** AUGUSTINE: It is not difficult to see why everlasting peace is signified
by the olive branch that the dove, returning,
brought back to the ark. For we know that the
smooth surface of oil is not readily hindered
by a different liquid. And the olive tree itself

is forever in leaf. CHRISTIAN INSTRUCTION
2.16.24.[7]

**THE DOVE AS A SYMBOL OF THE HOLY
SPIRIT.** AMBROSE: The oil is not for the synagogue, since it does not possess the olive and
did not understand the dove that brought
back the olive branch after the flood. For that
dove descended afterwards,[8] when Christ was
being baptized and dwelt with him, as John
brought witness in the Gospel saying, "I saw
the Spirit descending from heaven as a dove,
and it remained upon him."[9] LETTERS 40.21.[10]

THE OLIVE BRANCH. BEDE: After [the raven]
he sent a dove, and it came to him in the
evening, carrying in its mouth an olive branch
with green leaves.[11]

You are paying attention, I believe, and
with your intellect you anticipate me as I
speak. The olive branch with green leaves is
the grace of the Holy Spirit, rich in the words
of life, the fullness of which rests upon Christ,
[as] the psalm says, "God, your God, has
anointed you with the oil of gladness above
your fellows."[12] Concerning this gift given to
Christ's fellows, John speaks: "You have the
anointing from the holy one, and you know all
things."[13] And by a most beautiful conjunction
the figure is in agreement with the fulfill-
ment—a corporeal dove brought the olive
branch to the ark which was washed by the
waters of the flood; the Holy Spirit descended
in the form of a corporeal dove upon the Lord
when he was baptized in the waters of the Jor-
dan. Not only the human beings but also the

---

[3]FC 52:179-80. [4]FC 82:153. [5]Latin: *cras, cras.* [6]FC 38:188. [7]FC 2:83*. [8]After the ascendancy of the law. [9]Jn 1:32. [10]FC 26:393*. [11]Gen 8:8-11. [12]Ps 45:7. [13]1 Jn 2:20.

living things which the ark contained, and also the very wood from which the ark was made, prefigure us members of Christ and of the church after our reception of the washing of the waters of regeneration. Through the anointing of the sacred chrism may we be signed with the grace of the Holy Spirit, and may he deign to keep it inviolate in us who himself gave it [to us], Jesus Christ our Lord who with the almighty Father in the unity of the same Holy Spirit lives and reigns for all ages. Amen. HOMILY 1.12.[14]

THE DOVE AS A SYMBOL OF CHRIST. MAXIMUS OF TURIN: Christ is a dove because he commands his holy ones to be as doves when he says, "Be simple as doves." But the prophet speaks of what Christ the dove is when, in his person, he describes his return to heaven after his suffering: "Who will give me wings like a dove, and I shall fly away and be at rest?" When Christ the Lord, therefore, initiated the sacraments of the church a dove came down from heaven. I understand the mystery, and I recognize the sacrament. For the very

dove that once hastened to Noah's ark in the flood now comes to Christ's church in baptism. SERMONS 64.2.[15]

8:11-12 The Dove Does Not Return

THE END OF THE DELUGE COMPARED WITH THE END OF PERSECUTIONS. AUGUSTINE: The secular powers often and for a long time spare the wicked from corporal punishment and relieve some of them from their harassments, but the hearts of holy men never have any respite until the end of the world from the sinful conduct of men. It is thus we have the fulfillment of what the apostle said, as I cited it, that "all who will live godly in Christ suffer persecution."[16] Their suffering is more bitter in proportion to its inwardness. This is so until a man[17] passes over the deluge where the ark shelters the raven and the dove. LETTERS 248.[18]

---

[14]HOG 122-23. [15]ACW 50:158. [16]2 Tim 3:12. [17]Noah. [18]FC 32:237.

8:13-19 NOAH, HIS FAMILY AND THE ANIMALS GO OUT OF THE ARK

[13]*In the six hundred and first year, in the first month, the first day of the month, the waters were dried from off the earth; and Noah* removed the covering of the ark, and looked, and behold, the face of the ground was dry.* [14]*In the second month, on the twenty-seventh day of the month, the earth was dry.* [15]*Then God† said to Noah,** [16] *"Go forth from the ark, you and your wife, and your sons and your sons' wives with you.* [17]*Bring forth with you every living thing that is with you of all flesh—birds and animals and every*

creeping thing that creeps on the earth—that they may breed abundantly on the earth, and‡ be fruitful and multiply upon the earth." ¹⁸So Noah* went forth, and his sons and his wife and his sons' wives with him. ¹⁹And every beast, every creeping thing, and every bird, everything that moves upon the earth, went forth by families out of the ark.§

*LXX Noe †LXX the Lord God ‡LXX omits §LXX And all the beasts and cattle, and every bird and every creeping thing that moves on the earth went out, according to their kind, from the ark.

OVERVIEW: When Noah disembarks after the deluge, God encourages him in everything (CHRYSOSTOM). Chastity was observed in the ark, but after the deluge marriage is permitted again (JOHN OF DAMASCUS). This is made clear even in the order of boarding and leaving the ark (AMBROSE). In order that they might multiply, Noah brings out two by two those whom he had brought in one by one (EPHREM). The ark prefigures deliverance through the church's baptism in preparation for the divine judgment (MAXIMUS OF TURIN). Noah proclaimed a new birth to the world (CLEMENT OF ROME).

8:15-19 *Everything Went Out of the Ark*

NOAH RECEIVES THE BLESSING OF MULTIPLICATION THAT ADAM HAD RECEIVED.

CHRYSOSTOM: Then all creation was cleansed as if of some blemish, removing all defilement caused in it by human wickedness. Its countenance was made resplendent; God then finally commanded the just man to disembark from the ark, freeing him from that awful prison with these words, "Then the Lord God said to Noah, 'Disembark, you and your sons, your wife and your sons' wives with you, as well as all flesh, from birds to cattle; take off with you every reptile that crawls upon the earth, and increase and multiply on the earth.'" Notice God's goodness, how in everything he encourages the good man. After ordering him to dis-embark from the ark along with his sons, his wife, his sons' wives and all the wild animals, then lest great discouragement should gradually overtake him by this further development and he become anxious at the thought that he would be on his own, dwelling alone in such a vast expanse of earth, with no one else existing, God first said, "Disembark from the ark, and take off everything with you," and then added, "Increase and multiply, and gain dominion over the earth." See how once again this good man receives that former blessing that Adam had received before the fall. The same words were as man heard when he was created: God blessed them in the words "increase and multiply, and gain dominion over the earth."[1] So too this man now hears the words "increase and multiply on the earth." In other words, just as the former man became the beginning and root of all creatures before the deluge, so too this just man becomes a kind of leaven, beginning and root of everything after the deluge. From this point on, what is comprised in the make-up of human beings takes its beginning, and the whole of creation recovers its proper order, both the soil reawakening to productivity as well as everything else that had been created for the service of human beings. HOMILIES ON GENESIS 26.16.[2]

[1]Gen 1:28. [2]FC 82:155-56.

THE ARK PREFIGURES DELIVERANCE THROUGH THE CHURCH. MAXIMUS OF TURIN: For as Noah's ark preserved alive everyone whom it had taken in when the world was going under,[3] so also Peter's church will bring back unhurt everyone whom it embraces when the world goes up in flames.[4] And as a dove brought the sign of peace to Noah's ark when the flood was over,[5] so also Christ will bring the joy of peace to Peter's church when the judgment is over, since he himself is dove and peace, as he promised when he said, "I shall see you again and your heart will rejoice."[6] SERMONS 49.3.[7]

MARRIAGE IS PERMITTED AGAIN. JOHN OF DAMASCUS: When Noah was ordered to enter the ark and was entrusted with the safeguarding of the seed of the earth, he was given this command, which reads, "Go forth from the ark, you and your wife, and your sons and your sons' wives with you." He had separated them from their wives, so that with the help of chastity they might escape the deep and that worldwide destruction. However, after the cessation of the flood, the command was "Go forth from the ark, you and your wife, and your sons and your sons' wives with you." Here, see how marriage was again permitted for the sake of increase. ORTHODOX FAITH 4.24.[8]

THE ORDER OF BOARDING AND LEAVING. AMBROSE: Now let us examine why, at the moment of entering the ark, the order of entry was that Noah entered first with his sons, then his wife and the wives of his sons,[9] but when they got out, the order of exit was changed. In fact it is written, "Go forth from the ark, you and your wife, and your sons and your sons' wives with you." According to the literal mean-

ing the Scripture wants to emphasize the abstinence from the faculty of generation at the moment of the boarding on the ark and the use of this faculty at the moment of disembarking. At the beginning of the deluge the father entered first with his sons and the sons with the father, secondly his wife and the wives of his sons. There is no mixing of the sexes at the boarding, but there is at the disembarking. In a plain way, through the order of the people boarding, it is being made clear to the righteous that the time when death loomed over everybody was not suitable to concubinage and erotic pleasures. . . . With good reason, later, after the deluge ended, marriage was again in use and considered for the generation of other men. ON NOAH 21.76.[10]

NOAH BRINGS FORTH THE ANIMALS IN FAMILIES. EPHREM THE SYRIAN: Those whom he had brought in "one by one" in order to maintain chastity on the ark, he now brought out "two by two" so that they might "be fruitful and multiply in creation." Even with respect to the animals that had preserved their chastity in the ark God said, "Bring forth with you every living thing that is with you of all flesh—birds and animals and every creeping thing that creeps on the earth—that they may breed abundantly on the earth." COMMENTARY ON GENESIS 6.12.2.[11]

NEW BIRTH TO THE WORLD. CLEMENT OF ROME: Let us fix our gaze on those who have perfectly served his magnificent glory. Let us take Enoch, who was found righteous in obe-

---

[3]Cf. Gen 8:10-11. [4]Cf. 1 Pet 3:20-21. [5]Cf. Gen 8:10-11. [6]Jn 16:22. [7]ACW 50:116. [8]FC 37:394-95. [9]Gen 6:18. [10]PL 14:417; CSEL 32:467. [11]FC 91:142.

dience and was taken up without there being a trace of his death.[12] Noah was found faithful by reason of his service; he proclaimed a new birth to the world, and through him the Lord saved the living creatures who entered in har-

mony into the ark.[13] THE LETTER TO THE CORINTHIANS 9.2-4.[14]

---

[12]Gen 5:24; Heb 11:5. [13]Gen 6:8, 7:1; Heb 11:7; 2 Pet 2:5. [14]FC 1:17.

8:20-22 NOAH OFFERS A SACRIFICE TO GOD

[20]*Then Noah* built an altar to the* LORD, *and took of every clean animal and of every clean bird, and offered burnt offerings on the altar.* [21]*And when the* LORD *smelled the pleasing odor, the* LORD *said in his heart, "I will never again curse the ground because of man, for the imagination of man's heart is evil from his youth; neither will I ever again destroy every living creature as I have done.* [22]*While the earth remains, seedtime and harvest, cold and heat, summer and winter, day and night, shall not cease."*

*LXX Noe

OVERVIEW: Noah offers sacrifices to God of the clean animals, not of the unclean (AUGUSTINE). "The Lord smelled the pleasing odor" means that he accepted the offerings (CHRYSOSTOM). The Lord does not smell the smell of the flesh of animals or the smoke of wood, but he looks out and sees the simplicity of heart with which Noah offers the sacrifice (EPHREM).

The words "I will never again curse the ground because of man" mean that God, after restraining human sinful nature through the fear of his punishment, now wants to change it through his forgiveness (AMBROSE). After Noah's sacrifice God restores to the earth the seasonal cycles that had been disturbed during the deluge (EPHREM).

8:20 Noah Builds an Altar

NOAH OFFERS SACRIFICES OF THE CLEAN.
AUGUSTINE: [The clean and the unclean] were together in the ark, but they were not equally pleasing to the Lord as a savor of sacrifice, for after the deluge Noah offered sacrifice to God of the clean, not of the unclean. LETTERS 108.[1]

8:21 A Pleasing Sacrifice

GOD ACCEPTS NOAH'S SACRIFICE. CHRYSOSTOM: The Scripture says, "And the Lord smelled a sweet odor," that is, he accepted the offerings. But do not imagine that God has nostrils, since God is invisible spirit. Yet what is carried up from the altar is the odor and smoke from burning bodies, and nothing is

---

[1]FC 18:237.

more malodorous than such a savor. But that you may learn that God attends to the intention of the one offering the sacrifice and then accepts or rejects it, Scripture calls the odor and smoke a sweet savor. AGAINST JUDAIZING CHRISTIANS 1.7.3.[2]

SEEING THE SIMPLICITY OF NOAH'S HEART, GOD PRESERVES A REMNANT. EPHREM THE SYRIAN: "The Lord smelled" not the smell of the flesh or the smoke of wood, but rather he looked out and saw the simplicity of heart with which Noah offered the sacrifice from all and on behalf of all. And his Lord spoke to him, as he desired that Noah hear, "Because of your righteousness, a remnant was preserved and did not perish in that flood that took place. And because of your sacrifice that was from all flesh and on behalf of all flesh, I will never again bring a flood upon the earth."[3] God thus bound himself beforehand by this promise so that even if mankind were constantly to follow the evil thought of their inclination, he would never again bring a flood upon them. COMMENTARY ON GENESIS 6.13.2.[4]

PUNISHMENT AND FORGIVENESS COMPLEMENTARY. AMBROSE: Let us examine with greater attention the meaning of the words "the Lord said in his heart, I will never again curse the ground because of man, for the imagination of man's heart is evil from his youth." He will not add that he intends to destroy again, as he had already done, every living creature for the entire duration of earth. Even though he had punished the whole of mankind, he knew that the punishment of the

law is more suitable to raise fear and to teach the doctrine than to change the nature that can be corrected in some people but not changed in everybody. Therefore God punished so that we might fear and forgave so that we might be preserved. He punished once in order to give an example that would have raised fear, but he forgave for the future, so that the bitterness of sin would have not prevailed. One who is intent upon punishing sins too often is considered to be more obstinate than strict. Therefore God says, "I will never again curse the ground because of man," that is, he punishes a few, forgives many, because he intended to show his mercy for the whole of mankind without the necessity of producing in human hearts a false security mixed with a kind of neglect. ON NOAH 22.80.[5]

8:22 "Seedtime and Harvest Shall Not Cease"

GOD RESTORES THE SEASONS TO THE EARTH. EPHREM THE SYRIAN: And because there was neither planting nor harvest during that year and the seasonal cycles had been disturbed, God restored to the earth that which had been taken away in his anger. God then said, "All the days of the earth, planting and harvest, cold and heat, summer and winter, day and night shall not cease from the earth." For throughout the entire year, until the earth dried up, winter, with no summer, had been upon them. COMMENTARY ON GENESIS 6.13.3.[6]

---

[2]FC 68:27. [3]Gen 9:11-15. [4]FC 91:142. [5]PL 14:418; CSEL 32:470. [6]FC 91:143.

9:1-7 GOD GIVES FOOD AND DECLARES
HIS CONDEMNATION OF MURDER

¹And God blessed Noah* and his sons, and said to them, "Be fruitful and multiply, and fill the earth.† ²The fear of you and the dread of you shall be upon every beast of the earth, and upon every bird of the air, upon everything that creeps on the ground and all the fish of the sea; into your hand they are delivered. ³Every moving thing that lives shall be food for you; and as I gave you the green plants, I give you everything. ⁴Only you shall not eat flesh with its life, that is, its blood.‡ ⁵For your lifeblood I will surely require a reckoning; of every beast I will require it and of man; of every man's brother I will require the life§ of man. ⁶Whoever sheds the blood of man, by man shall his blood be shed;# for God made man in his own image. ⁷And you, be fruitful and multiply, bring forth abundantly on the earth and multiply in it."

*LXX Noe †LXX and rule on it ‡LXX with blood of its life (or soul) §LXX (or soul) #LXX for his blood shall [his blood] be shed

OVERVIEW: God gives human beings every herb for sustenance (JUSTIN MARTYR). He orders that people drain the blood of the beasts that they will eat (EPHREM) because the blood is the beast's soul and must be set aside for him (CHRYSOSTOM). The murder of human beings is condemned by God (CHRYSOSTOM, EPHREM). When God proclaims that he will require the blood of humans at the hand of every beast and person, he means that he compares human wickedness in the act of murder to the wildness of beasts (AMBROSE). By requiring the blood of persons at the hand of every beast, God intends to say that he will resurrect the bodies of those who die (JOHN OF DAMASCUS).

9:3 God Gives Noah Plants and Animals for Food

THERE IS NO UNCLEAN HERB OR PLANT.
JUSTIN MARTYR: You [Trypho, a Jew] object that Noah was ordered to make a distinction between the herbs, because we do not now eat every kind of herb. Such a conclusion is inadmissible. I could easily prove, but we will not spend the time now in doing so, that every vegetable is an herb and may be eaten. Now, if we make a distinction between them and refuse to eat some of them, we do so not because they are common and unclean but because they are bitter, or poisonous or thorny. DIALOGUE WITH TRYPHO 20.[1]

9:4 Not Eating the Blood of Animals

THE BLOOD OF ANIMALS MUST BE DRAINED. EPHREM THE SYRIAN: God also blessed Noah and his sons that they might be fruitful and multiply and that fear of them should fall upon all flesh both in the sea and

---

[1]JMO 2:454.

on dry land. "Only you shall not eat flesh with its life." That means you shall eat no flesh that has not been slaughtered and whose blood, which is its life, has not been drained. COMMENTARY ON GENESIS 6.14.1.[2]

ANIMAL'S BLOOD IS ITS SOUL. CHRYSOSTOM: From this the eating of meat takes its beginning, not for the purpose of prompting them to gluttony. But since some of the people were about to offer sacrifices and make thanksgiving to the Lord, he grants them authority over food and obviates any anxiety about foods lest they seem to be abstaining from foods because they were not properly consecrated. "I have given you them all," he says, "as I did the green grass." Then, as in the case of Adam when he instructed him to abstain from the one tree while enjoying the others, so in this case too. After permitting the consumption of all foods without hesitation, he says, "except you are not to eat flesh with its lifeblood in it." So what does this statement mean? It means "strangled," for an animal's blood is its soul. So since they were about to offer sacrifices in the form of animals, he is teaching them in these words that as long as the blood has been set aside for me, the flesh is for you. In doing so, however, he is intent upon resisting in advance any impulse toward homicide. HOMILIES ON GENESIS 27.13.[3]

9:5-6 Requiring a Reckoning

THE MURDER OF HUMAN BEINGS IS CONDEMNED BY GOD. CHRYSOSTOM: "Whoever sheds someone's blood, his own will be shed in payment for that person's blood, because I have made the human person in God's image." Consider, I ask you, how much fear he struck

in them with that remark. He is saying even if you are not restrained from murderous hands by kinship or by a sense of fellowship of nature, and even if you thrust aside all brotherly feeling and become completely committed to a bloody murder, you must think twice. Consider the fact that the person has been created in God's image. Mark the degree of honor accorded him by God! Think on the fact that he has received authority over all creation. Then you will give up your murderous intent. So what does he mean? If someone has committed countless murders and shed so much blood, how can he give adequate satisfaction simply by the shedding of his own blood? Do not have these thoughts, human being that you are. Instead you do well to consider in advance that you will receive an immortal body that will have the capacity to undergo constant and everlasting punishment. HOMILIES ON GENESIS 27.15.[4]

GOD REQUIRES SATISFACTION. EPHREM THE SYRIAN: God requires the blood now and in the future. He requires it now in the case of a death that he decreed for a murderer, and also a stoning with which a goring bull is to be stoned.[5] At the end, at the time of the resurrection, God will require that animals return all they ate from the flesh of man. God said, "From the hand of a man and of his brother I will require the life of a man," just as satisfaction for the blood of Abel was required from Cain, that is, "whoever sheds the blood of man, by man shall his blood be shed." COMMENTARY ON GENESIS 6.15.1-2.[6]

MURDER IS AN ACT OF INHUMAN AND

---

[2]FC 91:143. [3]FC 82:172. [4]FC 82:173*. [5]Ex 21:28. [6]FC 91:143.

BEASTLY CRUELTY. AMBROSE: "For your life-blood and your souls I will require a reckoning of every beast and of the hand of man." He compared human iniquity to beastly wickedness and considered it to be even more culpable than the wildness of the beasts. For he added, "of every man's brother I will require the life of man." Actually beasts have nothing in common with us, are not united to us by any fraternal bond. If they harm a man, they harm somebody who is stranger, do not transgress the rights of nature, do not obliterate the affection of brotherhood. Therefore one who makes an attempt on his brother's life commits a more serious sin. For this reason the Lord threatened a more severe punishment by saying "of the hand of his brother I will require a reckoning of the blood of man." Is not perhaps a brother someone of a rational nature come forth from a certain womb, so that we are united by a generation from the same mother? One single nature is mother of all humanity. Therefore we are all brothers generated by one and the same mother and united by the same kinship. ON NOAH 26.94.[7]

THE RESURRECTION OF THE BODY IS TESTIFIED BY THE WORDS OF THE LORD. JOHN OF DAMASCUS: Moreover, sacred Scripture, too, testifies to the fact that there will be a resurrection of the body. Indeed, God already had said to Noah after the flood, "Even as the green herbs have I delivered them all to you: saving that flesh with blood of its life you shall not eat. And I will require your blood of your lives, at the hand of every beast I will require it. And at the hand of every man I will require the life of his brother. Whosoever shall shed man's blood, for that blood his blood will be shed: for I made man to the image of God." How can he require the blood of men at the hand of every beast, unless he raises the bodies of those who die? For beasts will not die in the place of human beings. ORTHODOX FAITH 4.27.[8]

---

[7]PL 14:425; CSEL 32:480. [8]FC 37:402*.

9:8-17 GOD MAKES A COVENANT WITH NOAH

[8]*Then God said to Noah* and to his sons with him, [9]*"Behold, I establish my covenant with you and your descendants after you,* [10]*and with every living creature that is with you, the birds, the cattle, and every beast of the earth with you, as many as came out of the ark.*[l] [11]*I establish my covenant with you, that never again shall all flesh be cut off by the waters of a flood, and never again shall there be a flood to destroy the earth."* [12]*And God*[†] *said, "This is the sign of the covenant which I make between me and you and every living creature that*

is with you, for all future generations: ¹³*I set my bow in the cloud, and it shall be a sign of the covenant between me and the earth.* ¹⁴*When I bring clouds over the earth and the bow is seen in the clouds,* ¹⁵*I will remember my covenant which is between me and you and every living creature of all flesh; and the waters shall never again become a flood to destroy all flesh.* ¹⁶*When the bow is in the clouds, I will look upon it and remember the everlasting covenant between God and every living creature of all flesh that is upon the earth."* ¹⁷*God said to Noah,* "This is the sign of the covenant which I have established between me and all flesh that is upon the earth."*

l *Gk: Heb repeats* every beast of the earth   *LXX Noe   †*LXX the Lord God*

OVERVIEW: God makes his covenant with Noah out of love and in order to eliminate all apprehension from his mind (CHRYSOSTOM). God promises that he will never again bring a flood upon earth, even if people become constantly habituated to following the evil thoughts of their inclination (EPHREM). This covenant, which God makes with Noah and with all those creatures that come out of the ark with him (EPHREM), will never be broken (GREGORY OF NAZIANZUS).

9:8-11 *Establishing a Covenant*

GOD MAKES HIS COVENANT WITH NOAH OUT OF LOVE. CHRYSOSTOM: God's purpose, therefore, was to eliminate all apprehension from Noah's thinking and for him to be quite assured that this would not happen again. He said, remember, "Just as I brought on the deluge out of love, so as to put a stop to their wickedness and prevent their going to further extremes, so in this case too it is out of my love that I promise never to do it again, so that you may live free of all dread and in this way see your present life to its close." Hence he said, "Behold, I make my covenant," that is, I form an agreement. Just as in human affairs when someone makes a promise he forms an agreement and gives a firm guarantee, so too the good Lord said, "Behold, I make my covenant." God did not say that this massive disaster might come again to those who sin. Rather he said, "Behold, I make my covenant with you *and your offspring after you.*" See the Lord's loving kindness: not only with your generation, he says, do I form my agreement, but also in regard to all those coming after you I give this firm guarantee. HOMILIES ON GENESIS 28.4.[1]

GOD WILL NEVER BRING A NEW DELUGE UPON EARTH. EPHREM THE SYRIAN: And his Lord spoke to [Noah], as he desired that Noah hear, "Because of your righteousness, a remnant was preserved and did not perish in that flood that took place. And because of your sacrifice that was from all flesh and on behalf of all flesh, I will never again bring a flood upon the earth." God thus bound himself beforehand by this promise so that even if mankind were constantly to follow the evil thoughts of their inclination, he would never again bring a flood upon them. COMMENTARY ON GENESIS 6.13.2.[2]

---

[1]FC 82:185-86. [2]FC 91:142.

9:12-15 *The Rainbow a Sign of the Covenant*

GOD ESTABLISHES HIS COVENANT WITH HUMANITY AND EVERY LIVING CREATURE. EPHREM THE SYRIAN: After these things God made a covenant with Noah and with all those who came out of the ark with him, saying, "All flesh shall never again perish in the waters of a flood. I will set my bow in the clouds, and it shall be a sign of the eternal covenant between God and all flesh that is on the earth." COMMENTARY ON GENESIS 6.15.3.[3]

9:16-17 *An Everlasting Covenant*

GOD WILL NEVER FORGET HIS COVENANT. GREGORY OF NAZIANZUS: Who "binds up the water in the clouds"?[4] The miracle of it—that he sets something whose nature is to flow, on clouds, that he fixes it there by his word! Yet he pours out some of it on the face of the whole earth, sprinkling it to all alike in due season. He does not unleash the entire stock of water—the cleansing of Noah's era was enough, and God most true does not forget his own covenant. THEOLOGICAL ORATIONS 28.28.[5]

---

[3]FC 91:143-44. [4]Job 26:8. [5]FGFR 241.

9:18-29 THE DRUNKENNESS OF NOAH

[18]*The sons of Noah* who went forth from the ark were Shem, Ham,[†] and Japheth. Ham[†] was the father of Canaan.* [19]*These three were the sons of Noah*; and from these the whole earth was peopled.*

[20]*Noah* was the first tiller of the soil. He planted a vineyard;* [21]*and he drank of the wine, and became drunk, and lay uncovered in his tent.* [22]*And Ham,[†] the father of Canaan, saw the nakedness of his father, and told his two brothers outside.* [23]*Then Shem and Japheth took a garment, laid it upon both their shoulders, and walked backward and covered the nakedness of their father; their faces were turned away, and they did not see their father's nakedness.* [24]*When Noah* awoke from his wine and knew what his youngest son had done to him,* [25]*he said,*

"Cursed be Canaan;
a slave of slaves shall he be to his brothers."

[26]*He also said,*

"Blessed by the LORD my God be Shem;[m] [‡]
and let Canaan be his slave.

[27]*God enlarge Japheth,*

and let him dwell in the tents of Shem;
and let Canaan be his slave."
[28]*After the flood Noah* lived three hundred and fifty years.* [29]*All the days of Noah* were*
nine hundred and fifty years; and he died.

m *Or Blessed be the LORD, the God of Shem*   *LXX Noe   †*LXX Cham*   †*LXX Blessed be the Lord God of Shem*

OVERVIEW: Noah's drunkenness was due to his ignorance (THEODORET). He got drunk because he spent a long time without drinking any wine (EPHREM). Wine is not evil in itself but rather in its abuse (CHRYSOSTOM). Noah's vulnerability symbolizes the passion of Christ (CYPRIAN, JEROME, AUGUSTINE). Wine made Noah vulnerable (LEANDER OF SEVILLE). The Lord blessed those who covered his shame (CLEMENT OF ALEXANDRIA).

After Ham sees Noah in his drunkenness and nakedness, his son Canaan is cursed, because Ham, who had been blessed by Noah when entering the ark, could not be cursed now (EPHREM). Canaan is cursed by Noah because the sons are bound by the sins of their parents (AUGUSTINE, JUSTIN MARTYR). Not only is Canaan subjected to punishment but also his father, and it is likely that Canaan himself committed sin (CHRYSOSTOM, EPHREM). Noah is naked, but he is not ashamed because he is filled with spiritual gladness, while the one who mocks him remains exposed to reproach. Canaan's punishment demonstrates to us above all else what great reverence is due to our parents (AMBROSE). The word *slave* is first used by Noah in connection with the curse on Canaan's wrongdoing (AUGUSTINE). After cursing Canaan, Noah blesses Shem and Japheth (EPHREM).

9:18-21 Noah Planted a Vineyard

NOAH'S DRUNKENNESS IS DUE TO IGNORANCE. THEODORET OF CYR: Why was Noah not blamed for falling into drunkenness? His falling was not due to intemperance but inexperience. For he was the first man[1] to press the fruit of the vine and was ignorant not only of the power of the drink but also of the kind of change it had undergone. Because it ought to be mixed first before being drunk, he suffered drowsiness. There was nothing new about the fact that he was naked. For even now some people sleep naked, sleep having taken away their consciousness. The drunkenness, added to sleep, makes easier a defense of his nakedness. QUESTIONS ON GENESIS 56.[2]

NOAH'S DRUNKENNESS IS MAGNIFIED BY LONG ABSTINENCE. EPHREM THE SYRIAN: Noah's drunkenness was not from an excess of wine but because it had been a long time since he had drunk any wine. In the ark he had drunk no wine. Although all flesh was going to perish, Noah was not permitted to bring any wine onto the ark. During the year after the flood Noah did not drink any wine. In that first year after he left the ark, he did not plant a vineyard, for he came out of the ark on the twenty-seventh of Iyor, the time when the fruit should be starting to mature

---

[1]The first man mentioned in Scripture to make wine.   [2]QG 53.

and not the time for planting a vineyard. Therefore, seeing that it was in the third year that he planted the vineyard from the grape stones that he brought with him on the ark and that it was three or even four years before they would have become a productive vineyard, there were then at least six years during which the just one had not tasted any wine. Commentary on Genesis 7.1.1.[3]

Wine Is Not Evil in Itself. Chrysostom: Perhaps, on the other hand, someone might say, "Why was vine dressing, source of such terrible wickedness, introduced into life?" Do not idly blurt out what comes into your head, O man: vine dressing is not wicked nor is wine evil—rather, it is use of them in excess. You see, dreadful sins arise not from wine as such but from intemperate attitudes of human depravity that undermine the benefit that should naturally come from it. The reason that now after the deluge he shows you the use of wine is that you may learn that before using wine the human race had to come to grief from it. Before wine had even appeared, human history gave evidence of the extremity of sinfulness and unbridled licentiousness. This was intended to teach you that when you see the way wine is used, you will not attribute it all to wine as such but to depraved human intention bent on evil. Consider especially where wine has proved useful, and tremble, O man. For wine is used in good things by which our salvation is made real. Those who have an insight into spiritual realities understand this saying. Homilies on Genesis 29.10.[4]

Wine Made Noah Vulnerable. Leander of Seville: "Woe to you that demand strong drink as soon as they rise in the morning, and linger into the night while wine inflames them!"[5] Noah drank wine and fell into a drunken stupor and became naked in the more shameful part of his body[6] so that you may know that the mind of man is so confounded by wine and the reason of the human mind is made so dull that it does not have concern even for itself, much less for God. . . . When Lot was soused with wine, he committed incest with his daughters and did not know his mistake; from that passionate union came the Moabites and the Ammonites. The Training of Nuns 19.9.[7]

The Lord Blessed Those Who Covered His Shame. Clement of Alexandria: That is why the drunkenness of Noah also has been described,[8] so that we may guard against drunkenness as much as possible, with the picture of such a fall clearly described before our eyes in Scripture. That is why, too, the Lord blessed those who covered the shame of his drunkenness.

Scripture, summing everything up in one succinct verse, has said, "Wine is sufficient for a man well taught, and upon his bed, he shall rest."[9] Christ the Educator 2.2.34.[10]

Chastity Covered What Drunkenness Had Exposed. Clement of Alexandria: The chaste son could not endure looking upon the immodest nakedness of a good man; chastity covered over what drunkenness had exposed in a transgression committed in ignorance but manifest to all. Christ the Educator 2.6.51.[11]

---

[3]FC 91:144. [4]FC 82:205*. [5]Is 5:11. [6]Cf. Gen 9:30-38. [7]FC 62:213. [8]Gen 9:21. [9]Cf. Sir 31:19. [10]FC 23:124. [11]FC 23:138.

NOAH'S DRUNKENNESS PREFIGURES THE PASSION OF CHRIST. CYPRIAN: When Christ says, "I am the true vine,"[12] the blood of Christ is assuredly not water but wine. We are redeemed and made alive by his blood. But in the cup it is not wine as such that redeems but his blood. This is declared by the sacrament and testimony of all the Scriptures. For we find this even in Genesis also, in respect of the sacrament prefigured in Noah. That he drank wine was to them a precursor and figure of the Lord's passion. Noah was made drunk by this wine, was made naked in his household, was lying down with his thighs naked and exposed, and the nakedness of the father was observed by his second son and was told abroad but was covered by two, the eldest and the youngest, and other matters which it is not necessary to follow out. It is enough for us simply to embrace the understanding that Noah set forth a type of the future truth. Noah did not drink water but wine and thus expressed in advance the figure of the passion of the Lord. LETTERS 63.2-3.[13]

NOAH'S DISHONOR PREFIGURES THE CROSS. JEROME: After the deluge Noah drank and became drunk in his own house, and his thighs were uncovered and he was exposed in his nakedness. The elder brother came along and laughed; the younger, however, covered him up. All this is said in type of the Savior, for on the cross he had drunk of the passion: "Father, if it is possible, let this cup pass away from me."[14] He drank and was inebriated, and his thighs were laid bare—the dishonor of the cross. The older brothers, the Jews, came along and laughed; the younger, the Gentiles, covered up his ignominy. HOMILIES ON GENESIS 13.[15]

9:22-25 Noah Curses Canaan

WHY CANAAN WAS CURSED. EPHREM THE SYRIAN: Noah cursed Canaan, saying, "Cursed be Canaan. A slave of slaves shall he be to his brothers." But what sin could Canaan have committed even if he had been right behind his father when Ham observed the nakedness of Noah? Some say that because Ham had been blessed along with those who entered the ark and came out of it, Noah did not curse Ham himself, even though his son, who was cursed, grieved him greatly. Others, however, say from the fact that Scripture says, "Noah knew everything that his youngest son had done to him," it is clear that it was not Ham who observed his nakedness, for Ham was the middle son and not the youngest. For this reason they say that Canaan, the youngest, told of the nakedness of the old man. Then Ham went out and jokingly told his brothers. For this reason then, even though it might be thought that Canaan was cursed unjustly in that he did what he did in his youth, still he was cursed justly for he was not cursed in the place of another. Noah knew that Canaan would deserve the curse in his old age, or else he would not have been cursed in his youth.[16] COMMENTARY ON GENESIS 7.3.1-2.[17]

---

[12]Jn 15:1. [13]ACW 46:98-99. [14]Mt 26:39. [15]FC 48:95. [16]Ephrem is exercised about the apparent injustice of Canaan's being cursed by Noah for the sin of Ham ("the father of Canaan," as the biblical passage repeatedly asserts). Ephrem makes two suggestions, both drawing on rabbinic exegesis (cf. Bereshith Rabba 37.11). The first invokes the irrevocability of a blessing (cf. Gen 27:30-40) and the son's identity with his father (cf. Heb 7:9-10). The second speculates that Ham could not be the one who saw his father naked because Noah blames his youngest son, and Ham was the middle son. *Son* must therefore be used in a loose sense and must refer to Canaan. [17]FC 91:145.

THE SINS OF THE PARENTS FALL ON THE CHILDREN. AUGUSTINE: Why did Ham sin and yet vengeance was declared against his son Canaan? Why was the son of Solomon punished by the breaking up of the kingdom?[18] Why was the sin of Ahab, king of Israel, visited upon his posterity?[19] How do we read in the sacred books, "Returning the iniquity of the fathers into the bosom of their children after them" and "Visiting the iniquity of the fathers upon the children unto the third and fourth generation?"[20] The number here can be taken for all the descendants. Are these statements false? Who would say this but the most open enemy of the divine words? Then carnal generation even of the people of God of the Old Testament binds children for the sins of their parents. AGAINST JULIAN 6.25.82.[21]

WHY THE CURSE BEGAN WITH THE SON'S SON. JUSTIN MARTYR: In the blessings with which Noah blesses his two sons, he also curses his son's son. For the prophetic Spirit would not curse that son himself, since he had already been blessed by God, together with the other sons of Noah. But, since the punishment of the sin was to be transmitted down to all the posterity of the son who laughed at his father's nudity, he made the curse begin with the son's son. DIALOGUE WITH TRYPHO 139.[22]

BOTH CANAAN AND HAM ARE SUBJECTED TO GOD'S PUNISHMENT. CHRYSOSTOM: To be sure, some will say, this shows that the reason he did not curse Ham was that he had enjoyed blessing from God. Nevertheless, why is it that though Ham was the sinner, Canaan had to pay the penalty? This does not happen idly either. Ham did not endure less punishment than his son. He too felt its effects. You know well, of course, how in many cases

fathers have begged to endure punishment in place of their children. Seeing their children bearing punishment proves a more grievous form of chastisement for the fathers than being subject to it themselves. Accordingly, this incident occurred so that Ham should endure greater anguish on account of his natural affection, so that God's blessing should continue without impairment and so that his son in being the object of the curse should atone for his own sins. You see, even if in the present instance he bears the curse on account of his father's sin, nevertheless it was likely that he was atoning for his own failings. In other words, it was not only for his father's sin that he bore the curse but perhaps also for the purpose of his suffering a heavier penalty on his own account. After all, for proof that parents are not punished for their children, nor children for their parents, each being liable for the sins he has committed, you can find frequent statements among the inspired authors—as, for instance, when they say, "The teeth of the one eating sour grapes shall be set on edge,"[23] "The soul that shall die is the soul that sins,"[24] and again, "Parents shall not die for their children, nor children for their parents."[25] HOMILIES ON GENESIS 29.21.[26]

THE GREATEST REVERENCE IS DUE TO OUR PARENTS. AMBROSE: When we read that he was blessed who was blessed by his father and that he was cursed who was cursed by his father, we learn above all else what great reverence to show our parents. And God gave

---

[18]1 Kings 12. [19]1 Kings 21:29. [20]Jer 32:18; Ex 20:5. [21]FC 35:394. [22]JMO 2:454. [23]Jer 38:30 LXX. [24]Ezek 18:20. [25]Deut 2:16. [26]FC 82:212-13.

this privilege to parents so as to arouse respect in the children. The formation of the children is, then, the prerogative of the parents. Therefore honor your father that he may bless you. PATRIARCHS 1.1.[27]

THE WORD SLAVE USED FOR THE FIRST TIME. AUGUSTINE: When subjection came, it was merely a condition deservedly imposed on sinful man. So, in Scripture, there is no mention of the word *slave* until holy Noah used it in connection with the curse on his son's wrongdoing.[28] CITY OF GOD 19.15.[29]

9:26-29 Noah Blesses Two Sons

NOAH BLESSES SHEM AND JAPHETH.
EPHREM THE SYRIAN: After Ham had been

cursed through his one son, Noah blessed Shem and Japheth and said, "May God increase Japheth, and may he dwell in the tent of Shem, and let Canaan be their slave." Japheth increased and became powerful in his inheritance in the north and in the west. And God dwelt in the tent of Abraham, the descendant of Shem, and Canaan became their slave when in the days of Joshua son of Nun, the Israelites destroyed the dwelling places of Canaan and pressed their leaders into bondage.[30] COMMENTARY ON GENESIS 7.4.1.[31]

---

[27]FC 65:243. [28]Thus slavery is not natural to the human condition but comes about only under sinful conditions. [29]FC 24:222*. [30]Josh 17:13. [31]FC 91:146.

10:1-32 THE DESCENDANTS OF JAPHETH, HAM AND SHEM

[1]*These are the generations of the sons of Noah,* Shem, Ham, and Japheth; sons were born to them after the flood.*
[2]*The sons of Japheth: Gomer, Magog, Madai, Javan,[†] Tubal, Meshech, and Tiras.* [3]*The sons of Gomer: Ashkenaz, Riphath, and Togarmah.* [4]*The sons of Javan: Elishah, Tarshish, Kittim, and Dodanim.* [5]*From these the coastland peoples spread. These are the sons of Japheth" in their lands, each with his own language, by their families, in their nations.[‡]*
[6]*The sons of Ham: Cush, Egypt,[§] Put, and Canaan.* [7]*The sons of Cush: Seba, Havilah, Sabtah, Raamah, and Sabteca. The sons of Raamah: Sheba and Dedan.* [8]*Cush became the father of Nimrod; he was the first on earth to be a mighty* man.* [9]*He was a mighty* hunter before** the LORD; therefore it is said, "Like Nimrod a mighty* hunter before** the LORD."* [10]*The beginning of his kingdom was Babel, Erech, and Accad, all of them[††] in the land of Shinar.* [11]*From that land he went into Assyria,[‡‡] and built Nineveh, Rehoboth-Ir,[§§] Calah,*

and ^{12}Resen between Nineveh and Calah; that is the great city. ^{13}Egypt§ became the father of$^{##}$ Ludim, Anamim, Lehabim, Naph-tuhim, ^{14}Pathrusim, Casluhim (whence came the Philistines), and Caphtorim.

^{15}Canaan became the father of Sidon his first-born, and Heth, ^{16}and the Jebusites, the Amorites, the Girgashites, ^{17}the Hivites, the Arkites, the Sinites, ^{18}the Arvadites, the Zemarites, and the Hamathites. Afterward the families of the Canaanites spread abroad. ^{19}And the territory of the Canaanites extended from Sidon, in the direction of Gerar, as far as Gaza, and in the direction of Sodom, Gomorrah, Admah, and Zeboiim, as far as Lasha. ^{20}These are the sons of Ham, by their families, their languages, their lands, and their nations.

^{21}To Shem also, the father of all the children of Eber, the elder brother of Japheth,*** children were born. ^{22}The sons of Shem: Elam, Asshur, Arpachshad, Lud, and Aram.††† ^{23}The sons of Aram: Uz, Hul, Gether, and Mash. ^{24}Arpachshad became the father of Shelah;‡‡‡ and Shelah‡‡‡ became the father of Eber. ^{25}To Eber were born two sons: the name of the one was Peleg,^{o} for in his days the earth was divided, and his brother's name was Joktan. ^{26}Joktan became the father of Almodad, Sheleph, Hazarmaveth, Jerah, ^{27}Hadoram, Uzal, Diklah, ^{28}Obal,§§§ Abima-el, Sheba, ^{29}Ophir, Havilah, and Jobab; all these were the sons of Joktan. ^{30}The territory in which they lived extended from Mesha in the direction of Sephar to the hill country of the east. ^{31}These are the sons of Shem, by their families, their languages, their lands, and their nations.

^{32}These are the families of the sons of Noah, according to their genealogies, in their nations; and from these the nations spread abroad on the earth after the flood.

n Compare verses 20, 31. Heb lacks These are the sons of Japheth o That is Division *LXX variants in spelling within this pericope: Noah (RSV)=Noe (LXX); Ham=Cham; Gomer=Gamer; Javan=Iovan; Tubal=Thobel; Meshech=Mosoch; Togarmah=Thorgama; Elishah=Elisa; Dodanim=Rodioi; Cush=Chous; Put=Phoud; Seba=Saba; Havilah=Evila; Sabtah=Sabatha; Raamah=Regma; Sabteca=Sabakatha; Dedan=Dadan; Nimrod=Nebrod; Babel=Babylon; Erech=Orech; Accad=Archad; Shinar=Sennaar; Calah=Calach; Resen=Dasem; Anamim=Enemetiim; Lehabim=Labiim; Naphtuhim=Nephtaliim; Pathrusim=Patrosoniim; Casluhim=Chasloniim; Het=Chettaion; Jebusites=Iebousaion; Amorites=Amorraion; Girgashites=Gergesaion; Hivites=Evaion; Arkites=Aroukaion; Sinites=Asennaion; Arvadites=Aradion; Zemarites=Samaraion; Hamathites=Amathi; Elam=Ailam; Asshur=Assur; Arpachshad=Arphaxad; Gether=Gather; Mash=Mosoch; Peleg=Phalek; Joktan=Iektan; Mesha=Elmodad; Sephar=Saleph; Hazarmaveth=Asarmoth; Jerah=Iarach; Hadoram=Odorra; Uzal=Aizel; Diklah=Dekla; Sheba=Sabeth †LXX adds Elisa ‡LXX from there were separated the islands of nations in their land, each according to language in their races and in their nations §LXX (+Heb) Mesraim ¶LXX giant **LXX could mean against, which is how VL took it. ††LXX and Chalanne ‡‡LXX Assur came §§LXX the city of Rooboth ##LXX adds the ***LXX suggests younger brother †††LXX adds and Kainan ‡‡‡LXX Kainan §§§omitted in LXX

OVERVIEW: The narrative of Genesis mentions only those descendants of Japheth, Ham and Shem who were able to form their own families and to spread in different areas of the Middle East (AUGUSTINE). One of the descendants of Ham was Nimrod, who chased out the different nations, so that they settled down in various regions that the Lord had assigned to them (EPHREM). Nimrod was the first to seize despotic rule over the people (JEROME) and was a slave of ambition; he wanted to become a ruler and a king (CHRYSOSTOM). Nimrod was not a servant of God but a tyrant who acted cruelly against his brothers (PRUDENTIUS).

The passages in Genesis 10:20, 10:31 and 10:32 (see also 10:5), in which the different nations formed by the descendants of Japheth, Ham and Shem are described, refer to the period following the fall of the tower, when these nations already spoke their own languages (AUGUSTINE). One of the descendants of Shem was Eber, from whom the Hebrews originate (JEROME).

10:1 *The Generations of Noah's Sons*

DESCENDANTS WHO FORMED FAMILIES AND NATIONS. AUGUSTINE: We must therefore introduce into this work an explanation of the generations of the three sons of Noah, insofar as that may illustrate the progress in time of the two cities. Scripture first mentions the youngest son, who is called Japheth, who had eight sons, and by two of these sons seven grandchildren, three by one son, four by the other; in all, fifteen descendants. Ham, Noah's middle son, had four sons, and by one of them five grandsons, and by one of these two great-grandsons; in all, eleven. After enumerating these, Scripture returns to the first of the sons and says, "Cush begat Nimrod; he began to be a giant on the earth." He was a giant hunter against the Lord God; hence they say, "Nimrod a mighty hunter before the Lord." And the beginning of his kingdom was Babylon, Erech, Accad and Calneh, in the land of Shinar. Out of that land went forth Assur, and built Nineveh, Rehoboth-Ir and Calah, and Resen between Nineveh and Calah: this was a great city." Now this Cush, father of the giant Nimrod, is the first-named among the sons of Ham, to whom five sons and two grandsons are ascribed. But he either begat this giant after his grandsons were born or,

which is more credible, Scripture speaks of him separately on account of his eminence, for mention is also made of his kingdom, which began with that magnificent city Babylon, and the other places, whether cities or districts, mentioned along with it. But what is recorded of the land of Shinar, which belonged to Nimrod's kingdom—that Assur went forth from it and built Nineveh and the other cities mentioned with it—happened long after. But he takes occasion to speak of it here on account of the grandeur of the Assyrian kingdom, which was wonderfully extended by Ninus son of Belus, and founder of the great city Nineveh, which was named after him, Nineveh, from Ninus. But Assur, father of the Assyrians, was not one of the sons of Ham, Noah's son, but is found among the sons of Shem, his eldest son. Whence it appears that among Shem's offspring there arose men who afterwards took possession of that giant's kingdom, and advancing from it, founded other cities, the first of which was called Nineveh, from Ninus. From him Scripture returns to Ham's other son, Mizraim. His sons are enumerated, not as seven individuals but as seven nations. And from the sixth, as if from the sixth son, the race called the Philistines are said to have sprung, so that there are in all eight. Then it returns again to Canaan, in whose person Ham was cursed, and his eleven sons are named. Then the territories they occupied, and some of the cities, are named. And thus, if we count sons and grandsons, there are thirty-one of Ham's descendants registered.

It remains to mention the sons of Shem, Noah's eldest son, for to him this genealogical narrative gradually ascends from the youngest. But in the commencement of the record of Shem's sons there is an obscurity that calls for explanation, since it is closely connected with the object of our investigation. For we read, "Unto Shem also, the father of all the children of Eber, the brother of Japheth the elder, were children born." This is the order of the words: And to Shem was born Eber, even to himself, that is, to Shem himself was born Eber, and Shem is the father of all his children. We are intended to understand that Shem is the patriarch of all his posterity who were to be mentioned, whether sons, grandsons, great-grandsons or descendants at any distance. For Shem did not beget Eber, who was indeed in the fifth generation from him. For Shem begat, among other sons, Arpachshad; Arpachshad begat Cainan, Cainan begat Salah, Salah begat Eber. And it was with good reason that he was named first among Shem's offspring, taking precedence even of his sons, though only a grandchild of the fifth generation. For from him, as tradition says, the Hebrews derived their name, though the other etymology that derives the name from Abraham (as if Abrahews) may possibly be correct. But there can be little doubt that the former is the right etymology and that they were called after Eber, Heberews, and then, dropping a letter, Hebrews; and so was their language called Hebrew, which was spoken by none but the people of Israel among whom was the city of God mysteriously prefigured in all the people and truly present in the saints. Six of Shem's sons then are first named, then four grandsons born to one of these sons; then it mentions another son of Shem, who begat a grandson; and his son, again, or Shem's great-grandson, was Eber. And Eber begat two sons and called the one Peleg, which means "dividing." Scripture subjoins the reason of this name, saying, "for in his days was the earth divided." What this means will afterwards

appear. Eber's other son gave birth to twelve sons; consequently all Shem's descendants are twenty-seven. The total number of the progeny of the three sons of Noah is seventy-three, fifteen by Japheth, thirty-one by Ham, twenty-seven by Shem. Then Scripture adds, "These are the sons of Shem, after their families, after their tongues, in their lands, after their nations." And so of the whole number "These are the families of the sons of Noah after their generations, in their nations; and by these were the isles of the nations dispersed through the earth after the flood." From which we gather that the seventy-three (or rather, as I shall presently show, seventy-two) were not individuals but nations. For in a former passage, when the sons of Japheth were enumerated, it is said in conclusion, "By these were the isles of the nations divided in their lands, every one after his language, in their tribes and in their nations."

But nations are expressly mentioned among the sons of Ham, as I showed above. "Mizraim begat those who are called Ludim; and so also of the other seven nations." And after enumerating all of them it concludes, "These are the sons of Ham, in their families, according to their languages, in their territories, and in their nations." The reason, then, why the children of several of them are not mentioned is that they belonged by birth to other nations and did not themselves become nations. Why else is it that though eight sons are reckoned to Japheth, the sons of only two of these are mentioned; and though four are reckoned to Ham, only three are spoken of as having sons; and though six are reckoned to Shem, the descendants of only two of these are traced? Did the rest remain childless? We cannot suppose so; but they did not produce nations so great as to warrant their being mentioned but were absorbed in the nations to which they belonged by birth. CITY OF GOD 16.3.[1]

THE PASSAGES IN GENESIS REFER TO THE PERIOD AFTER THE FALL OF THE TOWER. AUGUSTINE: In the same book [of Genesis], when the generations of the sons of Noah are recalled to our minds, we read, "These are the children of Ham in their tribes according to their tongues, in their lands and nations."[2] Also, in enumerating the sons of Shem, it is said, "These are the children of Shem in their tribes according to their tongues, in their lands and nations."[3] And this is added in reference to all of them: "These are the tribes of the sons of Noah, according to their generations and according to their nations. From these were the islands of the nations scattered over the earth after the flood. And the whole earth was one tongue, and there was one speech for all."[4] And so, because this sentence was added: "And the earth was one tongue and there was one speech for all" (that is, one language for them all), it could be inferred that at that time, when human beings had been scattered according to the islands of the nations over the earth, there was one language common to all of them. Without a doubt, this contradicts the words used above, "according to their tribes and tongues." For, each single tribe that had formed individual nations would not be said to have had its own tongue when there was a common one for all. So it is by way of recapitulation that there is added: "And the earth was one tongue, and there was one speech for all." The narrative, without mentioning it, goes back to tell how it came about that the one language common to all men was broken up into many tongues. And immediately we are told about the building of

the tower, when this punishment for their pride was inflicted upon them by the divine judgment. After this event they were scattered over the earth according to their languages. CHRISTIAN INSTRUCTION 3.36.53.[5]

10:6-14 *The Descendants of Ham*

NIMROD CHASES OUT THE NATIONS ACCORDING TO GOD'S WILL. EPHREM THE SYRIAN: Concerning Nimrod, Moses said, "He was a mighty hunter before the Lord," because, according to the will of the Lord, it was he who fought with each of these nations and chased them out from there, so that they would go out and settle in the regions that had been set apart for them by God. "Therefore it is said, like Nimrod a mighty hunter before the Lord." One used to bless a chief or a ruler by saying, "May you be like Nimrod, a mighty hunter who was victorious in the battles of the Lord." COMMENTARY ON GENESIS 8.1.2.[6]

NIMROD IS THE FIRST TO RULE OVER THE PEOPLE. JEROME: "And Chus [Cush] begat Nimrod. This man began to be powerful in the earth." And after a little while, it says, "And the beginning of his kingdom was Babel and Arach and Achad and Chalanne in the land of Senaar [Shinar]." Nimrod, son of Chus, was the first to seize despotic rule over the people, which men were not yet accustomed to; and he reigned in Babylon, which was called Babel, because the languages of those building the tower were thrown into confusion there. For Babel signifies confusion.

---

[1]NPNF 1 2:311-12. [2]Gen 10:20. [3]Gen 10:31. [4]Gen 10:32—11:1. [5]FC 2:163-64. [6]FC 91:146-47.

Then he also reigned in Arach, that is, in Edissa; and in Achad, which is now called Nisibis; and in Chalanne, which was later called Seleucia after king Seleucus when its name had been changed and which is now in actual fact called Ctesiphon. HEBREW QUESTIONS ON GENESIS 10.8-10.[7]

NIMROD DESIRED TO BECOME A KING. CHRYSOSTOM: Then sacred Scripture goes on from this point to tell of the children born to the sons in these words: "Now, Ham became the father of Cush"; and further, "Now, Cush became the father of Nebrod (Nimrod), who began to be a giant on earth. He was a giant hunter before the Lord." While some people say the phrase "before the Lord" means being in opposition to God, I on the contrary do not think sacred Scripture is implying this. Rather, it implies that [Nimrod] was strong and brave. But the phrase "before the Lord" means created by him, receiving from him God's blessing. Or it may mean that God was on the point of arousing our wonder through him by creating such a remarkable creature and displaying him before us on the earth. Nimrod too, however, in his turn in imitation of his forebear did not take due advantage of his natural preeminence but hit upon another form of servitude in endeavoring to become ruler and king. You see, there would not ever be a king unless there were people being ruled. But in that case freedom is seen for what it really is, whereas slavery is the most

galling obstacle to conditions of freedom, when all the more power is exercised over free people. See what ambition is guilty of. Observe bodily strength not keeping to its limits but constantly lusting after more and clutching for glory. You see, the orders [Nimrod] gave were not those of a leader. Rather, he even builds cities with a view to ruling over the enemy. HOMILIES ON GENESIS 29.29.[8]

NIMROD IS A TYRANT WHO FIGHTS AGAINST HIS BROTHERS. PRUDENTIUS:
A Nimrod, who goes round the world, made rough
With deep ravines and wooden crags, and strives
To waylay some by fraud and secret wiles,
To vanquish others by his giant arms
And spread his deadly triumphs far and wide.
ORIGIN OF SIN 144-48.[9]

10:24-25 Eber and His Sons

THE HEBREWS DESCEND FROM EBER. JEROME: Eber, from whom the Hebrews descended, because of a prophecy gave his son the name Peleg, which means "division," on account of the fact that in his days the languages were divided up in Babylon. HEBREW QUESTIONS ON GENESIS 10.24-25.[10]

---

[7]HQG 40-41. [8]FC 82:218. [9]FC 52:49. [10]HQG 42.

11:1-9 THE TOWER OF BABEL

¹Now the whole earth had one language and few words.* ²And as men migrated from the east, they found a plain in the land of Shinar† and settled there. ³And they said to one another,‡ "Come, let us make bricks, and burn them thoroughly."§ And they had brick for stone, and bitumen for mortar. ⁴Then they said, "Come, let us build ourselves a city, and a tower with its top in the heavens, and let us make a name for ourselves, lest we be scattered abroad upon the face of the whole earth." ⁵And the LORD came down to see the city and the tower, which the sons of men had built. ⁶And the LORD said, "Behold, they are one people, and they have all one language; and this is only the beginning of what they will do; and nothing that they propose to do will now be impossible for them. ⁷Come, let us go down, and there confuse their language, that they may not understand one another's speech." ⁸So the LORD scattered them abroad from there over the face of all the earth, and they left off building the city.# ⁹Therefore its name was called Babel,** because there the LORD confusedᵖ the language†† of all the earth; and from there the LORD scattered them abroad over the face of all the earth.

p *Compare Heb* balal, *confuse* *LXX one speech for all †*LXX* Sennaar ‡*LXX* And a man said to his neighbor §*LXX* with fire #*LXX adds* and the tower **LXX confusion (Synchysis) ††*LXX* languages

OVERVIEW: The Septuagint renders Babel as Babylon[1] and in this passage translates it as "confusion." The men who migrate from the east in order to found Babylon are led by ambition and pride (CHRYSOSTOM). Babylon is founded by Nimrod, as the capital of his kingdom. The inhabitants of Babylon construct the tower because in their pride they want to defy the power of God (AUGUSTINE). The inhabitants of Babylon are giants who build the tower for their own salvation (PSEUDO-DIONYSIUS).

When God says, "Come, let us go down and there confuse their language," he is addressing the other persons of the Trinity (AUGUSTINE). The Son is the one who is sent to the earth in order to confuse the language (NOVATIAN). Since the inhabitants of Babylon use the privilege of having a single language for evil purpose, God confuses their speech so that they are not able to understand each other anymore (CHRYSOSTOM). God sees that they are able to build the tower because they speak the same language. Therefore he confuses their language in order to prevent them from finishing their building (COMMODIAN).

When the inhabitants of Babylon lose their language, a war breaks out among them. Nimrod is the one who wins this war and becomes the ruler of Babylon after he has scattered the population of the city throughout the earth (EPHREM). The inhabitants of Babylon are scattered for their welfare (JEROME). The

[1]Cf. Gen 10:10.

doom of the tower of Babylon is a constant warning for those who want to achieve fame by building splendid houses (CHRYSOSTOM).

11:1-4 *The Tower of Babel*

THOSE WHO FOUNDED BABYLON LED BY AMBITION. CHRYSOSTOM: "When they traveled from the east, they found open country in the land of Sennar [Shinar] and settled there." Notice how the human race, instead of managing to keep to its own boundaries, always longs for more and reaches out for greater things. This is what the human race has lost in particular, not being prepared to recognize the limitations of its own condition but always lusting after more, entertaining ambitions beyond its capacity. In this regard, too, when people who chase after the things of the world acquire for themselves much wealth and status, they lose sight of their own nature, as it were, and aspire to such heights that they topple into the very depths. You could see this happening every day without others being any the wiser from the sight of it. Instead, they pause for a while but immediately lose all recollection of it and take the same road as the others and fall over the same precipice. This is exactly what you can see happening to these people in the present instance: "When they traveled from the east, they found open country in the land of Sennar [Shinar] and settled there." See how in gradual stages it teaches us the instability of their attitude. When they saw the open country (the text says), they packed up and left their previous dwelling and settled down there. HOMILIES ON GENESIS 30.5.[2]

NIMROD IS THE FOUNDER OF BABYLON. AUGUSTINE: This city named "Confusion" was none other than Babylon, to whose marvelous construction pagan history brings testimonies. For Babylon means "confusion." It would seem that the founder of the city was the giant Nimrod, as was noticed above.[3] In mentioning him, the Scripture tells us that Babylon was the head of his kingdom, meaning at the head of all the other cities, the capital where the government of the kingdom had its seat. However, the city never reached the kind of completion that the pride of impious men had dreamed. The actual plan called for an immense height—it was meant to reach the sky. This perhaps refers to one of its towers, which was to be higher than all the others, or perhaps the word *tower* may mean all the towers much as "horse" can mean thousands of horsemen. CITY OF GOD 16.4.[4]

THE BUILDERS OF THE TOWER DEFY GOD. AUGUSTINE: After the flood, as if striving to fortify themselves against God, as if there could be anything high for God or anything secure for pride, certain proud men built a tower, ostensibly so that they might not be destroyed by a flood if one came later. For they had heard and recalled that all iniquity had been destroyed by the flood. They were unwilling to abstain from iniquity. They sought the height of a tower against a flood; they built a lofty tower. God saw their pride, and he caused this disorder to be sent upon them, that they might speak but not understand one another, and tongues became different through pride. TRACTATES ON THE GOSPEL OF JOHN 6.10.2.[5]

---

[2]FC 82:222-23. [3]See Gen 10:10. [4]FC 14:495*. [5]FC 78:138-39.

THE TOWER IS BUILT BY THE GIANTS.
PSEUDO-DIONYSIUS: What about the war of
the giants, described in Genesis? It is said,
God was afraid of those powerful men and
tricked them, even though they were building
their tower not to harm anyone but for their
own preservation. LETTERS 9.1105B.[6]

11:4-8 God Confuses Their Language

**GOD REFERS TO THE TRINITY WHEN HE
SAYS "LET US GO DOWN."** AUGUSTINE: It is
conceivable that here there may have been an
allusion to the Trinity, if we suppose that the
Father said to the Son and the Holy Spirit,
"Come, let us descend and confound their
tongue." The supposition is sound. But if so,
we must rule out the possibility that angels
were meant. And surely it is more proper for
the angels to come to God unbidden, moved
by grace, that is, by the thoughts that make
them devoutly submissive to unchanging
truth, as to the eternal law that rules their
heavenly court. The angels are not their own
criterion of truth, but, depending on creative
truth, they move unbidden toward it as
toward a fountain of life from which they
must imbibe what they do not have of themselves. And their motion is without change,
since they keep coming, never to depart. CITY
OF GOD 16.6.[7]

**THE SON IS THE ONE WHO DESCENDS TO
EARTH AND CONFUSES THE LANGUAGE.**
NOVATIAN: Moses represents God as descending to the tower that the sons of men were
building, seeking to inspect it and saying,
"Come, let us go down quickly, and there confuse their language, so that they may not
understand one another's speech." Who do
the heretics think was the God that descended

to the tower in this passage and then sought to
visit these men? Was he God the Father? In
that case, God is enclosed in a place. If so,
how then does he embrace all things? Or is it
possible that he speaks of an angel descending
with other angels and saying, "Come, let us go
down quickly, and there confuse their language"? On the contrary, we note in Deuter-
onomy that it was God who recounted these
things and God who spoke, where it is written: "When he scattered abroad the sons of
Adam, he set up the boundaries of the people
according to the number of the angels of
God."[8] Therefore the Father did not descend,
nor did an angel command these things, as the
narrative clearly indicates. Accordingly, the
only remaining conclusion is that he
descended of whom the apostle Paul says, "He
who descended, he it is who ascended also
above all heavens, that he might fill all
things,"[9] that is, the Son of God, the Word of
God. ON THE TRINITY 17.7.[10]

**WHY DOES GOD CONFUSE THE LANGUAGE
OF THE CITIZENS OF BABYLON?** CHRYSOS-
TOM: This in fact is the way the Lord is accustomed to behave. This is what he did in the
beginning in the case of the [first] woman as
well. She had abused the status conferred on
her, and for that reason he subjected her to
her husband. Again, too, in the case of Adam,
since he drew no advantage from the great
ease he enjoyed and from life in the garden
but rather rendered himself liable to punishment through the fall, God drove him out of
the garden and inflicted on him everlasting
punishment in the words "thorns and thistles

---

[6]PSD 282. [7]FC 14:498-99*. [8]Deut 32:8. [9]Eph 4:10. [10]FC
67:66-67.

let the earth yield."[11] So when the people in the present case, who had been dignified with similarity of language, used the privilege given them for evil purposes, he put a stop to the impulse of their wickedness through creating differences in language. "Let us confuse their speech," he says, "so that they will be unable to understand one another's language." His purpose was that, just as similarity of language achieved their living together, so difference in language might cause dispersal among them. HOMILIES ON GENESIS 30.13.[12]

GOD PREVENTS THEM FROM FINISHING THEIR TOWER. COMMODIAN: They foolishly began to build a tower that touched the stars and thought they might be able to climb the skies with it. But God, seeing that their work proceeded because they spoke the same language, intervened and caused them to speak different languages. Then he scattered them by isolating them in the islands of the earth, so that nations speaking different tongues arose. SONG OF TWO PEOPLES 165-69.[13]

11:9 God Scatters the People Throughout the Earth

AFTER GOD CONFUSES THE LANGUAGE, A WAR BREAKS OUT. EPHREM THE SYRIAN: It is likely that they lost their common language when they received these new languages. For if their original language had not perished their first deed would not have come to nothing. It was when they lost their original language, which was lost by all the nations, with one exception, that their first building came to nought. In addition, because of their new languages, which made them foreigners to each other and incapable of understanding one another, war broke out among them on

account of the divisions that the languages brought among them. Thus war broke out among those who had been building that fortified city out of fear of others. And all those who had been keeping themselves away from the city were scattered throughout the entire earth. It was Nimrod who scattered them. It was also he who seized Babel and became its first ruler. If Nimrod had not scattered them each to his own place, he would not have been able to take that place where they all had lived before. COMMENTARY ON GENESIS 8.3.2-8.4.2.[14]

THE BUILDERS ARE DISBANDED FOR THEIR OWN WELFARE. JEROME: Just as when holy men live together, it is a great grace and blessing; so, likewise, that congregation is the worst kind when sinners dwell together. The more sinners there are at one time, the worse they are. Indeed, when the tower was being built up against God, those who were building it were disbanded for their own welfare. The conspiracy was evil. The dispersion was of true benefit even to those who were dispersed. HOMILIES 21.[15]

THE DOOM OF THE TOWER MUST BE REGARDED AS A WARNING. CHRYSOSTOM: There are many people even today who in imitation of them want to be remembered for such achievements, by building splendid homes, baths, porches and avenues. I mean, if you were to ask each of them why they toil and labor and lay out such great expense to no good purpose, you would hear nothing but these very words. They would be seeking to

---

[11]Gen 3:18. [12]FC 82:229. [13]CCL 128:79. [14]FC 91:147-48. [15]FC 48:170.

ensure that their memory survives in perpetuity and to have it said that "this is the house belonging to so-and-so," "this is the property of so-and-so." This, on the contrary, is worthy not of commemoration but of condemnation. For hard upon those words come other remarks equivalent to countless accusations— "belonging to so-and-so the grasping miser, despoiler of widows and orphans." So such behavior is calculated not to earn remembrance but to encounter unremitting accusations, achieve notoriety after death and incite the tongues of onlookers to calumny and condemnation of the person who acquired these goods. But if you are anxious for undying rep-

utation, I will show you the way to succeed in being remembered for every achievement and also, along with an excellent name, to provide yourself with great confidence in the age to come. How then will you manage both to be remembered day after day and also become the recipient of tributes even after passing from one life to the next? If you give away these goods of yours into the hands of the poor, letting go of precious stones, magnificent homes, properties and baths. HOMILIES ON GENESIS 30.7.[16]

---

[16]FC 82:224.

11:10-28 THE NARRATIVE RETURNS TO SHEM AND HIS DESCENDANTS

[10]*These are the descendants of Shem. When Shem was a hundred years old, he became the father of Arpachshad two years after the flood;* [11]*and Shem lived after the birth of Arpachshad five hundred years, and had other sons and daughters.*[†]

[12]*When Arpachshad* had lived thirty-five*[‡] *years, he became the father of Shelah;*[§] [13]*and Arpachshad lived after the birth of Shelah*[§] *four hundred and three years, and had other sons and daughters.*[†#]

[14]*When Shelah had lived thirty** years, he became the father of Eber;* [15]*and Shelah lived after the birth of Eber four hundred*[††] *and three years, and had other sons and daughters.*[†]

[16]*When Eber had lived thirty-four*[‡‡] *years, he became the father of Peleg;* [17]*and Eber lived after the birth of Peleg four hundred*[††] *and thirty years, and had other sons and daughters.*[†]

[18]*When Peleg had lived thirty years,** he became the father of Reu;* [19]*and Peleg lived after the birth of Reu two hundred and nine years, and had other sons and daughters.*[†]

[20]*When Reu had lived thirty-two*[§§] *years, he became the father of Serug;* [21]*and Reu lived after the birth of Serug two hundred*[##] *and seven years, and had other sons and daughters.*[†]

²²*When Serug had lived thirty years, he became the father of Nahor;* ²³*and Serug lived after the birth of Nahor two hundred years, and had other sons and daughters.*†

²⁴*When Nahor had lived twenty-nine**** *years, he became the father of Terah;* ²⁵*and Nahor lived after the birth of Terah a hundred and nineteen*††† *years, and had other sons and daughters.*†

²⁶*When Terah had lived seventy years, he became the father of Abram, Nahor, and Haran.*

²⁷*Now these are the descendants of Terah. Terah was the father of Abram, Nahor, and Haran; and Haran was the father of Lot.* ²⁸*Haran died before his father Terah in the land of his birth, in Ur*††† *of the Chaldeans.*

*LXX variants in spelling within this pericope: Arpachshad (RSV)=Arphaxad (LXX); Shelah=Sala; Peleg=Phalek; Reu=Ragau; Serug=Serouch; Nahor=Nachor; Terah=Thara; Haran=Arran †LXX adds and died ‡LXX a hundred and thirty-five §LXX Kainan *LXX adds And Kainan lived a hundred and thirty years and begot Sala (=Shelah). And Kainan lived three hundred and thirty years after the birth of Sala and other sons and daughters and died. **LXX a hundred and thirty ††LXX three hundred ‡‡LXX a hundred and thirty-four §§LXX a hundred and thirty-two **LXX one hundred ***LXX seventy-nine †††LXX a hundred and twenty-nine ‡‡‡LXX the land

OVERVIEW: After describing the earthly city of Babel, Scripture reverts to the pious patriarch Shem, whose line of descendants leads to Abraham. The years from the flood to Abraham are 1,072. Abraham was born in the land of the Chaldeans, who were deeply immersed in unholy superstitions. Only the family of Abraham worshiped the true God (AUGUSTINE) and therefore was persecuted by the Chaldeans, who even executed Haran, the brother of Abraham (JEROME).

11:10-23 The Descendants of Shem

SCRIPTURE REVERTS TO SHEM AND HIS DESCENDANTS. AUGUSTINE: It is necessary, therefore, to preserve the series of generations descending from Shem, for the sake of exhibiting the city of God after the flood. As before the flood it was exhibited in the series of generations descending from Seth, now it is descending from Shem. And therefore does divine Scripture, after exhibiting the earthly city as Babylon or "Confusion," revert to the patriarch Shem and recapitulate the generations from him to Abraham, specifying the year in which each father gave birth to the son that belonged to this line and how long he lived. And unquestionably it is this that fulfills the promise I made, that it should appear why it is said of the sons of Eber, "The name of the one was Peleg, for in his days the earth was divided."[1] For what can we understand by the division of the earth, if not the diversity of languages? And, therefore, omitting the other sons of Shem, who are not concerned in this matter, Scripture gives the genealogy of those by whom the line runs on to Abraham, as before the flood those are given who carried on the line to Noah from Seth. Accordingly this series of generations begins thus: "These are the generations of Shem: Shem was a hundred years old and begat Arpachshad two years after the flood. And Shem lived after he begat Arpachshad five hundred years and

---

[1]Gen 10:25.

begat sons and daughters." In like manner it registers the rest, naming the year of his life in which each begat the son who belonged to that line that extends to Abraham. It specifies, too, how many years he lived thereafter, begetting sons and daughters, that we may not childishly suppose that the men named were the only men, but that we may understand how the population increased and how regions and kingdoms so vast could be populated by the descendants of Shem. Especially this is true of the kingdom of Assyria, from which Ninus subdued the surrounding nations, reigning with brilliant prosperity and bequeathing to his descendants a vast but thoroughly consolidated empire, which held together for many centuries. CITY OF GOD 16.10.[2]

11:24-28 The Ancestors of Abram

THE TIME SPAN BETWEEN THE FLOOD AND ABRAHAM. AUGUSTINE: But to avoid needless prolixity, we shall mention not the number of years each member of this series lived but only the year of his life in which he gave birth to his heir, that we may thus reckon the number of years from the flood to Abraham and may at the same time leave room to touch briefly and cursorily upon some other matters necessary to our argument. In the second year, then, after the flood, Shem when he was 100 years old begat Arpachshad; Arpachshad when he was 135 years old begat Cainan; Cainan when he was 130 years begat Salah. Salah himself, too, was the same age when he begat Eber. Eber lived 134 years and begat Peleg, in whose days the earth was divided. Peleg himself lived 130 years and begat Reu; and Reu lived 132 years and begat Serug; Serug 130, and begat Nahor; and

Nahor 79, and begat Terah; and Terah 70, and begat Abram, whose name God afterwards changed into Abraham. There are thus from the flood to Abraham 1,072 years, according to the common or Septuagint versions. In the Hebrew copies far fewer years are given, and for this either no reason or a not very credible one is given. CITY OF GOD 16.10.[3]

ABRAHAM WORSHIPED THE TRUE GOD. AUGUSTINE: When, therefore, we look for the city of God in these seventy-two nations, we cannot affirm that while they had but one tongue, that is, one language, the human race had departed from the worship of the true God. Nor can we conclude that genuine godliness had survived only in those generations that descend from Shem through Arpachshad and reach to Abraham. But from the time when they proudly built a tower to heaven, a symbol of godless exaltation, the city or society of the wicked becomes apparent. Whether it was only disguised before or nonexistent, whether both cities remained after the flood—the godly in the two sons of Noah who were blessed and in their posterity, and the ungodly in the cursed son and his descendants, from whom sprang that mighty hunter against the Lord—is not easily determined. CITY OF GOD 16.10.[4]

THE FAMILY OF ABRAHAM WAS PERSECUTED FOR ITS PIETY. JEROME: "And Aran [Haran] died before his father in the land in which he was born in the territory of the Chaldeans." In place of what we read [in the LXX] as "in the territory of the Chaldeans," in

---

[2]NPNF 1 2:316. [3]NPNF 1 2:316. [4]NPNF 1 2:316*.

the Hebrew it has "in ur Chesdim," that is, "in the fire of the Chaldeans." Moreover the Hebrews, taking the opportunity afforded by this verse, hand on a story of this sort to the effect that Abraham was put into the fire because he refused to worship the fire, which the Chaldeans honor, and that he escaped through God's help and fled from the fire of idolatry. What is written [in the LXX] in the following verses, that Thara [Terah] with his offspring "went out from the territory of the Chaldeans,"[5] stands in place of what is contained in the Hebrew, "from the fire of the Chaldeans." And they maintain that this refers to what is said in this verse: "Aran died before the face of Thara in the land of his birth in the fire of the Chaldeans"; that is, because he refused to worship fire, he was consumed by fire. HEBREW QUESTIONS ON GENESIS 11.28.[6]

---

[5]Gen 11:31. [6]HQG 43.

11:29-32 ABRAHAM AND HIS FATHER, TERAH, MOVE TO MESOPOTAMIA

[29]*And Abram and Nahor* took wives; the name of Abram's wife was Sarai, and the name of Nahor's wife, Milcah, the daughter of Haran the father of Milcah and Iscah.* [30]*Now Sarai was barren; she had no child.*

[31]*Terah took Abram his son and Lot the son of Haran, his grandson, and Sarai his daughter-in-law, his son Abram's wife, and they went forth together from Ur*[†] *of the Chaldeans to go into the land of Canaan; but when they came to Haran,*[‡] *they settled there.* [32]*The days of Terah were two hundred and five years; and Terah died in Haran.*[‡]

**LXX variants in spelling within this pericope:* Nahor (RSV)=Nachor (LXX); Sarai=Sara; Milcah=Melcha; Haran=Arran; Iscah=Iescha; Terah=Thara †*LXX the land* ‡*LXX Charran*

OVERVIEW: Abraham and his brother Nahor marry Sarai and Milcha. Sarai is also called Iscah in the biblical narrative (AUGUSTINE, JEROME). Terah, Abraham and his family leave the land of the Chaldeans and move to Mesopotamia (AUGUSTINE). Abraham is the one who leads his father and his family to Meso- potamia after God had appeared to him (CHRYSOSTOM). Nahor, Abraham's brother, lapses into the superstition of the Chaldeans and later, by reason of his repentance, emi- grates into Mesopotamia as Abraham had done before (AUGUSTINE). Terah dies in Meso- potamia, but it is not possible to establish the

173

exact number of years that he had spent in that land (AUGUSTINE).

11:29-30 Abram and Nahor Take Wives

ISCAH IS THE SAME AS SARAI. AUGUSTINE: "And Abram and Nahor took them wives: the name of Abram's wife was Sarai; and the name of Nahor's wife Milcah, the daughter of Haran, the father of Milcah, and the father of Iscah." This Iscah is supposed to be the same as Sarai, Abraham's wife. CITY OF GOD 16.12.[1]

11:31 Terah Leaves Ur and Settles in Haran

TERAH, ABRAHAM AND THEIR FAMILY LEAVE UR. AUGUSTINE: Next it is related how Terah with his family left the region of the Chaldeans and came into Mesopotamia and dwelt in Haran. But nothing is said about one of his sons called Nahor, as if Abram had not taken him along with him. For the narrative runs thus: "And Terah took Abram his son, and Lot the son of Haran, his son's son, and Sarah his daughter-in-law, his son Abram's wife, and led them forth out of the region of the Chaldeans to go into the land of Canaan; and he came into Haran, and dwelt there." Nahor and Milcah his wife are nowhere named here. CITY OF GOD 16.13.[2]

RELATIONSHIPS WITHIN THE EMIGRATING FAMILY. JEROME: Aran [Haran] was the son of Thara [Terah], the brother of Abram and Nachor [Nahor], and he fathered two daughters, Melcha [Milcha] and Sarai who, surnamed Jesca [Iscah], had two names. Of these, Nachor took Melcha as wife, and Abram took Sarai, because marriages between uncles and brothers' daughters had not yet been forbid-den by the law. Even marriages between brothers and sisters were contracted among the first human beings. HEBREW QUESTIONS ON GENESIS 11.29.[3]

ABRAHAM LEADS HIS FAMILY OUT OF THE LAND OF THE CHALDEANS. CHRYSOSTOM: Since, however, I have made mention of the patriarch, let us put before your good selves today's reading, if you do not mind, so as to explain it and thus see the extraordinary degree of the good man's virtue. "Thara [Thera]," the text says, "took his sons Abraham and Nachor, his son's son Lot, and his daughter-in-law Sarah, his son Abram's wife, and led them from the land of Chaldea to journey into the land of the Canaanites. He went as far as Charran [Haran] and settled there. Thara lived two hundred and five years in Charran, and died in Charran."[4] Let us attend precisely to the reading, I beseech you, so as to manage to grasp the plain sense of the writings. Note, in fact, right in the beginning there seems to be a question in the words used. This blessed author—Moses, I mean—says, "Thara took Abraham and Nachor and led them from the land of Chaldea to journey into the land of the Canaanites. He went as far as Charran and settled there." The blessed Stephen would later use the following words in praising the Jews: "The God of glory appeared to our father Abraham when he was in Mesopotamia before he settled in Charran ... and after his father died he led him there to settle."[5] So what does that mean? Is sacred Scripture inconsistent with itself? Not at all; rather, you need to understand from this that

---

[1]NPNF 1 2:318. [2]NPNF 1 2:318-19. [3]HQG 43. [4]Note the variants in the LXX that Chrysostom was reading. [5]Acts 7:2, 4.

since the son was God-fearing, God appeared to him and called upon him to move there. His father Thara, though he happened to be a heathen, nevertheless for the affection he had for his son agreed to accompany him in his migration. He went to Charran, settled there and thus ended his life. Then it was that the patriarch moved to Canaan at God's bidding. Of course, God did not transfer him from there until Thara passed on. HOMILIES ON GENESIS 31.7.[6]

NAHOR LATER JOINS HIS RELATIVES IN MESOPOTAMIA. AUGUSTINE: But afterwards, when Abraham sent his servant to take a wife for his son Isaac, we find it thus written: "And the servant took ten camels of the camels of his lord, and of all the goods of his lord, with him; and arose, and went into Mesopotamia, into the city of Nahor."[7] This and other testimonies of this sacred history show that Nahor, Abraham's brother, had also left the region of the Chaldeans and fixed his abode in Mesopotamia, where Abraham dwelt with his father. Why, then, did the Scripture not mention him when Terah with his family went forth out of the Chaldean nation and dwelt in Haran, since it mentions that he took with him not only Abraham his son but also Sarah his daughter-in-law and Lot his grandson? The only reason we can think of is that perhaps he had lapsed from the piety of his father and brother, and adhered to the superstition of the Chaldeans and had afterwards emigrated there, either through penitence or

because he was persecuted as a suspected person. CITY OF GOD 16.13.[8]

11:32 Terah Dies in Haran

THE CONTINUITY OF TIME FROM ADAM TO ABRAHAM. AUGUSTINE: On Terah's death in Mesopotamia, where he is said to have lived two hundred and five years, the promises of God made to Abraham now begin to be clarified. So it is written, "And the days of Terah in Haran were two hundred and five years, and he died in Haran." This is not to be taken as if he had spent all his days there but that he there completed the days of his life, which were two hundred and five years. Otherwise it would not be known how many years Terah lived, since it is not said in what year of his life he came into Haran. And it is absurd to suppose that in this series of generations, where it is carefully recorded how many years each one lived, his age was the only one not put on record. For although some whom the same Scripture mentions do not have their age recorded, they are not in this series, in which the reckoning of time is continuously indicated by the death of the parents and the succession of the children. For this series, which is given in order from Adam to Noah and from him down to Abraham, contains no one without the number of the years of his life. CITY OF GOD 16.14.[9]

---

[6]FC 82:242. [7]Gen 24:10. [8]NPNF 1 2:319. [9]NPNF 1 2:319*.

Early Christian Writers and the Documents Cited

The following table lists all the early Christian documents cited in this volume by author. Where available, Cetedoc and TLG digital references are listed.

Ambrose

"Flight from the World" (*De fuga saeculi*)	Cetedoc 0133
"Hexaemeron" (*Hexaemeron*)	Cetedoc 0123
"Isaac, or the Soul" (*De Isaac vel anima*)	Cetedoc 0128
"Jacob and the Happy Life" (*De Jacob et vita beata*)	Cetedoc 0130
"Letters" (*Epistulae*)	Cetedoc 0160
"Letters to Bishops" (*Epistulae*)	Cetedoc 0160
"Letters to Laymen" (*Epistulae*)	Cetedoc 0160
"Letters to Priests" (*Epistulae*)	Cetedoc 0160
"On Belief in the Resurrection" (*De excussu fratris Satyri*)	Cetedoc 0157
"On Noah" (*De Noe*)	Cetedoc 0126
"Paradise" (*De paradiso*)	Cetedoc 0124
"Patriarchs" (*De patriarchis*)	Cetedoc 0132

Anonymous

"Letter of Barnabas" (*Barnabae epistula*)	TLG 1216.001
"Letter to Diognetus" (*Epistula ad Diognetum*)	TLG 1350.001

Aphrahat

"Demonstrations"

Athanasius

"Festal Letters" (*Epistulae festales*)	TLG 2035.x01
"On the Incarnation" (*De incarnatione verbi*)	TLG 2035.002

Augustine

"Against Julian" (*Contra Julianum*)	Cetedoc 0351
"Christian Instruction" (*De doctrina christiana*)	Cetedoc 0263

"City of God" *(De civitate Dei)* Cetedoc 0313

"Confessions" *(Confessionum libri tredecim)* Cetedoc 0251

"Eighty-three Questions" *(De diversis quaestionibus octoginta tribus)* Cetedoc 0289

"Faith and Works" *(De fide et operibus)* Cetedoc 0294

"Letters" *(Epistulae)* Cetedoc 0262

"On Faith and the Creed" *(De fide et symbolo)* Cetedoc 0250

"On Nature and Grace" *(De natura et gratia)* Cetedoc 0344

"On the Literal Interpretation of Genesis" *(De Genesi ad litteram imperfectus liber)* Cetedoc 0268

"On the Literal Interpretation of Genesis" *(De Genesi ad litteram libri duodecim)* Catedoc 0266

"On the Trinity" *(De Trinitate)* Cetedoc 0329

"Sermons on the Liturgical Season" *(Sermones)* Cetedoc 0284

"Tractates on the Gospel of John" *(In Johannis Evangelium tractatus)* Cetedoc 0278

"Two Books on Genesis Against the Manichaeans" *(De Genesi contra Manichaeos)* Cetedoc 0265

Basil the Great

"Hexaemeron" *(Homiliae in hexaemeron)* TLG 2040.001

"Homilies on the Psalms" *(Homiliae super Psalmos)* TLG 2040.018

"Homily 20, Of Humility" *(De humilitate)* TLG 2040.036

"Letters" *(Epistulae)* TLG 2040.004

"On the Holy Spirit" *(De spiritu sancto)* TLG 2040.003

Bede the Venerable

"Homilies on the Gospels" *(Homiliarum evangelii libri ii)* Cetedoc 1367

"On the Tabernacle" *(De tabernaculo et vasis eius ac vestibus sacerdotum libri iii)* Cetedoc 1345

Caesarius of Arles

"Sermons" *(Sermones)* Cetedoc 1008

Clement of Alexandria

"Christ the Educator" *(Paedagogus)* TLG 0555.002

"Exhortation to the Greeks" *(Protrepticus)* TLG 0555.001

"Stromateis" *(Stromata)* TLG 0555.004

Clement of Rome

"The Letter to the Corinthians" *(Epistula i ad Corinthios)* TLG 1271.001

Commodian

"Song of Two Peoples" *(Carmen de duobus populis)* Cetedoc 1471

Cyprian

"Letters" *(Epistulae)* Cetedoc 0050

"On Mortality" (*De mortalitate*)   Cetedoc 0044

Cyril of Jerusalem
"Catechetical Lectures" (*Procatechesis*)   TLG 2110.001
"Catechetical Lectures' (*Catecheses ad illuminandos 1-18*)   TLG 2110.003

Diadochus of Photice
"On Spiritual Perfection"

Dorotheus of Gaza
"Spiritual Instructions"

Ephrem the Syrian
"Commentary on Genesis"
"Hymns on Paradise"

Fulgentius of Ruspe
"To Peter on the Faith" (*De fide ad Petrum*)   Cetedoc 0826

Gregory of Nazianzus
"About the Lord's New Day" (*In novam Dominicam [orat. 44]*)   TLG 2022.051
"Dogmatic Hymns" (*Carmina dogmatica*)   TLG 2022.059
"Second Oration on Easter" (*In sanctum pascha [orat.45]*)   TLG 2022.052
"Theological Orations 28" (*De theologia [orat. 28]*)   TLG 2022.008
"Theological Orations 29" (*De filio [orat. 29]*)   TLG 2022.009

Gregory of Nyssa
"Address on Religious Instruction" (*Oratio catechetica magna*)   TLG 2017.046
"On the Creation of Man" (*De opificio hominis*)   TLG 2017.079
"On the Origin of Man" (*De creatione hominis sermo primus [Sp.]*)   TLG 2017.034*
"On the Origin of Man" (*De creatione hominis sermo alter [Sp.]*)   TLG 2017.035*
"On the Soul and the Resurrection" (*Dialogus de anima et resurrectione*)   TLG 2017.056
"On Virginity" (*De virginitate*)   TLG 2017.043

Irenaeus
"Against Heresies" (*Adversus haereses*)   TLG 1447.008

Isaac of Nineveh
"Ascetical Homilies"

---

*TLG lists this work as spurious. It has also been attributed to Basil the Great.

Jerome

"Hebrew Questions on Genesis" (*Liber quaestionum hebraicarum in Genesim*)　　　Cetedoc 0580
"Homilies"
    Homily 1—On Psalm 1 (*Tractatus lix in Psalmos*)　　　Cetedoc 0592
    Homily 10—On Psalm 76 (77) (*Tractatus lix in Psalmos*)　　　Cetedoc 0592
    Homily 21—On Psalm 91 (92) (*Tractatus lix in Psalmos*)　　　Cetedoc 0592
    Homily 66—On Psalm 88 (89) (*Tractatuum in Psalmos series altera*)　　　Cetedoc 0593
    Homily 84—On Mark (*Tractatus in Marci evangelium*)　　　Cetedoc 0594
    Homily 93—On Easter Sunday (*In die dominica Paschae*)　　　Cetedoc 0603 & 0604

John Cassian

"Conferences" (*Collationes*)　　　Cetedoc 0512

John Chrysostom

"Against Judaizing Christians" (*Adversus Judaeos*)　　　TLG 2062.021
"Baptismal Instruction" (*Catechesis ultima ad baptizandos*)　　　TLG 2062.381
"Catechetical Lectures" (*Catecheses ad illuminandos 1-8*)　　　TLG 2062.382
"Homilies on Genesis" (*In Genesim [homiliae 1-67]*)　　　TLG 2062.112
"Homilies on John" (*In Joannem [homiliae 1-88]*)　　　TLG 2062.153
"Sermons on Genesis" (*In Genesim [sermones 1-9]*)　　　TLG 2062.113

John of Damascus

"Orthodox Faith" (*Expositio fidei*)　　　TLG 2934.004

Justin Martyr

"Dialogue with Trypho" (*Dialogus cum Tryphone*)　　　TLG 0645.003

Leander of Seville

"The Training of Nuns"

Marius Victorinus

"Against Arius" (*Adversus Arium*)　　　Cetedoc 0095

Maximus of Turin

"Sermons" (*Collectio sermonum antiqua*)　　　Cetedoc 0219a

Maximus the Confessor

"Book of Difficulties" (*Ambiguorum liber*)　　　TLG 2892.051

Nemesius of Emesa

"On the Nature of Man" (*De natura hominis*)　　　TLG 0743.001

Novatian

"Jewish Foods" (*De cibis judaicis*)	Cetedoc 0068
"On the Trinity" (*De Trinitate*)	Cetedoc 0071

Origen

"Against Celsus" (*Contra Celsum*)	TLG 2042.001
"Commentary on John" (*Commentarii in evangelium Joannis*)	TLG 2042 005
"Exhortation to Martyrdom" (*Exhortatio ad martyrium*)	TLG 2042.007
"Homilies on Genesis" (*Homiliae in Genesim*)	TLG 2042.022
"Homilies on Leviticus" (*Homiliae in Leviticum*)	TLG 2042.024
"On First Principles" (*De principiis*)	TLG 2042.002
"On Prayer" (*De oratione*)	TLG 2042.008

Potamius of Lisbon

"Letter on the Substance"

Prudentius

"Origin of Sin" (*Amartigenia*)	Cetedoc 1440
"Poems" (*Liber Apotheosis*)	Cetedoc 1439
"Scenes from Sacred History" (*Tituli historiarum siue Dittochaeon*)	Cetedoc 1444

Pseudo-Dionysius

"Celestial Hierarchies" (*De caelestine hierarchia*)	TLG 2798.001
'Divine Names" (*De divinis nominibus*)	TLG 2798.004
"Letters" (*Epistulae*)	TLG 2798.006

Pseudo-Macarius

"Fifty Spiritual Homilies" (*Homiliae spirituales 50*)	TLG 2109.002

Quodvultdeus

"Book of Promises and Predictions of God" (*Liber promissionum et praedictorum Dei*)	Cetedoc 0413

Sahdona

"Book of Perfections"

Salvian the Presbyter

"The Governance of God" (*De gubernationes Dei*)	Cetedoc 0485

Severian of Gabala

"On the Creation of the World"

Symeon the New Theologian
"Discourses"

Tertullian

"Against Marcion" *(Adversus Marcionem)*	Cetedoc 0014
"On the Crown" *(De corona)*	Cetedoc 0021
"On the Soul" *(De anima)*	Cetedoc 0017

Theodoret of Cyr

"Compendium of the Heretical Myths" *(Haereticarum fabularum compendium)*	TLG 4089.031
"On the Incarnation of the Lord" *(De incarnatione domini)*	TLG 4089.021
"Questions on Genesis" *(Quaestiones in Octateuchum)*	TLG 4089.022

CHRONOLOGICAL LIST OF PERSONS & WRITINGS

The following chronology will assist readers in locating patristic writers, writings and recipients of letters referred to in this patristic commentary. Persons are arranged chronologically according to the terminal date of the years during which they flourished (fl.) or, where that cannot be determined, the date of death or approximate date of writing or influence. Writings are arranged according to the approximate date of composition. This list is cummulative with respect to volumes of the ACCS released to date.

Josephus, Flavius, 37-c. 101

Clement of Rome (pope), regn. 92-101?

Ignatius of Antioch, d. c. 110-112

Letter of Barnabas, c. 130

Didache, c. 140

Shepherd of Hermas, c. 140/155

Marcion of Sinope, fl. 144, d. c. 154

Second Letter of Clement (so-called), c. 150

Polycarp of Smyrna, c. 69-155

Justin Martyr (of Flavia Neapolis in Palestine), c. 100/110-165, fl. c. 148-161

Montanist Oracles, c. latter half-2nd cent.

Theophilus of Antioch, late second century

Tatian the Syrian, c. 170

Athenagoras of Athens, c. 177

Irenaeus of Lyons, b. c. 135, fl. 180-199; d. c. 202

Clement of Alexandria, b. c. 150, fl. 190-215

Tertullian of Carthage, c. 155/160-225/250; fl. c. 197-222

Callistus of Rome (pope), regn. 217-222

Hippolytus of Rome, d. 235

Minucius Felix of Rome, fl. 218/235

Origen of Alexandria, b. 185, fl. c. 200-254

Novatian of Rome, fl. 235-258

Cyprian of Carthage, fl. 248-258

Dionysius the Great of Alexandria, fl. c. 247-265

Gregory Thaumaturgus (the Wonderworker), c. 213-270/275

Commodian, c. third or fifth century

Euthalius the Deacon, fourth century?

Victorinus of Petovium (Pettau), d. c. 304

Methodius of Olympus, d. c. 311

Lactantius (Africa), c. 250-325; fl. c. 304-321

Eusebius of Caesarea, b. c. 260/263; fl. c. 315-340

Aphrahat (Aphraates), c. 270-c. 345

Pachomius, c. 292-347

Hegemonius (Pseudo-Archelaus), fl. c. 325-350

Cyril of Jerusalem, c. 315-386; fl. c. 348

Eusebius of Emesa, c. 300-c. 359

Marius Victorinus, c. 280/285-c. 363; fl.

355-363

Acacius of Caesarea, d. 366

Macedonius of Constantinople, d. c. 362

Hilary of Poitiers, c. 315-367; fl. 350-367

Potamius of Lisbon, fl. c. 350-360

Athanasius of Alexandria, c. 295-373; fl. 325-373

Ephrem the Syrian, b. c. 306; fl. 363-373

Macrina the Younger, c. 327-380

Basil the Great of Caesarea, b. c. 330; fl. 357-379

Gregory of Nazianzus, b. 329/330, fl. 372-389

Macarius of Egypt, c. 300-c. 390

Pseudo-Macarius, fl. c. 390

Gregory of Nyssa, c. 335-394

Amphilochius of Iconium, c. 340/345-post 394

Paulinus of Nola, 355-431; fl. 389-396

Ambrose of Milan, c. 333-397; fl. 374-397

Didymus the Blind, c. 313-398

Evagrius of Pontus, 345-399; fl. 382-399

Syriac *Book of Steps (Liber Graduum),* c. 400

Apostolic Constitutions, c. 400

Severian of Gabala, fl. c. 400

Prudentius, c. 348-after 405

John Chrysostom, 344/354-407; fl. 386-407

Jerome, c. 347-420

Maximus of Turin, d. 408/423

Pelagius, c. 350/354-c. 420/425

Sulpicius Severus, c. 360-c. 420

Palladius, c. 365-425; fl. 399-420

Theodore of Mopsuestia, c. 350-428

Honoratus of Arles, fl. 425, d. 429/430

Augustine of Hippo, 354-430; fl. 387-430

John Cassian, c. 360-432

Fastidius, c. fourth-fifth centuries

Hesychius of Jerusalem, fl. 412-450

Eucherius of Lyons, fl. 420-449

Valerian of Cimiez, fl. c. 422-439

Sixtus III of Rome (pope), regn. 432-440

Cyril of Alexandria, 375-444; fl. 412-444

Pseudo-Victor of Antioch, fifth century

Ammonius, c. fifth century

Peter Chrysologus, c. 405-450

Leo the Great of Rome (pope), regn. 440-461

Theodoret of Cyr, 393-466; fl. 447-466

Basil of Selucia, fl. 440-468

Salvian the Presbyter of Marseilles, c. 400-c. 480

Hilary of Arles, c. 401-449

Euthymius (Palestine), 377-473

Diadochus of Photice, c. 400-474

Gennadius of Constantinople, d. 471; fl. 458-471

Pseudo-Dionysius the Areopagite, c. 482-c. 532; fl c. 500

Symmachus of Rome (pope), regn. 498-514

Jacob of Sarug, 451-521

Philoxenus of Mabbug, c. 440-523

Fulgentius of Ruspe, c. 467-532

Severus of Antioch, c. 465-538

Caesarius of Arles, 470-542

Dorotheus of Gaza, fl. c. 525

Cyril of Scythopolis, b. 525; fl. c. 550

Paschasius of Dumium, c. 515-c. 580

Leander, c. 545-c. 600

Oecumenius, sixth century

Gregory the Great (pope), 540-604; regn. 590-604

Isidore of Seville, c. 560-636

Sahdona (Martyrius), fl. 635-640

Braulio of Saragossa, c. 585-651

Maximus the Confessor, c. 580-662

Andreas (c. seventh century)

Isaac of Nineveh, d. c. 700

Bede the Venerable, 673-735

John of Damascus, c. 645-c. 749

Isho'dad of Merv, fl. c. 850

Symeon the New Theologian, c. 949-1022

Theophylact of Ohrid, c. 1050-c. 1108

This listing is cumulative, including all the authors and works cited in this series to date.

Alexander of Alexandria (fl. 312-328). Bishop of Alexandria and predecessor of Athanasius, upon whom he asserted considerable theological influence during the rise of Arianism. Alexander excommunicated Arius, whom he had appointed to the parish of Baucalis, in 319. His teaching regarding the eternal generation and divine substantial union of the Son with the Father was eventually confirmed at the Council of Nicea (325).

Ambrose of Milan (c. 333-397; fl. 374-397). Bishop of Milan and teacher of Augustine who defended the divinity of the Holy Spirit and the perpetual virginity of Mary.

Ambrosiaster (fl. c. 366-384). Name given by Erasmus to the author of a work once thought to have been composed by Ambrose.

Ammonius (c. fifth century). An Aristotelian commentator and teacher in Alexandria, where he was born and of whose school he became head. Also an exegete of Plato, he enjoyed fame among his contemporaries and successors, although modern critics accuse him of pedantry and banality.

Andreas (c. seventh century). Monk who collected commentary from earlier writers to form a catena on various biblical books.

Aphrahat (c. 270-350 fl. 337-345). "The Persian Sage" and first major Syriac writer whose work survives. He is also known by his Greek name Aphraates.

Apollinarius of Laodicea (310-c. 392). Bishop of Laodicea who was attacked by Gregory of Nazianzus, Gregory of Nyssa and Theodore for denying that Christ had a human mind.

Apostolic Constitutions (c. 381-394). Thought to be the work of the Arian bishop Julian of Neapolis. The work is divided into eight books, and is primarily a collection of and expansion on previous works such as the *Didache* (c. 140) and the *Apostolic Traditions*. Book 8 ends with eighty-five canons from various sources and is elsewhere known as the *Apostolic Canons*.

Arius (fl. c. 320). Heretic condemned at the Council of Nicaea (325) for refusing to accept that the Son was not a creature but was God by nature like the Father.

Athanasius of Alexandria (c. 295-373; fl.

325-373). Bishop of Alexandria from 328, though often in exile. He wrote his classic polemics against the Arians while most of the eastern bishops were against him.

Athenagoras (fl. 176-180). Early Christian philosopher and apologist from Athens, whose only authenticated writing, *A Plea Regarding Christians*, is addressed to the emperors Marcus Aurelius and Commodius, and defends Christians from the common accusations of atheism, incest and cannibalism.

Augustine of Hippo (354-430). Bishop of Hippo and a voluminous writer on philosophical, exegetical, theological and ecclesiological topics. He formulated the Western doctrines of predestination and original sin in his writings against the Pelagians.

Babai the Great (d. 628). Syriac monk who founded a monastery and school in his region of Beth Zabday and later served as third superior at the Great Convent of Mount Izla during a period of crisis in the Nestorian church.

Basil the Great (b. c. 330; fl. 357-379). One of the Cappadocian fathers, bishop of Caesarea and champion of the teaching on the Trinity propounded at Nicaea in 325. He was a great administrator and founded a monastic rule.

Basilides (fl. second century). Alexandrian heretic of the early second century who is said to have believed that souls migrate from body to body and that we do not sin if we lie to protect the body from martyrdom.

Bede the Venerable (c. 672/673-735). One of the most learned men of his age and author of *An Ecclesiastical History of the English People*. Born in Northumbria, at the age of seven Bede was put under the care of the Benedictine monks of Saints Peter and Paul at Jarrow and given a broad classical education in the monastic tradition.

Book of Steps (c. 400). Anonymous Syriac work consisting of thirty homilies or discourses and which specifically deal with the more advanced stages of growth in the spiritual life.

Benedict of Nursia (c. 480-547). Considered the most important figure in the history of Western monasticism. Benedict founded many monasteries, the most notable found at Montecassino, but his lasting influence lay in his famous Rule. The Rule outlines the theological and inspirational foundation of the monastic ideal while also legislating the shape and organization of the coenobitic life.

Braulio of Saragossa (c. 585-651). Bishop of Saragossa 631-651 and noted writer of the Visigothic renaissance. His *Life* of St. Aemilianus is his crowning literary achievement.

Caesarius of Arles (c. 470-542). Bishop of Arles from 503 known primarily for his pastoral preaching.

Cassian, John (360-432). Author of a compilation of ascetic sayings highly influential in the development of Western monasticism.

Cassiodorus (c. 485-c. 540). Founder of Western monasticism whose writings include valuable histories and less valuable commentaries.

Chromatius (fl. 400). Friend of Rufinus and Jerome and author of tracts and sermons.

Clement of Alexandria (c. 150-215). A highly educated Christian convert from paganism, head of the catechetical school in Alexandria and pioneer of Christian scholarship. His major works, *Protrepticus*, *Paedagogus* and the *Stromata*, bring Christian doctrine face to face with the ideas and achievements of his time.

Clement of Rome (fl. c. 92-101). Pope whose *Epistle to the Corinthians* is one of the most important documents of subapostolic times.

Commodian (c. third or fifth century). Poet of unknown origin (possibly Syrian?) whose two surviving works focus on the Apocalypse and Christian apologetics.

Cyprian of Carthage (fl. 248-258). Martyred bishop of Carthage who maintained that those baptized by schismatics and heretics had no share in the blessings of the church.

Cyril of Alexandria (375-444; fl. 412-444). Patriarch of Alexandria whose strong espousal of the unity of Christ led to the condemnation of Nestorius in 431.

Cyril of Jerusalem (c. 315-386; fl. c. 348). Bishop of Jerusalem after 350 and author of *Catechetical Homilies*.

Diadochus of Photice (c. 400-474). Anti-monophysite bishop of Epirus Vetus whose work *Discourse on the Ascension of Our Lord Jesus Christ* exerted influence in both the East and West through its Chalcedonian Christology. He is also the subject of the mystical *Vision of St. Diadochus bishop of Photice in Epirus*.

Didache (c. 140). A text of unknown authorship, that intertwines Jewish ethics with Christian liturgical practice to form a whole discourse on the "way of life." It exerted an enormous amount of influence in the patristic period and was especially used in the training of catechumen.

Didymus the Blind (c. 313-398). Alexandrian exegete who was much influenced by Origen and admired by Jerome.

Dionysius the Areopagite. The name long given to the author of four mystical writings, probably from the late fifth century, which were the foundation of the apophatic school of mysticism in their denial that anything can be truly predicated of God.

Dorotheus of Gaza (fl. c. 525). Member of abbot Serido's monastery and later leader of a monastery where he wrote *Spiritual Instructions*. He also wrote a work on traditions of Palestinian monasticism.

Epiphanius of Salamis (c. 315-403). Bishop of Salamis in Cyprus, author of a refutation of eighty heresies (the *Panarion*) and instrumen-

tal in the condemnation of Origen.

Ephrem the Syrian (b. c. 306; fl. 363-373). Syrian writer of commentaries and devotional hymns which are sometimes regarded as the greatest specimens of Christian poetry prior to Dante.

Eucherius of Lyons (fl. 420-449). Bishop of Lyons c. 435-449. Born into an aristocratic family, he, along with his wife and sons, joined the monastery at Lérins soon after its founding.

Eunomius (d. 393). Bishop of Cyzicyus who was attacked by Basil and Gregory of Nyssa for maintaining that the Father and the Son were of different natures, one ingenerate, one generate.

Eusebius of Caesarea (c. 260/263-340). Bishop of Caesarea, partisan of the emperor Constantine and first historian of the Christian church. He argued that the truth of the gospel had been foreshadowed in pagan writings but had to defend his own doctrine against suspicion of Arian sympathies.

Eusebius of Emesa (c. 300-c. 359). Bishop of Emesa from c. 339. A biblical exegete and writer on doctrinal subjects, he displays some semi-Arian tendencies of his mentor Eusebius of Caesarea.

Eusebius of Vercelli (fl. c. 360). Bishop of Vercelli who supported the trinitarian teaching of Nicaea (325) when it was being undermined by compromise in the West.

Fastidius (c. fourth-fifth centuries). British author of *On the Christian Life*. He is believed to have written some works attributed to Pelagius.

Faustinus (fl. 380). A priest in Rome and supporter of Lucifer and author of a treatise on the Trinity.

Filastrius (fl. 380). Bishop of Brescia and author of a compilation against all heresies.

Fulgentius of Ruspe (c. 467-532). Bishop of Ruspe and author of many orthodox sermons and tracts under the influence of Augustine.

Gaudentius of Brescia (fl. 395). Successor of Filastrius as bishop of Brescia and author of numerous tracts.

Gennadius of Constantinople (d. 471). Patriarch of Constantinople, author of numerous commentaries and an opponent of the Christology of Cyril of Alexandria.

Gnostics. Name now given generally to followers of Basilides, Marcion, Valentinus, Mani and others. The characteristic belief is that matter is a prison made for the spirit by an evil or ignorant creator, and that redemption depends on fate, not on free will.

Gregory of Elvira (fl. 359-385). Bishop of Elvira who wrote allegorical treatises in the style of Origen and defended the Nicene faith against the Arians.

Gregory of Nazianzus (b. 329/330; fl. 372-389). Bishop of Nazianzus and friend of Basil and Gregory of Nyssa. He is famous for maintaining the humanity of Christ as well as the orthodox doctrine of the Trinity.

Gregory of Nyssa (c. 335-394). Bishop of Nyssa and brother of Basil. He is famous for maintaining the equality in unity of the Father, Son and Holy Spirit.

Gregory the Great (c. 540-604). Pope from 590, the fourth and last of the Latin "Doctors of the Church." He was a prolific author and a powerful unifying force within the Latin Church, initiating the liturgical reform that brought about the Gregorian Sacramentary and Gregorian chant.

Hesychius of Jerusalem (fl. 412-450). Presbyter and exegete, thought to have commented on the whole of Scripture.

Hilary of Arles (c. 401-449). Archbishop of Arles and leader of the Semi-Pelagian party. Hilary incurred the wrath of Pope Leo I when he removed a bishop from his see and appointed a new bishop. Leo demoted Arles from a metropolitan see to a bishopric to assert papal power over the church in Gaul.

Hilary of Poitiers (c. 315-367). Bishop of Poitiers and called the "Athanasius of the West" because of his defense (against the Arians) of the common nature of Father and Son.

Hippolytus (fl. 222-245). Recent scholarship places Hippolytus in a Palestinian context, personally familiar with Origen. Though he is known mostly for *The Refutation of All Heresies*, he was primarily a commentator on Scripture (especially the Old Testament) and other sacred texts.

Ignatius of Antioch (c. 35-107/112). Bishop of Antioch who wrote several letters to local churches while being taken from Antioch to Rome to be martyred. In the letters, which warn against heresy, he stresses orthodox Christology, the centrality of the Eucharist and unique role of the bishop in preserving the unity of the church.

Irenaeus of Lyon (c. 135-c. 202). Bishop of Lyons who published the most famous and influential refutation of Gnostic thought.

Isaac of Nineveh (d. c. 700). Also known as Isaac the Syrian or Isaac Syrus. This monastic writer served for a short while as bishop of Nineveh before retiring to live a secluded monastic life. His writings on ascetic subjects survive in the form of numerous homilies.

Isho'dad of Merv (fl. c. 850). Nestorian commentator of the ninth century. He wrote especially on James, 1 Peter and 1 John.

Jerome (c. 347-420). Gifted exegete and exponent of a classical Latin style, now best known as the translator of the Latin Vulgate. He defended the perpetual virginity of Mary, attacked Origen and Pelagius and supported extreme ascetic practices.

John Chrysostom (344/354-407; fl. 386-407).

Bishop of Constantinople who was famous for his orthodoxy, his eloquence and his attacks on Christian laxity in high places.

John of Damascus (c. 650-750). Arab monastic and theologian whose writings enjoyed great influence in both the Eastern and Western Churches. His most famous writing was the *Orthodox Faith*.

John the Elder (c. eighth century). A Syriac author who belonged to monastic circles of the Church of the East and lived in the region of Mount Qardu (north Iraq). His most important writings are twenty-two homilies and a collection of fifty-one short letters in which he describes the mystical life as an anticipatory experience of the resurrection life, the fruit of the sacraments of baptism and the Eucharist.

Josephus, Flavius (c. 37-c. 101). Jewish historian from a distinguished priestly family. Acquainted with the Essenes and Sadducees, he himself became a Pharisee. He joined the great Jewish revolt that broke out in 66 and was chosen by the Sanhedrin at Jerusalem to be commander-in-chief in Galilee. Showing great shrewdness to ingratiate himself with Vespasian by foretelling his elevation and that of his son Titus to the imperial dignity, Josephus was restored his liberty after 69 when Vespasian become emperor.

Justin Martyr (c. 100/110-165, fl. c. 148-161). Palestinian philosopher who was converted to Christianity, "the only sure and worthy philosophy." He traveled to Rome where he wrote several apologies against both pagans and Jews, combining Greek philosophy and Christian theology; he was eventually martyred.

Leander (c. 545-c. 600). Latin ecclesiastical writer, of whose works only two survive. He was instrumental is spreading Christianity among the Visigoths, gaining significant his-torical influence in Spain in his time.

Leo the Great (regn. 440-461). Bishop of Rome whose *Tome to Flavian* helped to strike a balance between Nestorian and Cyrilline positions at the Council of Chalcedon in 451.

Letter of Barnabas (c. 130). An allegorical and typological interpretation of the Old Testament with a decidedly anti-Jewish tone. It was included with other New Testament works as a "Catholic epistle" at least until Eusebius of Caesarea (c. 260/263-340) questioned its authenticity.

Letter to Diognetus (c. third century). Essentially a refutation of paganism and an exposition of the Christian life and faith. The author of this letter is unknown, and the exact identity of its recipient, Diognetus, continues to elude patristic scholars.

Lucifer (fl. 370). Bishop of Cagliari and fanatical partisan of Athanasius. He and his followers entered into schism after refusing to acknowledge less orthodox bishops appointed by the Emperor Constantius.

Macarius of Egypt (c. 300-c. 390). One of the Desert Fathers. Accused of supporting Athanasius, Macarius was exiled c. 374 to an island in the Nile by Lucius, the Arian successor of Athanasius. Macarius continued his teaching of monastic theology until his death.

Macrina the Younger (c. 327-380). The elder sister of Basil the Great and Gregory of Nyssa. She is known as "the Younger" to distinguish her from her paternal grandmother. She had a powerful influence on her younger brothers, especially on Gregory, who called her his teacher and relates her teaching in *On the Soul and the Resurrection*.

Manichaeans. A religious movement that originated c. 241 in Persia under the leadership of Mani but was apparently of complex Christian origin. It is said to have denied free will and the universal sovereignty of God, teaching that kingdoms of light and darkness are coeternal and that the redeemed are particles of a spiritual man of light held captive in the darkness of matter (*see* Gnostics).

Marcion (fl. 144). Heretic of the mid-second century who rejected the Old Testament and much of the New Testament, claiming that the Father of Jesus Christ was other than the Creator God (*see* Gnostics).

Marius Victorinus (b. c. 280/285; fl. c. 355-363). Grammarian who translated works of Platonists and, after his late conversion (c. 355), used them against the Arians.

Mark the Hermit (c. sixth century). Monk who lived near Tarsus and produced works on ascetic practices as well as christological issues.

Maximus of Turin (d. 408/423). Bishop of Turin who died during the reigns of Honorius and Theodosius the Younger (408-423). Over one hundred of his sermons survive.

Maximus the Confessor (c. 580-662). Greek theologian and ascetic writer. Fleeing the Arab invasion of Jerusalem in 614, he took refuge in Constantinople and later Africa. He died near the Black Sea after imprisonment and severe suffering. His thought centered on the humanity of Christ.

Methodius of Olympus (fl. 290). Bishop of Olympus who celebrated virginity in a *Symposium* partly modeled on Plato's dialogue of that name.

Montanist Oracles. An apocalyptic and strictly ascetic movement begun in the latter half of the second century by a certain Montanus in Phrygia, who, along with certain of his followers, uttered oracles they claimed were inspired by the Holy Spirit. Little of the authentic oracles remains and most of what is known of Montanism comes from the authors who wrote against the movement. Montanism was formally condemned as a heresy before by Asiatic synods.

Nemesius of Emesa (fl. late fourth century). Bishop of Emesa in Syria whose most important work, *Of the Nature of Man*, draws on several theological and philosophical sources and is the first exposition of a Christian anthropology.

Nestorius (b. 381; fl. 430). Patriarch of Constantinople 428-431 and credited with the foundation of the heresy which says that the divine and human natures were associated, rather than truly united, in the incarnation of Christ.

Nicetas of Remesiana (fl. second half of fourth century). Bishop of Remesiana in Serbia, whose works affirm the consubstantiality of the Son and the deity of the Holy Spirit.

Novatian of Rome (fl. 235-258). Roman theologian, otherwise orthodox, who formed a schismatic church after failing to become pope. His treatise on the Trinity states the classic Western doctrine.

Oecumenius (sixth century). Called the Rhetor or the Philosopher. Oecumenius wrote the earliest extant Greek commentary on Revelation. Scholia by Oecumenius on some of John Chrysostom's commentaries on the Pauline Epistles are still extant.

Origen of Alexandria (b. 185; fl. c. 200-254). Influential exegete and systematic theologian. He was condemned (perhaps unfairly) for maintaining the preexistence of souls while denying the resurrection of the body, the literal truth of Scripture and the equality of the Father and the Son in the Trinity.

Pachomius (c. 292-347). Founder of cenobitic monasticism. A gifted group leader and author of a set of rules, he was defended after his death by Athanasius of Alexandria.

Paschasius of Dumium (c. 515-c. 580). Translator of sentences of the Desert Fathers from Greek into Latin while a monk in Dumium.

Pelagius (c. 354-c. 420). Christian teacher whose followers were condemned in 418 and 431 for maintaining that a Christian could be perfect and that salvation depended on free will.

Peter Chrysologus (c. 380-450). Latin archbishop of Ravenna whose teachings included arguments for the supremacy of the papacy and the relationship between grace and Christian living.

Philoxenus of Mabbug (c. 440-523). Bishop of Mabbug (Hierapolis) and a leading thinker in the early Syrian Orthodox Church. His extensive writings in Syriac include a set of thirteen *Discourses on the Christian Life*, several works on the incarnation and a number of exegetical works.

Poemen (c. fifth century). A common title among early Egyptian desert ascetics. One-seventh of the sayings in the *Sayings of the Desert Fathers* are attributed to Poemen, which is Greek for shepherd. It is unknown whether all of the sayings come from one person.

Polycarp of Smyrna (c. 69-155). Bishop of Smyrna who vigorously fought heretics such as the Marcionites and Valentinians. He was the leading Christian figure in Roman Asia in the middle of the second century.

Potamius of Lisbon (fl. c. 350-360). Bishop of Lisbon who joined the Arian party in 357, but later returned to the Catholic faith (c. 359?). His works from both periods are concerned with the larger Trinitarian debates of his time.

Prudentius (c. 348-c. 410). Latin poet and hymnwriter who devoted his later life to Christian writing. He wrote didactic poems on the theology of the incarnation, against the heretic Marcion and against the resurgence of paganism.

Pseudo-Dionysius the Areopagite (fl. c. 500). Author who assumed the name of Dionysius the Areopagite mentioned in Acts 17:34, and who composed the works known as the *Corpus Areopagiticym* (or *Dinysiacum*), although the author's true identity remains a mystery.

Pseudo-Macarius (fl. c. 390). An imaginative writer and ascetic from Mesopotamia to eastern Asia Minor with keen insight into human nature and clear articulation of the theology of the Trinity. His work includes some one hundred discourses and homilies.

Quodvultdeus (fl. 430). Carthaginian deacon and friend of Augustine who endeavored to show at length how the New Testament fulfilled the Old Testament.

Rufinus of Aquileia (c. 345-411). Orthodox Christian thinker and historian who nonetheless translated Origen and defended him against the strictures of Jerome and Epiphanius.

Sabellius (fl. 200). Allegedly the author of the heresy which maintains that the Father and Son are a single person. The patripassian variant of this heresy states that the Father suffered on the cross.

Sahdona (fl. 635-640). Known in Greek as Martyrius. This Syriac author was bishop of Beth Garmai for a short time. His most important work is the deeply scriptural *Book of Perfection*, which ranks as one of the masterpieces of Syriac monastic literature.

Salvian the Presbyter of Marseilles (c. 400-c. 480). An important author for the history of his own time. He saw the fall of Roman civilization to the barbarians as a consequence of the reprehensible conduct of Roman Christians.

Second Letter of Clement (c. 150). The earliest surviving Christian sermon probably written by a Corinthian author, though some scholars have assigned it to a Roman or Alexandrian author.

Severian of Gabala (fl. c. 400). A contemporary of John Chrysostom. Severian was a highly regarded preacher in Constantinople, particularly at the imperial court, and ultimately sided with Chrysostom's accusers. His sermons are dominated by antiheretical concerns.

Severus of Antioch (c. 465-538). A monophysite theologian, consecrated bishop of Antioch in 522. Severus believed that Christ's human nature was an annex to his divine nature and argued that if Christ were both divine and human, he would necessarily have been two persons.

Shepherd of Hermas (second century). A Christian apocalypse divided into five *Visions*, twelve *Mandates* and ten *Similitudes*. Written by a former slave and named for the form of the second angel said to have granted him his visions, this work was highly esteemed for its moral value and was used as a textbook for catechumens in the early church.

Sulpicius Severus (c. 360-c. 420). An ecclesiastical writer born of noble parents. Devoting himself to monastic retirement, he became a personal friend and enthusiastic disciple of St. Martin of Tours. His ordination to the priesthood is vouched for by Gennadius, but no details of his priestly activity have reached us.

Symeon the New Theologian (c. 949-1022). Compassionate spiritual leader known for his strict rule. He believed that the divine light could be perceived and received through the practice of mental prayer.

Tertullian of Carthage (c. 155/160-225/250; fl. c. 197-222). Brilliant Carthaginian apolo-

gist and polemicist who laid the foundations of Christology and trinitarian orthodoxy in the West, though he himself was estranged from the main church by its laxity.

Theodore of Mopsuestia (c. 350-428). Bishop of Mopsuestia, founder of the Antiochene, or literalistic, school of exegesis. A great man in his day, he was later condemned as a precursor of Nestorius.

Theodoret of Cyr (c. 393-466). Bishop of Cyr (Cyrrhus). He was an opponent of Cyril, whose doctrine of Christ's person was finally vindicated in 451 at the Council of Chalcedon.

Theophylact of Ohrid (c. 1050-c. 1108). Byzantine archbishop of Ohrid (or Achrida) in what is now Bulgaria. Drawing on earlier works, he wrote commentaries on several Old Testament books and all of the New Testament except for Revelation.

Valentinus (fl. c. 140). Alexandrian heretic of the mid-second century who taught that the material world was created by the transgression of God's Wisdom, or Sophia (*see* Gnostics).

Valerian of Cimiez (fl. c. 422-439). Bishop of Cimiez. He participated in the councils of Riez (439) and Vaison (422) with a view to strengthening church discipline. He supported Hilary of Arles in quarrels with Pope Leo I.

Vincent of Lérins (d. 435). Monk who exerted considerable influence through his writings on orthodox dogmatic theological method, as contrasted with the theological methods of the heresies.

BIBLIOGRAPHY

Ambrose of Milan. "De excussu fratris Satyri." In *Sancti Ambrosii opera*. Edited by Otto Faller. Corpus Scriptorum Ecclesiasticorum Latinorum, vol. 73. Vienna, Austria: Hoelder-Pichler-Temsky, 1955.

———. "De fuga saeculi." In *Sancti Ambrosii opera*. Edited by Karl Schenkl. Corpus Scriptorum Ecclesiasticorum Latinorum, vol. 32, pt. 2. Vienna, Austria: F. Tempsky; Leipzig, Germany: G. Freytag, 1897.

———. "De Iacob et vita beata." In *Sancti Ambrosii opera*. Edited by Karl Schenkl. Corpus Scriptorum Ecclesiasticorum Latinorum, vol. 32, pt. 2. Vienna, Austria: F. Tempsky; Leipzig, Germany: G. Freytag, 1897.

———. "De Isaac vel anima." In *Sancti Ambrosii opera*. Edited by Karl Schenkl. Corpus Scriptorum Ecclesiasticorum Latinorum, vol. 32, pt. 1. Vienna, Austria: F. Tempsky; Leipzig, Germany: G. Freytag, 1896.

———. "De Noe." In *Sancti Ambrosii opera*. Edited by Karl Schenkl. Corpus Scriptorum Ecclesiasticorum Latinorum, vol. 32, pt. 1. Vienna, Austria: F. Tempsky; Leipzig, Germany: G. Freytag, 1896.

———. "De paradiso." In *Sancti Ambrosii opera*. Edited by Karl Schenkl. Corpus Scriptorum Ecclesiasticorum Latinorum, vol. 32, pt. 1. Vienna, Austria: F. Tempsky; Leipzig, Germany: G. Freytag, 1896.

———. "De patriarchis." In *Sancti Ambrosii opera*. Edited by Karl Schenkl. Corpus Scriptorum Ecclesiasticorum Latinorum, vol. 32, pt. 2. Vienna, Austria: F. Tempsky; Leipzig, Germany: G. Freytag, 1897.

———. "Epistulae." In *Sancti Ambrosii opera*. Edited by Otto Faller. Corpus Scriptorum Ecclesiasticorum Latinorum, vol. 82, pt. 1. Vienna, Austria: Hoelder-Pichler-Temsky, 1968.

———. "Epistulae." In *Sancti Ambrosii opera*. Edited by Michaela Zelzer. Corpus Scriptorum Ecclesiasticorum Latinorum, vol. 82, pt. 2. Vienna, Austria: Hoelder-Pichler-Temsky, 1990.

———. "Epistulae extra collectionem traditae." In *Sancti Ambrosii opera*. Edited by Michaela Zelzer. Corpus Scriptorum Ecclesiasticorum Latinorum, vol. 82, pt. 3. Vienna, Austria: Hoelder-Pichler-Temsky, 1982.

———. "Exameron." In *Sancti Ambrosii opera*. Edited by Karl Schenkl. Corpus Scriptorum Ecclesiasticorum Latinorum, vol. 32, pt. 1. Vienna, Austria: F. Tempsky; Leipzig, Germany: G. Freytag, 1896.

Aphraat. "Demonstrationes." In Patrologia Syriaca, vol. 1. Edited by R. Graffin. Paris: Firmin-Didot et socii, 1910.

Athanasius. "De incarnatione verbi." In *Sur l'incarnation du verbe*. Edited by C. Kannengiesser. Sources Chrétiennes, vol. 199. Paris: Cerf, 1973.

————. "Epistulae festales." In *Opera omnia*. Edited by J.-P. Migne. Patrologiae Cursus Completus; Series Graeca, vol. 26. Paris: Migne, 1865.

Augustine of Hippo. "Confessionum libri tredecim." In *Aurelii Augustini opera*. Edited by Lucas Verheijen. Corpus Christianorum, Series Latina, vol. 27. Turnhout, Belgium: Typographi Brepols Editores Pontificii, 1981.

————. "Contra Julianum Pelagianum." In *Opera omnia*. Edited by J.-P. Migne. Patrologiae Cursus Completus, Series Latina, vol. 44. Paris: Migne, 1865.

————. "De civitate Dei." In *Aurelii Augustini opera*. Edited by Bernardus Dombart and Alphonsus Kalb. Corpus Christianorum, Series Latina, vols. 47, 48. Turnhout, Belgium: Typographi Brepols Editores Pontificii, 1955.

————. "De diversis quaestionibus octoginta tribus." In *Aurelii Augustini opera*. Edited by Almut Mutzenbecher. Corpus Christianorum, Series Latina, vol. 44a. Turnhout, Belgium: Typographi Brepols Editores Pontificii, 1975.

————. "De doctrina christiana." In *Aurelii Augustini opera*, pp. 1-167. Edited by J. Martin. Corpus Christianorum, Series Latina, vol. 32. Turnhout, Belgium: Typographi Brepols Editores Pontificii, 1962.

————. "De fide et symbolo." In *Sancti Aureli Augustini opera*. Edited by Joseph Zycha. Corpus Scriptorum Ecclesiasticorum Latinorum, vol. 41. Vienna, Austria: F. Tempsky, 1900.

————. "De Genesi ad litteram imperfectus liber." In *Sancti Aureli Augustini opera*. Edited by Joseph Zycha. Corpus Scriptorum Ecclesiasticorum Latinorum, vol. 28, pt. 1. Vienna, Austria: F. Tempsky, 1894.

————. "De Genesi ad litteram libri duodecim." In *Sancti Aureli Augustini opera*. Edited by Joseph Zycha. Corpus Scriptorum Ecclesiasticorum Latinorum, vol. 28, pt. 1. Vienna, Austria: F. Tempsky, 1894.

————. "De Genesi contra Manichaeos." In *Opera omnia*. Edited by J.-P. Migne. Patrologiae Cursus Completus, Series Latina, vol. 34. Paris: Migne, 1865.

————. "De natura et gratia." In *Sancti Aureli Augustini opera*. Edited by Carl Franz Urba. Corpus Scriptorum Ecclesiasticorum Latinorum, vol. 60. Vienna, Austria: F. Tempsky, 1913.

————. "De trinitate." In *Aurelii Augustini opera*. Edited by W. J. Mountain. Corpus Christianorum, Series Latina, vols. 50, 50a. Turnhout, Belgium: Typographi Brepols Editores Pontificii, 1968.

————. "Epistulae." In *Sancti Aureli Augustini opera*. Edited by A. Goldbacher. Corpus Scriptorum Ecclesiasticorum Latinorum, vol. 34, pt. 2. Vienna, Austria: F. Tempsky, 1895.

————. "In Johannis euangelium tractatus." In *Aurelii Augustini opera*. Edited by Radbodus Willems. Corpus Christianorum, Series Latina, vol. 36. Turnhout, Belgium: Typographi Brepols Editores Pontificii, 1954.

————. "Sermones." Patrologiae Cursus Completus, Series Latina, vol. 38. Edited by J.-P. Migne. Paris: Migne, 1861.

Barnabas. "Barnabae epistula." In *Épître de Barnabé*. Edited by R. A. Kraft. Sources Chrétiennes, vol. 172. Paris: Cerf, 1971.

Basil the Great (of Caesarea). "De humilitate." In Patrologia Cursus Completus; Series Graeca, vol. 31. Edited by J.-P. Migne. Paris: Migne, 1857.

―――. "De spiritu sancto." In *Basile de Cesaree: Sur le Saint-Esprit*, 2nd ed. Edited by B. Pruche. Sources Chrétiennes, vol.17. Paris: Cerf, 1968.

―――. "Epistulae." In *Saint Basile. Lettres*, 3 vols. Edited by Y. Courtonne. Paris: Les Belles Lettres, 1957, 1961, 1966.

―――. "Homiliae in hexaemeron." In *Basile de Cesaree: Homelies sur l'hexaemeron*, 2nd ed. Edited by S. Giet. Sources Chrétiennes, vol. 26. Paris: Cerf, 1968.

―――. "Homiliae super Psalmos." In *Opera omnia*. Edited by J.-P. Migne. Patrologia Cursus Completus; Series Graeca, vol. 29. Paris: Migne, 1865.

Bede the Venerable. "De tabernaculo et euasis eius ac vestibus sacerdotem libri iii." In *Bedae Venerabilis opera*. Edited by D. Hurst. Corpus Christianorum, Series Latina, vol. 119a. Turnhout, Belgium: Typographi Brepols Editores Pontificii, 1969.

―――. "Homiliarum evangelii libri ii." In *Bedae Venerabilis opera*. Edited by D. Hurst. Corpus Christianorum, Series Latina, vol. 122. Turnhout, Belgium: Typographi Brepols Editores Pontificii, 1953.

Caesarius of Arles. "Sermones." In *Caesarii Arelatensis opera*. Edited by D. Germani Morin. Corpus Christianorum, Series Latina, vols. 103, 104. Turnhout, Belgium: Typographi Brepols Editores Pontificii, 1953.

Cassian, John. *Iohannis Cassiani Conlationes XXIIII. Iohannis Cassiani opera* Pars II. Edited by Michael Perschenig. Corpus Scriptorum Ecclesiasticorum Latinorum, vol. 13. Vienna, Austria: C. Geroldi Filium, 1886.

Clement of Alexandria. "Paedagogous." In *Le pédagogue [par] Clement d'Alexandrie*. 3 vols. Edited by M. Harl, H. Marrou, C. Matray and C. Mondésert. Sources Chrétiennes, vols. 70, 108, 158. Paris: Cerf, 1960, 1965, 1970.

―――. "Protrepticus." In *Le protreptique*, 2nd ed. Edited by C. Mondésert. Sources Chrétiennes, vol. 2. Paris: Cerf, 1949.

―――. "Stromata." In *Clemens Alexandrinus*, vols. 2, 3rd ed., and 3, 2nd ed. Edited by O. Stählin, L. Früchtel and U. Treu. Die griechischen christlichen Schriftsteller 52 (15), 17. Berlin: Akademie-Verlag, 1960, 1970.

Clement of Rome. "Epistula i ad Corinthios." In *Clément de Rome: Épître aux Corinthiens*. Sources Chrétiennes, vol. 167. Paris: Cerf, 1971.

Commodian. "Carmen de duobus populis (Carmen apologeticum)." In *Commodiani carmina*. Edited by Joseph Martin. Corpus Christianorum, Series Latina, vol. 128. Turnhout, Belgium: Typographi Brepols Editores Pontificii, 1960.

Cyprian. "De mortalitate." In *Sancti Cypriani episcopi opera*. Edited by C. Moreschini and M. Simonetti. Corpus Christianorum, Series Latina, vol. 3a. Turnhout, Belgium: Typographi Brepols Editores Pontificii, 1972.

―――. *Sancti Cypriani episcopi epistularium*. Edited by G. F. Diercks. Corpus Christianorum, Series Latina, vol. 3c. Turnhout, Belgium: Typographi Brepols Editores Pontificii, 1994.

Cyril of Jerusalem. "Catecheses ad illuminandos 1-18." In *Cyrilli Hierosolymorum archiepiscopi opera quae supersunt omnia*, 2 vols. Edited by W. C. Reischl and J. Rupp. Munich: Lentner, 1848, 1860.

———. "Procatechesis." In *Cyrilli Hierosolymorum archiepiscopi opera quae supersunt omnia*, vol. 1. Edited by W. C. Reischl and J. Rupp. Munich: Lentner, 1848.

Diadochus of Photike. "Capita Centrum de perfectione Spirituali." In *Oeuvres*. Edited by E. Des Places. Sources Chrétiennes, vol. 5. Paris: Cerf, 1966.

Dorotheus of Gaza. "Instructiones." In Patrologiae Cursus Completus; Series Graeca, vol. 88. Edited by J.-P. Migne. Paris: Migne, 1860.

Ephrem the Syrian. "Hymni de Paradiso." In *Des Heiligen Ephraem des Syrers Hymnen de Paradiso und Contra Julianum*. Edited by E. Beck. Corpus Scriptorum Christianorum Orientalium, vol. 174. Louvain, Belgium: Secretariat du Corpus SCO, 1957.

———. "In Genesim Commentarii." In *Sancti Ephraem Syri in Genesim et in Exodum*. Edited by R. M. Tonneau. Corpus Scriptorum Christianorum Orientalium, vol. 152. Louvain, Belgium: Secretariat du Corpus SCO, 1955.

———. *Sancti patris nostri Ephraem Syri et Jacobi episcopi Edesseni interpretationum in Genesim collectanea*, 1. Edited by J. A. Assemani. Sancti Patris Nostri Ephraem Syri Opera Omnia. Tomus I. Rome, 1737.

Fulgentius of Ruspa. "De fide ad Petrum seu de regula fidei." In *Opera*. Edited by J. Fraipont. Corpus Christianorum, Series Latina, vol. 91a. Turnhout, Belgium: Typographi Brepols Editores Pontificii, 1968.

Gregory of Nazianzus. "De filio [oration 29]." In *Gregor von Nazianz. Die fünf theologischen Reden*. Edited by J. Barbel. Düsseldorf, Germany: Patmos-Verlag, 1963.

———. "De substantiis mente praeditis [carm. 7]." In *Carmina dogmatica*. Edited by J.-P. Migne. Patrologiae Cursus Completus; Series Graeca, vol. 37. Paris: Migne,

———. "De theologia [oration 28]." In *Gregor von Nazianz. Die fünf theologischen Reden*. Edited by J. Barbel. Düsseldorf, Germany: Patmos-Verlag, 1963.

———. "In Sanctum Pascha [oration 45]." In Patrologiae Cursus Completus; Series Graeca, vol. 36. Edited by J.-P. Migne. Paris: Migne, 1862.

Gregory of Nyssa. "De creatione hominis sermo alter [Sp.]." In *Gregorii Nysseni opera, suppl.* Edited by H. Hoerner. Leiden: Brill, 1972.

———. "De creatione hominis sermo primus [Sp.]." In *Gregorii Nysseni opera, suppl.* Edited by H. Hoerner. Leiden: Brill, 1972.

———. "De opificio hominis." In Patrologiae Cursus Completus; Series Graeca, vol. 44. Edited by J.-P. Migne. Paris: Migne, 1865.

———. "De virginitate." In *Grégoire de Nyssé. Traite de la virginité*. Edited by M. Aubineau. Sources Chrétiennes, vol. 119. Paris: Cerf, 1966.

———. "Dialogus de anima et resurrectione." In Patrologia Cursus Completus; Series Graeca, vol.. 46. Edited by J.-P. Migne. Paris: Migne, 1863.

———. "Oratio catechetica magna." In *The Catechetical Oration of Gregory of Nyssa*. Edited by J. Strawley. Cambridge: Cambridge University Press, 1903.

Irenaeus. "Adversus haereses (liber 5)." In *Contre les hérésies [par] Irénée de Lyon, livre 5*, vol. 2. Edited by A. Rousseau, L. Doutreleau and C. Mercier. Sources Chrétiennes, vol. 153. Paris: Cerf, 1969.

Isaac of Nineveh. "Asketica." In *Isaak—Asketika*. Edited by Nikephoros Hieromonachos. Athens, 1895.

Jerome. "In die dominica Paschae." In *Tractatus sancti Hieronymi presbyteri in librum Psalmorum*. Edited by D Germanus Morin. In *S. Hieronymi presbyteri opera*. Corpus Christianorum, Series Latina, vol. 78. Turnhout, Belgium: Typographi Brepols Editores Pontificii, 1958.

———. "Liber quaestionum hebraicarum in Genesim." In *S. Hieronymi presbyteri opera*. Edited by Paul de LaGarde. Corpus Christianorum, Series Latina, vol. 72. Turnhout, Belgium: Typographi Brepols Editores Pontificii, 1959.

———. "Tractatus lix in Psalmos." In *Tractatus sancti Hieronymi presbyteri in librum Psalmorum*. Edited by D Germanus Morin. In *S. Hieronymi presbyteri opera*. Corpus Christianorum, Series Latina, vol. 78. Turnhout, Belgium: Typographi Brepols Editores Pontificii, 1958.

———. "Tractatus in Marci Euangelium." In *Tractatus sancti Hieronymi presbyteri in librum Psalmorum*. Edited by D Germanus Morin. In *S. Hieronymi presbyteri opera*. Corpus Christianorum, Series Latina, vol. 78. Turnhout, Belgium: Typographi Brepols Editores Pontificii, 1958.

———. "Tractatuum in Psalmos Series Altera." In *Tractatus sancti Hieronymi presbyteri in librum Psalmorum*. Edited by D Germanus Morin. In *S. Hieronymi presbyteri opera*. Corpus Christianorum, Series Latina, vol. 78. Turnhout, Belgium: Typographi Brepols Editores Pontificii, 1958.

John Chrysostom. "Adversus Judaeos." In *Opera omnia*. Edited by J.-P. Migne. Patrologiae Cursus Completus; Series Graeca, vol. 48. Paris: Migne, 1863.

———. "Catechesis ultima ad baptizandos." In *Varia graeca sacra*. Edited by A. Papadopoulos-Kerameus. St. Petersburg: Kirschbaum, 1909.

———. "In Genesim (homiliae 1-67)." In *Opera omnia*. Edited by J.-P. Migne. Patrologiae Cursus Completus; Series Graeca, vol. 53. Paris: Migne, 1865.

———. "In Genesim (sermones 1-9)." In *Opera omnia*. Edited by J.-P. Migne. Patrologiae Cursus Completus; Series Graeca, vol. 54. Paris: Migne, 1865.

———. "In Joannem (homiliae 1-88)." In *Opera omnia*. Edited by J.-P. Migne. Patrologiae Cursus Completus; Series Graeca, vol. 59. Paris: Migne, 1865

John of Damascus. "Expositio fidei." In *Die Schriften des Johannes von Damaskos*. Edited by B. Kotter. Patristische Texte und Studien, vol. 2. Berlin: De Gruyter, 1973.

Justin Martyr. "Dialogus cum Tryphone." In *Die altesten Apologeten*. Edited by E. J. Goodspeed. Gottingen: Vandenhoeck & Ruprecht, 1915.

Leander of Seville. "De institutione virginum et contemptu mundi." In Patrologiae Cursus Completus, Series Latina, vol. 72. Edited by J.-P. Migne. Paris: Migne, 1865.

Letter to Diognetus. "Epistula ad Diognetum." In *Á Diognete*, 2nd ed. Edited by H.-I. Marrou. Sources Chrétiennes, vol. 33. Paris: Cerf, 1965.

Marius Victorinus. "Adversus Arium." In *Marii Victorini opera*. Edited by Paul Henry and Peter Hadot. Corpus Scriptorum Ecclesiasticorum Latinorum, vol. 83, pt. 1. Vienna, Austria: Hoelder-Pichler-Tempsky, 1971.

Maximus the Confessor. "Ambiguorum liber." In Patrologiae Cursus Completus, Series Graeca, vol. 91. Edited by J.-P. Migne. Paris: Migne, 1860.

Maximus of Turin. "Collectio sermonum antiqua." In *Maximi episcopi Taurinensis sermones*. Edited by Almut Mutzenbecher. Corpus Christianorum, Series Latina, vol. 23. Turnhout, Belgium: Typographi Brepols Editores Pontificii, 1962.

Nemesius of Emesa. "De natura hominis." In *Nemesius of Emesa*. Edited by B. Einarson. Corpus Medicorum Graecorum (in press).

Novatian. "De cibis iudaicis." In *Opera*. Edited by G. F. Diercks. Corpus Christianorum, Series Latina, vol. 4. Turnhout, Belgium: Typographi Brepols Editores Pontificii, 1972.

———. "De trinitate." In *Opera*. Edited by G. F. Diercks. Corpus Christianorum, Series Latina, vol. 4. Turnhout, Belgium: Typographi Brepols Editores Pontificii, 1972.

Origen. "Commentarii in evangelium Joannis (lib. 1, 2, 4, 5, 6, 10, 13)." In *Origine: Commentaire sur saint Jean*, 3 vols. Edited by C. Blanc. Sources Chrétiennes, vols. 120, 157, 222. Paris: Cerf, 1966, 1970, 1975.

———. "Contra Celsum." In *Origine: Contre Celse*, 4 vols. Edited by M. Borret. Sources Chrétiennes, vols. 132, 136, 147, 150. Paris: Cerf, 1967, 1968, 1969.

———. "De principiis." In *Origenes Werke*. Edited by Paul Koetschau. Die griechischen christlichen Schriftsteller der ersten drei Jahrhunderte, vol. 22. Leipzig, Germany: J. C. Hinrichs, 1913.

———. "De oratione." In *Origines Werke*. Edited by Paul Koetschau. Die griechischen christlichen Schriftsteller, vol. 2. Leipzig, Germany: J. C. Hinrichs, 1899.

———. "Exhortatio ad martyrium." In *Origines Werke*. Edited by Paul Koetschau. Die griechischen christlichen Schrifsteller, vol. 1. Leipzig, Germany: J. C. Hinrichs, 1899.

———. "Homiliae in Genesim." In *Origenes Werke*, vol. 6. Edited by W. A. Baehrens. Die griechischen christlichen Schriftsteller, vol. 29. Leipzig, Germany: Teubner, 1920.

———. "Homiliae in Leviticum." In *Origenes Werke*, vol. 6. Edited by W. A. Baehrens. Die griechischen christlichen Schriftsteller der ersten Jahrhunderte, vol. 29. Berlin: Akademie-Verlag, 1920.

Potamius of Lisbon. "Epistula de substantia." In *Potami episcopi Olisponensis opera omnia*. Edited by J. N. Hillgarth and M. Conti. Corpus Christianorum, Series Latina, vol. 69a. Turnhout, Belgium: Brepols, 1999.

Prudentius. "Amartigenia." In *Aurelius Prudentius Clemens*. Edited by Maurice P. Cunningham. Corpus Christianorum, Series Latina, vol. 126. Turnhout, Belgium: Typographi Brepols Editores Pontificii, 1966.

———. "Liber apotheosis." In *Aurelius Prudentius Clemens*. Edited by Maurice P. Cunningham. Corpus Christianorum, Series Latina, vol. 126. Turnhout, Belgium: Typographi Brepols Editores Pontificii, 1966.

———. "Tituli historiarum." In *Aurelius Prudentius Clemens*. Edited by Maurice P. Cunningham. Corpus Christianorum, Series Latina, vol. 126. Turnhout, Belgium: Typographi Brepols Editores Pontificii, 1966.

Pseudo-Dionysius. "De caelesti hierarchia." In *Corpus Dionysiacumi: Pseudo-Dionysius Areopagita. De coelesti hierarchia, de ecclesiastica hierarchia, de mystica theologia*. Edited by A. M. Ritter. Patristische Texte und Studien. Berlin: De Gruyter, 1991.

————. "De divinis nominibus." In *Corpus Dionysiacumi: Pseudo-Dionysius Areopagita. De divinis nominibus*. Edited by B. R. Suchla. Patristische Texte und Studien. Berlin: De Gruyter, 1990.

————. "Epistulae." In *Corpus Dionysiacumi: Pseudo-Dionysius Areopagita. De coelesti hierarchia, de ecclesiastica hierarchia, de mystica theologia*. Edited by A. M. Ritter. Patristische Texte und Studien. Berlin: De Gruyter, 1991.

Pseudo-Macarius. "Homiliae spirtuales 50." In *Die 50 geistlichen homilien des Makarios*. Edited by H. Dorries, E. Klostermann and M. Kroeger. Patristische Texte und Studien 4. Berlin: De Gruyter, 1964.

Quodvultdeus. "Liber promissionum et praedictorum Dei." In *Opera Quodvulteo Carthaginiensi episcopo tributa*. Edited by R. Braun. Corpus Christianorum, Series Latina, vol. 60. Turnhout, Belgium: Typographi Brepols Editores Pontificii, 1976.

Sahdona. "Liber de perfectione." In *Oeuvres Spirituelles*. Edited by André de Halleux. Corpus Scriptorum Christianorum Orientalium, vol. 200. Louvain, Belgium: Secretariat du Corpus SCO, 1960.

Salvian. "De gubernatione Dei." In *Oeuvres*. Edited by George LaGarrigue. Sources Chrétiennes, vol. 220. Paris: Cerf, 1975.

Severian of Gabala. "De mundi creatione." In *Opera omnia*. Edited by J.-P. Migne. Patrologiae Cursus Completus; Series Graeca, vol. 56. Paris: Migne, 1862.

Symeon the New Theologian. "Catecheses." In Sources Chrétiennes, vols. 96, 104. Edited by H. de Lubac, J. Daniélou et al. Paris: Cerf, 1964.

Tertullian. "Adversus Marcionem." In *Opera*, pp. 437-726. Edited by Aem. Kroymann. Corpus Christianorum, Series Latina, vol. 1. Turnhout, Belgium: Typographi Brepols Editores Pontificii, 1954.

————. "De anima." In *Opera*, pp. 779-869. Edited by J. H. Waszink. Corpus Christianorum, Series Latina, vol. 2. Turnhout, Belgium: Typographi Brepols Editores Pontificii, 1954.

————. "De corona." In *Opera*, pp. 1037-65. Edited by Aem. Kroymann. Corpus Christianorum, Series Latina, vol. 2. Turnhout, Belgium: Typographi Brepols Editores Pontificii, 1954.

Theodoret. "Haereticarum fabularum compendium." In Patrologiae Cursus Completus; Series Graeca, vol. 83. Edited by J.-P. Migne. Paris: Migne, 1859.

————. "Quaestiones in Octateuchum." In *Theodoreti Cyrensis quaestiones in Octateuchum*. Edited by N. Fernandez-Marcos and A. Saenz-Badillos. Textos y Estudios "Cardenal Cisneros," vol. 17. Madrid: Poliglota Matritense, 1979.

Authors/Writings Index

Subject Index